Barnstorming to Heaven

BARNSTORMING to HEAVEN

Syd Pollock and His Great Black Teams

ALAN J. POLLOCK
Edited by James A. Riley

The University of Alabama Press • Tuscaloosa

Copyright © 2006
The University of Alabama Press
Tuscaloosa, Alabama 35487-0380
All rights reserved
Manufactured in the United States of America

Typeface: Minion and Triplex

∞

The paper on which this book is printed meets the minimum
requirements of American National Standard for Information
Science—Permanence of Paper for Printed Library Materials,
ANSI Z39.48-1984.

Library of Congress Cataloging-in-Publication Data

Pollock, Alan J.
    Barnstorming to heaven : Syd Pollock and his great Black teams / Alan J. Pollock ; edited by
James A. Riley.
        p.   cm.
    Includes index.
    ISBN-13: 978-0-8173-1495-8 (cloth : alk. paper)
    ISBN-10: 0-8173-1495-4
    1. Pollock, Syd. 2. Baseball team owners—United States—Biography. 3. Negro leagues—History.
4. Indianapolis Clowns (Baseball Team)—History. I. Riley, James A. II. Title.
    GV865.P65A3 2006
    338.7'61796357'092—dc22

                                                                                        2005014446

This book is dedicated to the entire Pollock family.

First and foremost to my parents, Villa and Syd Pollock.

Also to my siblings and their spouses
Don and Jane
Estelle and Al
Valaria and Tom
Jerry and Jeanne
and to their families.

Most especially, this is dedicated to my wife, Marti, to our children,
Theresa, Anna, Valeria, Karen, and to all our grandchildren.

CONTENTS

ACKNOWLEDGMENTS

This book would not have been possible without the support of my wife, Marti. Without her love, understanding and encouragement, this work would never have been brought to fruition.

Many others provided generous measures of assistance.

Jim Riley shared his Negro Leagues research, helped conduct player interviews and served as a proofreader and editor for the early versions of the manuscript. Troy Soos also provided cogent suggestions on various aspects of the narrative. Lenny Kleinman's assistance proved invaluable in preparing the manuscript in a viable format.

My brothers, Don and Jerry, and my sisters, Estelle and Valaria, shared their memories of both Dad and the Clowns to complement my own recollections.

Interviews with former Clowns players, including Sherwood Brewer, Jim Cohen, Jim Colzie, Leroy Cromartie, Frank Ensley, Felix "Chin" Evans, Jim Everett, Carl Forney, Dirk Gibbons, John Gray, Sam Hairston, Art Hamilton, Buster Haywood, Gordon Hopkins, Rufus McNeil, Connie Morgan, Ray Neil, Len Pigg, Charlie Rivera, Ed Scott, Allen Smith, Eugene "Chivo" Smith, Armando Vasquez and Billy Vaughn were very helpful in providing additional perspectives.

This is also true for others from the sports world who knew Dad from his association with the Clowns. Sue Barnhill, Col. Charles B. Franklin, Joyce Hamman, Buck O'Neil, Cliff Robinson, Monk Silva and Ted Worner shared memories which were beneficial in telling the complete story.

I extend an apology to anyone I may have overlooked who contributed thoughts or reminiscences that helped make this memoir—in Dad's words—"as round as a baseball."

Barnstorming to Heaven

Introduction

There was a time! A time when baseball was king and a typical American boy dreamed of being a baseball player. A time when major league baseball was restricted exclusively to ten of our largest cities, and these favored venues were all located in the Northeast or Midwest. A time when there was no major league baseball either west or south of St. Louis, but there were countless minor league, semi-pro and amateur teams in towns all across the country. A time when professional traveling teams traversed the country playing these local teams, a practice that was called "barnstorming." A time when there was no television and the barnstorming teams often represented the highest level of baseball skills that the local populace had ever seen.

During this time baseball was separated by a color line, and black ballplayers were denied the opportunity to play in white leagues. This practice, although not written, had the impact of law and was firmly entrenched in America's mindset. Thus black players were forced to play in separate black leagues on all-black teams, some of which were among the touring teams that traveled across the country.

The most popular and longest surviving of these black barnstorming teams was the Indianapolis Clowns, a team that featured an entertaining blend of comedy, showmanship and good baseball. It was the superb quality of the comedic component that elevated them above other barnstorming ball clubs. Some teams imitated the Clowns, but none captured the true essence that made them genuinely unique.

It has been stated—often and accurately—that baseball is a microcosm of society. In a world of racial prejudice, injustice and adversity, the Clowns traveled across the country for four decades, carrying laughter and goodwill wherever they went. They epitomized the positive aspects of barnstorming and generally served as a prototype for traveling athletic teams. They are often called the Harlem Globetrotters of baseball and, like the "Trotters," captured the affection of America. They were beloved by people of many ethnicities and classes all across America. Their appeal transcended baseball, and proved a common ground for bringing diverse groups together.

The man who made the Clowns the great baseball ambassadors that they were was Syd Pollock. Pollock was Jewish, his wife was Irish Catholic, and his business partner a black Protestant. The story of Syd and the Clowns is more than a baseball story. It is a montage of America from the end of the Roaring Twenties, through the years of the Great Depression and World War II, on into the civil rights movement. One constant during these changing times was Syd Pollock and the Indianapolis Clowns, who were always on the cutting edge of societal change as they crisscrossed America.

The story of the Clowns is told by Syd's son, Alan Pollock, who shared his father's love of America, family and baseball. Even more important was the special place in his heart that he reserved for the Clowns. From his childhood, when he idolized the players, through his early adult years, when he traveled with the team and worked with his father, Alan was an eyewitness to this distinctive segment of baseball history. In addition to his own personal perspective, Alan also had access to the recollections of his siblings and his wife, Marti, and to his father's files. While working on his manuscript, Alan gained greater depth for the story through interviews with many of his father's business associates and former Clowns players.

Never before have the comedic routines of King Tut been described so vividly and in so much detail. As you read, Tut comes alive in your imagination, and it is almost like stepping inside a time machine and going back as an eyewitness to a slice of Americana that cannot be replicated.

You are also given glimpses into Syd Pollock's lifelong quest to integrate baseball and his underacknowledged support for Civil Rights before it became politically correct. The apple didn't fall far from the tree, and Syd's son, Alan, embodied these same attributes in his life.

When I first met Alan, I felt that I had always known him. We both liked sports, especially baseball, and each of us had a special interest in the Negro leagues. His interest came from growing up with the Clowns, while mine came from extensive research, interviews and writing on the subject. Since we were the same age, we also shared common life experiences of our generation, and we bonded instantly.

For Alan, work on his memoir was a labor of love. He was in the final stages of editing his manuscript when he suffered a sudden and fatal heart attack. I was asked by his widow to complete the editorial task and shepherd the manuscript into publication. In the process, his monumental work, which was almost twice conventional book size, was converted into the book that you are now reading.

Initially, Alan presents the entertainment element of the Clowns' performances that defined their uniqueness. Next he introduces his father, who was the force that provided the impetus to transform a baseball team into an American institution. Finally, he embarks on a road trip with the team through the decades until the inevitable conclusion that there was no longer a place for the Clowns in the world of baseball.

While writing his memories of the Clowns, Alan had sometimes read parts of his manuscript to our Central Florida SABR (Society for American Baseball Research) chapter, and they were always well received. Occasionally, Alan's recollections go beyond the confines of black baseball and touch on other aspects of our national pastime. At a breakfast following Ted Williams' Shoeless Joe Jackson Symposium, Alan read a selection—his childhood memory of meeting Ted Williams—to Ted himself.

Alan's memoir is an invaluable source for us because it preserves an integral part of baseball history. As I read it, I again hear him speaking as he did to our SABR group and to Ted Williams. The story, as told in his voice, is a book that you will not soon forget.

James A. Riley

PART ONE

CELEBRATION

The Essence of the Clowns

Every Clowns game I ever attended, I went to the top step of the dugout
or turned around on the bench to see the laughing faces and thought,
"These people would never know the joy of this moment without Dad."
It was a glimpse at universal love.

—Alan Pollock

1

The Heart and Soul of Black Baseball

Once I watched the laughing bride at a wedding reception romp and strut to rock music, wedding gown held high off the floor, legs flashing—the same electric, irreverent joy and energy the Clowns gave baseball. Urban Negro league games were celebrations. Men wore straw boaters, fedoras and Stetsons, suspenders, dress pants and shirts and ties; women were in dresses, hats, jewelry, perfume and full makeup. Fans had sirens, cowbells, horns and spinning noisemakers. Hard liquor passed freely, and bets were openly made on anything from game results to whether the batter would get a hit to whether the next pitch would be a fast ball or a breaking pitch to whether the ball, if fouled, would be foul left or foul right. Games were social events.

Yankees fans in New York or Cardinals fans in St. Louis had seventy-six chances to see their teams at home. Clowns fans in New York or St. Louis had once or twice a year at most to see their team, absent rainout, and fans in the Clowns' hometown usually had less than a half dozen chances. Black children played with white dolls. Blacks saw white movies. Black schools stocked white books. Blacks heard white actors portray blacks on radio. But blacks could celebrate the greatness of black baseball live, and no fans were wilder, louder, or happier than Clowns fans.

I was a family legend for my ability to guess paid attendances of huge crowds of blacks within a few hundred fans, but I missed by thousands at Yankees games. The decibel level at a Clowns game nearly caused middle ear nausea, and I sometimes crossed my eyes to double crowd size to match sightsize with soundsize. Every Clowns game I ever attended, I went to the top step of the dugout or turned around on the bench to see the laughing faces and thought, "These people would never know the joy of this moment without Dad." It was a glimpse at universal love.

If Cool Papa Bell with his speed was the legs of black baseball and Satchel Paige with his fastball its arm, if Rube Foster, its founder, was its head, and Buck Leonard, Oscar Charleston and Josh Gibson with their Hall of Fame ability its body, lean and athletic, then King Tut with his charisma, creativity and acting ability was its heart and soul, wild and poetic and funny. He wasn't just watched and enjoyed. Tut was flat out loved by everybody. In 1950 at a game in Victory Field in Indianapolis, a black man in his eighties, sitting next to Mom and me, told Mom, "I saw Tut from my Mama's lap. He gets right in beside your heart, don't he?" And we understood. He couldn't have seen Tut that long ago, but Tut wasn't just seen and heard. He was felt inside, fresh and young as a timeless, ageless spring bubbling joy. He was a drink from childhood's stream.

Tut was a genius, and I guess I'll never stop missing him. I grew up with his comedy. He was with the Clowns from 1936 until 1958. Tut traveled the nation so thoroughly, players reported no need to carry a road map on the bus. According to Clowns' lore, lost, even in the night, the team chauffeur could wake Tut to determine location at a glance and unerring directions to the journey's end.

Once Dad and I watched Ringling Brothers and Barnum & Bailey Circus stars Felix Adler and Emmitt Kelly state and nod respectively, during a TV interview, that many of their ideas and attitudes originated with Tut, and they considered him the best clown ever. First a ballplayer, then a ball handler in Clowns pepperball and other comedic juggling routines, Tut became an actor probably capable of playing Shakespeare in pantomime, but, of course, as a black man in his day, he likely would not have been permitted to play even a silent Othello, if he were so inclined. Tut loved and was loved in his own theater circuit—ballparks all over the continent. Silently he could entertain 20,000 fans or more from 30 to 150 yards away with routines they'd seen dozens of times before and have them roaring.

Whenever Tut saw Dad, his first words were always the same, "Skip, I got to have a raise." He always deserved one; he sometimes got one. He was perhaps the highest paid player in black baseball, receiving a salary from Dad and more from fans as he passed through the stands giving baseballs to kids and doing comedy. Fans often paid Tut a dime each for postcards of him that Dad had made for him. During the off-season, he sold numbers in Philadelphia, and given his ability to work a crowd close up, he must have enjoyed successful winters.

His real name was Richard King, and he and his wife, Bea, were family friends as long as we could remember. Bea too called him Tut.

Unless my brothers and I joined Dad in the dugout, the most exciting games for our family were always those at which Mom sat with Bea King and Pauline Downs, the wife of Clowns' manager Bunny Downs. The cheering and laughter of the three women spread through the section they sat in like good news. This, despite the fact Mom disliked baseball and considered 18 men playing with a little white ball absurd.

Before large, black, big-city crowds, Tut's entrance never varied. After batting practice and before infield practice and as the crowd filed in, a chain of firecrackers exploded, amplified like gunshots in the Clowns dugout, and Tut bounded from a smoking dugout onto the field, clothed in prisoner's black and white striped suit and hat, and shackled by ball and chain, wide-eyed, body flexed in tension, searching urgently behind in fear and ahead for escape. Some thought it was racial, stereotypical imagery, among them Dad, but Dad saw surrealistic anti-racist overtones. He felt Tut was stating, "This the way they see us—startin' out shackled, but before this game is over my brothers and sisters, I gonna take you everyplace we gonna be, and we gonna leave this ball and chain behind. Ain't nothin' really back of me but noise and smoke, and next time I come out the dugout, I gonna be free."

Of Tut's sketches, his most obvious low comedy acts were fan favorites, but Tut's subtlety lent a beauty that even when such earthy routines were repeated, they were creative, inspiring, different and funny, and his artistic use of face and body blended to give life to routines that were nothing short of pure genius.

Tut worked solo and in tandem with Peanuts Davis, Goose Tatum and others. Peanuts and Goose, who later became famous with basketball's Harlem Globetrotters, were both good ballplayers and talented comedians, but Tut's most memorable companion for rehearsed two-person sketches was Spec Bebop, who never played. Bebop joined the Clowns in 1949, and his real name was Ralph Bell. He was a dwarf from Daytona Beach, Florida, standing just over three feet tall, and because he was short-limbed, stubby and pudgy, and Tut was tall, slim, graceful and long-limbed, the physical contrast highlighted the humor. Bebop's drinking sometimes caused non-appearances, but infrequently enough that Dad was unafraid to advertise Bebop's appearances.

Bebop's rookie year, Pauline Downs reported to Mom, "Wait till you see

Spec Bebop. He's so cute, you'll just want to pick him up in your arms and love him," an urge Mother easily overcame. But as I grew up, I learned through team saga that Bebop was a lady's man, so I guess there were those who did pick him up in their arms and love him.

Tut and Bebop's comedy routines were great crowd pleasers and never failed to "bring down the house." The fishing sketch was Tut's popular favorite. Each game, between a random set of innings, Tut and Bebop sat on the infield grass, Tut in front. With two sets of bats as oars, they cut through imaginary waters to their fishing spot and rested their bats on the bottom of their invisible boat. Peacefully, each picked up a bat as a pole, cast an imaginary line and fished. As they waited for a bite, Bebop pointed up to the beauty of the day, and, as Tut scanned the skies contentedly appreciating, he suddenly flinched, snapped one eye shut and wiped his angry face clean as he shook his other fist at an imaginary bird, a portent of worse things to come. Then—the unexpected—Tut hooked a monster fish, and, with Bebop a clinging appendage to his back, he quaked and shook from front to back and side to side with the ebb and flow of the huge invisible beast, fishing pole flicking and seeming to bend, until the creature pulled the boat under, throwing Tut and Bebop separate ways into menacing currents. As they swam for their lives across the infield toward shore, and as their strokes brought their heads above water, each spit an impossible number of streams high in the air, seemingly from reservoirs unknown to even gluttonous camels.

Tut swam safely ashore, exhausted and almost drowned near the pitcher's mound, and as he came to and gathered his strength and resources and arose, he noticed Bebop prone, unmoving, heaped on the shore several feet away. A stethoscope pulled from a pocket affirmed life, but the joy of Tut's face again clouded as, pulling off his baseball cap, he scratched his head, risked a look upward, to contemplate means and perhaps divine assistance to restore consciousness to his small companion.

First, he sat on Bebop's waist and pumped his chest, becoming doused anew with each thrust as a still comatose Bebop sprayed him from some improbable reserve source of water in his mouth.

Each subsequent treatment involved odors. And ecumenical and selfless in thought, Tut pre-checked each remedy. He unbuttoned the top of his baseball shirt, put his nose in the armpit of his underlying sweatshirt, held his nose, again looking to the heavens as if to ask for this task to pass from his nostrils, and almost joined Bebop in the nether world. Then he subjected the dwarf to the therapy. Bebop's legs rose and shook, then fell, and his body convulsed, but his eyes stayed closed and there was no respite from his near-death experience.

Finally, less extreme anatomical rescue possibilities were tried and narrowed to Tut's foot, and the pre-operative anxiety of a neurosurgeon could be read in Tut's eyes from as far as the bleachers as the comedian committed to the ultimate final cure and removed his shoe, and the shock of his pre-administration test nearly killed him. He threw the shoe upward, recoiled from it and ran from it momentarily. Then he turned to face it and confront what he must do: altruistically sneak up on his shoe on tiptoes, no matter the risk to self, grab it, and place it under the moribund Bebop's nose.

And this he did. Again, Bebop's legs rose, and his feet shook, and his body quaked with spasms. His arms jerked and twisted, and his body flapped, and at last he jumped to life, and the two ran to the dugout smiling to start their lives anew.

One summer a dachshund, name later repressed by those who knew him, traveled with the Clowns. Between innings, a player placed a tiny plastic fire hydrant behind home plate. Tut then walked the dog leisurely, eventually approaching the hydrant. Pointing to the hydrant, Tut, in pantomime, instructed the dog to relieve himself. Irritated at the dachshund's failure, Tut illustrated the technique on one tiptoe while raising his opposite leg over the hydrant. The dog looked at him even more quizzically. Still restrained, Tut illustrated again by gently lifting the dog's right rear leg over the hydrant but again failed to obtain the desired result. Figuring he had a left-legged dog (Dad once claimed Michelangelo had a left-legged dog who wet wild high), Tut manually helped the dog with the left leg. Always grantor of a last chance, Tut rose ominously to full height and pointed dramatically at the hydrant like Sitting Bull—had he chosen to give Custer warning, would have pointed at the border of Indian territory—as though by raw will Tut could make the dachshund voluntarily vacate its bladder politely. Again failing, he waved Bebop out of the dugout carrying a three-foot by two-foot red wooden box with a flip top, a hole at one end, and a crank at the other. Tut placed the dachshund in the box and lowered the lid over him as Bebop turned the crank, and a string of a dozen hot dogs rolled one by one from the hole.

"We could carry an extra pitcher-outfielder and the bus would smell better," one Clowns player observed during the year of the hot dogs.

Bebop started the dentist sketch in the dugout, filling his mouth with large kernels of blanched corn as Tut strolled the sidelines dressed in his trademark tailed tux coat over the Clowns uniform and carrying a severely scuffed black leather bag with "DENTIST" on each side. Over the seasons, Tut acquired his bags from doctors who had overused them through years of house calls, and got his tux coats from undertakers. His original sartorial inspiration came in an alley behind a Philadelphia funeral home sometime off-season during the 1930s. As Tut was walking down the alley, an undertaker emerged and threw an old cutaway on the trash pile, and Tut spontaneously conceptualized it on the baseball diamond and picked it up. Sewing up the back, Tut finalized the image that all who saw him would always remember—Tut in Clowns uniform wearing tailed tux coat and double-billed Clowns cap turned sideways, a peak shading each side of his head.

And that was the Tut fans saw as Bebop climbed the dugout steps, holding his towel-encased head in agony, and approached the circuit dentist with a toothache bigger than self, pointing to the upper right side of his mouth. Tut pulled a pre-placed folding chair from the stands, and Bebop sat, rocking back and forth in pain. Tut unstrapped the towel from Bebop's head and, as Bebop opened his mouth, seemingly wide enough to take in Tut's entire head, close exam revealed an abscessed tooth, but as Tut pulled pliers from his bag with one hand, with the other he had to shove a rapidly panicking Bebop back into the chair. Again, as Tut clanked the pliers loudly, he had to restrain the patient by force. Finally, the pliers entered the dwarf's mouth, but the tooth was tough. Bebop's body rocked in rhythm with Tut's, hands grasping Tut's arms in futile resistance, as Tut alternately pulled on the tooth, leaning backwards to put all his weight into it, and shifted forward to allow slack. Finally, Tut put one foot on the chair for extra leverage and shook back and forth and side to side yanking on the tooth as Bebop swayed in reaction like a seated dance partner.

And at last, the pliers came free, as Tut fell back on the ground, a blanched corn tooth in the pliers, and Bebop smiled. Tut proudly threw the tooth in the air for all potential patients to see, as Bebop walked away confidently, but before Tut could fold up the chair, Bebop was returning, again clenching his mouth in agony, this time pointing at the lower left, indicating the wrong tooth had been pulled. He sat, and Tut confirmed the self-diagnosis, and as he test-clanged the hammer and chisel newly removed from the bag, he again had to make a one-handed catch of the nervous patient to seat him.

The chisel slid into Bebop's mouth and the metallic sound of the tripping hammer echoed to the farthest bleacher seats. Each time Tut pounded, Bebop's feet flew up off the ground. And when the hammering finally stopped, Tut reached in Bebop's mouth and flicked a second tooth high in the air.

Bebop staggered toward the dugout, dazed and worn, but in obvious relief, then, before Tut could fold the chair, Bebop again clutched his mouth in agony, this time pointing at the upper middle, sitting again to submit to expert examination. With a smile, Tut snapped his fingers at the ultimate why-didn't-I-think-of-it-sooner dental plan.

He inserted a metal funnel into Bebop's mouth, and this time, before the patient had chance to bolt, he dropped a lit firecracker into the funnel. With the explosion, Bebop spit a cloud of smoke and dozens of blanched teeth into the air, and the two ran happily into the dugout.

Dad's own comedy career began spontaneously when I was six, at a Puerto Rican Winter League game. Mom and I watched Tut stroll the sideline with his dentist bag. Complacently, we turned toward the dugout and saw Dad emerge, towel around his head, as Tut's stooge. Rum and the heat had victimized the scheduled patient. Later during the game, a slight earthquake stirred the crowd, but I was more stunned by Dad's comedy debut.

A few years later the Clowns played their longtime rivals, the Brooklyn Bushwicks, at Dexter Park in Brooklyn. Mom and Dad wouldn't let me go because it was a school night, but the game was televised live in the New York metropolitan area. Mom was cleaning dishes as the camera panned to Dad in a business suit, towel around his head, again leaving the dugout for the dentist sketch and looking like a forlorn figure out of a

B movie. "Mom!" I hollered in disbelief, "Come quick! Dad's on TV!" Dad later told me Bebop had not been feeling well and that when I next went to see Dr. Leibowitz, our family dentist, I was not to mention that Dad had seen another dentist.

Both times Dad was an excellent patient and probably would loved to have performed more. I never saw him do any other Clowns act. Other players or comedians stood in for Bebop. I suspect, though, that, besides Bebop, no one but Dad was willing to face the funneled firecracker.

No film footage exists to commemorate the between-innings boxing sketch, but it entertained millions over the years. The bout featured a wildly swinging Bebop unable to reach Tut, futile roundhouse rights and lefts merely stirring the air under Tut's arm, as Tut held Bebop away with a hand on the top of Bebop's head. Tut followed with a sweeping uppercut knockdown, delivered off the hold. As Tut bowed toward the crowd in assumed victory, Bebop arose and lifted Tut off his feet and decked him forward with a thunderous, crushing right to the backside. The act ended with Bebop fleeing with glee into the dugout as Tut removed his boxing gloves and threw them at the retreating champion.

Comedy pepperball and shadowball date back before World War I, and the House of David teams and the "Gashouse Gang" St. Louis Cardinals of the 1930s incorporated comedy pepperball, but the Clowns perfected both events and carried them to center stage as art forms on the strong shoulders of King Tut.

Peppperball was a standard pregame warmup throughout baseball during the Clowns years. Three or four players lined up about 30 feet from a batter, lobbing the ball and fielding everything hit toward them. The hitter used loose, easy swings, placing the ball so that, in theory, each fielder would have an equal number of chances. But the Clowns lent the drill improvised juggling and unprecedented comedy. The batter was really ancillary to Clowns pepperball. After a few hits, the warm-up disappeared into the comedy juggling act, with each player in the line outdueling the next with increasingly difficult and funny ball-handling feats. Baseballs whirled over, around and between bodies. One player would roll the ball down his arm, from shoulder to hand, rocking it on and bouncing it up and down off his biceps, then his forearm, then turning to face a teammate to hand him the ball, but as the teammate reached, he'd roll the ball away back up his arm or flip the ball over his head to the player behind, while the one in front got a handshake. The next player in line who had received the ball would roll it down and juggle it around and between his legs, dropkicking it backwards to the next player when he was done. The ball was passed from the crook of the back of a leg up to be wedged between the hollow of the neck and the head of the next man. Players juggled while tumbling, drinking water, dancing or faking sleep. The few dropped balls became part of the act. Ed Hamman, who worked with Dad for many years and eventually became a part owner, was a master at incorporating a miscue into the routine. Whenever Ed missed, he wedged the dropped ball between his heels and, jumping, tossed it with his feet over his head into his glove.

Counterdirection was part of pepperball, and each player had to stay alert, because the least suspecting player received the ball at the least likely time from the least likely place and direction, and the action was fast. The crispness of Clowns pepperball prevented its speed from becoming a blur, and only lengthy preseason workouts and daily practice maintained the requisite skill levels. Pepperball, which never happened the same way twice, always ended with Tut's special touches, the last of which was to deliver the ball down his back, with a rear end flip to a teammate. Pepperball was particularly brilliant during the 1940s in the hands of Tut, Goose Tatum, Ed Hamman and Peanuts Davis.

Shadowball was the Clowns' trademark. Most team publicity releases referred to "The Clowns famous Shadowball and diamond Funshow." During phase I infield practice before games, Tut took a turn at first, and infielders intentionally threw in the dirt so Tut could show off his never-diminished fielding arsenal, including last-second traps, eyes-closed pickups and backhanded scoops with his back to the ball. When he was with the Clowns, Goose generally played first for shadowball, and later others filled the role.

At the end of the seventh inning, Clowns players took the infield for a second infield practice. After a few rounds, the batter discovered a scuff on the ball and threw to a player on the dugout steps, who reached into a ball bag, pulled out an invisible ball, polished it with his hands and threw it to the catcher. And shadowball exploded in a blaze of dancing hands and feet, clouds of dirt flying. With silent-movie speed, Clowns players made spectacular plays, rifling the nonexistent ball around the horn with behind-the-back throws, 90-foot kicks, behind-the-back catches, pivot plays in which the second baseman used his backside to bump the shortstop's toss to first, and throws caught by Tut on his back with his glove on his foot (during infield practice, he often did the same with a real ball).

Then, as suddenly as shadowball had begun, it switched to slow motion, and with ballet precision, the players made even finer plays off speed. Goose's incremental split receiving a throw from deep third evidenced his superb physical condition and comedic body control.

Before the infielders left the field, the batter, always the Clowns' manager, hit one deep outfield fly, whistling and pointing, and Bebop, dressed in a grass skirt, sprinted from the bullpen and made a running, somersaulting catch, rolling to his feet and making a 400-foot peg to home, forcing Tut to run back to the foot of the stands to jump to make the catch.

As shadowball infield practice ended, each player, at normal speed, charged an invisible chopper and tossed the ball home as he left the field, and after all had done so, Tut remained on the field for the ultimate big league fungo. The batter hit a phantom pop-up, and Tut circled home plate watching and waiting and looking skyward. Bebop, who had returned to the dugout after his outfield heroics, ran onto the infield near first base, pointing the ball out to Tut. Tut raced to the dwarf and watched and waited and shook his head in disgust at his inability to spot the ball. Scanning the skies, Bebop ran toward third, again pointing straight up. Tut raced to Bebop, but the ball remained invisible as the two men searched. Then, Tut squinting toward heaven, at last made a true sighting, raising his arm to point, and drifted slowly toward home, at the last second, running and jumping and sliding across the ground to make an incredible rolling catch.

From prone position, he pulled a real ball from his mitt and tossed it casually to the batter, and shadowball was ended.

Shadowball was followed by a raucous jitterbug dance by Tut and Bebop, showcasing Tut's inimitable moves, including rhythmic, hand-to-hand passes of Bebop around Tut's body and under each raised leg. In the early years, various theme songs were used. During the late 1950s, Tut's genius again took an unexpected turn when he selected Elvis Presley's "All

Shook Up." The biggest laugh was when Tut and Bebop, hands on knees, wagged backsides in unison to the words "All shook up."

Mom complained year after year of baseballs Tut gave fans each game we saw. "It costs you money, Sydney," she told Dad. "Ask him to stop."

"Tut's Tut, and the gifts are great advertising," Dad answered. "Every fan gets a ball from Tut will be back multiplied, with his kids and friends."

"And Tut will give all of them balls next time," Mom responded, disdaining public relations. Whenever Mother and Dad argued, they took untenable positions. "They'll pay $1.25 each to get in and cost you $1.50 each for a baseball. You can do without advertising that loses a quarter a customer."

But Tut worked the stands and gave out balls every game, never many, and Dad never complained, and Mom never stopped. Dad loved the laughter within the laughter of the crowd as Tut worked the stands. Dad's favorite was the changing of the hats. Weekend crowds in cities were best. Every fan wore a hat. Tut would take a straw hat off a thin man and put in on the head of a fat woman, after removing her white pillbox. He'd take her white pillbox and put it on a minister, taking the cleric's black hat and putting it on a staggering drunk roaming the crowd. Men with moustaches ended up wearing women's feathered hats. As laughter swelled, Tut streaked through the crowd changing fans' hats with a creative eye only he had for the most incongruous mixture of body, face and hat. If a nun were in the crowd, Tut would try to unscrew her habit, a fedora or homburg in his hand to put on her head if he succeeded. And each changing of the hats, he'd put a hat on a woman and hoist his hand with—instead of the anticipated woman's hat—a huge bra, which he'd embarrassingly tuck into his tux coat, then grab her hat to move on.

More often than not, the source of laughter in the stands was Tut in someone's lap. Usually the fan was hugging him. Buster Haywood, longtime player and manager for the Clowns, recalled the funniest thing he ever saw:

We were killing the Monarchs in Dallas, Texas. Plenty of betting. A Monarchs fan pulled a gun. Fans screamed. The cops disarmed him.

Tut waits thirty seconds, goes up into the stands and lights a chain of firecrackers under the seats in the row where the cops had just hauled off the Monarchs fan. People scattered, diving over seats, jumping, running. Tut too ran and caused more commotion, looking back at the smoke and hollering, "What's that! What's that!" He ended up in a fat woman's lap, shaking.

Tut was one of the sharpest dressers in all of sports, impressive considering team bus space limitations. Clowns players recall Tut's humor keeping them as happy on the bus as it did crowds in the stands. And when the bus arrived in town, he was always the first one off, smiling and reaching out to those who met the Clowns. He kept in top physical condition through his comedy and pregame workouts and comedic infield practice at first.

According to outfielder Erwin Ford, who roomed some of the summer of '54 with Tut, "Off the field Tut was a father. He was a teacher, talked with you like a daddy if you was down. He told each young player what the Clowns had done for him and what the Clowns could do for them if they kept themselves under control. Wasn't a problem in the world you couldn't take to Tut."

Tut took his job seriously. "You're the sorriest ball club I ever saw," he admonished after losses. "You're the best team on earth," he boasted after wins. If the Clowns were behind, he often curled into a corner of the dugout, muttering, "Get some damn runs so I can do my damn act. I can't do my damn act with shit like this."

Tut's close-game disposition irritated Dad. If Tut were happy, his timing was as good or better than Goose Tatum's or Peanuts Davis' or any of the Clowns entertainers who came later. If Tut had a tragic flaw, it was his longevity with and resulting love for the Clowns, and in a close game, his attitude was sometimes counterproductive. He took being the Clowns number one fan slightly more seriously than Roosevelt viewed being president.

Tut was involved in every Clowns game, and some of his finest comedy revolved around his involvement. Universally, players grouped for pats and handshakes for home run hitters crossing the plate. Tut's post–home run congratulation was unique. As the mobbed player crossed the plate, Tut removed the player's cap, and, with his hands on both sides of the player's head, kissed him on top of the head.

Tut had Dad order a custom-made giant first baseman's mitt, three and one-half times normal size. After an opponent's error, Tut was in the fielder's face offering the giant glove. The first day Dad delivered the giant mitt to a Clowns game, Tut brought it to first for infield practice, lay down with his head on the bag, put the mitt on his foot, and caught the first throw from third in the mitt with his foot.

Clowns' equipment included a giant bat, which Tut and Bebop would together haul to any opposing batter who had just dramatically missed with an apparent home run swing.

Tut was part of every opposing mound conference, hand cupping the conversation to his ear, and, at conference end, he rushed to the batter and pantomime-whispered enemy strategy, while pointing at the mound.

Selecting at least one inning a game to mimic the home plate umpire, Tut lined himself behind the ump rear to rear, bent as the ump crouched, watched the delivery under his arm, turned away with eyes winced closed as pitch popped mitt, and raised his hand for a ball if the Clowns were batting and a strike if not. With each close call against the Clowns, he suspended a different sign swaying from the umpire's backside on two strings. The signs varied from "Pencils—help the blind" to "Jesse James," from "Out to lunch" to "Gone fishing" or "For Rent." At times Tut would mirror umpire actions nearly simultaneously, scratching whatever delicate place the umpire scratched, and stopping only when the ump turned to him to see what all the laughter was about. If the ump swept the plate, Tut kicked dirt back on. On badly missed calls, Tut offered giant eyeglasses.

During Clowns halves of late innings of particularly close games, Tut walked determinedly to the foul side of the first or third base line, knelt, and, with a giant two-armed sweep, clapped his hands into praying position, face raised wagging at Heaven beseechingly. The roar of crowd laughter reached ear-splitting crescendo with a key base hit, and Tut would leap high, waving base runners, tossing his two-billed hat spinning in the air and generally leading crowd pandemonium. But his praying was so real that a rally-killing strikeout or double play jolted him from his knees to kick the dirt and swear or throw his hat on the ground and kick it and stomp into the dugout, further dampening the spirits of Clowns fans. And Dad would say, "Your timing is bad in close games. Get less involved."

"Shit, Skip. Ain't right, ending a rally like that. Send that man home, Skip. Send him home."

Tut's most lyrical routine resulted from Dad's suggestion that he replace one frayed and torn tailed tux coat. Instead, Tut approached home plate one night with the coat slung over his arm. He sat on the ground and tried to put the coat on, but ended up with hands through wrong holes and caught in tatters and the coat on backwards. Subsequent tries ended with both arms together in the remains of one sleeve, then the other—or a leg through a sleeve—with the coat on upside down. Leaving the coat on the ground, Tut walked sadly, thoughtfully to the dugout, returning with a folded road map and flashlight. Spreading the road map on the ground next to him, he studied the map and examined the coat with the flashlight, traced the map with his fingers, caressed the corresponding parts of the coat, and, gradually, going from map to coat, and weaving hands and arms through fabric hole by hole, properly put on the coat, put out the flashlight, folded the map, stood, fluffed out the coattails, pulled the old garment as straight as it would go, shook out as many wrinkles as he could, and walked, tall, proud and dignified, into the dugout, carrying the map and flashlight.

White major league baseball was like apple pie for whites only. There can be no more glaring example of racial prejudice, no more obvious segregation as a national mind-set, than the very existence of the Negro leagues. That the national pastime was divided between black and white on the professional level should forever memorialize the nearness in any society of potential holocaust of some magnitude in one form or another.

In the case of the Clowns, Tut was a symbol. He was proud, not humble. He was confident, not fearful. He was certain, not confused. He was lively, not passive. He was whimsical, not regimented. He was colorful, not withdrawn. He was passionate, not detached. He was hopeful, not depressed. He was joyful, not sad. He could pray for a rally before tens of thousands. He could swim the infield nightly and never drown. He could watch smoke diffuse behind him and move ahead. He could make new use of an old tux coat. He was Tut, not Uncle Tom. He could laugh at anything, and nothing was sacred to him but the game. He was black, not white. He was the soul of black baseball.

Not just Tut, but all Clowns; not just all Clowns, but all Negro leaguers, were symbols of joy, the celebration within the national disgrace of segregated baseball. And their fans knew that.

Most Clowns humor revolved around Tut. If he didn't perform it and it wasn't spontaneous, he usually originated it. One example was the hidden ball trick. Every player and every fan would swear the first baseman threw the pickoff throw back to the pitcher. The runner on first took his lead, and was promptly tagged out by the first baseman with a hidden ball. As the Clowns threw the ball around the infield, the shortstop or second baseman dropped a surreptitious second ball. The opposing manager, informed of the gag even before the pickoff attempt, angrily demanded searches of all Clowns infielders. Frisking umpires confiscated extra balls from each Clowns infielder as the crowd roared, and the runner was returned to first on a reversal of ruling.

Tut was the essence of the Clowns and the heart and soul of black baseball. He blazed the trail and set the standard for all other performers who came after him. Peanuts Nyassas, Goose Tatum, Ed Hamman, Nature Boy Williams, Prince Jo Henry and Birmingham Sam Brison were all good—but there was only one King Tut!

2

Peanuts, Goose and Ed

If Tut were not the Clowns' essence, Peanuts Davis might have been. Known also as Peanuts Nyasses on the Ethiopian Clowns, he and Goose Tatum were two of the best athletes ever to play baseball, good enough to make comedy part of every Clowns game from the time Peanuts joined the team in 1938 until illness forced his retirement after the 1950 season.

Dad described one Clowns incident from the mid-1940s as the funniest:

> Against a strong semi-pro club, we were bunching so many hits that we had already knocked three pitchers off the mound when a fourth was called in from the bull pen. As he warmed up, King Tut mimicked his every move, while Peanuts snuck behind the mound and set a pile of newspapers ablaze.
>
> It was a hot afternoon anyway, and the pitcher began to perspire freely, aided by the fire behind him. Fans laughed hysterically, and the pitcher looked at them quizzically, oblivious yet to the roaring flames.
>
> Finally, he became unnaturally hot, turned and saw the blaze and panicked, threw his glove in the air and ran to the center field clubhouse, trailed by King Tut and Peanuts, who failed to persuade him to leave the clubhouse and return to the mound.

The comedy of Peanuts is described in newspapers and magazines of his times. One 1939 source wrote:

> "Peanuts" Nyasses, the Clown prince of baseball, is the funniest of the funny men who call themselves the Ethiopian Clowns baseball team. But he is also one of the best pitchers in baseball today and a star utility player for the top-notch Clowns team. "Peanuts" was the big attraction of the day. He kept the crowd howling with his shipwreck

walk and continued jeering of opposing players and the umpires. In the sixth inning of the second game he was substituted in center field for the Clowns. He went out there wearing a cut-away coat over his uniform, two baseball gloves and he was smoking a long cigar.

The June 26, 1941, edition of the *Winnipeg Tribune* stated:

Baseball showmen like an operative choosing to call himself Peanut Nyasses come along only once in a decade, even among Negro ball players, perhaps the most colorful in the world. . . . Peanut is a skinny, loose-limbed bird who possesses all the hilarious antics usually owned by a top-flight circus clown. In addition, he is one of the most able pitchers ever to appear in Winnipeg and that, perhaps, is why the touring Negro teams, Ethiopian Clowns and Kansas City Monarchs (Negro American League champs), provided an estimated crowd of 4,000 with the best diamond exhibition of the season last night. . . . The Clowns triumphed 7-4 with Peanut Nyasses keeping the customers in a continuous uproar. He drew a great hand every time he shuffled up to the plate and one of the loudest to applaud was Peanut Nyasses. . . . He delivered an endless chain of witty comment and unbelievable contortions . . . The Clowns, bearing war-paint and fictitious names, neatly managed the joint roles of comedians and ball players. Their baserunning was a revelation, their fielding at times miraculous. . . . Shortstop Rivera of the Clowns pulled off two electrifying fielding plays, throwing out a runner from deepest short once and racing in behind the mound, head down, to snap up a ground ball and beat a fast runner another time.

The other Winnipeg daily wrote of the same game:

The Ethiopian Clowns certainly lived up to their name last night at Osborne Stadium. . . . While that old master, Satchel Paige, was billed as the feature attraction, it was Peanuts Nyasses, right-handed ace of the Clowns, who stole the show. . . . Peanuts, who literally had the crowd in fits with his slow motion antics and unconcerned attitude, gave the impression he couldn't even throw a ball from the pitchers' box to home plate. However, looks were deceiving in his case, for with all his clowning (and he didn't stop during the whole game) he could really fog 'em through. . . . The pepper game staged by the Clowns prior to the game was really a treat to watch. . . . Tackelac, Mofike and Wahoo did everything but make the ball talk. . . . the crowd enjoyed their clever performance and wasn't slow in showing their appreciation. . . . the same went for the Shadowball game staged by the Clowns at the end of the seventh inning. . . . We've seen Shadowball games before, but last night's exhibition goes down as the best yet in our books. . . . The crowd was the largest to see a ball game here this season.

Ted Shane captured Peanuts best, with a glimpse at life on a black traveling team, in his article in the September 19, 1942, issue of *Liberty Magazine*:

In the dignified precincts of St. Louis' Sportsman Park one day last summer a long, loose, lugubrious colored gentleman in a cutaway and a plug hat stepped to the plate. The bases were loaded. Bang!—and he sent a ball zooming off the pitcher's shins.

Promptly the runner on first cut straight across the diamond for third, the gent on third headed for first, while the man on second dashed straight for the plate. Instead of sprinting for first, the batter legged it Corrigan-style for third—then kept right on for second. Meanwhile his teammates, faces chalked and in clown-colored uniforms, rushed from their dugout and with sympathetic cries began massaging and applying shinguards to the legs of the dumfounded pitcher.

Well, when you see Peanuts Nyasses and his screwballs of pasture pool—known en masse as the Miami-Cincinnati Ethiopian Clowns— play ball, these are exactly the sort of horsehide shenanigans you pay your money for to see, and are extremely annoyed if you don't. Last year Peanuts was pitching and clowning against Brooklyn's famed Dexter Park Bushwicks—with considerable success. This so irked the Bushwicks that their manager demanded the umpires force Peanuts to cut the comedy and play ball. Result—heartfelt boos from the stands.

The Clowns are currently the colored sensation of independent baseball. With their flashy support, Peanuts claims but five losses in 206 games in four years. Last year he pitched thirty-seven scoreless innings against the great Satchel Paige, best Negro pitcher of all time. In other words, Peanuts Nyasses is currently the best pitcher in Negro baseball.

He was born, not in the African bush but in the N'Orleans fish-fry belt, on August 26, 1917, and was baptized Edward A. Davis. His first job was to pack peanuts in bags at the Jackson, Mississippi, Southeastern League ball park just seventeen years ago. Graduating from the Jackson High School, he debuted in baseball with the Gobbers Grade-8 Feed Company of Jackson, playing any position except catcher against other commercial colored teams.

One day in 1937 a strange collection of colored players came to Jackson to play the Gobbers. They were the Zulu Cannibal Giants. Stripped to the waist, their faces chalked, they dashed about in bare feet and Hawaiian grass skirts, hooting and clowning their way through the game—meanwhile playing excellent ball. They made fools of the poor Gobbers. That is, until Peanuts took charge. When all the Jackson hurlers were pasted out of the box, the Gobbers' manager sent him in. Equipped with a blazing fast ball, a gift for pantomime, and a bag of peanuts, he mixed all three. It resulted in his becoming a full-fledged member of the Zulu Giants for sixty dollars a month and all the hot dogs he could eat. When the Zulu Giants folded, he joined the Louisville Black Spiders, summering with them in the ball park and wintering as a baggage pitcher in a New Orleans hotel.

In 1938 a lunatic outcropping of the Zulu Giants, calling themselves the Miami Ethiopian Clowns, passed through Louisville. Peanuts outgagged and outpitched this comedy aggregation, and again he wound up with it—this time as star knockabout and pitcher. A small financial deal accompanied this change. Pop Coons, manager of the Spiders, refused Peanuts permission to jump to the Clowns unless he paid back ten dollars he owed the club. Pop has been kicking himself ever since.

"I could easily have gotten $100 for Peanuts," he mourns. Rechristened Peanuts Nyasses, he literally pitched and clowned his way to stardom. Let us go backstage and study the technique by which he's made himself the Showboat King of Baseball, as he modestly dubs himself.

SUMMONED to the rubber to start the game, Peanuts is invariably discovered snoozing somewhere in the stands. Half asleep, he warms up, his arm as loose as a goose's neck. Suddenly he is whipping them in with the zip of something shot from a rifle. After such goonishness, what batter can be sure of what will be projected from behind his size-16 shoe?—especially since Peanuts has a habit of waving his team-mates to sit down behind him while he proceeds to fan you with the world's weirdest change-of-pace ball.

During double-headers, when he isn't pitching Peanuts installs himself as third-base coach decked out in an ancient cutaway and silk katy, mocking opponents with burlesques of their play. Now and then he climbs into the stands for a chat and to share your goobers. Comes a tight spot in the game, Peanuts invariably signals to the stands to have himself sent in as a pinch hitter. Invariably the stands chant, "We want Peanuts!"

Umpires, of course, are his dish. He delights the customers by creeping up on an umpire with bat in hand and feigned murder in his eye—to play innocent when the ump suddenly whirls around and catches him at it. . . . With another man on base with him, he will start either a bullfight or a long distance crap game.

Today, his puzzling, clowning, crowd-milking style and timing at perfection, he is probably one of the highest paid Negro players in baseball. His sixty dollars plus hot dogs has swelled considerably—and may go still higher. Because he pitched the Clowns to victory in the Denver Post Annual Invitation Semi-pro Tournament last year—incidentally helping draw in three games 6,000 more fans than the 24,000 the Denver team of the Western League drew in forty-three home stands at the same park—this spring Peanuts wrote his own ticket. He held out four times before he signed. While he may now shuffle physically, he doesn't mentally.

This season Peanuts has had six separate offers to jump the Clowns for other Negro major league teams. But he has refused them all. He knows he'd be out of place with a serious team. As co-owner Syd Pollock puts it: "Peanuts needs the Clowns and they need him."

Nevertheless, behind the grease paint and the laughter Peanuts has his share of headaches. Chief weakness is his unfortunate fondness for ponies. . . . "I was born medium bad luck," he sighs in his slow drawl, "and have never lost over $179 or won over $500 in my financial investments!" Peanuts, in other words, is usually broke, and at the time of this writing he had already tapped his staggering salary for two months' advance! Incidentally, he has a wife and a little daughter, Wilmer Gene Davis, who live in Jackson.

And there is the matter of the bus. All his life Peanuts has had to travel in buses. Usually they've been weary old jaloppies with athlete's phutt, which he and his fellow players have had to take turns driving, repairing or pushing to garages. Though the bus the Clowns now travel in is a $5,000 ex-Greyhound, and though they make enough to afford a real chauffeur to pilot them around . . . during the season Peanuts averages about twenty hours of sleep a week—and this of the half-vertical variety on the bus's reclining chairs. For directly after a game he often has to climb into the bus in his uniform and hotfoot it to the next town, usually from 300 to 400 miles away. "I get so," Peanuts explains, "I can't sleep horizontal. . . . just the same, sleep doesn't do any good. Last year we came to New York to play the Bushwicks. It rained for two days, so we slept for two days. I never did get in the groove. I pitched good—but I just didn't get the laughs."

Winters he plays some professional basketball, lives quietly in Jackson, Mississippi. His driving ambition is to own a giant bowling alley some day. At present this is but a dream, as Hunter Campbell, the Clowns' colored promoter and part owner, has tried vainly to preach thrift to Peanuts, who, he says, is "a human financial sieve."

Meanwhile, the driving ambition of Syd Pollock, sad-eyed white co-owner of the Clowns, is some day to convince big-league moguls there is a place in the major leagues for a team like the Clowns. Pollock is firmly convinced that his beloved Clowns, given a little genuine sleep in Pullmans and some decent food, could—with Peanuts in the box—give the Yanks and Dodgers something to think about. "But try and get a line in the New York papers about Peanuts," he sighs.

We were seated in Pollock's cramped office in his simple home in Tarrytown, New York. A special delivery interrupted our talk. It was from Peanuts asking a twenty-five dollar advance. "Nothing doing," said Pollock firmly. Then he read on: "He says he has a great idea. Wants to walk three batters on purpose—then strike out the next three! Say"—and Pollock's tired eyes suddenly awoke and lit up— "wouldn't that be something! Peanuts Nyasses walks Hassett, Rolfe and Henrich to strike out DiMaggio, Keller, and Gordon!" And I watched his hand reach slowly for his checkbook.

Goose Tatum's élan is well documented in Harlem Globetrotters literature. Born and raised in Eldorado, Arkansas, Goose was 6'3" and had huge, nimble hands. Joyce Hamman, wife of Ed Hamman, recalls that she could press the outside of her thumbs in a cross against the inside of her second fingers and spread both hands as far as she could, set them against a single hand of Goose, fingers spread, and her two hands would have the same span as his one.

During the late 1930s, Colonel Charles B. Franklin, who promoted the Clowns several times annually in Louisville from 1936 to 1964, was putting together his own short-lived team, the Louisville Black Lookouts. Colonel Franklin, a white man, placed player ads in several regional black papers. Goose answered by letter from Eldorado, and Colonel Franklin called him and said, "If you feel you can play pro ball and pay your way into Louisville, I'll reimburse you if you make my club."

A few days later, answering a knock on his front door, Colonel Franklin first saw Goose, age 17, and immediately noticed the player's long arms.

"Col. Franklin, I'm Reece Tatum, El Dorado, Arkansas. Want me go 'round back?" "No need for that. Come right in, Mr. Tatum," Colonel Franklin said.

Asked what position he played, Goose replied, "Shortstop."

Goose proved inadequate at short. His long arms precluded quick release, and fast runners routinely beat out slow rollers to short. So, thinking of the obvious long stretch, Colonel Franklin moved Goose to first. "From the start, Goose was the best fielding first baseman in baseball," he said.

Tom Hayes later signed Goose to a Birmingham Black Barons contract, but when the Cincinnati Clowns entered the Negro American League in 1943, Goose Tatum was the Clowns regular first baseman. He remained at that position through the end of the 1949 season, after which he played basketball full-time for the Globetrotters.

"After Goose was with the Clowns a few years, around 1945 or 1946, Goose went with the Globetrotters winters. They were nothing till they got Goose. He made the Trotters, and no one since has done his job so well,"

Colonel Franklin summarized, "but he was something to see on the diamond too.

"King Tut was an original, a one of a kind, once in a generation performer, with Birmingham Sam close second," he said, "but Goose Tatum provided my Clowns highlight: the funniest thing I ever saw.

"Goose was a good hitter, not a great one. One mid-'40s game here in Louisville, he swung at a curve and missed badly. Stepping out of the batter's box, he placed his bat on the ground, and, imitating King Tut, knelt and prayed. Next pitch he hit 40 feet over the left field wall, and the cheering and laughter were explosive and deafening. The fans went berserk."

Often, as part of the show, Goose's legs shook and his knees bumped in his stance as he awaited the pitch. He was as good a fielder as imaginable. Comedic timing was a strength, spontaneity a trademark. Unusually long arms, a running strut and an infectious grin, all part of his basketball repertoire, served him as well in baseball. He was a key performer in pepperball, shadowball and some of Tut's routines.

Sometimes, Goose would step in front of the bag to receive a throw, watching the runner advance, until, at the last possible moment, Goose tapped first with his toe with a flick of his foot. Sometimes he twitched out four or five staccato taps. Other times, he took the throw with a bullfighter's pass as the runner went by. Other times, he stretched, then caught the ball behind his back. Other times he took the throw in a split, backs of both legs and crotch forming a straight line across the ground.

My brother Jerry's favorite memory of Goose involved a caught foul ball. Instead of running over at the proper angle and leaning into the stands, which would have been a great play by anyone on this particular foul ball, Goose ran to the stands at a 90 degree angle, then, running toward the dugout grinning and reaching his long left arm into the stands, he caught the ball as he highstepped past, timing it all so that his pace never changed.

The Harlem Globetrotters comedy evolved from the Clowns. Their "Sweet Georgia Brown" pregame warm-up was Clowns pepperball without a bat, with a basketball instead of a baseball. Tut originated many ball-handling tricks and almost all comedy in the routine. For example, the ball rolling down the back and flipped off the rear end to the waiting teammate was

Tut; the ball offered forward and flipped over the head to the hand behind the back, resulting in a handshake with the tossing hand, was Tut.

Tut's water fight was long a part of Clowns entertainment. He and a crony carried a bucket of water from the dugout, wiping sweaty brows. Alongside Sunday-best-dressed fans in crowded box seats they rested for a cool drink, scooping paper cups of drinking water from the bucket and sipping, but eventually arguing until the water fight erupted using full paper cups as launchers. Tut escalated the battle, bucket raised, and confetti floated harmlessly from the pail as Tut heaved the contents toward his cohort ducking in front of the flinching fieldside fans. It was a part of every Clowns' appearance, and just when fans who'd seen it before expected confetti, Tut would douse them with real water. The Globetrotters popularized the routine worldwide once Goose Tatum joined them.

A substantial number of Globetrotters routines originated with Tut and the Clowns, and the looping foul shot with weighted ball and the ball on elastic were created by Ed Hamman, who spent decades as a comedian and business manager with Negro league teams including the Clowns and Kansas City Monarchs. For several key basketball seasons, Ed was owner Abe Saperstein's business manager and comedy coordinator for the Trotters; he was Dad's second and last partner in operating the Clowns. As a player, Ed had toured for years with the House of David, the independent, bearded, white team that was sponsored by and popularized a religious sect in Michigan and often played the Clowns and other Negro league teams. Ed was an integral part of their pepperball routines and lent his own style to the Globetrotters' "Sweet Georgia Brown" warm-up. Reese "Goose" Tatum was the Clowns' greatest contribution to the "Funnymen of Basketball" (taken from the Clowns' self-designated "Funnymen of Baseball"). A gifted athlete with natural comedic timing and a wonderfully malleable face, Goose used his long arms (84-inch "wingspan"), huge hands and lithe grace with the Clowns at first base and during intra-squad pickup basketball games. Clowns players reported Goose's prowess on the court, and Dad suggested to Abe that he use Goose with the Trotters. Goose proved even better at basketball than baseball. As catalyst to Globetrotters success, he was frequently referred to in the press as "The Goose Who Laid the Golden Egg."

Goose played only baseball before 1945, both sports from 1945 to 1949, and only basketball after that, until he tried baseball again after he left the Trotters.

His factory manager/semi-pro ballplayer job eliminated by the depression, Ed Hamman toured during 1932 with his Nebraska Indians team, consisting of Ed and native American Indians. In 1933, Dad helped him form the Canadian Clowns, a white spinoff of Dad's Havana Red Sox–Cuban House of David–Cuban Stars teams. In 1934, Ed joined the bearded House of David club, where he remained for years, sharpening his pepperball skills. Partway into the 1944 season, he signed with Dad as an entertainer with the Clowns, and reported to the club at Mudhen Stadium in Toledo, Ohio, a day well remembered by Joyce, whom he had married the prior year: "The Clowns were in a class by themselves. It was baseball with a definite difference. It was exciting. It was great baseball. Crowd noise and involvement were unbelievable. I began to anticipate the unexpected. It was joyful. I had never seen anything like it."

Caledonia the trained duck was Ed's most famous routine. Ed performed with Caledonia at the 1948 Cleveland Indians–Boston Braves World Series game that drew the largest crowd in baseball history at that time. Caledonia traveled with Ed and the Clowns for years. Waddling from the dugout between innings, Caledonia was trained to set up shop between the lines. Players running to positions pointed at the duck and complained. At unpredictable intervals, Caledonia wiggled a few steps, wings flapping, and surveyed the world with malice and defiance. Reacting to player requests, the umpire motioned to the dugout for some zoological authority to remove the creature. Ed Hamman, in traditional circus clown suit, complete with white greasepaint face and painted red smile, emerged and approached the duck. Caledonia's basic training was to wait until Ed came within a few feet and then to run away, wings flapping, casting about defiant looks like royalty looking down on a rabble crowd. Caledonia was an actress who always portrayed herself. She was typecast as one angry, acidic, put-upon, dyspeptic duck. For four or five minutes, as Ed got next to her, Caledonia ran and flapped her wings and looked around malevolently. He got a broom and dustpan and tried to sneak up on her from behind to sweep her off her webbed feet, but still at the last second, she flapped and ran. A net proved useless. The grounds crew then took the field to assist in her capture, but Caledonia engaged in skilled broken field waddling, eluding all like some winged, lopsided All-American halfback.

Finally, on cue from Ed, a player took the field oblivious to Caledonia, and Caledonia happily waddled over to him and climbed into his arms for the ride to the dugout ending the act.

Caledonia was not alone in the Hamman petting zoo. For a few years, Ed carried a coin-collecting monkey that sat on the wooden book box suspended from Ed's neck as he passed through the stands selling souvenir joke books. Apparently bored with the off-season, the monkey once ate a considerable portion of paint off the outside of the Hammans' home and, a short time later, ate their cupboard. "I was always happy when Jocko went on the road," Joyce said. One day Ed called home, sobbing uncontrollably. When he could talk, he told Joyce, "I accidentally locked Jocko in the car in the hot sun. He didn't make it—poor, innocent creature. Jocko's dead and it's my fault."

The pseudo-scientific aspect of baseball appealed to Ed. His daughter, Louise, said, "Our garage never housed a car. It was a baseball laboratory, under control of my mad-scientist father and strewn with the body parts of baseball equipment and whatever material would hold together my father's inventions."

The simplest was the ball balance, which consisted of a baseball screwed onto the knob end of a bat. Ed staggered across the field balancing the ball on the bat and the bat upside down on the palm of his hand, and when the crowd finished applauding, he tilted the bat back over his shoulder, ball defying gravity, bowed and walked happily into the dugout.

An umbrella popped out of the end of another bat, just in time to protect against a sprinkling of water also generated from the top of the bat.

Ed meandered through foul territory smoking a Camel cigarette from the mouth of a perfectly painted wooden camel, a cigarette holder three-quarters of a foot long and a foot high.

He ate popcorn from a spring-operated box that showered the snack over the umpire trying to accept the tendered treat.

Between innings once a game, he stood atop the pitcher's mound with a mechanical arm, realistic hand with ball painted on wood at the end of the sleeve. He wound up and delivered, but the ball was never released. Rather it stayed, and the mechanical arm slid to a length of eight or nine feet and formed one side of a grotesque obtuse triangle, with Ed's forward-leaning body and the ground forming the other two sides. Ed's painful cries for help brought Tut and Bebop. Tut unstuck him and administered first aid to Ed's shoulder as Bebop walked under Ed's outstretched arm, supporting it on his head with both hands.

Between another set of innings, Ed approached the plate for batting practice, but as the pitch was delivered, his bat wilted and bent into an almost sexual arch at the label, like a Freudian disaster. The expression on the clown's face matched the event, as he walked sad and embarrassed back to the dugout.

Ed designed Tut's giant bat, which was made by Joyce's father, Tony Pillsburg, a carpenter and contractor. Ed also developed safe use of special percussion firecrackers strapped into gloves for Clowns infielders.

He entertained most years for the Clowns until his 1958 heart attack ended his performing career. He excelled at ball-handling feats, and his last season as an entertainer, at age 51, he could still throw a strike from home to second behind his back. Once during the late 1940s, Clowns first baseman Armando "Bocci" Vasquez was riding from one Deep South game to the next with the Hamman family in Ed's car. A state highway patrolman pulled them over to find out why a black man was riding with a white family in a car with an Ohio license plate. The officer's anger further ripened when he realized the black man spoke little English. But when Ed told him they were all headed to a comedy baseball game, and the patrolman asked Ed to tell him about it, Ed briefly summarized Clowns' activities.

"What do you mean, you fellas throw differently?" the officer asked.

Ed picked up a rock, and the officer nodded when Ed asked him if he saw the telephone pole across the street and down the block. Ed then hit the pole with a behind-the-back throw, and the patrolman let the party pass, but not before getting the Clowns' regional schedule.

3

Nature Boy, Prince Jo and Birmingham Sam

The comedy of James "Natureboy" Williams was part of Dad's Clowns from 1955 to 1964. Initially, he played barefooted, in a dress, wearing falsies, and was billed as "Clowns Firstbase Ma'am." He wore a question mark for a number on his back. No one seriously thought he was female, and no one took him as a female impersonator. He simply played baseball well, but in different clothing.

Natche was a combination of all prior Clowns entertainers. His first few years, he performed with Tut and Ed Hamman and learned from them. After Tut was gone, he was part of many Tut routines in either the Tut or the Bebop role. The hilarious incongruity of his portly physique and deft athleticism was personified by his ability to leap high in the air as an infielder's throw approached and come down in a perfect split while making the catch. Once a game, Natureboy batted with his back to home plate, jumping around to hit only after the offering left the pitcher's hand.

His antics cannot be separated from those of infielders Prince Jo Henry and Birmingham Sam Brison. Prince Jo Henry said his ideas came from God. If Mozart was right that he merely scored the music God put in his head, maybe Prince Jo was right too. The most popular skit for Prince Jo was the bats-in-the-pants routine. Customarily, Prince Jo played in checkered Bermuda shorts, a Clowns jersey and a white navy rain hat pulled down around his head. Usually the second at bat of each game, he wore loose-fitting flannel coveralls held up by suspenders, and took a called first strike. Stepping out of the batter's box, he put the knob of the bat against his eye like a wooden spyglass, closed the other eye and squinted up the surface of the bat like a carpenter inspecting a board, turning it gently in caressing hands. Perceiving an imperfection invisible to others, he tossed the bat toward the dugout, reached into his pants, seeming to try to hide his actions as though doing something illicit, looked both ways to assure himself no one was watching, and slowly and seductively slid a second bat up out of his pants. As crowd laughter approached crescendo, he surveyed the second bat, discarded it, and slid out a third, then a fourth, then a tiny souvenir bat, then the leg of a female mannequin, taking his stance and wildly swinging the appendage menacingly toward the pitcher, then pounding it on the plate, swaying his body wildly and defiantly like an elastic wand. Only when the umpire confiscated it did Prince Jo realize what it was and cringe in embarrassment. Sometimes, he'd augment the plate appearance by pulling something else out of his pants: a broom, a fishing rod, an oar, a pool cue, and then he'd slide out two more bats before he finally had a keeper and finished his at bat.

Prince Jo, whose early career in the Negro American League with the Philadelphia Stars was followed by two years of minor league ball, joined the Clowns in 1955, the year after they left the Negro American League. He was a good-fielding, weak-hitting third baseman his first two seasons with the Clowns, before turning to comedy to seek a raise and assure presence in the starting lineup, if not at God's behest, certainly bestowing grace on the Clowns' comedy sanctuary. He got his starting position and his raise.

Whenever caught in a rundown, almost always intentionally, Prince Jo pulled a base from his pants, stood on it and argued he was safe.

One of the Clowns' great improvising comics, he took a bad call strike at a 1957 game I attended in a poorly lit former minor league ballpark in Fort Lauderdale, Florida. As the pitcher released the next pitch, Prince Jo pulled a lit flashlight from his uniform and followed the pitch into the catcher's mitt with the light, piercing the umpire with a baleful look as though stating, "I damn sure hope you got a better look at that one!" The umpire called ball, and the fans howled. It was the only time he ever did that, and the crowd of just over 1,500 were the only ones who ever saw that particular piece of comedy genius.

And that was Prince Jo, always something different, fresh, outrageous, unpredictable. And just because something worked once didn't necessarily mean he'd do it again. Some things, like the flashlight, were, like fine art, created only once.

Prince Jo, who played with the Clowns only through the end of the 1959 season, and Natche coupled for ultimate use of Ed Hamman's percussion firecrackers. Sometimes Prince Jo fielded a hard-hit grounder at third and attempted to race the runner to first for an unassisted putout, throwing to a leaping, splitting Natureboy Williams at the last possible second. As the ball hit Natureboy's mitt and Natureboy's crotch hit the dirt, the firecracker exploded, and after the putout, Natche threw the smoking glove into the air, then shook his hand and worked his fingers, dancing around in apparent pain. Sometimes both men fielded their positions in chairs, and, occasionally, when things went perfectly, someone hit a one-hopper to Prince Jo in the chair and he tossed to Natureboy's exploding mitt, with neither player leaving his chair. Occasionally there were seated double plays.

Bobo Nickerson learned ball handling as a pitcher-pepperballer for the House of David clubs of the late 1940s and early 1950s, and appeared at least part of most seasons with the Clowns from 1959 to 1964.

One of two players ever to catch a ball dropped from the Washington Monument (the other was major leaguer Gabby Street), Bobo juggled bats and balls. He was one of two white performers to travel regularly with the Clowns, the other being Ed Hamman. Bobo's bat juggling extended to tower-high tosses caught behind the back like an expert twirler. His juggling of four and five balls around and between his legs, as he bent forward, was particularly impressive. He often threw balls simultaneously to three different players lined up side by side.

Bobo was known for his pantomime imitation of a nervous rookie pitcher, and, unexpectedly, was the only comedian, other than Tut, to ever successfully perform Tut's changing of the hats through the stands. But Bobo did it rarely, only as the mood took him. His chances were limited anyway because, by his time, crowd dress had become far less formal for most games.

Bobo was truly one of those "unforgettable characters" that are encountered along the way in life's journey, and there will be more about him later.

Birmingham Sam Brison added his own magic to the legacy of all who preceded him as Clowns. A 1962 rookie, Sam, like Prince Jo, was a mediocre-hitting, sharp-fielding, intuitive player-comedian. He was distinguished by nonstop creativity and an ability to slide like no one else.

Belly sliding into third, Sam became a comedian when he moved hands and feet through the dirt in a freestyle swimming motion. After that, Ed Hamman, then road business manager, offered him two dollars a day extra to clown, and Sam became so successful, his pay rose accordingly. Eventually, he worked year around, touring basketball seasons with the Harlem Globetrotters.

A shortstop–third baseman, Sam excelled at Prince Jo's field antics of trying to outrun runners to first and fielding from a chair. His creativity revolved around his ability to slide. His swimming slide became a staple along with his slide through the second baseman's legs.

Sam originated some set routines. Once each game during Sam's at bat, he argued a call, and Natureboy Williams retaliated against the home plate ump by lighting a superloud firecracker behind him, but without telling Sam. At the explosion, Sam threw his bat in the air and ran down the first base line, leaping parallel to the ground into the first base coach's arms, hugging the coach's neck and hiding his quivering face in the nape, while the coach cuddled him and patted his head, assuring him everything was all right.

Sam's ability to mimic rivaled Tut's, and in Grand Island, Nebraska, when I was with the team as temporary road business manager in 1962, the power company sent a truck to a Clowns night game to repair a light tower. Sam mimicked the lineman move for move from the time the worker left the truck, and crowd laughter reached a frenzy when, as Sam put one foot on the pole to climb after the lineman, he intentionally activated a field watering well pump with his foot, sending a geyser of water up the pole, drenching the lineman and Sam.

But the funniest sight gag I ever saw happened about a week after that in St. Joseph, Missouri. During May and June of 1962, St. Joe underwent a month-plus drought. City Stadium there had been used for tournament after tournament, game after game—a college regional championship tournament, then a Little League Tournament, then a Pony League Tournament, then a Babe Ruth League Tournament, then an American Legion Tournament, then a semi-pro tournament, plus regular games, then the Clowns.

Because of water use restrictions, the groundskeeper responded with promises only to my intermittent pleas to water down the infield, so that the whole game was played in dust. Running created bursts of smoky clouds that blended into fog. Breezes stirred fog and coughing. The groundskeeper probably had some form of lung disease himself, as he disappeared shortly after the game started, undoubtedly to check into a hospital for dust inhalation.

Toward the end of the game, "Midget" Billy Vaughn, the Clowns 4'5" shortstop, batted with Sam at first on a single. Billy was a fair hitter without power. With one out, the outfield was drawn in. Sam wore the twin-billed cap invented by Tut and a circus-clown suit. Billy lofted a fastball over the leftfielder's head. Sam rounded third in staccato puffs of dust knowing he faced a play at the plate. He started his slide at least 15 feet from home, and the throw from left went into a cloud that enveloped the sliding Sam, the catcher, the umpire—all invisible until the umpire's hands, poking out through the haze, signaled safe, and as the cloud drifted quickly apart, Sam was uncovered resting on his back, his left foot on home plate, his right leg nestled relaxed across his left, head on his hands behind his head, puffing on a lit cigar. The crowd of about 2,500 laughed like thunder.

With the skill of a TV talent show host, Dad presented a variety of acts over the years, none of whom had the staying power of the baseball comedians. Juggling Joe Taylor and Paul Batholemay, a one-man band billed as Boogie-Woogie Paul, entertained during the late 1940s. Juggling Joe was an exceptionally good juggler, but his talent didn't relate to baseball.

Dero Austin, a nonplaying midget, joined the team in 1964, Dad's last year. Each game, he initially appeared as Birmingham Sam opened a rattling steamer trunk rocking near home plate, and the midget popped out like a baby dinosaur out of a giant, misshapen, hinged egg, scaring Sam head over heels backwards. A discovery of Ed Hamman, Dero was heir apparent to Spec Bebop, but unlike Bebop, he had no Tut, had no long-term Syd Pollock to publicize his career and had no Negro leagues, and he never shared the popularity or longevity attained by his predecessor.

PART TWO

SYD POLLOCK
The Man Behind the Clowns

Mystifies me mightily how your daddy always run hisself so well so clean.
                                                                —Satchel Paige

Two and two don't make four on the road.

                                                                —Ed Hamman

4

Dad and Baseball

In Municipal Stadium, Kansas City, on the afternoon of June 10, 1962, before 4,553 paid, Dad's Indianapolis Clowns beat Satchel Paige and the Kansas City Giants 9-2. Satchel wasn't bad, considering his age and the pregame events. In five innings, he allowed six hits and seven runs behind four Giants' errors.

Before the game, Dad showed me how to set up the gate at a large stadium, then we met with the old-time Negro leaguers at the gate, among them Satchel Paige in his Kansas City Giants uniform.

"So what you want to do now that you finished college, Little Syd?" Satchel asked me.

"Run the Clowns," I said.

"Shit," Satchel said, "got to watch yourself there. A dirty business this, far as that concerned. You got people loves womens much as baseball—might not show when you figger. Ain't that right, Syd?" he asked Dad.

"Or you got people off fishing," Dad said.

"Or off fishing," Satchel echoed. "Worse, you got thieves, you got numbers people in this here business. Shit, you get people shot dead up in the crowd bettin' on our goddamn games. Mystifies me mightily how your daddy always run hisself so well so clean. But you ought to think twice, Little Syd, before you go mixin' with nasty people in a dyin' business. You daddy tell you I ain't lyin'."

Having issued his warning, Satchel shook my hand, announced warm-up time, said his goodbyes and gently jangled down through the stands to the Kansas City Giants' dugout, which amplified his anguished roar. Someone had stolen his glove from the Kansas City Giants' bench.

"Someone stole my glove, Little Syd," Satchel told me later. "Look like I should have been off fishin' or lovin'."

At that moment, Dad's black comedy teams had been traveling the continent averaging over 200 games a year for 33 seasons. The Negro leagues and the great Clowns teams were past. I was 21, and about to hit the road with the Clowns as temporary road business manager. In under a month, M. H. Winston would drive us 500 miles on a tough nighttime jump from hate to love. And in less than seven years, Dad would die, and I would fully know how well he understood life, and how he "always run hisself so well so clean."

Diogenes' lantern burned out, and he died about 23 centuries too soon to find Dad. In fifth grade, I listed the greatest people who ever lived. The best was Dad, and that never changed. He wasn't perfect. For publicity, he exaggerated Toni Stone's salary as the first female professional baseball player in a male major league. He was earthy, and once had Mom rearranging shopping plans to go to a certain neighborhood grocer, who, he told her, with a five dollar order, would take her out back and give her a free goose. But he was good, he worked hard, and he was devoted first to family, then to others, and last to self. He taught what was right not by saying it, but by doing it. Traveling baseball offered almost limitless opportunity for dirty dealing, and Dad always declined. Instead, he put aside opportunism in his peers and dealt with them on the basis of their good qualities and with a sense of humor reflecting his team. He didn't think in terms of race except when prejudices demanded confrontation. He saw things as they were and as they ought to be. He lived the way we should.

It was hard to think of Dad and not the Clowns or the Clowns without Dad. And Dad and the Clowns shaped our family's world, as Dad would say, "as round as a baseball."

In turn, to understand how our family was shaped, we should begin with my grandmothers, Theresa Sussman Pollock and Estella O'Connor Carroll.

Potato noodles hung over the edge of the bowl on Grandma Pollock's kosher table, and the family spoke German and stood and ate them using fingers, rural Middle European style. Nearby on Pine Street, Nana Carroll read her family's fortunes from teacup bottoms and told how Roderick O'Connor, the last pagan king of Ireland, was blasted between the eyes by a lightning bolt. Grandma never left the Temple on Yom Kippur, the Day of Atonement, and Nana went to daily Mass.

On November 11, 1923, Dad first died when he told Grandpa Pollock he had that day married a Catholic, and Grandpa threw him down the stairs from the apartment and told him he was dead. The Pollock family sat shiva, the balm for surviving Jews. Although the Carrolls acknowledged that both Dad and Mother lived, they had room for one only. So for months Mom stayed home and Dad lived with his friend Moe Levy and family until Dad and Mom could afford their own apartment. With the birth of my brother Don, as firstborn son a Messianic candidate, Dad became a born-again Orthodox Jew, rewelcomed into the Pollock home.

Years later, whenever we were lost and used someone's driveway to turn around, Dad said toward the house, "Don't put the coffee on, we're not staying."

Sydney Samuel Pollock and Villa Carroll Pollock stayed. They were married three times: by a justice of the peace, by a priest, by a rabbi. They had Diocesan dispensation to marry, and to secure it Dad gave the Church his written promise to raise the children Catholic. Only then did the Catholic ceremony occur—in the back of the church. We were raised Catholic, and as long as Dad lived, the Church told us it would be a sin for us to attend synagogue with him. When he went, he went alone. Dad attended all our family religious ceremonies, including First Holy Communions and, occasionally, Midnight Mass.

Because it involved joy and giving, Dad loved Christmas. We all went to the lot, but he selected our Christmas tree. And each Christmas Eve as we slept, he decorated it. He gave us money for Church collections, won a $500 raffle one year at the Carmelite Church and donated $100 of it back to the Church. He selected Patrick as my confirmation name. He always remained Jewish, ultimately switching from Orthodox to Conservative. We went to family Bat Mitzvahs, Bar Mitzvahs and weddings, but no other Jewish ceremonies. Mother and Dad stayed married until Dad died on November 21, 1968.

Just before I married Marti at a High Mass in 1962, her sister-in-law Susan, a non-Catholic bridesmaid, who had never attended Mass, suddenly realized she didn't know when to sit, stand, kneel, bless herself or otherwise act Catholic. Fearing that she might inadvertently commit a felony under canon law, she sought procedural advice from a non-Catholic who had been through it all, one with a Catholic wife and five Catholic children—Dad.

"When in doubt, genuflect," he said.

Dad once concluded that Christians were Jews who believed the Messiah had come.

That conclusion typified Dad. He sought harmony, adjustment, and ecumenism. He viewed all as companions, not competitors. He found strengths, not weaknesses. He valued positive things. His terms were always fair. Most of that had to do with what was inside him. Some of that had to do with where and when he lived.

In the 1890s Austria-Hungary, Cossacks and anti-Semites raided farms along the Danube, raping, killing, stealing and destroying. The Sussmans sent their children by twos to the safety of New York City. Theresa Sussman came to the United States an indentured servant to her uncle, a Manhattan physician, and in New York City, she met Edward Pollock, an immigrant from Budapest employed as a machinist in what was to become the Maxwell-Briscoe Motor Company car plant in North Tarrytown, New York (since renamed Sleepy Hollow).

In 1898 they were married and moved to the second story flat at 74 Beekman Avenue in North Tarrytown, an apartment building they would later own and live in the rest of their lives. Dad, the oldest of six children from this union, was born March 20 or 22, 1901. He always requested two gifts, settled for one, and never knew his birthday.

With an indentured servant's work ethic and schedule (later adopted by Dad), Grandma developed a dry goods store into ownership of a significant number of apartment buildings and commercial properties, including the Strand Theater. Entertainment in the Tarrytowns changed forever on October 7, 1915, when Grandpa Pollock opened the Strand Theater, with silent movies flickering to Aunt Dot's raucous piano playing and with vaudeville.

Twenty-five miles south, New York City was the world entertainment center. Grandpa operated the Strand into the 1940s. Movie pickup in New York City was one of Dad's duties, and his standard answer to Grandpa's question about what movies were in the cans was "Charlie Chaplin in 'His Pants' and Tom Mix in 'Concrete.'"

Although early clarity was needed for forbidden notes carried back and forth by Beth Levy between Dad at North Tarrytown Elementary and Mother at St. Theresa's School, the clarity of Dad's letters as an adult belies his beginnings. He spoke German, Hebrew and Yiddish until he learned English to begin school, and his formal education ended at age fourteen, when Grandma and Grandpa took him from school to help run the Strand. But the theater exposed him to show business and added passion for entertainment to his existing love for baseball, so that the future wedding of Dad to the Clowns was mere ceremony celebrating two existing loves.

Dad young was like an artist collecting colors to paint a masterpiece. Business acumen expanded from Grandma and in the Strand. Love blossomed with Mom. The theater sharpened his sense of humor. His town and reactions to the mixed marriage affected his perspective, his generosity, his tolerance, his integrity. And the state of American sports defined his love for baseball.

Dad was a journeyman amateur men's basketball player. Sometimes he raced through traffic along Manhattan streets against long distance club runners. But his sport was baseball.

Baseball was the national pastime. There were two major leagues, hundreds of minor league teams, hundreds of traveling pro and semi-pro clubs and thousands of local semi-pro nines. Every city and almost every town had at least one enclosed baseball park where admissions could be charged for fans eager to see their favorite local or traveling team. Commentators noted that the game's ebb and flow, rules, drama, free choice, unpredictability, political structure, mythology, character, egalitarianism, reward for excellence and element of chance mirrored America. America loved a raw sport with an intensity that might never again occur.

In Poughkeepsie, New York, in 1928, when Dad, then an established baseball entrepreneur, was awarded a bouquet of flowers as the youngest promoter in baseball, his professional promoting career already spanned 12 years, back to age 15.

As early as the mid-1920s Dad was sending out postcards as exclusive booking agent for the Maggie Riley Devil Dogs, a "Semi-Pro Male Club—One of the Fastest Out of Metropolitan District—with Baseball's $10,000 Female 'Wonder Girl.'"

Dad studied the game as few others and knew its every nuance. He watched a player bat once and forever recalled his tendencies. He had both a sense of the game and an acquired knowledge. Forty years after he stopped playing, he could often predict a home run by a hitter's body language and attitude.

During the 1930s, when Babe Ruth, Lou Gehrig, Tony Lazzari, Earl Combs, Frankie Crosetti and Bill Dickey were Yankees, Dad weekly took my brother Don and *Tarrytown News* sports editor Larry Angel to Yankee Stadium. The Philadelphia Athletics, with Lefty Grove, Mickey Cochrane and Jimmy Foxx, were the Yankees' strongest rivals, and Dad chose those games whenever possible. Don recalls the two men talking strategy, and Dad told Don things like "The batter's supposed to hit behind the runner to advance him, but watch Lefty pitch inside to prevent it, and watch the second baseman move two steps to his right because he knows Lefty has the control to do it." He was usually right, and the second baseman would prevent a hit by barely reaching a grounder through the box.

I was 11 in 1952, striking out the first eight times I'd faced curve balls. My ninth chance came against Tarrytown Red Birds' curve baller Joe Rucker. Between innings, Dad called me over to the stands.

"Rucker's struck you out twice on curves," he said. "What size bat you using?

"Thirty-five inch," I said.

"Switch to a thirty-three. It's lighter. And if he throws a fast ball, wait for the curve, then whip that thirty-three through it." I did, and laced a triple over the left fielder's head.

After the inning, I went to Dad. "The thirty-three works great!"

"Now go back to the thirty-five. You get better bat speed."

"But you said thirty-three."

"You were striking out looking at the curve. I had to tell you something to make you swing. Hitting—come to think of it, everything—is 90 percent confidence."

Dad organized, operated and played for the semi-pro Westchester Blue Sox. He was a good fielder and base runner, a smart player, an adequate hitter. He played confidently, and said, "Hitting's hard, for me near impossible, but bunting's easy. Easiest thing there is. Just hold the bat and wait for the pitch to hit it. And so many major leaguers can't do it. I would have hit .180 in the majors, but between swings I'd have bunted 1.000."

Former Blue Sox teammate Leaguer Marasco told me, "I never saw your father swing at a pitch and miss." Dad's reaction: "But I never hit it far, and was called out a lot on strikes."

The team was a powerhouse in southeastern New York during the early 1920s. Dad played for the Blue Sox from his early teens until 1923, when he broke his leg sliding into third.

Mom and Dad had just moved into their first home, a one-bedroom apartment over the U.S. Post Office on Cortlandt Street.

Dad recalled the brilliant red of Mom's hair that morning and her blue eyes matching the sunlit sky. It was warm and midsummer, and he clacked the fat end of the bat along the glistening cobblestones of Cortlandt Street as he walked to the ballpark for the game against the Catholic Lyceum team. He felt like something good would happen, and fantasized that someone from New York would spot him that day and sign him for the Yankees.

Mom later cited the day as evidence of the truth of her eternally optimistic Irish adage that bad things always happen for the best.

Dad's leg broke when he slid into third on a triple in the right center field gap. He was later told that had he held his foot slightly higher, the damage might not have been career ending. But that break benefitted all who sought joy in sports. It changed Dad's emphasis from playing to business. Instead of dividing time among playing, promoting and player placement, he now focused on the latter two aspects. Many semi-pro teams early in the century were sponsored by factories, which hired ballplayers as workers. Unlike professional players, semi-pros were salaried as workers only. Their pay-to-play came from team division of a share of the gate. If a plant needed a foreman-shortstop, Dad reviewed inventoried applications for the best available player skilled also as a plant foreman. For making the placement, Dad received a commission.

But the heart of his baseball business was booking and promoting. Early local efforts expanded as he played around the state with the Blue Sox and booked their schedule. By the time he was injured, he was booking not only the Blue Sox and other semi-pro nines, but such nationally known barnstorming novelty teams as the House of David with its long-haired and bearded ballplayers, the New York Bloomer Girls and Negro league teams.

Booking and promoting was done by fractions. The ball park got a cut, the teams took percentages and the booker and promoter, often the same person, had a share. The number of ball-yards where paid admissions could be controlled had peaked in those days, and in that sense, booking was at its easiest, but it was more difficult for the booker to keep his cities after his first try. Competition was fierce among promoters, and fans were often lost to other nearby contests. The booker had to maintain a good reputation with those who owned or controlled ballparks; otherwise, if his attraction didn't appear or didn't draw well or if he was a cheat, he would not be able to book the city again.

Baseball mirrored American segregation and racial prejudice.

Jackie Robinson's 1947 debut with the Brooklyn Dodgers is celebrated for breaking baseball's color barrier. It was more of a hole in the dike. I was with Dad and Braves farm system director John Mullen on an elevator in the Commodore Hotel in New York City during the 1954 World Series. Ray Neil, perennial Negro American League All-Star second baseman, had joined the Clowns in 1942, and spent the next thirteen seasons riding highways parallel to the major leagues. The first three innings of each game were sliced forever away from Neil in 1953 for the drawing power playing time of Toni Stone and in 1954 for her successor, Connie Morgan. Neil led the Negro American League in eight different offensive categories in 1953, including highest batting average and most doubles. A quiet, smooth player, he had to be seen over a period of time for proper evaluation. The aging Neil still could have started on most major league clubs in 1954, and Dad wanted him in the majors for his remaining career.

"Your people ought to look at Ray Neil and several other players I have," Dad said.

"Syd, management tells me our system has its quota of Negroes," Mullen replied.

If Dad thought it unusual to form a partnership with a black man in the 1930s, race didn't enter the decision. It was the naturally right thing to do. Dad had operated Cuban comedy teams, black teams, beginning in 1929. In the spring of 1936 Hunter Campbell, financed by Johnnie Pierce, left South Florida in two Cadillacs on tour through the darkness of the Great Depression and the deeper darkness of baseball's segregated world, with a newly named black aggregation, the Miami Ethiopian Clowns.

Mostly South Floridians, Clowns players bore names presumed African: Impo, Kalahari, Mofike, Selassie, Tarzan, Khora, Aussa, Sardo. Whether wearing grass skirts or clown suits and red wigs, they wore neither baseball shirts nor numbers, and their faces were unrecognizable under greasepaint or war paint. When behind white teams, they batted only their three or four best hitters around until they were back in the game, and their opponents never noticed the difference.

They were a major league quality baseball club. And Dad, who booked them throughout the Northeast earlier as the Miami Giants, was delighted that the Clowns, like his Cuban teams, now featured comedy. He booked the Clowns for his eight best New York spots. Crowds were slim as the Clowns played north, and two days before the first of Dad's bookings, Hunter Campbell called to cancel Dad's eight dates because the team was heading home to disband for want of funds.

Avoiding damage to reputation and loss of his eight best cities, Dad asked Hunter what amount he needed to make the eight dates before disbanding, and Dad sent the money. The eight games in New York State drew more than the Clowns had attracted from Florida to Pennsylvania, and Dad and Hunter saw that their talents were complementary. They agreed that Hunter would run the team on the field and handle road business management and Dad would book and promote. They became partners.

Dad's other booking and promoting diminished; his player placement service ended.

5

View from the Office

To New York Yankees fans outside American League metropolitan areas, the Yankees remained abstractions on sports pages or in occasional newsreels.

The Clowns were America's living team; they brought the taste and smell and sound and feel of baseball into every part of every state, from big cities to small towns. During the decades when Babe Ruth, Lou Gehrig, Joe DiMaggio, Yogi Berra and Mickey Mantle played on familiar grounds in Yankee Stadium, King Tut, Buster Haywood, Speed Merchant, Verdes Drake and Peanuts Davis labored everywhere from Yankee Stadium to a Little League Field in Deming, New Mexico, from Comiskey Park to airplane hangars on military bases or steel mill yards or picnic fields. Anyone anywhere in the United States could see the Clowns someplace some season without waiting too long to see them again.

The Clowns were history's most financially successful and dependable road team in part because their schedule consumed Dad. He considered every factor and started inquiries months before the season began. A family man first, Dad had his office in our home once Mom and Dad moved into 27 Maple Street in 1932. Mail was so voluminous and timing so important that, with the exception of Sundays, Dad visited the Clowns post office box at least four times daily, year around. He forwarded player mail to general delivery in one or two predetermined cities weekly for mail calls. Incoming correspondence numbered as many as hundreds of pieces in a single day, including fan mail and player family mail and letters from other teams, players and prospective players, scouts, local promoters, news people and suppliers.

Most mail involved booking and promoting. Big draw cities were set first. Over the years the Clowns drew crowds ranging from 5,000 to more than 31,000 in major cities. Dates available to a traveling team at a given park in such cities usually totaled less than seven in a given season, so that early,

Dad tried to obtain one or two dates for each such city plus a rain date in case of a rainout.

The rest of the schedule was set between those dates, but with consideration of many factors. It was necessary to obtain either a flat fee or an enclosed park where paid attendance could be controlled. Then the issue became whether the park was available when desired. So the home team had to be away at the right time, and no other attraction booked first for the appropriate date. The next factor was the availability of a follow-up booking within a reasonable jumping time or distance.

Weather patterns were crucial. Dates in an area during its rainy season would be wasted.

Availability and quality of roads were important. In the Dewey Decimal System of Clowns literature, book number one was the well-worn road atlas Dad kept in his office. Routes over routes were penciled in red, black and blue on each rumpled, kaleidoscopic page, to distinguish one planned or proposed trip from the next. Mileage was added in margins. A replacement was bought annually. Terrain was the related geographical factor. A 100-mile jump across mountains could take as long as a 400-mile jump across the plains. Flooded rivers could cause a missed date, and the Clowns never missed a booking in the thirty-five seasons Dad operated the team. No other road team could make such a claim, and more than once the Clowns arrived for their appearance only because Dad was aware of weather conditions and geography between one game and the next, and phoned a warning to the team.

In 1955, the first year after the Clowns left the Negro American League, their traveling partners were the New York Black Yankees, managed by former Negro leagues great Dick Lundy, who roamed the continent during the 1920s for the Bacharach Giants of Atlantic City, and was considered as fine a shortstop as ever played. Lundy had family in Connecticut. Mom and Dad and I spent the night before the Clowns–Black Yankees game in Poughkeepsie with Estelle and Al, my sister and brother-in-law, who operated their first dancing studio there. Dad called the team's hotel in Montreal, warning Dick to avoid Connecticut next day because of local rains. He didn't, and the Black Yankees were flooded into place overnight.

Two local black teams volunteered to play the Clowns four and a half innings each that night, and money was refunded to ticket holders who wanted to leave. Most stayed. Both local teams claimed to feature comedy.

The Poughkeepsie Clowns played straight baseball, but in Bermuda shorts. The Poughkeepsie Winos too played humorless baseball, but after one inning, their catcher announced that Doc Wino would perform.

A stooped old man of average size materialized and stood at home plate in a rumpled tuxedo. His arthritic swing missed two straight pitches by more than a foot and more than a tick of the clock. He then called time, reached under his coat, took out a flask and drained it, rising straight to a height of at least six feet seven inches and gaining youth as he stretched, and, without taking another swing, dashed around the bases with long, loping strides, and without breathing hard, like a reincarnation of the god Bacchus with the foot speed of his co-god Mercury.

"I don't know whether the miracle's the wine or Poughkeepsie," Dad said.

"Don't think I'll use that routine," King Tut said.

Clowns' manager McKinley "Bunny" Downs simply shook his head. "What would Casey Stengel do against the Poughkeepsie Winos?" he asked of the night.

Regional economic factors and current events affected itineraries. Dad daily read several newspapers to keep informed generally and to determine team travel. The Clowns often began and ended each season in North Carolina to coincide with tobacco harvests, when fans had ticket money.

Cost and availability of hotel rooms was a major consideration, especially for black teams. Often, there was no room for the Clowns at the inn. They spent thirty-five seasons as nomads on the road before passage of the Civil Rights Act of 1964. Hotels they could stay in were limited by racial policy or cost, and often hotels and local restaurants, aware of limited markets imposed by segregation, raised prices for black teams. It was the law of supply and demand in black and white.

Sometimes special summer events were regional draws, and Dad had to be aware because supply and demand could inflate seasonal expenses during special events. Clowns' attendance might also suffer when competing with local attractions or traditions. Conversely, in some cases, it might pay the Clowns to play a small town momentarily overpopulated by a regional public for some local affair.

Availability of competition was another consideration. Dad was concerned with the schedule of potential competition for most bookings, especially when the Clowns weren't in the Negro American League. There had to be a local team worthy of playing the Clowns, or there had to be a traveling team driven by similar factors to share the date with the Clowns. The worthiness of competition was important, because the Clowns sometimes had a few chances a year and sometimes a chance every few years to impress fans enough to see their next appearance. Playing down to competition would not enhance the Clowns' reputation.

Sometimes the schedule had to be adjusted to travel plans of rival teams. This was certainly so once the Clowns joined the Negro American League. Owners met several times each season in Chicago to discuss league matters, including team pairings for scheduling. At the meetings, owners planned traveling from a few days to a few weeks against one rival, then meeting two other paired teams to switch opponents. The exchange of opposition usually occurred in a big draw city and was accompanied by a four-team doubleheader. For example, the Clowns and Memphis Red Sox might cap a two-week tour in the first game of a doubleheader in Kansas City, with the Kansas City Monarchs and Birmingham Black Barons ending a six-day tour in the second game. The teams would then exchange and the Clowns and Monarchs would leave the city on their next tour and the Red Sox and Black Barons on theirs.

League scheduling difficulties were compounded by the popularity of different teams in different cities and by the desirability of Sunday bookings in big cities. Dad always wanted the most popular opponent in a given city, but that team might have its biggest draw of the season elsewhere at the time. At league meetings, clubs argued to travel with the Clowns because Clowns comedy made them fan favorites and they drew far better than others.

Without a good, reliable promoter, an otherwise qualified city was considered unbookable by Dad, unless it was close enough to home that he could handle promotion himself. His early promoting days qualified him to book the Clowns effectively because he could transmit experience to his promoters. With few exceptions, Dad wrote his own publicity. He alone decided photo use; letterhead, windowcard and handbill formats; advance ticket and press pass design; color and design of uniforms; and other matters involving promotion and image. Dad did all shipping instructions for all windowcards and handbills for all Clowns games. He did all their bookkeeping. He generally operated as a one-man office and saw the world through typewriter keys from early spring through late fall. As fast a typist as imaginable, he typed as most of us talk. He typed as he thought. The result was not always perfect English, but was always absolutely clear.

Bothered, Dad had a way of typing angry. If one of us asked for movie money and infringed on his thoughts, he'd read his typing in a tone of voice most men reserve for profanity, and we knew to leave. Road baseball was mail-order baseball conducted by typewriter, and Dad's typewriter sat sacred as a monument at the center of his desk, as sustaining as a beating heart.

Maybe coincidental physical layout of our houses dictated the location of Dad's offices or maybe office location was determined by design facilitating one of his favorite activities; each office was adjacent to our eat-in kitchen. On Maple Street, he was mere steps from Mom's cooking. When we moved to Tarrytown, his office sat on the golden oak floor at the open end of the central hall next to the kitchen. When we moved to Hollywood, Florida, the Florida room served as Dad's most spacious office, and his typing resonated off the pink tile floor like the sound of a machine gun in a gym. Sliding glass doors separated family room and kitchen. Less than a year later, we moved across town, and the office was in a small detached building two steps off the exterior door into the kitchen. He soon enclosed the area between so trips to the kitchen were not rain delayed. Dad's planning of crisp jumps and rain contingencies served him well at home.

His work day extended from before 6 A.M. until well after midnight. He set up the office each morning, worked briefly, then left for the post office, morning paper and bakery rolls, and, as part of breakfast, we dunked the rolls in tea in the Irish way.

Dad then settled into the office. First, he had a rolltop desk, a chair and a file cabinet. Over the years he added a mimeograph machine, and there were publicity shelves on which piles of duplicate releases were arranged so that he could pull a sheet off each pile to accompany mats, prints or glossy photos in the publicity kit mailed to promoters weeks before game time, with instructions on how to use and time the releases.

Publicity kits included radio spots and later a short TV film. Dad wrote weekly news releases covering Clowns games in the national press. Early he learned that white papers excluded or trivialized black sports, so his file cabinet contained a "colored press" folder, but no "white press" file. Attendances in large cities swelled with coverage in white daily papers, if not because of greater circulation, then because articles appearing game day eve had more immediacy than those days before in weeklies. Non-black papers generally carried Negro baseball news, if at all, only when the black teams appeared locally, and big city coverage, when given, was generally filler material.

Dad knew the importance of words. He said, "Negro leaguers call Oscar Charleston the black Ty Cobb. If Ty Cobb were a decent person, he'd be worthy of being called the white Oscar Charleston. Press can make a guy like Cobb idol of millions, Jackie Robinson demeaned for taking out runners on double plays and Hank Aaron hated for hitting. Same as a pitcher can make a mediocre team invincible, a poem can make Tinkers to Evers to Chance errorless." He added, "There's no bad publicity. Anything written about colored baseball is good if it gets attention."

One of Dad's ongoing struggles was to convert postgame coverage to pregame publicity. "It mystifies me nothing is published about our games until we're on the bus and gone with just a box score to remember us by," he said. "Too often our publicity trailed us instead of preceded us, and fans learned what they missed, not what they could see."

By train and car, Dad traveled to nearby or key distant Clowns games and to league meetings in Chicago, and he annually attended the East-West Game (the Negro leagues' all-star game) in Chicago, but more often he traveled the continent by mail, and results gathered in his file cabinet. The things he did were best performed at home, and for the most part he lived Clowns life vicariously from business manager reports, news clippings and conversations with the team field manager, players, writers, promoters, fans and entertainers. Sometimes he rode the bus with the team for days at a time and tasted the flavor of life on the road. As youngsters, my brothers and I joined him from time to time. But his bread and butter travel for the Clowns was between home and post office, and those trips were family tradition. He went early morning, late morning, early evening and late night, with occasional extra trips as needed. He seldom went alone all trips in a day; usually, he had one or more of us with him and, in later years, grandchildren.

Rides presented a chance to talk to Dad as parent, to seek advice about personal or family matters or his views on national or international affairs. Clowns news was updated on the way to the post office. Almost daily, one trip included a visit to a drugstore soda fountain. He loved ice cream sodas, sundaes and malteds with relaxed conversation. Problems led him to suggest, "Let's go to the post office and discuss this over a banana split."

If files grew during the off-season, from spring to fall carbon copies seemingly reproduced their kind. Correspondence was grouped by cities within larger files alphabetical by state. Such files held booking and promoter correspondence along with notes on factors affecting crowd size, such as weather, strikes, crop failures or competing events.

A player file contained an inventory of players available at each position along with scouting reports, applications and background narratives. Bus capacity limited manpower as well as equipment. Because of lack of room on the bus, Dad's booking contracts provided that the promoter supply baseballs.

Clean uniforms were a problem. The Clowns played almost every day every season, sometimes twice daily, and occasionally three times, almost always in different cities or towns. It was a luxury to arrive in town in the morning with a laundry deposit to be ready for the night's game. One solution Dad had was the navy blue uniforms associated with the Clowns. Dirt didn't show nearly as much on navy blue.

There were rarely enough bats to keep all players happy until Dad finally bought a Flxible bus in 1948 with sufficient storage. It was one of the first of its kind in traveling baseball, with passenger compartment forward and baggage room aft, in a long and streamlined body.

But players were the largest problem. Roster numbers were limited, and injured players had to be replaced in remote areas. There was no room for a weak player on the roster. Versatility resulted. Perhaps the greatest example was Ted "Double Duty" Radcliffe, who pitched and caught for 22 years for 12 Negro league teams. "Double Duty," brother of Clowns all-star third baseman Alex Radcliffe, sometimes pitched the first game and caught the second game of a double header, and excelled at both positions. Every traveling team had players skilled at more than one position and billed as pitcher-outfielder or infielder-outfielder or catcher–first baseman. Dave Hoskins, primarily an outfielder with the Clowns, was one of the first blacks in the American League, as a pitcher for the Cleveland Indians.

One oddity in the Negro leagues was using individual players on an ad hoc basis. One team depleted of shortstops might use its traveling companion's backup until its own replacement arrived. Big draw players were paid per diem by opposing teams for big dates. For example, Satchel Paige, who pitched primarily for the Kansas City Monarchs, sometimes pitched one-day stints for other teams for sizeable sums to help draw large crowds in big cities.

A separate, related file folder was titled "Player Contracts" and included original signed current player agreements, and between seasons included a list of prospective contracts for the following year. Sets of ledger books contained payroll records and advances drawn against pay. The Clowns were possibly the only team in the history of black baseball never to have missed a payday.

Of Dad's functions, the most difficult may have been compiling and maintaining a roster. Players arrived at spring training (usually in Virginia, North Carolina or Florida) from around the country by bus. Players from South America and the islands were flown in. Each spring we went with Dad, in his role as travel agent, to the train station, bus stations and airline ticket offices, as he arranged to transport his team from paper to field, and we went with him to Ben Cohen's sports shop in nearby Elmsford, New York, to arrange shipment of equipment not already on the bus with uniforms.

Negro leaguers accepted organized baseball (O.B.) as consisting of the white major leagues and their minor leagues systems. Within O.B., teams were not raided for players. Black teams, however, historically slipped out of town with their opposition's talent, and players in the United States sometimes jumped to teams in Canada, Mexico, the Dominican Republic, Venezuela and, to a lesser extent, other Latin American countries. Black teams in the United States, dating back to the 1880s, faced ever-changing rosters. Players followed money. Strong Clowns teams developed during the late 1930s when Dad could afford to hire top players from other teams.

In 1920, Rube Foster organized the Negro National League, and one reason was to stabilize rosters through league nontampering rules. The Eastern Colored League was a companion from 1923 to 1928, and the Negro American League began in 1937.

Player jumps still occurred, even after the Negro leagues were well established. In 1950, the Clowns shortstop was Pablo Sama. Before Hank Aaron, Sama appeared to be the Clowns best shortstop prospect. In July, just days after his ninth-inning home run beat the New York Cubans before a huge crowd at the Polo Grounds, he jumped the club to return to play in his native Venezuela. There, he was killed when his new Corvette catapulted over a cliff. The Corvette had been his signing bonus for jumping.

In July 1951, Clowns shortstop Len "Preacher" Williams was arrested in Indianapolis as a "fugitive" from North Dakota. The outlaw Minot, North Dakota, Baseball Club had sent Williams $500 to jump to their team and to induce other Clowns to do so. Players informed Dad, who raised salaries to avoid roster depletion. Apparently, the Minot General Manager felt Williams took the money and did nothing for it.

North Dakota police officials sent the state attorney's office in Indianapolis a telegram stating that Williams was a fugitive wanted in Minot on fraud charges. An affidavit was filed by an Indiana official, and Williams was picked up. Dad paid attorney's fees, and the matter came to trial in August. No witness appeared from North Dakota. Williams, who had been out on bail paid by Dad, was acquitted.

The attorneys pointed out that the Minot Club could use this tactic again and again under the principle of comity (under which one state honors the laws and decisions of another) wherever the Clowns appeared, and the Clowns could not enjoin the activity, since it was lawful under North Dakota statutes—this, even though Williams had not even been in North Dakota that season.

Lawyers, players, management, publicity, housing, food, equipment, transportation, and office operation all cost money. As money spun through turnstiles, daily reports—sent to Dad by the road business manager and checked as received—itemized daily expenses and translated gross gate to net. Federal income tax audits never revealed error in Clowns books. At the end of each season, using the daily reports and office records, Dad prepared an annual report showing gross income, expenses and net income. Annual reports were used for income tax preparation, planning and, during years of partnership, division of profits and losses.

And, at the end of each season, like a bear, Dad's baseball income hibernated until spring.

6

View from the Bus

The story is told that when Abe Lincoln practiced law, he appeared before the same circuit judge two consecutive days in two separate towns, each day arguing opposite sides of the same issue on essentially the same facts involving different parties. When questioned about that by the judge, Lincoln said, "Yesterday I thought I was right, but today I know I'm right." He understood the math of the road.

Viewing the world through the windshield of the Clowns bus, Hunter Campbell saw the same shimmering mirage puddle crossing the highway at the horizon no matter what jump, no matter what state, no matter what day. Dad's last partner, Ed Hamman, who doubled as road business manager, often said, "Two and two don't make four on the road."

In 35 years under Dad, the Clowns had four road business managers: Ramiro Ramirez from 1929 to 1935; Hunter Campbell from 1936 to 1942, the year he died; McKinley "Bunny" Downs from 1943 to 1955; and Ed Hamman from 1956 to 1964. Ramirez, Hunter and Bunny were black, Ed white. All were former ballplayers—Bunny the best, as long-term star infielder for the Hilldale Club starting before World War I.

The road business manager had to excel at business ability, dealing with people, traveling the same roads year after year and staring at the same hot mirage, forsaking family and friends for the road half the year, being honest, dealing with racial bias with the calm determination of a Jackie Robinson and having the knack for accepting five or three from time to time as the sum of two plus two. He had to know baseball. And he had to have all those abilities on the run in pressure situations in many different environments.

In some cases, with white promoters, Hunter and Bunny in doing their jobs were perceived as "uppity" blacks, Ramirez as a temperamental Cuban, Hamman as a "nigger lover."

Hunter Campbell was a father figure for the Miami Ethiopian Clowns.

Felix "Chin" Evans, later an all-star pitcher for the Memphis Red Sox, pitched for Hunter as Kalahari on the 1940 Ethiopian Clowns, and he said, "Hunter tended toward profanity on the bus and in the dugout, but there were few finer men, and as business manager, he was a gentlemen and checked the four-letter words in at the door of the ballpark office."

In public, Hunter wore a white shirt and a dark suit and tie. He was impressive and well groomed. He wore no jewelry. He tried not to look monied because he often carried large amounts of cash, and he couldn't always get to a bank to convert his cash to a cashier's check.

As part of Dad's policy, the cash was in Hunter's money belt under his clothes, not in the briefcase he carried containing his paperwork and rolls of tickets. Traveling teams dealt with money in motion. The manager, the chauffeur and the team captain carried replenishable banks. The manager's bank was sufficient to pay for meal money, hotel, laundry and equipment. The team captain carried roughly one-third that amount for equipment replacement or repair or some emergency expense should the manager be unavailable or short on cash. The chauffeur carried enough for gas, oil and emergency repairs. When I was temporary road business manager in 1963, chauffeur M. H. Winston carried a $500 bank, Carl Forney kept a $500 manager's bank, and team captain Freddie Battle had a $150 bank.

Daily, each banker presented receipts to the business manager for reimbursement to replenish the bank to the prior day's starting level. The business manager had to maintain sufficient funds to replenish the three other banks, cover his own expenses and, sometimes, to advance players money against pay. When cash sufficiently exceeded that level and he had time, he posted a cashier's check from a local bank to Dad, who used road funds for office expenses and any player advances, loans or bonuses made directly to players' families. At season's end, the total of Dad's surplus and the business manager's was team profit.

Excessive road cash resulted from big crowds and jumps too long to allow time for a cashier's check. Extra cash was carried near paydays, which were biweekly. The business manager's hotel room, the dugout or the bus served as his office, and pay was given in the hotel room whenever practical. It was team policy not to reveal one player's salary to another. Further, some players and entertainers, such as King Tut, kept only partial salaries, balances sent by Dad directly to their wives or parents. That was between Dad, the business manager and the player or performer. Use of the hotel room allowed the business manager privacy to deal with players individually and to confidentially discuss deductions or advances. Players were paid in cash.

Sometimes, long jumps precluded the niceties of a hotel room, and payday, like sleep, was on the bus. Time permitting, the business manager used a parking lot for bus paydays so that confidentiality could be preserved by taking players one by one back into the bus once they disembarked.

Players generally bought their own gloves and spikes, which were unique to the player and, like his toothbrush, left with him if he was traded or released or if he jumped or quit. The Clowns supplied room and board, uniforms, jackets, caps, socks, bats, masks, bat bags, belts, shin guards, jockstraps, sliding pads, rosin bags, neat's-foot oil, saddle soap, body soap, athlete's foot powder, practice baseballs, liniment, first aid needs and all other equipment. Sometimes, if a player could not afford a suitcase to report to camp, the Clowns would provide one, cheap but adequate. That was the extent of a signing bonus in black baseball.

The business manager had to guard against losing money he wasn't even carrying yet. Negro league tickets, with few exceptions, were generic ticket rolls. While numbered in sequence, the tickets contained neither name of team nor designation of event. They did not even contain the word "baseball," but rather were close kin to the rolls of tickets used at carnivals. Color varied from time to time, but there was no foolproof way to stop dishonest promoters or gate attendants from selling from their own rolls or taking cash to pass someone through ticketless. Ticket numbers purported to control attendance, but there was even more control if the ticket takers were Clowns pitchers not expected to see action that date.

Players often had secondary duties dictated by economics and limited bus space. Sometimes Clowns players relieved a weary chauffeur. Pitchers Jim Colzie and Big John Williams, Buster Haywood (even when he managed), James "Nan "Natureboy" Williams and all-star Clowns pitcher Jim "Fireball" Cohen were licensed chauffeurs and sometimes drove the bus. Fireball once wondered aloud if Cy Young ever had to use his golden arm to swerve a bus to miss a drunk.

Catching gate thieves was a continuing challenge never fully successful for long. In 1962, Dad and Tom Baird, who started the Kansas City Monarchs with cofounder J. L. Wilkinson, recalled a Clowns-Monarchs game in the late 1930s when Dad and Tom trapped a ticket seller in Lawrence, Kansas, by posing as ticket-buying fans. More than a quarter century later, laughing and thanking Dad for grabbing his raised hand to prevent assault and battery, Tom clenched his fist and said, "But somehow, Syd, I still wish you'd have let me hit the son of a bitch."

Some Negro league teams had no insurance. Some carried minimal insurance. The Clowns were always fully insured while traveling, and later Clowns teams, with the advent of workman's compensation laws, were insured for nontravel injuries. Decisions had to be made by the road business manager and Dad as to whether to pay extraordinary medical expenses in a given instance. Player importance to the team, likelihood of recovery, the player's own financial circumstances, the need for immediate treatment, present availability of funds and the manner in which the injury or illness occurred were considered. Clowns' business managers were under orders to pay for emergency medical treatment. But too often, black players played at their own risk.

Traveling teams were always at the mercy of the weather. Dad sometimes bought rainout insurance for big games. Otherwise, the Clowns and other black teams were virtually uninsured against loss of income from game cancellations.

Player morale was a concern for Dad and business and player managers. Of the variables affecting morale, the most obvious was racial prejudice. Sometimes the Clowns traveled a day hungry because no white would sell them food. And sometimes they spent a night in the bus because no white would sell them sleep. Once, in the 1940s, in Memphis, his hometown, M. H. Winston was driving the bus down a one-way street the wrong way. "One way street, nigger!" shouted a white pedestrian. "I guess I'll make it," Winston said out the bus window with his usual calm dignity, and traveled on.

And the bus always rolled on, blacks only.

In southern stands, crowds were segregated by law. In southern cities, and to a lesser extent nationwide, the Clowns dressed in hotel rooms or on the bus. They were not permitted to use ballpark dressing rooms. They were daily reminded they were segregated players.

Black players received low pay compared with their white counterparts, and Dad always placed priority on making paydays. Negro leaguers slept in transit, and played in different parks in different cities each game. In 1954, the Clowns came to Tarrytown, where the ballpark had a rocky infield and minimal dirt basepaths. The grass had been uncut for weeks when the

Clowns arrived about 4 P.M. for a 7 P.M. game. When I saw the bus pass, I ran home from the ball park to meet the players.

"I was just playing where you're gonna play tonight," I said to Frank Carswell, a Clowns pitcher.

"You're lucky you weren't killed," he replied.

Black players were away from home and family half the year. Because they shared love of baseball with their teammates didn't mean they had anything else in common. Being teammates does not guarantee friendship. It only ensures 24-hours-a-day intimacy half the year, like it or not. Players were away from the women they loved and sometimes children. All black teams knew Jody and discussed him regularly. He was as feared in 1964 as he was in 1929, and he probably plagued the Cuban X-Giants in the 1800s. I never heard of Jody until I was on the road in 1962; he was mentioned daily then, and second baseman Jim "B. D." Bland gave me what other players have since acknowledged as the ultimate definition of Jody: "He's the man at home, the one comes in the back door when you go out the front," B. D. said.

Jody crossed racial lines one night in 1962 on the bus when I told Birmingham Sam Brison, "I'll probably marry Marti. I miss her out here," and someone else said, "Don't you worry 'bout Marti. Jody makin' sure she okay."

Dad and Hunter made every effort to retain players of good character and ability and to do all they could to keep players with common interests. As Buster Haywood said, "We had a nice ball club—good people or your Daddy wouldn't keep them." Clowns players selected their own roommates, and that helped morale. Road problems assailed the Clowns from every angle every day. Retaining players with good character was good geometry and helped keep the angles of approaching problems at least sometimes in peripheral view.

The nature of the Clowns created a problem other clubs didn't face—entertainers. Good baseball entertainers were not quite as hard to find as practicing Druid brain surgeons or retired ace kamikaze pilots. Many players wouldn't do comedy, even for more pay. Others would, but lacked the style or timing to do it successfully. Dad interviewed or tried out dozens for each one able to successfully blend the caliber of play necessary for Negro American League competition with the requisite comedic gifts.

Once found, the good entertainer was not only cultivated, but often tolerated. Behavior intolerable in good baseball players was often overlooked in good entertainers. Drinking ballplayers were often given unconditional releases; drinking entertainers were not. Activities of a womanizing infielder were often curtailed, but promiscuity by a leading entertainer was not. Some Clowns entertainers, such as Tut or Birmingham Sam Brison, sought no special favor, but most demanded pampering.

Of the Negro leaguers, Peanuts Davis and Goose Tatum with the Clowns and Satchel Paige of the Kansas City Monarchs would probably rate as three of the more difficult people to manage. All three were outstanding ballplayers, Satchel, of course, the best of the trio. With his flair, Satchel too was an entertainer. He and Peanuts featured windmill windups for some deliveries. Satchel departed from his fastballs with the hesitation pitch, and Peanuts changed speeds with baseball's best knuckleball. Both occasionally sat down fielders while they struck out the side. Dad nervously advertised any of the three for a given game, because it was unknown when Satchel would miss a game for a girlfriend or a nearby lake stocked with fish. If Peanuts had a girlfriend (he didn't fish), he'd miss a game. Goose, when he didn't feel like playing, claimed a variety of ailments. All three were demanding and slow to pay back frequent loans. Satchel was a problem only occasionally when signed to pitch for the Clowns for a single date, but Goose and Peanuts were daily problems for years, tolerated because they brought in fans. Clowns' managers had to handle Goose and Peanuts without alienating other players. "It was hard to say anything to Goose or Peanuts. They were our attractions, along with Tut," Clowns' manager Buster said. "I just had to pet them along."

An entertainer was sometimes given more playing time than a better player, as when Natureboy Williams began his Clowns career. A gifted athlete, Natureboy was 5′8″ and weighed 220 pounds, some of the surplus weight attributable to love of beer, not workouts. But he ran with track and field speed, and almost everything he did was funny on and off the field. He came to the Clowns in 1955 with insufficient baseball ability to survive a tour with the Clowns in the Negro American League, but he was kept because he was a comedian and the Clowns had left the league. By 1957, he was one of the best baseball players outside the major leagues and became year-by-year one of the best first basemen anywhere. But sometimes, before 1957, his presence caused dissension.

A series of lines, angles and shapes spanning the years 1961 through

1964 in the life of Natureboy Williams proved Ed Hamman's two-plus-two theorem.

From 1960 through 1964, Malcolm Poindexter, a black Philadelphia journalist, was the Clowns' public relations director, preparing some publicity releases sent to promoters and some weekly news stories released to Negro Associated Press affiliates.

In a February 18, 1961, letter to Malcolm, Dad stated (not for publication) that Natureboy's days with the Clowns were numbered. Worried about the rotund first baseman's negative effect on morale and morals, Dad had privately discussed with him his concern about Natureboy's "wives" in places visited by the Clowns and the effect they had on his play and potentially his health and the outlook of Clowns teammates. Further, during the 1960 season, Ed Hamman confiscated a gun "Natche" pulled on a drunk trying to pick a fight. Referring specifically to the comedy dance performed with Birmingham Sam following shadowball each game after the seventh inning, Dad wrote to Malcolm, "He not only hurt kid prospects with his talk, threats, goings on . . . but we also had difficulty trying to keep him from being suggestive on his dance." Natureboy privately promised Dad reform. He would no longer carry a gun. He would try to be a positive force. Dad signed him for the 1961 season.

On July 2, 1962, while I was temporary road business manager and following the memorable Clowns' victory over Mel Clark's All Stars in Mason, West Virginia, we stopped for supper shortly after midnight at an all-night restaurant across the river in Gallipolis, Ohio. I sat with outfielder-manager Carl Forney, shortstop Haley Young and Natureboy, and as we were finishing, a passing white family, who had attended the game, stopped, and the father introduced his son to Natureboy. After they left our table, as the father was paying the bill, the mother returned to thank Natche for talking to her son, explaining the boy was terminally ill and probably wouldn't survive the summer. Natureboy asked the boy's name, position and team affiliation, and in a few minutes, as the family opened the door to leave, Natche called the boy by name, and the youngster returned self-consciously to us.

"You the Jimmy McCoy plays short for the Gallipolis Eagles?" Natche asked.

"Yes."

"Thought I knew the name. You should have said so. Wouldn't have been braggin'. We got to write back and forth, at least two, three times a week. Give me your address," Natche said.

Radiant, the boy complied, and Natche wrote it on his paper napkin.

On the bus I told Carl Forney that Natureboy shouldn't make promises lightly. "He doesn't," Carl replied. "He has five or six dying kids a year he writes to almost daily. They all know right to the end that at least Natche loves 'em."

Dad's reaction was to assure me that while Dad ran the Clowns, James Natureboy Williams had a job as long as he wanted one.

That winter, Natureboy was chipping ice at work, and a sliver slashed into his right eye, causing total loss of sight in the eye. He played the 1963 season and, in 1964, returned as player-manager, Dad's last field manager. On June 15, 1964, Dad wrote to Malcolm:

Natureboy Williams . . . is . . . doing a terrific job this year.

You'll recall he lost complete sight of one eye during the winter of 1962 working on his job, played through entire 1963 season under this adverse condition, without fans or press knowing or realizing his handicap.

On June 1st, I believe it was, at Carlsbad, N.M., Natureboy cracked three ribs, in an accidental collision making a play at first base . . . and heavily taped, against advice of physicians, has been playing at least 5-innings daily, refusing to stay out of games.

Days later, the Clowns were first at the scene of a terrible accident at the Canadian border. Clowns players, led by Natureboy, lifted the car off a woman, and Natche administered first aid and resuscitation efforts until paramedics arrived. On June 24, 1964, Dad wrote to Malcolm:

The rescue incident took place at Blaine, B.C. at Canadian Customs as our teams were checking through customs, headed for a 2-day engagement at Capilano Stadium in Vancouver. Note James (Natureboy) Williams, Clowns' manager's sad face, when photographed after reaching Vancouver by The Sun, and informed Miss Sylvia Henry had died, that team's rescue attempt had been in vain.

I believe this rates AP, UP coverage . . . since it involves our nationally famous American . . . Indianapolis Clowns, opening their 35th annual tour entering . . . Canada. . . . since Natureboy and his players never questioned the color of the girl trapped underneath the over-turned car . . . who happened to be white . . . were the first on the scene in their frantic effort to save a life . . . after all we're just human beings . . . altho there's too many want us to believe otherwise, as you well know.

Neither AP nor UPI carried the story. And two plus two didn't always make four in road baseball.

PART THREE

THE TWENTIES AND THIRTIES
Road Map

During the late 1920s and early 1930s, Clowns' origins bubbled from dissimilar men like waters from springs separated in space and time but trickling, then rushing in streams to form one wide, blacklight, joyful river. . . .

—Alan Pollock

7

Blue Sox, Red Sox and Cuban Stars

Dad's 1920 Westchester Blue Sox was a decent local semi-pro team warranting a column inch or two in the Monday *Tarrytown Daily News*. All players held primary jobs, so games were Saturdays and Sundays. By 1922, the Blue Sox were a local favorite and quite skilled.

Dad's Blue Sox days shaped his promotional and booking ability and typing speed, and his own style of play became a working drawing for players later hired for the best Clowns teams. The Blue Sox scored when Dad stole home, or on a single driving in someone in scoring position because Dad had made contact on a hit-and-run or a grounder behind the runner or a sacrifice bunt. Dad scored on singles after he walked or beat out an infield hit and stole second. "I was a pest," he said. "Took advantage of everything, learned every phase of the game so I could do the little things others didn't bother with. Often I outplayed guys better than me."

Initially the Blue Sox played within Westchester County. In 1920, the team lost its opener 16-9 to Sing Sing Prison. Dad's black teams would later play the prison periodically for decades. Sing Sing games were for inmates only, not open to the general public.

By 1921, the Blue Sox played a more cosmopolitan schedule, including the Buffalo Colored Giants, and the *Tarrytown Daily News* carried team box scores.

In 1922, Dad introduced vaudeville acts at his semi-pro bookings, and as a result of his promotional skills, Blue Sox crowds swelled to paid attendances exceeding 2,000, and *Tarrytown Daily News* articles expanded to play-by-play coverage under the byline "Sid."

Once, Dad learned something of the hardships of the road before there was much of a road. In covering a 1922 Blue Sox win over Tannersville, the *Tarrytown Daily News* reported, "The trip into the heart of the Catskills, where . . . Tannersville is located, was made by touring cars and considerable time was lost climbing the steep incline to the top of the hills where the contest took place." Luckily, a forfeit was averted because wet grounds from early rains forced rescheduling of the game from early afternoon to evening. But Dad learned the lesson well—never assume the road allows travel to match map time. Later Clowns teams timely made games because of that lesson. Clowns personnel knew as much as possible of the travel conditions ahead, and allowed extra time. Every ten days or two weeks each Clowns season, Dad forwarded anticipated travel conditions and local contacts and phone numbers to his road business manager care of general delivery. Any change in conditions was related by phone.

Dad ran the Strand during the early 1920s and promoted traveling teams as well as the Blue Sox. His player placement service was active. One 1922 article reported that "[Georgie] Speno secured his position through the Syd Pollock Agency, which is the first baseball bureau to open in Westchester County." In a move reverse—paralleling his 1953 signing of Toni Stone as the first female player on a professional male team—Dad, through his agency, placed local pitcher John Joe Dwyer for a game on the New York Bloomer Girls against an all-male semi-pro club in Portchester. The August 13, 1922, promotion was Dad's and resulted in a record crowd. John Joe struck out nine, and led till the seventh, when the Bloomer Girls' shortstop made an error, allowing the tying and winning runs.

In *Tarrytown Daily News* articles, Dad described Strand movies. Double features changed three times weekly. Combining those duties with his promoting and booking and the placement service and his inning-by-inning reports of the Blue Sox games, often for the next-day edition following a late game well upstate, he developed two lifelong abilities: speed typing and keeping score on the bench. Later, as Clowns' owner, he was never on the bench without a scorebook in his hands.

Dad dated the Clowns to 1929. But there was no 1929 team called the Clowns. During the late 1920s and early 1930s Clowns' origins bubbled from dissimilar men like waters from springs separated in space and time but trickling, then rushing in streams to form one wide, blacklight, joyful river: Ramiro Ramirez in Havana; Charlie Henry in Louisville; Richard King in Philadelphia; Buck O'Neal, Johnnie Pierce and Hunter Campbell in Miami; and Syd Pollock in North Tarrytown.

For years, Dad booked and promoted the Havana Red Sox, and after the 1928 season, purchased the team from Ramiro Ramirez, who stayed on as business manager, field manager and outfielder. It was Dad's first black team, and his 1929 edition featured comedy and shadowball and the navy blue uniforms with red lettering and trim later popularized by the Clowns (and in the 1990s adopted with variations by the Cleveland Indians). The Havana Red Sox was one of few semi-pro teams with its own bus and was the only club backed by Dad's signature promotional techniques. Dad booked the team throughout the South, East, Midwest and Canada. Brief press notice was given games as booked. Then pregame publicity was designed to produce news articles daily with photos starting about ten days before game date. Timing and type of coverage varied little from later Clowns press releases and publicity recommendations. Dad knew how to run a road club before he bought one, but for 35 years, he constantly adjusted to things he learned and to changes in society, prices, highway quality, politics, geography, personnel and the thousands of factors that made up the math of the road.

In 1931, the Havana Red Sox became the Cuban House of David, which became the 1932 Cuban Stars. Dad's early black teams played primarily Negro league teams, local semi-pro clubs, minor league aggregations, county all-stars, factory nines and other traveling teams, such as the House of David or the Zulu Cannibal Giants. From 1929 on, his Cuban teams had more and more American players. To Dad, his teams from 1929 on were one. It is difficult to read of the 1929 Havana Red Sox without thinking of them as the Clowns. To Dad they were the same just as the American League Washington Senators became the Minnesota Twins.

Because of comedy, Dad's teams outdrew and outlasted most. Quality baseball was consistently foremost to Dad, and he was amazed at what his black teams accomplished. "They had something special," Dad once told me. "It came from the comedy and from traveling together and playing under the toughest conditions without rest and being told they can't stay here, they can't eat there, they got to wet behind a tree if there's no colored-only rest-room, the kind of adversity that brings people together proud and tough and makes them win. And later, the something special came too from Tut."

Steak and leg of lamb were 39 cents a pound, a nurse's uniform $3.95, and a new Dodge $1,495 on March 23, 1929, when Syd Pollock's Havana Red Sox played their first game, ironically at the City Park (later named Dorsey Park) at NW 17th Street and First Avenue, Miami, the same park in which Johnnie Pierce and Hunter Campbell originated the Miami Ethiopian Clowns seven years later. Prohibition had four more years to run, and the Great Depression was a half year away. Al Capone was talking to grand juries in Chicago. Fannie Brice starred at Miami's Rosetta Theater in "My Man," billed as "A 100% All-Talking Picture." And at the City Park at 17th and First, a grandstand was reserved for whites only.

Yielding three ninth-inning runs in a 4-3 loss to the Miami Red Sox, Lefty Tiant pitched the complete game. Lefty was the father of Luis Tiant, who pitched for the Boston Red Sox after baseball was integrated, and when Dad spoke of the best pitchers he ever saw, he ranked Lefty Tiant at the top. My brother Don was there the day Lefty Tiant gave Mom the beautiful silver crucifix on a silver chain she kept until she died. As star of Dad's Cuban teams, he was billed as Lefty Grove Tiant, and the irony of the billing echoes in words my brother Don once wrote me: "Lefty [Tiant] was the greatest pitcher I ever saw, better than Lefty Grove or Lefty Gomez." Tiant played for Dad until Alejandro Pompez stole him in 1935 for the New York Cubans, where Lefty was a Negro National League All-Star his first year.

The other star hurler with Dad's Havana Red Sox, Andrew "Stringbean" Williams, was a top pitcher from before World War I until the mid-'20s, allegedly winning more than 90 percent of his career decisions. He was the only American on Dad's 1929 team. A tall skinny right-hander, also dubbed "Iron Man," he sometimes pitched doubleheaders and sometimes five complete games in a week. At age 55, with Dad's Havana Red Sox, he pitched a nine-inning shutout one day in northern New York, a nine-inning shutout next day in Canada and five innings of shutout relief the following day in western New York. "I don't think anyone on a major league team staying put could do that," Dad said. "Whenever I think of the spirit of the Clowns and special performances in road baseball, I recall Stringbean Williams doing that at his age."

Needing equipment and new uniforms for their 1929 team, Tarrytown's Rotary Club turned to Dad, and the Havana Red Sox scheduled a benefit against the Tarrytown Rotary All-Stars May 31. Dad had mixed emotions. During his playing days, he was a Tarrytown All-Star and some of his closest friends were on the team.

After their opening series in Miami, the Red Sox played north for a month. As the Tarrytown game drew closer, it was switched from May 31, a Friday, to Saturday, June 1, so Tarrytown commuters working in New York City could attend.

Tarrytown added the best players countywide to their roster, including players from the International League.

As the Red Sox inched north, they notched 21 straight victories. Tarrytown's player-manager Dick Graveson told the *Tarrytown Daily News* that "There is a way to beat these Cubans and my teammates know the way." Dad's response published two days later was that his team expected to "take the Rotarians for a ride."

Dick was right. Dad was wrong. Dick's homer and a four-run eighth inning gave the All-Stars a 13-10 win before just over 700 paid. The *Tarrytown Daily News* reported, "The pep in the game was injected by the comedy antics of the Cubans and three fast double plays at critical moments by the Rotary team."

Cited for the lackluster play of his charges in early innings, Ramiro Ramirez referred to the all-night bus ride from Philadelphia to Tarrytown for the local appearance and suggested that perhaps such bus rides had taken their toll.

Dad probably would have traded the 21-game win streak for a victory in Tarrytown.

While the All-Stars could socialize postgame or rest at home, the Red Sox could not. Highways then were still two lanes, dark and winding and dotted with potholes and stops, and the Red Sox loaded their bus and left town on another long night bus ride jumping toward their Midwest tour, and would next play Tarrytown in 1931 as the Cuban House of David, an improved road club.

The 1930 edition of the Havana Red Sox, the first during the Great Depression, won their 100th game of the season during a late August–early September tour of New Hampshire, Vermont and Canada. On September 18 and 19, 1930, the nearest they would get to Tarrytown, they visited New Rochelle for successive shutout victories over the New Rochelle Athletic Club.

During the 1930–1931 off-season, the Havana Red Sox became the Cuban House of David, and strengthened the roster. Reportedly the only Cuban team permitted to enter the United States in 1931, having to post a bond for the distinction, the Cuban House of David still featured shadowball and comedy. The primary newcomer was legendary Tetelo Vargas, the greatest player in the history of the Dominican Republic and maybe the fastest runner ever to play. Dad once said Tetelo would not only beat out routine grounders to third and short, but sometimes take second on the throw to first.

Vargas was joined on the roster by power hitters Jacinto "Battlin' Siki" Roque and Corporal Charlie Mason, former star of the famed Lincoln Giants, based at the Protectory Oval in the Bronx and one of the great black teams of the first third of the century. Siki was billed as "The Babe Ruth of Cuba." Fermin Valdez, who would play during the 1940s for Dad's Clowns in the Negro American League was starting second baseman. The roster also featured quick-handed infielder Cleo Smith, formerly of the Hilldale Club, opponent of the Kansas City Monarchs in the first Negro World Series.

As earlier with Stringbean Williams, the presence of Mason and Smith resulted from businesslike, altruistic signings characterizing Dad's career. Both players were past their primes, but still had ability and wanted to play. Each represented name recognition and residual talent. Each made decent money with Dad. He signed both as much for their benefit as for his own.

Booked into Tarrytown again against local all-stars on Saturday afternoon, June 6, 1931, Dad's club started the season in Tampa and played north with impressive wins over top Negro league and minor league teams including the Three-I League Decatur Club, the Homestead Grays, the Birmingham Black Barons, the St. Louis Stars (World Negro Champions) and the Baltimore Black Sox.

Despite another home run by Tarrytown's Dick Graveson, the Cuban House of David pounded the All-Stars 7-1 before just over 300 fans. That night Dad's team added an 8-0 win over the nearby Ossining All-Stars before packing the bus for that night's ride into the rest of the season.

Along with teams representing Pittsburgh, Cleveland, Detroit, Newark, Philadelphia, Baltimore and Washington, in 1932, the Cuban House of David, also playing as the Cuban Stars, competed in the short-lived East-West Colored League, set up by Cum Posey to fill the void left by the demise of the first Negro National League. Dad's team that season helped pioneer night games by carrying their own portable "floodlight system for night baseball." Dad's letterhead promoted the league as "serving the public in baseball." For once that year, in the *Tarrytown News* at least, it seemed black baseball might get consistent white press.

On April 6, the paper reported two Cuban House of David wins: an 8-2 lacing of the Birmingham Black Barons won by Lefty Tiant and a 16-2 drubbing of the Black Barons behind Barney Brown and Lazaro Salazar. (In 1954, Salazar was inducted into the Mexican Baseball Hall of Fame.)

On April 11, the paper reported the Cuban House of David's 4-3 loss to Montgomery of the Southern Association, following a 15-3 win in Thomaston, Georgia, pitched by Jimmy Claxton, an Indian, and Lazaro Salazar, and a 10-5 win tossed by Barney Brown in Daytona Beach, Florida. In Montgomery, seven-foot sidearmer Cuneo Galves had a two-hitter until the ninth.

On April 14, the paper reported that the Cuban House of David lost 4-2 to the Memphis Red Sox the prior Sunday, then came back and beat the Red Sox 6-1 the next day behind Cuneo Galves. The April 18 issue reported that the Cuban House of David took the series with a 4-0 win over the Red Sox, as Lefty Tiant threw a three-single shutout. On April 29, the paper reported,

"The Cubans defeated the Blackcaps of the Southern League 3-0, yesterday at Louisville, with Lefty Tiant on the mound, and on Wednesday turned in a 5-3 victory over the same team. Cuneo Galves hurled." On May 9, the paper reported:

> Syd Pollock's Cuban House of David club Saturday got off to a flying start in the new East-West Colored League by defeating the Wolverines of Detroit, 4-1. Lefty Tiant was on the mound.
>
> The Havana nine broke even yesterday, losing to Detroit in the opener 13-3, and then coming back in the nightcap 4-2. The score was 2-2 in the sixth when Etchegoyen's home run with one aboard broke up the game.

Then, the 1932 *Tarrytown News* stopped its coverage. Before mid-June, Dad pulled his team out of the league to eliminate league scheduling and to book dates he knew would draw with shorter jumps. By mid-June, the league folded, victim of the depression. Dad issued a release carried in major black newspapers:

> The Cuban Stars, like everyone else, lost money and plenty of it attempting to establish a real colored league in the wrong year. It's tough scraping by this year, many miles of travel, many grinding overnight jumps. Something is bound to happen on the political horizon real soon to bring some changes for a weary, but courageous, world to go on to secure a better foothold and lease on life. Let's hope for future seasons which will bring a better fare to baseball, which is now undergoing a severe strain.

Credited with being a visionary integrationist, Bill Veeck, Jr., reportedly tried to integrate baseball by buying the Philadelphia Phillies to convert them into an all-black team for the 1943 season, a move vetoed by Baseball Commissioner Kenesaw Mountain Landis. The story may have been a Veeck fabrication.

A decade earlier, on August 23, 1933, in a letter to Bill Veeck, Sr., then president of the Chicago Cubs, Dad began a real 14-year quest to integrate baseball, not with a black individual, but with a black team. The letter, re-printed with Dad's permission in the August 24, 1933, *Tarrytown News*, read as follows:

Your statement "Major League baseball must do something drastic in order to revive interest in 1934" and "only one big league club out of 16 made money last year" has come to my attention through the press. As owner and president of the Cuban Stars, Inc., an independent semi-pro baseball club, which has played exhibition games through-out 31 States of the Union during the past season, defeating all oppo-sition, including every Minor League club played, may I offer one so-lution and the only one capable of reviving the waning interest, not only in the Majors, but baseball in general. Baseball has come to a point where semi-pro and Minor League ball cannot successfully carry on financially. The Majors are in the same predicament. Baseball next season will go into an additional slump if something drastic is not done about it.

My solution is simple, yet would meet with plenty of opposition from the league moguls, but only because of social pride. Social pride and prejudice must be overlooked where a business enterprise is at stake, and no one can dispute the fact that Major League ball is a busi-ness, a business that furnishes sport and entertainment to an Ameri-can public and expects to be rewarded at the box office by a substan-tial return for the investment at stake.

Your problem can be solved by placing an entire colored club to represent a city like Cincinnati in the National League and Boston in the American League. Instead of these two clubs being lodged in or near a cellar berth, a real colored aggregation would bring them into the first division and make a first place contender throughout the season.

Imagine the drawing power of a formidable colored aggregation playing in New York, Pittsburgh, Brooklyn, Chicago, Philadelphia, St. Louis, Detroit, etc. Imagine the interest they would stimulate by their colorful playing and dash around the diamond. Imagine the in-crease in attendance at their home parks in Cincinnati or Boston, two spots lacking sadly in attendance figures both at home and abroad.

Babe Ruth recently stated, "The colorfulness of Negroes in baseball and their sparkling brilliancy on the field would have a tendency to increase attendance at games." Hans Wagner, Pirates coach, stated, "The good colored clubs play just as good baseball as seen anywhere." Cy Perkins, Yankee coach, says, "When I played for Eddie Mack's All Stars against the Homestead Grays, Vic Harris and [Oscar] Charleston would grace the roster of any big league club." He also thought that Johnny Beckwith could hit a ball harder than any man he ever saw.

One of my Cuban Stars in 1931, Tetelo Vargas, at Sioux City, Iowa, broke the world's record for circling the bases, and in either Major League circuit would steal more bases during the length of a season than any two present players combined. This same player only a week prior, hit seven (7) consecutive home runs in two days against tough semi-pro competition, yet his feats were entirely ignored by the white press. With a colored club in either or both circuits, these feats, common among colored ball players, would not go unnoticed and bring greater interest in baseball with the necessary publicity to go with it. If there is any doubt about the ability of colored teams, look back over the results in fall exhibitions between the pick of Major League talent and the colored clubs they played. You will find that the colored teams won 90% of these exhibition games versus all-star Major League line-ups. Such teams as the Cuban Stars, Inc., Homestead Grays, Pittsburgh Crawfords, Kansas City Monarchs, Chicago American Giants, could today defeat either the Washington Senators or the New York Giants in a series of seven games, and yet all of these mentioned colored clubs could be improved upon if considered for a Major League berth.

The writer would be only too glad to go further into detail on the above subject, if any of your league officials should be interested. I am in a position to place a real select colored or Cuban club into the weakest spot of your circuit and can secure the foremost colored talent in the country to play for me.

May I have your personal views on the subject by return mail?

Within a week, Margaret Donahue, secretary to Bill Veeck, Sr., acknowledged receipt of Dad's letter while Mr. Veeck was on the road with the Cubs, and she promised the letter would be given to him for personal attention. There is no record of any other response. Dad worked verbally thereafter through all his major league contacts, trying to secure integration of baseball through an all-black team, and, while he hoped his club would break the racial barrier, he offered any other, and would have been delighted at any team selected so long as the barrier crumbled.

For 14 more years, the white press would virtually ignore the tremendous accomplishments of black players. For example, in 1937, the World Negro Champion Homestead Grays, with future Hall of Famers Josh Gibson catching and Buck Leonard at first, opened their season in West Palm Beach with a 7-7 tie against the Miami Ethiopian Clowns. The *Miami Herald* carried a pre-Clowns-Grays-series article, but didn't cover one game of the subsequent three in Miami, despite the fact that Impo (Dave "Skinny" Barnhill), one of baseball's best pitchers, started the opener for the Clowns against what may have been the greatest team ever assembled in any sport. The Grays won the Negro National League pennant for nine straight seasons, from 1937 to 1945.

The 1933 Cuban Stars had won more than 125 games. Manuel Rivero, assistant football coach at Columbia University and former football star there, also considered the best baseball player at Columbia since Lou Gehrig, played third for the 1933 Stars.

Stars first baseman was the spectacular Lionel Jackson. My brother Don recalls Jackson's huge, dark pink mitt. Don thought it was a magical weapon because of Jackson's impossible pickups and almost errorless play. Whenever the family was near a sporting goods store or a magic shop, Don looked for a pink first baseman's mitt, but never found one. He once told me, "You saw Goose Tatum play in later years with the Clowns and while he was considered the best defensive first baseman of his time, he didn't come close to Jackson."

Late in the season, before a crowd of 1,800 paid, the Cuban Stars beat a black all-star team 3-1 in White Plains, seven miles from Tarrytown. Luther Farrell, star New York Black Yankees pitcher, was the loser. The winner was Otis "Lefty" Stark, for years a hurler for top black teams, and admired by white fans who knew of him as the man who once struck out Babe Ruth three times in one game.

8

Enter the Clowns

The 1929 Miami Giants, operated by Buck O'Neal, a second base-man and bootlegger–numbers man, was Miami's best.

In May, they had a series with the same Miami Red Sox that ruined the season opener for Lefty Tiant and Dad's Havana Red Sox that March. The Giants–Red Sox matchup was described by the *Miami Herald* as one "to settle the supremacy of Miami's negro baseball circles." It reported, "The war is on folks and it will be worth seeing too. The Miami Red Sox and Miami Giants, our two colored baseball teams and bitter rivals all season, have decided to play it out." A section was reserved for whites.

After 5-4 and 6-2 wins, the Giants were declared "colored city champs," and left town on tour against "some of the best negro teams in the country." They won 12 straight through north Florida, Georgia and Alabama before returning home for a win over the U.S. Army team from Ft. Benning, Georgia.

Dad was the Northeast booking agent for the Miami Giants.

By the early 1930s, Johnnie Pierce, a numbers man, joined Buck O'Neal as a Miami Giants owner. Pierce was the money man and O'Neal was field manager and business manager. In 1934, they signed Sarasota's John O'Neil to play first base. Dad persistently confused owner Buck O'Neal with John O'Neil. After John completed his only season in Miami, following the course of least resistance, he adopted the owner's name and became the John "Buck" O'Neil of Kansas City Monarchs fame.

After the 1934 season, Buck O'Neal, the owner, moved to New York City, and died following a stint as groundskeeper at Yankee Stadium. Starting the 1935 season, Hunter Campbell replaced Buck O'Neal as Miami Giants' co-owner and business manager.

Richard King, a young, weak-hitting first baseman–pitcher, with prospects of a brief and routine playing career, left his native Philadelphia in the early

1930s and played his way south with independent black teams, washing clothes in bathroom sinks, drying freshly washed uniforms out touring car windows and otherwise learning road ways. He settled briefly in Miami with Roderick "Monk" Silva's West Indies Royals before joining the Zulu Cannibal Giants.

In Louisville, Kentucky, during the early 1930s, Charlie Henry, a former Negro league pitcher, launched the Zulu Cannibal Giants, a road club known for grass skirts, assumed African names, warpaint, foreign chatter, comedy and shadowball. Occasionally, Charlie Henry still pitched.

The Zulus christened Richard King "King Tut." During the 1940s, in telling Indianapolis Clowns star righthander Jim "Fireball" Cohen about his days with the Zulus, Tut reported that the African gibberish was maintained in public. Tut slipped up once with a woman on his arm in a Jacksonville hotel lobby. Passing a teammate, Tut said, "She sure was good."

"I made one of them talk! I made one of them talk!" the woman shouted.

Dad was the Northeast booking agent for the Zulu Cannibal Giants.

A road club like no other, the Zulu Cannibal Giants carried only five or six players and traveled in two cars, one carrying all equipment and uniforms and Charlie Henry, also known under his Zulus pitching name, King Shabambi.

When the Zulus hit town, to flesh out the lineup, Henry hired local players otherwise unengaged on game day. Players were to be paid at dinner after the game. That he spent time negotiating the day's pay was often irrelevant. One crucial employment tenet was that players not eat before games, so they were ravenous postgame. After the game, Charlie would drive the locals to a restaurant, give them orders for himself and the nucleus traveling with him, then tell the locals he and the others would go gas up the cars while the food was being prepared, and the Zulu Cannibal Giants would promptly leave town.

At the end of his Zulus career in 1937, Charlie Henry sold the Zulu Cannibal Giants to Louisville's Colonel Charles B. Franklin, after which Colonel Franklin received a call from Chicago's Abe Saperstein about booking Saperstein's Zulu Cannibal Giants. Charlie Henry had conveyed the team to Abe too. Dad apparently also bought the Zulu Cannibal Giants from Charlie Henry. In fact, history does not provide a complete list of those who contributed to the Charlie Henry retirement fund buying the Zulu Cannibal Giants. Sometimes I picture Dad and Abe and Colonel Franklin and a couple unidentified guys emerging from a car in front of a fancy restaurant somewhere, Charlie Henry behind the wheel saying, "Men, order us big, soup to nuts; I'll be right back soon as I gas up."

In 1935, tired of the hunger pangs of Charlie Henry's posthaste post-game exits from town, Tut got out of Henry's car with the locals at a restaurant in Miami following a Zulu Cannibal Giants–Miami Giants game, and joined the Miami Giants.

Tut retained his nickname and the spark of comedy from the Zulu Cannibal Giants, as well as some teammates. In a wholesale defection, center fielder L. C. Williams, second baseman Sylvester Snead and catcher Luther Halton left the Zulus to join Tut on the Miami Giants.

During the 1935–1936 off-season, the Miami Giants became the Miami Ethiopian Clowns. Monk Silva recalled the pageantry of the 1936 Miami home opener at Dorsey Park: "One by one, each Clowns player was given his African name over the loudspeaker. It was quite a ceremony and quite a crowd reaction," he said. In marked contrast, the team honored the black African Kingdom of Coptic Christians by using the word "Ethiopian," but players wore circus clown suits and red fright wigs.

In 1936 or 1937, the Clowns played north in two Cadillacs with Hunter Campbell and ran out of money just before Dad's bookings. That's when Dad and Hunter became partners.

Some report that Dad paid Johnnie Pierce a nominal amount for his interest. Johnnie Pierce's daughter, Sue Pierce Barnhill, who married pitcher Dave "Skinny" Barnhill, said that Hunter Campbell sold her father out dealing with Dad and that Dad never knew her father or that her father had an interest in the team. It is unlikely Dad paid Johnnie Pierce, who financed the team and generally left management, booking and promotion to Hunter Campbell. Some have reported that Johnnie Pierce became bitter as Clowns fame grew.

But according to Sue Barnhill, her father was never angry at Dad. Hunter Campbell was the target of his bitterness. The Clowns were at an end without Dad's money and promotions, and would never have grown without

Dad's talent. Their value depended on Dad, and Dad's value became interwoven with the Clowns.

It is unclear what team Dad owned during 1934–1936, and just exactly when he became an owner of the Clowns. It is likely he had the Cuban Stars until he became part owner of the Miami Ethiopian Clowns during the 1936 season, but that cannot be ascertained. Dad bought Hunter Campbell's interest in the Clowns during the 1938–1939 off-season, after they had been partners at least two years. He once told me, "Doesn't matter to me when we started except it matters we did things the right way under the same ownership starting in 1929."

Sometimes in response to the cost of supporting a large family during the depression, Dad told Mom, "Villa, we don't have a money tree," and one afternoon, Mom caught my brother Don planting a dime to grow a money tree to end family fiscal concerns.

As with other small towns during the depression, the Tarrytowns had armies of tramps passing through. Many stayed in lean-tos or boxes in the Sleepy Hollow Cemetery or in tents in open fields or in caves in the woods on the Rockefellers' property, and searched garbage cans or begged food from back doors throughout town. It seemed like every neighborhood in nearby New York City had block-long soup lines. People lined up hundreds of yards for an apple or a slice of bread. Others picked through garbage or gutters. Men used wads of gum stuck to the ends of poles to fish through subway grates for coins.

Thanks to Dad, even without a money tree, our family had soup, apples, bread, and coins. As with most who headed families then, Mother and Dad reacted to the depression until they died. Dad kept $500 emergency cash in an envelope in his current XYZ file folder in case banks closed. Mom made at least occasional casseroles, hot dogs and kale and boiled potatoes mashed together, bird's nest stew, a main entree of homemade tomato and rice soup, potato noodles from Grandma Pollock's recipe, rice and cinnamon in milk and other European peasant dishes and economy meals.

During the depression, Grandma Pollock let some indigent tenants stay in family apartments rent-free to help prevent pipes from freezing in winter. Dad applied the principle to baseball. He promoted the Clowns throughout organized ball by explaining that the Clowns helped fans attain the habit of coming out to the home ballpark, and he argued that high rental fees preventing Clowns' use of stadiums in organized ball left an idle park, and that an idle park produced no rent, no concessions income and no good will.

The depression that dominated the '30s did not adversely affect Dad's teams as most others. His teams provided a cheap seat for great entertainment, and gave laughs during an era provoking too many tears.

Still, Dad worked three jobs throughout the decade, and whenever my sister Estelle danced at Clowns games, she passed the hat through the crowd for her pay. Without a word being said for or against, Estelle integrated the more tolerant world of black baseball more than a decade before Jackie Robinson first played for the Dodgers. During the 1930s, starting when she was still in elementary school, Estelle performed acrobatics whenever our family attended Dad's teams' games. At the same games, my brother Don was paid in cracked bats for being batboy, a job he broke in for Jerry and me, who later worked for the same pay. As Don nailed together his broken bats for his future use, Estelle became one of few Tarrytowners to save money.

Family transcended politics for Dad, so when Grandpa Carroll ran as Republican candidate for the North Tarrytown Board of Trustees, Dad, a lifelong Democrat, was his campaign manager. Except for that and two votes for Dwight David Eisenhower, Dad's loyalty to the Democratic Party was constant. He was an active Democrat with a lifetime of interest in politics and a litany of letters to the editor, a superhighway of paper stretching into LBJ's full term. Early, his letters extolled the virtues of Franklin Delano Roosevelt and attacked the policies of Herbert Hoover and the Republicans. Dad's involvement in the party following the crash in 1929 resulted in his appointment as clerk in the Tax Collector's Office in the First National Bank Building a half block from his parents' home and the Strand Theater. As tax clerk he worked 8:00 A.M. to 5:00 P.M.; then, five days a week following supper at home, he ran the Strand from 6:45 P.M. until it closed about 11:00 P.M. Weekends he worked full time in the Strand. He operated his baseball teams and promoted around the other two jobs and duties as a volunteer fireman for the village.

Christmas morning, 1932, there was no gift under the tree for Mom from Dad. Later, just up the hill from the Hudson, Mom and Dad strolled Beekman Avenue holding hands with Don and Estelle and pushing Valaria in a perambulator through the crisp, clean air, and as they neared Pocantico Street, Don saw the Tarrytowns' most beautiful car at the curb, a navy blue Desoto sedan, and Dad told Mom, "It's a shame you leave your car out like that gathering dust." It was his Christmas gift to her, the car Don, Estelle and Valaria later rode in to see Dad's teams play. Don recalls many times lying in bed, supposedly asleep, listening to the night until he heard the unique sound of the Desoto—Dad coming home at night's end from the Strand—and moments later, the rhythms of Dad's Underwood put Don to sleep, and he woke next morning for school to the same staccato sounds.

But somehow, Dad found time for family even during baseball season. All recall summer family trips to Coney Island, Radio City Music Hall, Palisades Park, the Bronx Zoo, Clowns games, family in the city.

Dad and Mom were like parent birds at the head of a loose V formation, children trailing them in flight.

Early low gate receipts prompted Mom to suggest Dad attend games on a spot basis, and the Pollocks' love of travel began.

The family rode to selected bookings, and receipts improved sufficiently to make such travel permanent policy. A family ritual began. Before we even thought about checking into a hotel, we drove black section streets, noting the placement of game placards. Status was acquired by the sibling spotting the first window card. Years later, when all the others were married and gone, and Mother and Dad and I traveled alone and I saw the first placard, I automatically thought, "I would have seen it first even if they were all here." Dad randomly stopped and asked pedestrians if they knew Clowns game time, both as a check to see if publicity had done its job and to gain a few more fans. If they knew the time, he was pleased; if not, he'd tell them the time and some team highlights, advising them they shouldn't miss it.

Sometimes detail of Dad's demographics overwhelmed Mom, and she'd say, "Sydney, don't talk baseball. We have to get these children to a hotel this week, unless that kind man wants to put us all up a few nights while you tell him your story."

In sharp contrast, Dad's brother Charlie, an undergraduate at the University of Alabama, returning there following spring vacation, was forcibly removed from the Cuban Stars bus during the early '30s by Alabama state troopers for violating racial custom by being with them or perhaps for not putting them all in the back of their own bus. Twenty-eight years after Dad died, '40s Clowns pitcher Jim Colzie told me, "Bet you can't remember your daddy coming below Washington, D.C., without his family to see the Clowns."

I couldn't. He went to Chicago alone, or Detroit, or St. Louis, or Cincinnati, or Indianapolis, or Buffalo, or Cleveland, or Pittsburgh, or Toledo, or even Washington, but never farther south that I could recall. "The reason was because he wouldn't go anywhere he couldn't stay wherever he wanted with his team," Colzie said.

Buster Haywood verified, adding, "Only times Syd came South alone was when we played my hometown of Portsmouth, Virginia, because he'd stay at my house because he loved my mother's cooking."

From 1929 on, Dad visited nearby players off-season. Don recalled early visits to Ramiro Ramirez and family in Spanish Harlem. Charlie Rivera of the 1941 National Champion Clowns remembered Dad's off-season visits: "Syd came into the City weekly to pick up films for his father's theater. We'd meet at the Woodside Hotel and go midtown for the films and talk baseball. Syd would take me to lunch or dinner either midtown or in Harlem. We all stayed close to Syd because what he said happened. He was a good, good man—the best."

Forties Clowns first baseman Armando Vasquez remembered Dad's Harlem visits to Clowns' business manager Bunny Downs, then Ramiro Ramirez, Vasquez, and finally Marcelino Bauza. Bauza was shortstop of the

1929 Havana Red Sox. Armando explained: "Most times Syd visited Bauza, he brought Estelle. Afro-Cuban jazz interpretive dancing was a big part of her act in the mid-'40s, and Marcelino's brother Mario played in a top Afro-Cuban jazz band. Estelle and Syd and Mario would kick around ideas."

Jim "Fireball" Cohen, ace pitcher for the Clowns from 1946 to 1952, said, "Syd often took me out to eat and brought me to one restaurant and introduced me to former world heavyweight champion Jack Johnson sitting at another table. There was never a dull moment around Syd."

There were changes in Harlem before I grew up. Don spoke of the glamour of Harlem's Hotel Theresa, the Cotton Club, the Apollo Theater and the sidewalk fashion parades—the colorful hats and dresses of the women and the zoot suits of the glide-walking day-strutters. Every day was Sunday.

We too walked Harlem streets comfortably until one day in the late 1940s. Mom and I were with Pauline Downs in her living room. Jerry was elsewhere in the apartment with Dad and Bunny, and Pauline wanted to go shopping. "Will we be okay?" Mom asked. "I hear it's not so safe anymore, the streets."

"We'll be fine with this," Pauline said. "Turn your head, Alan." Later Mom told us Pauline had hiked her skirt, revealing a straight razor taped to her right thigh.

Off-seasons were almost as busy as seasons. Each year, Dad improved the team, and by the end of the decade, the Miami Ethiopian Clowns were among baseball's best. John "Buck" O'Neil told me:

Oh, yes! Yes! I remember well the first time the Monarchs played the Clowns. Surely do. Your Daddy and Hunter Campbell had the Clowns then. Our fellas were whoopin' it up about how we were gonna play clowns, the Miami Ethiopian Clowns, sayin' how we're gonna do this, gonna do that to a bunch of clowns.

First time the Monarchs played the Clowns was in Minneapolis. I think maybe it was after their club came from the Denver Post Tournament one year. But you know the Monarchs kept talkin' about beating up on them and runnin' them out the ball park, so I told them not to be taking that ball club lightly. Said I'd played for them in '34 when they were still the Miami Giants, and they were Major League caliber then, and Syd and Hunter improved them since, so everybody laughed, and Skinny Barnhill struck out 17 Monarchs and beat us 2-1. Lord, yes! The only laughin' about the Clowns the Kansas City Monarchs did after that was at King Tut drownin' out there when his boat sunk.

According to Louisville promoter Colonel Charles B. Franklin:

The Clowns could win games like no other team in baseball. During the '30s and '40s, the Clowns revolutionized sports entertainment.

One game Tut played all nine positions. Beaned or brushed back early in a game, Clowns players later came to bat wearing chest protectors, shin guards and catcher's mask.

The Clowns busted a double steal one time in Louisville. Men on first and third. Man on first steals second to draw a throw so the man on third could steal home. Didn't work, so next pitch the man on second steals first to try again.

In close games, after close calls against the Clowns, King Tut came at umpires with progressively larger axes, 'til Peanuts or Goose or Bebop had to help him carry out the last one. And when Peanuts Davis pitched, it was something to see you just couldn't believe. He'd pick an inning to throw butterflies (four-finger knucklers) and the catcher caught from a rocker, Tut and Goose played craps on the ground behind Peanuts, the second baseman pulled out a newspaper and sat and read it, and the shortstop had the batboy bring him a fishing rod so he could cast into left field, fishing with his back to the plate as Peanuts struck out the side. Didn't matter who was hitting. Coulda been Babe Ruth, Ted Williams and Hank Aaron—one, two, three. That's how good Peanuts was.

The Clowns were the most innovative team in sports. There was something different every time. Even when [they] did fishing or boxing or the dentist, no matter how often you saw it, it was funnier this time than last, and you knew it would be funnier next time.

The late '30s Clowns could have fit in the Negro leagues. Then Syd replaced the older players with speed men with bat control and contact hitters who could bunt and run the bases. And the Clowns drove everybody who played them crazy. The late '40s, early '50s Clowns,

I'm saying '49, '50, '51, would have won championships in any league anywhere, anytime. They played baseball as well as it could be played. Those years and the year they won the Denver Post, they were the best baseball team in the world. Negro leaguers will tell you, but I was one of the few whites knew it.

But it was never just baseball, not in 1929, not in the '30s or '40s, not in the '50s or '60s. It was black life. It was road life. Sometimes, the road crackled lonely like the echoes of batting practice in an empty stadium. Ed Scott, who discovered Hank Aaron for Dad and played a tour with the 1939 Miami Ethiopian Clowns, recalled:

I was with Tut in Jacksonville on the sidewalk at the hotel, just down from the tap room. Tut tells each passing lady, say, "How do?" Some said, "How do?" back and smiled and sashayed on. Some lingered to talk a spell. Some passed before Tut could catch their eye, so he coughed, a coy, sexy kinda cough, and when they turned around, he said, "How do?"

So the prettiest of all the ladies come by, and Tut caught her eye, said, "How do?"

Her nose went in the air. She smirked. She looked straight ahead and kept walkin', and Tut, he start coughin'. She turned around, said, "My husband's got somethin'll kill that cough."

PART FOUR

THE FORTIES

With Fire

We played with fire and always took the extra base. . . . The Clowns were fire and hustle. . . . The thing was to draw people. . . . the Clowns out-drew every team in both leagues. We brought money and good baseball into the League. . . .

—Buster Haywood

9

Denver Post Tournament Champions

As the '40s began, not all loved the Clowns. Foremost among Clowns detractors was Homestead Grays owner Cum Posey. Posey doubled as a columnist for the *Pittsburgh Courier,* the world's largest black weekly, and was also creator of the short-lived 1932 East-West League. His motives may have been fear of losing crowds, games and players to the Clowns and a remembrance that Dad was slow to put his Cuban Stars in the East-West League and quick to pull them out because Dad made more money with his own schedule as an independent club.

Posey's opposition to the Clowns was echoed by Alejandro Pompez, owner of the New York Cubans, who likely feared Dad would reclaim players Pompez stole from the Clowns. Posey, by 1945, was great friends with Dad. But in the late '30s and early '40s, he and *Courier* editor Wendell Smith berated the Clowns with sizzling hometown pens in *Courier* columns for mocking the African heritage with African names and painted faces, providing a "minstrel show." Using their exclusive forum, they told readers Dad was white but did not report that in 1933, Dad helped Ed Hamman start Ed's Canadian Clowns, a white semi-pro comedy team. The Clowns' entry into the league was delayed because the Clowns, according to Posey, acted contrary to league principles. The *Courier* columns did not report that Posey had built his imposing team with numbers money. So much for league principles.

Criticism of the names, warpaint and use of "Ethiopian" had merit, but the source and forum resulted in unjust attacks. Clowns humor was nothing like a minstrel show. The team was good or great. The players were black and proud, and Dad loved the level of play and entertainment they achieved. In one 1940 article sent to all promoters for pregame release, Dad stated, "The Clowns, who sport humorous monikers merely to accentuate their painted faces and numerous pregame stunts, are in reality the pick of players from many outstanding Negro clubs." Lacking in dignity and frankly causing confusion and contributing to the lack of recognition of individual talents of black players so sought by Dad, the names and paint were meant as fun, not to demean or deceive, and certainly weren't Dad's invention. He could have ended the names and the warpaint when he became Hunter Campbell's partner. Likely he'd have ended them after a few icy blasts from Cum Posey and Wendell Smith, but *Courier* readers nationwide came to the ballparks to see what it was they shouldn't see. Cum Posey and Wendell Smith had inadvertently produced the Clowns' best publicity.

The importance of the Clowns as one of the best and most influential and compelling black teams has been obscured through the years by the *Courier* columns, given credibility in some histories of black baseball like echoes of dead scoldings. This adherence to the *Courier* perspective has in effect put the Clowns in the back of the bus by either ignoring the Clowns or stating as unqualified fact the Cum Posey/Wendell Smith myth that the Clowns were a minstrel show, a perpetrator of stereotypical concepts and a perverter of black baseball. As a result, individual Clowns greats and great Clowns teams remain virtually unknown and unrecognized among those who never saw them play.

Eventually led by J. L. Wilkinson and Tom Baird of the Kansas City Monarchs, Tom Hayes of the Birmingham Black Barons and Tom Wilson of the Baltimore Elite Giants, the majority of Negro leagues owners favored the Clowns. The Clowns entered the Negro American League in 1943, agreeing to call Cincinnati home and to drop the names, warpaint and "Ethiopian" portion of their moniker.

Some have since reported that owners came down on the Clowns because Clowns comedy betrayed league principles and that the Clowns stopped comedy once they entered the league. None of that is true. The truth is that black baseball was never hypocritical. It was always joyous. It was never mercenary. It always struggled to survive. And while black baseball was played seriously, with risk, improvisation, aggressiveness and daring seldom seen in white baseball, it was always fun. And that was exactly how the Clowns played baseball. Negro leagues owners no more stopped Clowns comedy than they did the windmill windups, showmanship and clowning of Satchel Paige with the Kansas City Monarchs. Clowns comedy was considered something negative only in the hyperbole of a few men of that time with their own causes to protect and in retrospect by some since who never saw them. As with any comedy, some criticized the quality of their humor from time to time for impugning baseball's purity, or over-doing things, or tastelessness. Such criticism was almost never warranted.

As Clowns catcher-manager Buster Haywood said, "The thing was to draw people. The Negro leagues weren't drawing. The Monarchs were. The Grays and Elite Giants did okay. But the Clowns outdrew every team in both leagues. We brought money and good baseball into the league, and that was our purpose, and the critics can say whatever they want about that!"

The Clowns answered their critics on the field, and the fans responded with attendance and joy.

As the decade began, Felix "Chin" Evans hurled as Kalahari for the Miami Ethiopian Clowns, still an independent semi-pro club. There were Kala-haris before Chin and after. Players came and went; the names stayed.

Chin, Lefty Bowe, Eddie "Peanuts" Davis (Nyasses) and Dave "Skinny" Barnhill (Impo) were the strength of the Clowns 1940 pitching staff. Ac-cording to Evans, who said he was 26-4 that year, the Clowns were 153-28-3 in 1940 "against the best colored, white, semi-pro and minor league clubs throughout the United States and Canada." He had a news article backup. I can't recall their 1940 record. It may have occurred on the field or in Dad's typewriter; I wasn't born that year till the day after Christmas. But the 1940 Clowns had an overwhelmingly winning record, as they did in 1941 and 1942. And they beat good teams, including a large percentage of wins against Negro leagues opposition. The Clowns never again had a pitching staff equal to the 1940 mound corps.

By 1941, the original Clowns lineup was significantly improved. Dad had added catcher Buster Haywood, first baseman Dave "Showboat" Thomas, shortstop Charlie Rivera, and pitchers Peanuts Davis (Nyasses) and Roose-velt "Duro" Davis (Macan) to the Clowns, and many considered them the best team in baseball. The 1941 Clowns were one of the great Clowns teams. In 1996, former Kansas City Monarchs manager John "Buck" O'Neil called the 1941 Miami Ethiopian Clowns "one of the greatest baseball teams ever assembled." Peanuts and Duro Davis were consistently beating all comers, including several one-run wins over Satchel Paige and the Kansas City Monarchs. The Clowns won 125 games in 1941, including victories over the Monarchs, Birmingham Black Barons, Memphis Red Sox, House of David, Brooklyn Bushwicks, Satchel Paige Stars and every Negro league and white minor league team they played.

Fay Young wrote in the June 14, 1941, issue of the *Chicago Defender* that "the Clowns have a ball club. . . . they can rightfully call themselves champions of independent ball clubs. . . . they make some of the dadgondest catches, the outfield moves at lightning speed to rob opponents of extra base hits." Another reporter wrote:

In spite of the antics which panicked the fans at High Rock Park this week, the Clowns have one of the two best semi-pro baseball aggregations in the entire country white or colored. . . .

For instance, "Showboat" Thomas, manager and ace first baseman, conducted his own show around the initial sack. Khora (Buster Haywood), Clown catcher, went to bat twice with his chest protector and shin guards on. He hit a single, stole two bases, and came home handicapped none by his extra gear.

One batter hit with one hand in his hip pocket and lined a double which knocked the left fielder down. The base runners ran when they wanted to. While a man on second was going to third, the runner on third would run to second then to first and so on. With many different variations of this backward baserunning, including one batter who bunted and ran to third base, the Clowns kept the fans in stitches.

In Denver each summer, the nation's top teams outside organized baseball met in the "Little World Series of the West," the *Denver Post* Tournament. Originated in 1915, the tournament was considered the most important series in baseball other than the World Series.

In 1931, Dad's Cuban House of David played in two lesser tournaments, winning the Southwestern Iowa Tournament and losing the championship game of the Eastern Nebraska Tournament to the Kansas City Monarchs.

As a result of that and their overall record against prime competition, in 1932, playing as the Cuban Stars of the East-West League, Dad's team was extended a *Denver Post* Tournament invitation; however, when tournament officials discovered the Cuban Stars were, according to a national release, "composed of dark-skinned islanders," the invitation was revoked. C. L. Parsons, *Post* sports editor, wired Dad that "the color line has been drawn" against his Cuban Stars because southern entries from past tournaments might be offended. The tournament remained segregated until the Kansas City Monarchs appeared in 1934. The Monarchs that year lost the championship game to the House of David, the long-haired, bearded, traveling team representing the conservative religious sect out of Benton Harbor, Michigan, and managed by Grover Cleveland Alexander. The 1934 tournament was the first top-flight black team–white team championship competition in U.S. history and marked the seepage of Satchel Paige's fame from the black world to the white. Ironically, Satchel pitched the tourney as a mercenary for the House of David.

The Negro League All-Stars, featuring the best of the Pittsburgh Crawfords, Washington Elite Giants and Homestead Grays, became the first black *Denver Post* Champions in 1936. Causing important defections from Negro league teams, Dominican Republic dictator Rafael Trujillo, in a 1937 political move designed to provide him public love as head of the world's best baseball team, imported Satchel Paige, Josh Gibson, Cool Papa Bell, pitcher Leroy Matlock and other Negro league stars, all of whom jumped their Negro league contracts to island hop. The nucleus of that aggregation returned to the United States and won the 1937 *Denver Post* Tournament.

Blacks were banned again in 1938. But in 1939 and 1940, the Clowns came and did well. They returned in 1941.

My brother Don described the August 14, 1941, phone call to Dad in his office surrounded by our family at championship game end as "the most exciting moment in Clowns history."

The Clowns had gone into the last day of the tournament unbeaten. But former Brooklyn Dodgers pitcher Boots Poffenberger, of the reigning champion Bona Allen club from Buford, Georgia, had beaten the Clowns

3-1 in the afternoon, and Dad and the family were sullen from the prior call. The Clowns were down 7-3 going into the ninth inning of the championship game.

In their first tournament game, brilliant pitching held the Clowns to a single run until they exploded in the seventh, eighth and ninth for an 11-2 win over the Fort Logan Soldier nine, one of the two best U.S. military teams. Peanuts Davis struck out nine and threw a six-hitter. L. C. Williams hit for the cycle. Showboat Thomas, heralded by the *Denver Post* as "the finest fielding first baseman in the game, bar none," had three hits.

A crowd of 6,000 cheered the Clowns to a 9-1 win over the Enid (Oklahoma) Champlin Refiners, national semi-pro champions, for their second win. The *Denver Post,* referring to the "once-mighty bats" of Enid, reported that "amazed fans waited expectantly all through the brilliantly played contest for the big berthas of the Champlin club to speak with authority as they always have done in the past, but it was not to happen." Duro Davis was mixing his usual fast ball, sharp curve, "jump-ball," knuckler and spitter. While the press proclaimed his pitches legal, and many were, his spitter and "jump ball" (Clowns called it a "cutball") were illegal. He would sometimes cut the ball with his ring or take advantage of a scuff from a throw in the dirt by Buster Haywood. The cutball required at least the scuff. The spitter started with an arm swiping sweat from his forehead. He struck out seven against Enid.

The Clowns took the defending champion Bona Allen club for the Funmakers' third win. More than 5,000 fans were turned away. A crowd exceeding 10,000 saw the game, the first loss in ten tournament games for the Georgia team, including seven wins for the 1940 championship and their first two in 1941. The game was scoreless through five. The Clowns' first rally was started by a Charlie Rivera liner blasted into left center, ruled a ground rule double because it disappeared into the overflowing standing-room-only crowd. Boots Poffenberger gave up three runs in relief. Duro Davis got the 6-1 win. The game featured what I grew up thinking of as "The Stop" by Charlie Rivera. The *Denver Post* reported, "Rivera, the Clowns speedy shortstop, made what easily was the best play of the tournament in the 8th, and incidentally took the spark out of what might have been a Buford rally, when he snagged a shot-out-of-a-gun bounder far to his right and regained his footing in time to make a forceout at second." Fifty-four years later, Charlie Rivera told me, "That ball was hit so hard it spun me around exactly where I had to be to throw to second to get the force."

The Clowns fourth tournament game was a ten-inning 12-7 win over Aurelia, the Iowa Champions. Behind early 7-0, the Funmakers scored two with one out in the top of the ninth to tie the contest. With two gone in the tenth, Buster Haywood singled to trigger a five-run shelling, featuring Blue Dunn's double and home runs by Showboat Thomas and L. C. Williams. Roosevelt Davis pitched two scoreless innings in relief to pick up his third tournament win.

A seven-run first highlighted the Clowns 14-5 win over the Wichita Stearmen Aviators in their fifth tournament game. The *Post* said:

From a baseball standpoint, the game offered everything from big league performance on down. The Clowns were great throughout. They hit the ball from one corner of the lot to the other. Then when they had the Stearmen backing up, they laid down a barrage of the most perfectly executed bunts Merchants Park has ever seen.

In the field the Clowns came up with everything, topped by Mofike's [L. C. Williams] running catch of Bates' tremendous 425-foot drive to the scoreboard—a homer in any man's league.

Following Boots Poffenberger's 3-1 gem beating the Funmakers, the championship game was played. The *Denver Post* reported:

The Clowns at 12:40 o'clock Thursday morning, August 14 . . . before more than 10,000 persons, hundreds of them sitting on the ground outside the jammed-packed grandstands and bleachers, won the title from the defending champion, the Bona Allen club (white) of Buford, Ga.

The Clowns wrote the most thrilling page in the 26-year history of the tournament into the books by rallying for 6 runs in the 9th inning of the final championship game to dethrone Bona Allen.

The Negro club can rightfully be called a champion in every sense of the word. They went into the 9th inning of the final game trailing 5-3. It was do or die for the Clowns as they came up for the last time.

Like the champions they are, the Clowns didn't let their followers down. Before the inning was over six runs had crossed the platter, Bona Allen had its third pitcher in the box, and the tourney was all but wrapped up for delivery to the deserving Clowns.

The final score was 9-7. The trophy read "Won by Syd Pollock's Ethiopian Clowns—Denver Post Champions." It came with a $4,729.66 winner's share divided by Dad, Hunter Campbell and the players. Buster Haywood was awarded a Gruen Curvex wrist watch as most valuable player; Showboat Thomas, a Gothic jarproof wrist watch as manager of the championship team; Peanuts Davis, a fielder's glove as "most entertaining coach."

Later, the Clowns awaited a flight to St. Paul, Minnesota, to resume their tour with a game against the Birmingham Black Barons, beginning a nine-game series against the Black Barons and Memphis Red Sox, both Negro American League teams. *Denver Post* columnist Jack Carberry caught up with Dave "Showboat" Thomas at the airport. In his "Second Guess" column, Carberry repeated this exchange:

I said: "Showboat, I want to tell you that the folk in this town think your boys are swell. Not only are you great ball players but we, who have dealt with you through this tournament, know you as gentlemen and sportsmen. You boys, Showboat, are a credit to your race."

Showboat said: "Thank you—and I want to say that means as much to us as does our winning the tournament."

The article continued, "You fans who saw the Clowns in their seven tournament games never once saw a single player voice a protest over an umpire's decision. . . . the Clowns . . . never replied when taunted by opposing players, or ever addressed a remark to a fan in the stands."

Clowns answers were sung in the silence of their response to the taunts. Their answers were written on the mound, in the basepaths, on the infield clay, behind the plate, in the outfield grass and within the coaches' boxes. Their answers were spoken in the backwards baserunning, the behind-the-back catches and throws and the laughter and cheers of the fans, and not just their fans. As the *Denver Post* pointed out in the championship game coverage, "the fans . . . cheered the two foes from the first pitch to the final out." Clowns answers were stained in black sweat into the fabric of backrests of the team bus and were framed by the ache of roads connecting borrowed ballparks.

Clowns answers almost slipped past white Miami. Annually tens of thousands of northern white tourists flocked to Miami Beach like migrating birds and perched poolside in the sun, trying to get darker, and accepted segregation on arrival. Most never understood that the only blacks on Miami Beach were there temporarily as entertainers, construction workers, waiters, cooks and servants. Only work permits allowed tourist industry workers on Miami Beach streets at night. The ordinance was enforced against blacks only. Internationally known black entertainers, such as Duke Ellington, Lionel Hampton, Count Basie, Ella Fitzgerald, Louis Armstrong, headlined at the best Beach hotels, but could not stay in any, best or worst. Instead, they slept across the water in the Sir John Hotel or the George Washington Carver in the Central Miami Negro District.

While Coconut Grove, South Miami, Liberty City and Brownsville all had black neighborhoods, they were a vascular system to the Central Miami Negro District, the heart of Dade County's black community. Renamed Overtown during the 1960s after inner city deterioration and urban renewal uprooted more than 10,000, overcrowding Liberty City and leading to the expression "Goin' over town this weekend," the section became a slum, one with a deep, but separate, Miami history. In October 1941, it was a beating heart inside a joyful, living body set aside by whites. Few whites knew that following their shows on the beach, the great black entertainers performed at the Knightbeat at the Sir John. Whites didn't buy their "threads" at Perry's Fashion Department Store. Whites couldn't tell you the way to Good Bread Alley, the block of residences graced by the baking aroma from the Holsum Bread plant.

On August 13, 1941, the Miami Ethiopian Clowns became the first team to win a national championship representing Miami, yet of the two white Miami dailies, the *Miami News* did not report the feat, and the *Miami Herald* mentioned it only in the "Spotlighting Sports" column by sports editor Everett Clay on September 23, 1941, nearly a month and a half after the tournament ended. If it weren't for Clay's backyard lawn "boy" George, the news might have stayed unnoticed on the back seat of the bus. Clay wrote:

"WAIT'LL THOS' Clowns git hom," George, the yard boy, was telling your correspondent the other day, "Tain't ev'r been or ev'r will be an'thin' like it. It'll be sumthin.'"

For, you see, there are big doings afoot, from Coconut Grove's Grand Avenue to the Liberty City Settlement, for those returning heroes—Miami's World's semi-pro Championship Ethiopian Clowns baseball team.

The Clowns, winners of the *Denver Post*'s tournament last month, will open a "miniature world series" with the Jacksonville Red Caps of the Negro American League Oct. 1 in Jacksonville. After three games there the scene will shift to Miami for the "big doin's" Sunday and Monday, Oct. 5 and 6.

Sunday, Oct. 5, has been designated as "Hunter Campbell Day" at Dorsey Park in honor of the manager of the Clowns, and 4,000 seats will be installed to take care of, what George vows will be, "bigges' cro'd o' folks ev'r had ther'."

Unquestionably, next to Satchel Paige, the Clowns are the No. 1 drawing card in negro baseball today, as testified by the size of the throngs which have been watching them on their barnstorming trip home.

Their only loss since the tournament has been to the Toledo Hens of the American Association. The score was 4-3. In recent games, the Clowns have whipped Birmingham, 7-1; Toledo All-Stars, 4-3; Charleston (W. Va.) A.S., 1-0, and Birmingham BB 6-5.

Neither the *Herald* nor the *News* carried another word about the Clowns that season, and on October 5, Hunter Campbell lost his day when a hurricane lashed ashore, its eye 13 miles south of Miami.

Developing the championship 1941 Miami Ethiopian Clowns required not just Dad's ability to spot and acquire talent supplementing the skills of Clowns players inherited from the Miami Giants, but luck as well.

Carlos "Charlie" Lavezzari Rivera, born in Puerto Rico in 1912, played with the Baltimore Elite Giants in 1940. Before the 1941 season, he was suspended because he played winter ball in Puerto Rico and reported to the Elite Giants later than owner Tom Wilson expected. Learning of the suspension, Ed Gottlieb wanted him for a tryout in Shibe Park with the Philadelphia Stars.

"Tryout? What for?" Charlie asked. "You saw me play all last year."

"Team policy," Ed replied.

"I'll think about it." While walking in Manhattan's Central Park and thinking about Ed Gottlieb, Charlie met Showboat Thomas, recently hired as Clowns' manager, himself out for a contemplative stroll, and at Showboat's suggestion, Charlie entered a verbal contract with Dad to play short for the Clowns.

As Clowns crowds grew during the late 1930s, cash flowed, and Hunter Campbell's betting on horse racing became serious. His debts took on so much body fat, a fiscal coronary prevented any contribution to Clowns capital, and eventually he sold his interest to Dad, but stayed on as business manager. By 1941, Dad was sole owner. The occasion was marked by the purchase of a used Greyhound bus and two sets each of two uniforms differing in color and style. Buster Haywood recalls the bus as the best in baseball "till Syd and I picked up the new Flxible in Loudonville, Ohio, in 1948."

"Once Syd bought Hunter out, we never again worried about bats. We always had enough," Buster said.

Hunter never saw the Clowns play a Negro league game. He died suddenly following the 1942 season, believing that his beloved independent Negro champion Clowns were the best team in baseball.

10

Bunny and Buster

McKinley "Bunny" Downs, once second baseman of the reknowned Hilldale ball club, was first hired in 1942 as Clowns' field manager, then replaced Hunter Campbell as business manager and remained in that post the entire time the Clowns were in the Negro American League.

A kind man, Bunny was light enough to pass for white. Almost always in suspenders, he had an ever-present toothpick wedged into the same crack between his teeth. When I was young, and Bunny caught me staring at it, which was wide-eyed and often, he clicked his teeth, and the toothpick moved with them. It stayed in place as he talked. I wanted to see him asleep to see if the toothpick retained its place. It did the one time I saw on the bus. My question was whether the toothpick was a permanent part of his anatomy—whether it was merely jammed between his teeth or actually grew there. Childless himself, Bunny loved kids, and Louise Hamman's childhood memories include hand-in-hand walks with him to the concession stand for peanuts. Mine include the official Negro American League balls Bunny had the big leaguers sign for me each autumn the Clowns had postseason tours against major league all-stars.

If Bunny drank, I never saw evidence, and I sat on the bench with him for hundreds of Clowns games and spent time with him in his home and ours almost as often. Buster Haywood and Jim Colzie, however, both report Bunny sometimes drank too much. Jim recalls a four-team double-header Yankee Stadium crowd that seemed like 60,000, with a gate of at least $50,000. "Bunny had sipped a few and asked me to go with him to settle up. I told him he best let someone else handle it, but Bunny says, 'Syd pays me to settle up and count his money, and I'm gonna settle up and count his money,' and he did, without error."

Walter "Dirk" Gibbons, who pitched for the 1948 and 1949 Clowns, remembered Bunny nearly a half century later: "Bunny was The-Man-in-the-Back-Seat. Back seat of that bus was his, and he had all he needed back there. Was back there Bunny taught me about eating pork and beans and sardines, Bunny and Goose. We'd go the grocery store, me and Bunny and Goose, and get us a loaf of bread, onions, pork and beans and sardines, and slice it all up on the back seat while we rode along. Imagine the smell on that bus! I still eat that today, and people think I'm crazy. Bunny was friendly, but strictly business. He was a good, honest man, a perfect man for Syd."

According to 1945 Clowns infielder Leroy Cromartie, Bunny was funny and fun, but firm. His terms prevailed when conflicting with the field manager's. Partyers and drinkers sat out the next day's game. Cromartie played part of one summer between school years at Florida A&M. "Bunny made sure I didn't drink or womanize by hanging around certain older players. Now Fred Wilson was alcoholic, and would soon cut you as look at you. A great hitter, he only liked you when you bought him whiskey. Bunny made sure to sit between me and Fred Wilson."

Once when the bus broke down, players caught cabs to the ballpark, and one cabbie gunned out of control, rolling the cab three times, and Bunny ended up in Cromartie's lap. Looking down into the infielder's eyes, Bunny said, "Guess the Lord don't want us yet."

"Bunny and Syd were like brothers," Jim Colzie said, an opinion confirmed by other Clowns players from the '40s and '50s. Pitcher Amos Watson once was given leave to go home to Florida for family reasons. He returned late without leave instead of calling Dad to alert the team through Bunny, and missed his turn in the rotation. Colzie was there when Bunny reprimanded Watson, and "Watson took a bat after Bunny. Syd promptly traded Watson to Baltimore for Lester Lockett."

Sometimes Bunny sat in the stands to soak in crowd reaction. Because he looked white, no one figured he was with the team, and people said things around him they might not say if they realized his affiliation. In 1946, Colzie broke a local player's arm with a pitch in Michigan City, Indiana. In the crowd, Bunny heard someone say, "That's one dead nigger pitcher," and he followed a group of six or seven white men and watched them enter their cars to go for weapons.

Bunny spoke to our bus driver, who was always called "Chauff," then rushed to the dugout and alerted the players. He said, "Win fast. Make damn quick outs. And when it's over, I got Chauff with the bus warmed up outside the locker room. We grab our clothes and pass right on through to the bus in uniform. No showers this game."

Colzie said, "The Clowns were 50 miles out of town by the time those guys got back to the ball park to kill me."

Unfortunately, during 1941 and 1942 before they entered the Negro American League, the Clowns lost players to Negro league raids and to World War II armed forces. When shortstop Livingston "Winkie" James was drafted before the 1941 season, Charlie Rivera replaced him. In 1942, Alejandro Pompez of the New York Cubans alone purged the Clowns roster of Charlie Rivera, Blue Dunn, Showboat Thomas, Roosevelt Cox and Buster Haywood. Uncle Sam took Ray Neil, Jim Oliver, Peanuts Davis, Goose Tatum (though Goose wasn't drafted until after the 1943 season), Jim Colzie, Sloppy Lindsay and Winkie James. So when the Clowns entered the Negro American League more than half the 1941 National Championship starting lineup was gone, along with the improved replacement double play combination, starting first baseman and backup and two starting pitchers, including Peanuts, considered by many the best pitcher then in baseball. Chin Evans went to the Memphis Red Sox after the 1940 season. According to Jim Colzie, Peanuts remained a top pitcher but was never the same hurler or person after the war. The nucleus of the Clowns had spun and shattered.

Isaac Newton might have expected his apple to rise on release had he watched Dad smoke and type. Wrapped by summer sun at his typewriter, glare cut by a green reporter's eyeshade tilted slightly up and toward the side of his head, Dad always had a lit cigarette dangling from the right corner of his mouth, and the length and curl of the ash defied the laws of physics, especially when the cigarette bobbed as he talked. He looked like a latent pyromaniac, but the ash never dropped. When the curve seemed at its maximum, it bent more, and when it almost creaked, Dad would curl his hand to catch whatever dropped, a movement always superfluous, di-

rect the cigarette over the ashtray on his desk, and safely flick in another
Guinness-record ash.

Buster Haywood remembered Dad's cigarette ash. "Syd would sit beside me
in the dugout when I was manager, cigarette curled out of his mouth with
the biggest curved ash you ever saw, scorebook in his lap, keeping score,"
Buster said.

Dad never told Buster what to do. "He made suggestions time to time. I
always took them. They always worked. Syd knew baseball."

Dad and Buster were like brothers. Buster didn't holler at players. To
Buster, a pro knew his own mistakes and needed to be encouraged, not dis-
couraged. "We all make mistakes. Get 'em next time!" he'd shout over the
roar of the crowd.

Dad taught us the same.

"Never worry about what the man beside you's making just so long as
you're paid fair," Buster told players.

Dad told us the same.

"You'll sleep if you go to bed at night with love in your heart, with hate
you'll toss and turn the night," Buster said.

Dad lived inducing sleep.

Buster and Dad grayed black and white.

The Clowns of the 1940s were clearly a harmonious ballclub, defined by
Dad, Buster, Bunny Downs and Tut.

White baseball was played methodically at a jog, black in a blur on the
run. The Clowns entered the Negro American League in 1943 figuring to
dominate. They couldn't. They lacked team speed and power and personnel
from 1940 and 1941. With games played against league teams always un-
equal in number, the Funmakers most frequently crossed bats with two of
the best: the Kansas City Monarchs and the Birmingham Black Barons.

The Monarchs had power hitting and power pitching. So during the decade, Dad slowly rebuilt the Clowns with youth, character, speed, the will
to win, contact hitting, defense, good pitching and intelligence. And at the
end of the decade, under Buster Haywood, considered by some the greatest
catcher ever to play, the Clowns became a dominant team, winning four
Negro American League pennants their twelve seasons in the circuit.

When Buster won Most Valuable Player designation in the Clowns' National Championship *Denver Post* Tournament performance in 1941, Joe McCarthy, manager of the great Babe Ruth–Lou Gehrig New York Yankees teams saw him play and said, "I'd give Babe Ruth and Ty Cobb in their primes plus $100,000 for Haywood Khora [Buster Haywood]." Likely if he could have, he wouldn't have, but he clearly considered Buster, then 31 years old, a great catcher.

Negro leagues statistics covered only a small portion of the season's games and were never complete, and therefore often meaningless. Any player could claim any batting average or pitching record or any number of home runs, especially considering the dominance over nonleague teams, and whether he was anywhere near truth or not, no one could disprove him. Accuracy of Negro league statistics is little better than the integrity of the player giving the account.

No one questioned Buster Haywood's integrity. He claims a lifetime batting average of .260–.265, though it was likely higher. No one questioned Buster Haywood's humility either.

"Buster was a singles hitter who really worked a pitcher," Kansas City Monarchs first baseman–manager John "Buck" O'Neil said. "Great arm. Top flight receiver. Very intelligent. Great clutch hitter. Extremely fast afoot."

Among Clowns contemporaries, Buster was considered the best clutch hitter in baseball. I was Clowns batboy for a 1953 game at Pittsburgh's Forbes Field. In the bottom of the ninth, score tied, the Clowns had runners on second and third, when Buster pinch-hit himself. As he strode toward the plate, pitcher Frank Carswell tapped my thigh and said, "Little Syd, pack up the bats. This game's ours."

"How do you know?"

"Skip's at the plate. He'll spray a single someplace. Best clutch hitter there is." Players at the other end of the dugout began putting bats into batbags.

As Buster's game-winning liner bounced into right center, Carswell said, "You should have seen him young. Same thing, day in day out. Always a gamewinner in Skip's bat itchin' to crack out."

Buster's will to win was as consuming as a Bedouin's thirst. He kept the side of his throwing hand touching the side of his mitt to eliminate the fractional second lost moving throwing hand to caught ball. No one knows how many runners he threw out by that same fraction of a second, but at various times over the years, Buster broke every finger on his throwing hand at least once.

In 1944, a remarkably talented young catcher–third baseman, Sam Hairston, was concerned with future paydays with the Birmingham Black Barons. The Black Barons played a double header against the Ft. Benning nine in Atlanta, Georgia, and former Clowns first baseman Leonard "Sloppy" Lindsay, playing for the military team, suffered through a seven-for-eight Hairston hitting barrage.

"But one man to play for makes every payday," Lindsay told a disgruntled Hairston after the games, "Let me talk to Syd Pollock about making a deal for you."

Dad soon traded Pepper Bassett for Hairston and sent Hairston a bus ticket to join the Clowns in Indianapolis, promising "You make my club, I'll give you a $25 dollar raise first paycheck."

A doubleheader in Indianapolis against the Detroit Stars provided Sam Hairston's first Clowns forum, and he duplicated his Atlanta feat with seven hits in eight at bats in a Clowns sweep. Next payday, he had his raise without request.

Sam's philosophy was to exceed all, friend and foe alike. If he lost his spot on the team, his family suffered the same whether he lost his spot to friend or foe. So Sam would do anything fair to stay and anything fair to win.

As a youngster, he began plant work at the Acipco Mill in his hometown Birmingham, Alabama. He severely injured the middle finger of his right hand in an on-the-job accident, and the company doctor wanted to amputate, but Sam ran away first and received other treatment, saving the finger. Before his Acipco career ended, he played beside future Birmingham Black Barons greats Piper Davis and Ed Steele, and one year the team won 50 straight games. His first game with the Acipco Mill team, Sam struck out in his only two at bats and was cut. Then, playing with the Sayreton Mines team outside town, he did nothing but hit, including a game winner against Acipco. An Acipco official told him he had to rejoin their team or be fired.

In 1943 the Black Barons won the Negro American League pennant, and Sam's 1944 tryout was jeopardized because the club was composed substantially of veterans and was cutting back personnel to economize. So when Ted "Double Duty" Radcliffe broke his finger, Sam said he could catch. He had never been behind the plate before in his life, and ironically his first game as backstop was against the Clowns. He caught a shutout.

By 1945, Sam was catching more than the 35-year-old Haywood. And Sam never forgot one crucial game during the late 1940s in Portsmouth, Virginia, Buster's hometown. A standing-room-only crowd, including Buster's

parents, chanted and cheered for their local catcher, but Buster, then manager, kept himself on the bench in favor of Hairston. "That was integrity
and will to win!" Sam recalled.

The same attributes ended Buster's Clowns career after the team's 1953
second-place finish. "That was the only year I was ever angry at your
daddy," Buster told me. "Ray Neil's the best second baseman I ever saw,
along with Dick Seay and Piper Davis, and I had to play Toni Stone at second the first three innings every game. She wasn't a ballplayer, and I'm playing to win," he said. "It was the worst season of my life; made me sick."

Buster's arm was generally considered best of any catcher. Jim Colzie recalls Buster catching speed demon Sam Jethroe stealing twice in one game,
after which Jethroe never ran on him again. In 1947, at age 36, Buster led
Negro American League catchers in assists with 42. Next closest was 33.
There was no better backstop.

"Intelligence made Buster the best catcher I ever saw," Dad said. While
others relaxed or exercised during opposition batting practice, Buster studied hitters. At 5'8", 160 pounds, he was one of baseball's smallest catchers.
"I was too little to block the plate, so I jumped on runners," Buster said.
"Weren't collisions around my home plate; just me lying on top of the runner after the tag."

Mask flipped off, Buster, to back up throws, mirrored runners on their
way to first on infield grounders.

Dad said Buster knew every baserunner's trends. "He always called the
pitchout right to stop the steal, and picked more guys off second and third
from a squat, even with bases loaded, than the next dozen catchers combined," Dad said. Buster had a nearly extrasensory ability to pick up signals
and an almost mystical knack for calling a pitchout on a hit-and-run or
suicide squeeze.

The Birmingham Black Barons were paying Buster $90 a month when
the Ethiopian Clowns came to town in 1940. Clowns' wallets bulged with
$200–$300 each.

Buster asked Clowns pitcher Dave "Skinny" Barnhill where the money
came from, and Barnhill reported that the Clowns were on "p.c." and drew
the best crowds in road baseball. In the players' vernacular of the time, p.c.
meant playing for a percentage of the gate. Negro league teams played on
salary, regardless of the attendance, whereas independent teams like the
Clowns could make more by attracting good crowds. As semi-pros, Clowns

players equally divided 60 percent of team cut, the other 40 percent going to Dad and Hunter Campbell. The winning team split 60 percent of teams' share, the loser 40 percent. Unlike league clubs, players with teams on p.c. paid their own room and board.

Buster wanted to play for the Clowns, and within a few days, Dave Barnhill persuaded Hunter Campbell to send a bus ticket so Buster could join them at Salem, Virginia. Because the Clowns were independent, the leagues didn't honor their contracts and they didn't honor the leagues'.

Black Barons owner Tom Hayes pulled Buster off the bus, claiming over $200 for loans for a glove, spikes and other items. Denying the debt, Buster called police, and when Hayes failed to produce a single note or receipt, Buster got a police escort out of town.

Regular backstop for the Clowns through the rest of 1940 and all of 1941, in 1942, he joined Barnhill on the New York Cubans in the Negro National League.

During the 1942 season, Clowns crowds and financial instability of the Negro leagues, plus a need for mutual honoring of player contracts, intensified Negro American League overtures to the Clowns.

The team moved its hometown to Cincinnati, and Dad agreed to comply with the league mandate that the Clowns cease applying warpaint. But Dad had some demands of his own, including freedom to schedule nonleague teams and including "the return of my catcher."

Buster rejoined the Clowns for the 1943 season, the Funmakers' first in the Negro American League, and as bad actors slow afoot, such as Fred "Evil" Wilson, were replaced with young, fast, intelligent players, the character of the Clowns slowly changed from warhorse to racehorse. Partway through the 1948 season, Buster replaced Ramiro Ramirez as Clowns' manager, and, so like Dad in temperament, philosophy and baseball intelligence, caressed the Clowns into champions.

11

Style Defined and Refined

The Clowns' will to win appears in photos of team altercations. Tut and Bunny were always central images. The team's business manager and chief entertainer took the field for every bad call, every argument, every melee, every brawl. If the Clowns lost, Tut used spare time to harangue them in the locker room or on the bus or in the hotel as "the sorriest bunch I ever saw." If they won, he proclaimed them the best baseball club ever, and his beautiful singing voice led the Clowns bus quartet.

So behind the comedy, the Clowns played not just with pride, but to win, to be best. And Buster set the pace.

Henry "Speed" Merchant, of God-given speed and God-given surname, was leading base stealer for the best Clowns teams, closely followed by Rienaldo Verdes Drake. Buster was probably the leading base stealer among league catchers, and he considered Ray Neil the team's finest base runner. Neil ran with speed and icy intelligence. Almost all Clowns players ran well.

"We played with fire," Buster said, "and always took the extra base. Merchant almost always looked for second on a single, and generally got it when he tried."

The Clowns featured the hit-and-run and sacrifice. Ray Neil, Verdes Drake, Speed Merchant, Buster, Honey Lott, Leo Lugo, Sam Hairston and Jim Oliver excelled as contact hitters, with Neil, Drake, Merchant and Buster tops at the hit-and-run. Merchant and Hairston hit with power too. Hairston was king of doubles.

Dad considered a man who couldn't bunt an incomplete ballplayer, so every Clowns player, including pitchers, mastered the bunt.

"The Clowns were fire and hustle," Buster said. "Once in Chicago, we got a standing ovation for infield practice. No other team's ever done that."

❖

Clowns league players were acquired through trades and a less regimented scouting system than found in organized ball, though as sophisticated as any outside organized ball. But most Clowns players came from teams played or from references from other players.

Clowns scouts were bird-dog scouts. Not on the payroll, a bird-dog scout is paid only for players found, and usually not until player retention exceeds a given period of time. The only exception I know of was a scout Dad had in Venezuela, who was so flawless so long, he was paid upon selection.

During war years, Sloppy Lindsay was Goose Tatum's backup at first, and started some once Goose went into the service, though that role was filled primarily by Armando Vasquez once Lindsay himself was drafted. Sam Hairston and ace righthander Jim "Fireball" Cohen both hooked up with Dad through Sloppy Lindsay. Cohen pitched against Lindsay in the service, and Sloppy brought him to our house in Tarrytown to meet Dad, who signed Jim to a 1946 contract.

Fermin "Striko" Valdez, Dad's second baseman with the Cuban Stars in the early '30s, returned for a two-year term at second beginning 1944, and introduced Dad to Armando Vasquez and Maximo Sanchez.

A high school English teacher in Havana, famous in his home city for being the first man to bring the Harlem Globetrotters to Cuba, Maximo Sanchez became the Clowns most important scout and more; he was focal point for the U.S. entry of the Clowns Latin players.

"The players all gathered with Maximo," Miami's Monk Silva explained. "They needed a certain amount of money to come into this country in those days. Syd wired the money to Sanchez, who gave it to the players. Once here, they gave the money to me, and I wired it back to Syd. It was like Visa lending."

While Monk was visiting with Maximo one year to sign a player for Dad, Maximo invited him to a high school game to see "a magnificent pitcher." So impressed by what he saw, Monk arranged for Raul Galata to complete high school in Miami. "His opening high school game in Florida, Galata struck out the first 21 batters to face him," Monk said. "When he graduated, I signed him for Syd."

Monk, who officiated all home games for Jake Gaither's great Florida A&M Rattlers football teams, also signed 1943 Rattlers' star quarterback Leroy Cromartie to a Clowns contract.

When the Miami Giants became the Clowns, Monk bought the Giants' uniforms from Johnnie Pierce, and started his own Miami Giants, often providing the Funmakers season-beginning, season-ending competition at the Clowns' birthplace, Dorsey Park. As diversified as any associate Dad ever had, Monk led his 1948 Miami Giants upstate to play a semi-pro club in Daytona Beach. A large crowd gathered to witness the comedy of a local dwarf named Ralph Bell. Monk signed him for Dad, and he became Spec Bebop.

Often, I think of understatements, real and imagined. Once I pictured a young man telling Juliet, "Look, I got this friend Romeo. I think you'd make an interesting couple." It seemed the best match for Monk's remark to Dad, "Syd, I think I signed someone's going to work quite well with my old team-mate Tut."

The majority of games played by Negro league teams were not league games. Most games between Negro league teams throughout the season were exhibitions. But most exhibitions were against semi-pro and all-star teams, and sometimes minor league teams. Major league baseball commissioner Judge Kenesaw Mountain Landis killed competition between Negro league nines and white major league teams during the 1930s, apparently because black teams were winning a majority of these games.

Negro league teams needed to play locals to improve rosters.

Buster Haywood tells the story of a pitcher in Greenwood, Mississippi: "One of the best I ever saw. Fastball over 100 miles per hour. Control. Greenwood was one place fans bet on locals. We tried to get him. Memphis Red Sox about baked cornbread for him. Black Barons did a dance to get him. No one could. He loved home, like our shortstop, Jim Oliver. Except you couldn't budge this kid from Greenwood. Townspeople bought him a car and whatever he wanted. The kid was a professional homeboy."

During World War II people followed the horrors of war through news photos, radio or theater newsreels. On the home front Dad was an air-raid warden, while Uncles Gabie and Charlie Pollock and Tom Carroll went to war.

Aunt Leah Pollock was in Europe with the WACS. Estelle danced at military bases coast to coast with the USO. Don's ship sailed for the Pacific. In our family's "God Bless Prayer," Mom had us add "God bless the sailors, soldiers and Marines" just after "God bless the policemen and firemen."

And each week, we visited the honor roll board on the small lawn in front of the Pocantico Hook and Ladder Firehouse, to see the names of local boys added to the list of those who gave their lives for their country.

America learned to adjust to rationing of a variety of materials deemed necessary for the war effort. Gasoline rationing limited most families to local travel. Traveling ball clubs, led by the Negro league teams, lobbied for and received preferential gasoline treatment so they could carry entertainment to all.

The Cincinnati Ethiopian Clowns met the Zulu Cannibal Giants in Louisville in 1942, their first matchup in five years. The flyer listed all grandstand seats at 80 cents, children under 12 years 25 cents and men in uniform 15 cents.

Releases in 1942 proclaimed the Clowns "lineup subject to change due to conscription of draftees." One 1943 Clowns release proclaimed the team's pitching staff tough despite "those lost to service." The war effort thinned baseball talent in the United States. From 1943 to 1944, the Clowns moved from near the bottom of the Negro American League to second place, largely because Dad signed five players from the Cuban Winter League— outfielder Leo Lugo, second baseman Fermin "Striko" Valdez, first baseman Armando Vasquez, outfielder Rafael Cabrera and pitcher Antonio Ruiz.

Every year they played, the Clowns traveled more than any other road team, next the Kansas City Monarchs, then the Homestead Grays, and, during the war black baseballers coined their own paraphrase, "Join the Clowns, Monarchs or Grays, and see the world." Most eastern Negro league teams stayed east, most western teams midwest. The Clowns covered traditional east and midwest and more, going into the Dakotas, the Canadian Rockies, the Far West, the Southwest, the Northwest and remote areas everywhere. Joyce

Hamman remembers a game in a town-off-in-a-corner in Saskatchewan, Canada, where the park was almost empty at game time. "Suddenly, people in waves of hundreds emerged from the forest, many on horseback, and, like attacking colonial militia suddenly pacified, formed ticket lines. The Clowns ended up with a crowd of many thousands."

Jim Colzie narrates a gift from Dad:

It was the strangest thing. Syd booked us a 1 P.M. game p.c., hours out of Lincoln, Nebraska, little group of a few houses with a Field-of-Dreams diamond. We didn't know why Syd offered us a percentage of the gate. We got out to where the highway was the only paved road, then left it. We got to this little place, Tut said, "Shit, I coulda stayed at the hotel listening to the radio." Half past noon no one in the ballpark but ballplayers and the promoter, smiling and squinting at the sun and rubbing his hands, saying, "This is gonna be great." We figured the promoter for a baseball purist booked us to see good ball, and we wondered what Syd was thinking, if anything. At 12:45 dust rose from every road coming in, as far as the eye could see, like multiple tornadoes coming from every direction. It was carloads of fans on all those dirt roads. Crowds up to the baselines, and we made $85.00 a man for our p.c. that day.

Many traditional Clowns rivalries were fixed by the time the war started. Besides their natural rivalry, as "World Colored Independent Champions," with Negro league teams and their road rivalry with the barnstorming House of David, which included not just baseball but pepperball competition, the Clowns visited many cities at least annually for existing rivalries. Perhaps the most intense was with the Brooklyn Bushwicks, but the longest was with the Kalamazoo, Michigan, All-City Stars.

Beginning in 1940, at the end of each summer, the Kalamazoo City League All-Stars, as selected by general vote of city residents, crossed bats with a selected quality opponent in the local season finale. In 1940, Kalamazoo beat the House of David 5-3, and the same team again, 12-2, in 1941. In 1942, they were one of few independent teams to beat the Miami Ethiopian Clowns. The score was 5-0. In 1943, the locals suffered their first loss of the series, 8-3 to the Chicago American Giants of the Negro American League. The Cincinnati Clowns were booked for 1944.

Attendance was not expected to match the Detroit Tigers appearance there earlier in the season, but exceeded it. The Kalamazoo roster included Chicago Cubs player Peanuts Lowery, who was absent from the major leagues due to military service. Clowns' manager Jesse "Hoss" Walker named Roosevelt "Duro" Davis starter against Kalamazoo, and the stage was set for one of baseball's strangest controversies.

Sometimes I watched teams debate Roosevelt Davis' cutball, expecting to see Lincoln and Douglas leading the factions, but in Kalamazoo it was his spitter got things going.

An overflow crowd, producing a large enough gate to provide each All-City Star a $25 war bond, looked on as Kalamazoo early questioned the ball's humidity. The *Kalamazoo Gazette* reported that "in the very first inning, Umpire Fred Spurgeon called time and charged Roosevelt Davis, Cincinnati's ace hurler, with using a spitball. This Davis didn't deny, claiming he was permitted to use it in the Negro league." The photo of the rhubarb at the plate shows Tut and Bunny in their accustomed place in the middle of things. According to the *Gazette,* the net result was that Kalamazoo let the incident pass, "figuring the All-City squad was keyed to the point it might win anyway."

Clowns All-Star third baseman Alex Radcliffe doubled to the left-field fence as a pinch hitter in the ninth to drive in the winning run in a 5-4 Clowns triumph. But as the *Gazette* stated, "The Cincinnati Clowns moved on to Indianapolis for a night game tonight that is important in the second half race of the Negro league. They ought to be glad to get out of Michigan, too, for they were forced 15 innings to beat Flint's State champions at Flint on Thursday night before moving into Kalamazoo for another nip-and-tuck battle."

Uncle Gabie returned to North Tarrytown by train on Yom Kippur of 1945. He had fought in the worst part of the Battle of the Bulge. Religious Jews spent Yom Kippur, the Day of Atonement, fasting in the temple in sorrow for sins. Grandpa Pollock, apparently a light sinner or maybe even limbered up to cast the first stone, spent little time there, but Grandma spent the day, refusing to leave even for Gabie's arrival. So Dad picked Gabie up at Tarrytown Station and drove him to the temple to see their mother. Soon Aunt Leah and Uncle Charlie were teaching school again, and Uncle Tom changed into his policeman's uniform. Soon Don was home, his ship short of the Pacific Theater at war's end. Soon Clowns players returned to the team.

Soon the final name was imprinted on the bronze Honor Roll.

12

Highlights and Insights

Pitching and comedy highlights provide insight into the Clowns of the '40s.

Jim Cohen sat on the bench next to Dad in a small park with a tin fence near Wilmington, Delaware, as Clowns hopeful Walter "Dirk" Gibbons worked in a dense fog against the Monarchs. "Kansas City was educating Dirk," Cohen said. "He threw a pitch—BOOM, off the tin. Another, BOOM, off the tin. Syd looks at me and says, 'Gibbons is throwing nothing but doubles.'"

Lazarus Medina, a Mexican right-hander with a good curve, wound up and began his delivery with his back to home plate, whirling plateward with a giant leg kick as he pitched like an uncoiling snake whipping out over its own tail with its head. He threw 98–100 mph fastballs. Manolo Godinez cut the ball on his belt, and floated pitches that hurtled like weighted beach balls.

Most Clowns pitchers fit between those two, but Dave Barnhill, 5'7", less than 150 pounds, threw as hard as Medina, Jim Cohen or any other Clowns hurler. Born and raised in Greenville, North Carolina, Barnhill, who always looked 18 years old, played as a young man in a Virginia–North Carolina League against future Homestead Grays great and Cooperstown Hall of Famer Buck Leonard and future Clowns star Buster Haywood. When the Clowns came to town in 1936, Barnhill beat them and soon got a telegram from Johnnie Pierce offering terms for him to report to the Clowns in Olean, New York. He accepted.

Considered the first legitimate ace of the Clowns staff since Lefty Tiant of the Cuban Stars, Barnhill struck out 18 one game and 16 in seven innings of the next during the Clowns' inaugural *Denver Post* Tournament appearance in 1939. Many tab Barnhill the best Clowns pitcher ever.

During a '40s black vs. white game, as the managers passed between innings, the white manager requested the removal of Satchel Paige so his team could hit for the fans. After the sixth, Satchel announced he was tiring, and, as the sides changed, the black manager said, "Satchel's tired. Who you want in?"

"How about the little, skinny kid throwing in the bullpen?"

"You got him."

Pitching the last three innings, Barnhill allowed a popout to third. He struck out the other eight. "Way I see it, you sawed off Satchel's legs and put him back out there," the white manager said.

Because of limitations imposed by bus space, versatility sometimes dictated the moundsman. Outfielder Speed Merchant occasionally pitched to rest regulars for big games. Dave Hoskins, who later pitched for the Cleveland Indians, threw some for the Clowns, but was primarily an outfielder.

Sometimes the whole battery was versatile. Buster Haywood once pitched. "I gave up nine runs without an out against the U.S. Army team at Ft. Knox, Kentucky," he said. "Had a week we played maybe ten games in ten cities. My staff was wore out. I just pitched Preacher Henry in a big game, and was saving Big John Williams for a league game in Chicago next day." Afterwards, he learned the military club was mostly major leaguers. Next time Buster started Peanuts Davis against Ft. Knox. Peanuts shut them out. When all-star outfielder Fred Wilson pitched, his favorite catcher was second baseman Ray Neil, who caught only for Wilson.

Big John Williams, Shreveport, Louisiana's gift to the Clowns, was a versatile, hard-driving man. He threw a first-class spitball, a cutball, a knuckler and a good fastball, and he drove the bus from time to time. A sometimes drinker, he kept opponents loose by throwing at heads, and batters never knew whether he meant it or just had a bad game after an evening of imbibing. He was sometimes ejected for throwing a spitter and once frivolously adopted the technical defense that it was a sweatball, not a spitball, and "ain't nothing illegal 'bout sweating, then grabbing the ball." Had his position held up, fellows like Big John and Duro Davis probably would have had to submit body fluid samples for analysis each start. But Johnny Williams was a serious pitcher, and a loss stayed with him for days.

Jim Colzie too drove the bus and learned to throw "the sweatball" from Big John Williams. He pitched part of three decades for the Clowns, joining the club for the summer at age 17 in 1937. He played for the Funmakers from time to time until the war, then regularly during 1946 and 1947 until a severe knee injury in a team bus wreck sidelined him. Wearing a knee brace, he made a brief comeback in the early 1950s. At 6'0", 152 pounds, Colzie was another slim hurler, and used an 85–90 mph fastball to set up his best pitch, the curve, and "other junk." Recalling his insistence on throwing his best pitch, Colzie said, "One game Buster wouldn't let me call off the fastball. I threw the curve anyway. He came out for a few words at the mound. He called fast ball again, and again I threw the curve. He came to the mound and called me everything but Colzie."

Known as the Kansas City Monarchs killer, Jim was part of one of manager Hoss Walker's favorite jokes. Pregames as Hoss came on the field from the locker room, Kansas City players asked who was starting pitcher. "Colzie," Hoss answered, whether Jim was pitching or not, giggling as the Monarchs squirmed.

Colzie had trouble though with Luke Easter. "Had to throw him high and hard," Colzie said. "I got one low in Terre Haute one night, and the damn thing was still going up when it left the park at the 375' sign."

"On the other hand," Colzie said, "one time I heard Willie Grace, the Cleveland Buckeyes outfielder, say he was glad I was pitching, because 'Hell, he can't pitch.' Struck him out four for four that game."

Colzie was born and raised in Montezuma, Georgia and, as a boy during the early 1930s, saw the strong, local, black, semi-pro team play the Miami Giants, and noted the unhittable drop thrown by 5'4" Miami righthander Leo "Preacher" Henry. Preacher moved up to the Jacksonville Red Caps, then, during the '40s, to the Clowns, where he spent years as a mainstay on the pitching staff.

Henry was born in Inverness, Florida, in 1910, and, according to Colzie, got his nickname there as a young boy. Jim relates something of Preacher's childhood:

> Preacher grew up in Inverness. Mom worked in the Sheriff's Depart-ment. As a kid, Preacher was a bootblack and sang and preached while he cleaned and polished and popped the rag. Time came some drunk white guys, grown, asked him to sing. Said get in the car, we're going for a drink. Took him in the woods. Said, "Sing and preach now, nig-ger, and when we say you're finished, then you leave—if you leave." Sang two, three hours. Preached. The men drank and drank, drunker and drunker. Preacher bolted and ran. Never stopped till the Sheriff's. Made him wait, silent, fifteen minutes before they gave him a listen. Deputies found those white men passed out in the woods. Judge gave them probation. Said they go around Preacher again, they get life.
>
> He stopped singing and preaching in Inverness after that. But what a voice that man had on the bus riding around the rest of the country, rang out like it was gliding up to heaven.

One Clowns player told pitcher Al Overton that a raised toilet seat back home meant a house visit from Jody, the man who comes in the back door when you go out the front. Overton got leave for a brief trip home to Texas, and never returned. After that, when opponents asked what had happened to Overton, Clowns players answered cryptically, "Went home and found his toilet seat up."

Roosevelt "Duro" Davis, son of a California vineyard worker, was born in Bartlesville, Oklahoma, in 1908, and left high school after two years to pitch for the Topeka, Kansas, Monrovians, a black semi-pro team. In 1923, at age 15, he started his professional career with the St. Louis Stars, after which he joined an integrated team from Tekamah, Nebraska, for a brief stint before becoming Satchel Paige's teammate with the Pittsburgh Crawfords. He then joined the Miami Ethiopian Clowns. Most teams arguing his spitter were really victims of his cutball. "His cutball is virtually unhittable," Dad often said, "and in a big game, I want Roosevelt Davis on the mound." Making reference to the ring Davis sometimes used to cut the ball, Dad once said, "Maybe I ought to have Duro's jeweler on the payroll."

Accused of spitters and "illegal jump balls" at the *Denver Post* Tournament, Davis responded, "I never use nothing on the ball but pitching. . . . I throw the kind of pitching that if you could hit it you would be in the big leagues—that is all there is to my pitching. It is just big league." It was that, and obviously more. His spitball too was technically a sweatball, beginning with an armwipe across the forehead. Big John Williams was a disciple.

On June 27, 1941, Duro outdueled Satchel Paige in a 2-1 Clowns win over the Kansas City Monarchs before 4,000 paid in St. Paul, Minnesota. The June 28 issue of the *St. Paul Pioneer Press* reported that "From beginning to end the Monarchs protested Macon's [Roosevelt Davis'] delivery, arguing he was throwing a spitter. And from beginning to end both teams harassed the umpire with calls for new balls which near the close of hostilities nearly found the supply diminished." It's likely there was a severe rainstorm somewhere in Minnesota June 28, 1941, just from whatever evaporated off Duro's pitches.

One mid-'40s night against the Birmingham Black Barons in Birmingham, Roosevelt Davis did want to run out of baseballs. As usual, in the dugout before the game he reminded teammates of nonexistent leadership possibilities. It was his "especially" clause that was different.

"Remember this, fellas. When I pitch, I run the show. Especially tonight—got me a new woman in the stands. Gonna take one run to get me to heaven." Throughout the later innings of a 0-0 tie, Duro repeated the game's refrain, "One run takes me to heaven. Get me that one run, fellas."

After the tenth and eleventh, "One run takes me to heaven. Get me that one run, fellas." After the twelfth, thirteenth and fourteenth, "One run takes me to heaven. Get me that one run, fellas." Duro gazed longingly into the stands, smiling seductively. The score stayed 0-0.

After the Clowns half of the fifteenth, the smile was gone from Duro's lips, his teeth were clenched in lust. "Shit, you fellas ain't gonna get me no run!" he said.

Bottom of the fifteenth, his first pitch floated homeward like a Rip Sewell blooper and Ed Steele ripped it over the roof for the game-winning run. Duro whooped, and ran to the shower. He later told Steele he "hung a knuckler," but once he left the locker room, he was gone till the bus left next day.

Jim "Fireball" Cohen's father was a coal miner, and Jim was raised around the Derry Township mines in western Pennsylvania. He played in the coal-mining camps until he was drafted into the army in 1942. Playing service ball, he met Sloppy Lindsay, who took him to Tarrytown on leave to meet Dad. Cohen pitched for the Clowns from 1946 through 1952. Sam Hairston and Armando Vasquez rated Cohen one of the best right-handers the Clowns ever had. Buster Haywood cited four pitchers as the best he'd seen: right-handers Satchel Paige, Hilton Smith and Jim Cohen, and left-hander Slim Jones. Another versatile acquisition, Fireball helped Bunny with the books when Bunny let things pile up, and he took his turn driving the bus. But his best asset was pinpoint control, his best pitch his fastball. He was one big Clowns fastballer. I remember seeing him pitch in Shibe Park in Philadelphia the weekend after I learned humans came from single cells, and thinking as I watched him stride from the dugout toward the mound sweating power, "How can a man that big come from a single cell?"

Probably the three toughest pitches to hit were Satchel Paige's nearly invisible fastball, Hilton Smith's knee-buckling curve and Peanuts Davis' butterfly or flutterball.

My earliest baseball memories are the legendary pitching duels between Satchel Paige and Peanuts Davis. Their windmill windups were unforgettable. Both played with unusual intensity. Both were comics. They had great control in common. Often before games, they jammed a wooden match into the ground, head up, walked back as far as they could—still able to make out the match—and bet $100 who could throw the most of ten over the match head. Satchel's speed made him memorable. I thought his name was Statue Paige because of the pause at the peak of his delivery. Peanuts' sideways hat and everything else about him made him unforgettable.

When the two went head to head, they sometimes picked an inning to sit down their fielders and strike out the side, Satchel with his fastball, Peanuts with his butterfly. Sometimes, Pepper Bassett would catch that inning for the Clowns sitting in a rocking chair.

Clowns catcher Leonard Pigg picked Peanuts as his all-time, all-star right-handed pitcher, and Pigg didn't see Peanuts pitch in his prime, only after the war. Colonel Charles B. Franklin of Louisville said the Clowns had three great players, and he gave them in order: Peanuts Davis, Hank Aaron, Buster Haywood. Clowns second baseman Ray Neil played from 1942 to 1954 in the Negro American League, and toured many years against major league all-stars and played against them winters in Latin America. He faced Bob Feller and Robin Roberts, Satchel Paige and Hilton Smith, and he said, "Peanuts was the best pitcher I ever saw. He had a decent fastball and an average curve, but he just showed them to set up the knuckler. His knuckler was unreal. Imagine the best knuckle ball you ever saw coming at you with speed, darting around like it's doing the jitterbug, and the man had perfect control of it. He could strike out man after man with it."

If you picture a man dressed in a parka with thick leggings and hip boots finishing a 50-mile walk through knee-deep water in 95-degree mid-August heat and sloshing through wave remnants from six-foot seas, you can picture how Peanuts walked to the mound, or the on deck circle, or the batter's box, lazy, slow, heavy, exhausted, off-balance. Reporter after reporter described it as "a shipwreck walk." Buster Haywood said, "Peanuts could run. Fooled locals. He walked around like an old man. But he could bunt, hit and run. He'd steal second, and stick his tongue out at the catcher, wagging his head."

Peanuts loved wine and women. "Peanuts might pitch and put on a show in St. Louis Sunday," Jim Colzie said, "and if the rotation called for him to pitch Wednesday, he'd find out where we were Wednesday, and that's when and where we'd see him next."

Clowns shortstop Sherwood Brewer said, "Peanuts never took care of himself, but he was very intense. You never knew what would happen to him after the ball game, but he was focused every moment of every game.

I don't know why his name's not mentioned more—great, great pitcher, and everyone knew he was."

Colzie said, "Peanuts threw an 85 mph fastball to set up one, two, three and four finger knucklers. The more fingers, the tougher on his hands. The four-finger was his butterfly or flutterball. Had he been able to throw the four-finger every pitch, no one ever would have hit him. If he'd been white, if he didn't do comedy, he'd have been one of the most famous pitchers of all time. He was notches above Wilhelm or Hough or Wakefield or any other knuckleballer ever pitched."

Chin Evans spoke of Josh Gibson: "Only fastball I ever threw Josh was for the Baltimore Elite Giants. Never saw a ball hit so hard. Just kept rising up. Started out a low liner. Pee Wee Butts told me later how it flicked off top of his glove when he leaped for it at short. That ball cracked like a gunshot off the wall 20' above the 425' sign in left center."

Sam Hairston noted how Peanuts loved to pitch to Josh and considered each game he bettered Gibson a career. Peanuts taunted baseball's hardest hitter. Before each start against the Grays, Peanuts wagged his glove at the big backstop, "Get up there all you want, you big son of a bitch. You ain't gonna hit shit today." Josh usually ignored him, and Peanuts usually did well. But the big guy must have seen a clairvoyant before one Washington, D.C., game.

Pregame posturing, Josh Gibson stood on the top step of the dugout, leaning cross-legged, with one hand on a bat. Peanuts wagged his glove fearlessly. "Get up there all you want, you big son of a bitch. You ain't gonna hit shit today," he roared.

Gibson calmly raised his bat to his shoulder in both hands. "For your disobedience, I'm going to homer three times today." He hit three progressively deeper home runs, the last sending Peanuts to the showers. As Peanuts walked sadly from mound to dugout, the crowd applauded politely, but Gibson climbed to the top step of the Grays' dugout. "Hey, Goobers," he called, and, when Peanuts looked, he raised one hand waving from knuckles to fingertips only, like a toddler. "Goodbye, Goobers," he chanted.

That was unusual for Peanuts. Ray Neil recalls at least three 1-0 wins Peanuts ground out over Satchel Paige. In a 1942 release, Dad described how more than 30,000 fans turned out to a 1941 game in Cincinnati. Peanuts beat Satchel and the Satchel Paige All-Stars 1-0 in ten innings, allowing but four hits. Three weeks later, he shut out Paige and the Havana Cuban Giants

9-0, and in his next start beat the Memphis Red Sox, allowing one run, un-earned.

But because of Peanuts' lifestyle, his greatness slipped away like sand passing through an hourglass.

According to Buster Haywood, when Hoss Walker was manager, the Clowns blew a 15-4 lead over the Chicago American Giants, and lost 16-15. Even Peanuts got bombed in relief. Like the Clowns, their pitching was some-times great, sometimes mediocre, sometimes poor. But it was always inter-esting, always fun.

13

More Tales of Goose and Tut

Like "Revelation" and the start of *Tale of Two Cities*, Reece "Goose" Tatum was a tangle of contradictions. Most say he played basketball best, some baseball. All say he was funny. He was mean. He was master of comedic timing. He often lacked the rhythm of ordinary human kindness. He was considerate. He was selfish. He was a loner. Kids loved him and flocked around him. He was violent and unpredictable. Fans loved him. Most players stayed clear of him. He was one man Dad didn't always like, but Dad loved him. He was everyman. He was a prima donna. He was an El Dorado, Arkansas, country kid suddenly world famous and taken to be cosmopolitan. "Maybe the only time you saw the real Goose was if you visited the family farm," Jim Colzie observed. "Nothing to be famous about there. He was just Goose."

Goose's comedy could be majestic. According to Jim Cohen, going one better than a home run Goose once hit in Louisville, Goose came to bat left-handed with bases loaded against the Chicago American Giants in Comiskey Park before a huge crowd. Chicago changed pitchers to a lefty. A switch-hitter, Goose walked around the plate, called time, knelt and prayed, hands folded, wagging his head skyward like the abbot at a monastery for demented monks, as Tut had taught him. He arose, shook his head yes and, right-handed, drove the first pitch into the upper deck for a grand slammer. Acting exhausted as he jogged the basepaths, he sat and rested on each base wiping his brow, as the crowd roared louder, and as he came home and the crowd thundered, he circled the plate with quick mincing steps as he leaned over it, at last tapping it for the run.

Goose Tatum was the consensus best fielding first baseman of the 1940s. Buck O'Neil of the Monarchs and Buck Leonard of the Grays could hit better, but Goose could hold his own at the plate with most, and in the field, as Sherwood Brewer said, "You could throw too high for Goose if you tried, but never too low. Nothing low got by him. And with that eight-foot wing-span and 6'3" height, it had to be awfully high to get over the top."

John "Buck" O'Neil, as Monarchs first baseman and manager, played against Goose for more than a decade. "Goose played basketball fall and winters," Buck said. "Had he gone to Latin America and played baseball year around like Buck Leonard and me, he'd have been good as anybody. As it was, he had as good a glove as any first baseman ever played the game."

Tatum's prowess was reported as follows in local coverage of a 1947 game in Tulsa, Oklahoma:

> Could Jesse Owens run?
>
> Could Bill Robinson tap dance? Could George Washington Carver do things with peanuts?
>
> History already has chronicled these great Negroes as tops in their respective fields—and the 2,500 fans who saw Reece (Goose) Tatum performing at first base last night at Texas League Park as the Kansas City Monarchs defeated the Indianapolis Clowns, 5 to 3—will help the historians label this long, lanky Negro as nothing short of miraculous. The six-foot, four-inch clown prince of Negro baseball did everything last night but make the ball talk. He made incredible stops with beautiful ease and grace, he juggled the ball until it appeared he had it on a string—and then in the eighth inning came up with a play that looked like something Orson Welles might have dreamed up.
>
> It was his last defensive gesture since the Monarchs did not have to bat in the ninth. Two were down, and Earl Taborn hit into the hole at shortstop.
>
> Newt Allen cut loose with a high throw that sent Tatum at least two feet into the air—but the lanky Negro speared the throw, and tagged Taborn in midair as the runner raced into the bag. And Tatum tagged him good, sprawling Taborn head over heels into right field.
>
> While Tatum kept the crowd in an uproar with his glovework at first, Henry Thompson, sensational 20-year old Monarch shortstop, and Lefty LeMarque, the Monarchs pitcher, turned in sparkling performances that would fit well into major league play.
>
> Thompson, a war veteran, hailed as another Jackie Robinson, ham-

mered out a single, a double and a triple in four trips—and was robbed of his fourth hit by a fancy piece of fielding by Tatum.

In addition Thompson handled six chances in the field and started two lightning double plays. The young shortstop played in the Cuban league last winter and was nosed out for the batting championship by Lou Klein of the St. Louis Cardinals.

LeMarque, another Cuban league veteran and one of the loop's leading pitchers, showed the Indianapolis Clowns a blazing fastball that they couldn't do anything with for six innings before he tired and yielded a run in the seventh and two more in the eighth. It was top flight baseball all the way—garnished with the clever antics of Tatum.

Occasionally Goose would bat one-handed with a hand in his back pocket, and once slapped a one-handed double. "He never pulled the hand from his pocket till after he slid in under the tag," Sam Hairston related.

Colonel Charles B. Franklin, who promoted sports in Louisville for more than half a century, rated Goose the top all-time basketball comic.

Buck O'Neil felt that while Tut was pure-versatile-all-around funny,

Goose Tatum was the funniest baseball comedian ever. Funniest thing I ever saw him do was read the newspaper during shadowball. Clowns shadowball was a wonder to see. So synchronized. People swore they saw the ball, but there was none. And there was Goose, sitting on a chair at first base, legs crossed, reading a newspaper. The shortstop speared one deep in the hole and whipped a nonexistent throw to first. Precisely when the ball would have arrived and just after he turned the page of the paper with tongue-wet finger, Goose flipped his mitt up for the silent no-look catch. He pulled the ball from the glove and tossed it home smooth as you please, legs still crossed, all without missing a lick of reading.

As Goose's basketball fame traveled worldwide, he became more diffi-cult. Increasingly, he declined to play, citing non-existent illnesses or inju-ries. Once during pregame warm-ups, his last pair of spikes broke. He wore size 16, and Dad had to special order his shoes out of St. Louis. Though he really couldn't play, and told the fan just that, a white man near the Clowns dugout kept asking when he would. After a while, Goose responded, "Next inning." After a few more innings of the same question, Goose, annoyed, said, "Look. I told you I can't play. My spikes broke. I got no shoes."

"Well, damn it, Goose. You come back here next time without shoes, you're playing barefoot."

Then there was the Leo Lugo incident. Verdes Drake and Leo Lugo, both Maximo Sanchez products from Havana, were outfielders. Lugo played left, and Drake center. Seatmates and roommates, both were good men and excellent players. Lugo spoke Spanish, English and French fluently, and Drake spoke Spanish and English fluently, and between the seatmates, they insulated young Latin players from temptations of travel and taught them the ways of the road.

At 3:00 A.M. on a jump from Minneapolis to Chicago, Goose decided he needed Lugo's seat. Awakened, Lugo refused and said Goose had best let him sleep. Goose had Chauff stop the bus. He took the keys, opened the outside baggage compartment and grabbed a bat. Back aboard, he raised the bat to club Lugo, but the bat hit the ceiling on the upswing as Chauff started the bus. Preacher Henry and Jim Colzie, in the seat in front of Lugo and Drake, caught Goose as he swayed when the bus bumped onto the highway, and that calmed Goose down.

"You're business manager, Bunny," Goose said, "And if I want a piece of money, you give it to me. Hoss, you're the manager, and you and Colzie and Preacher alright." And he lay the bat on the luggage rack, and went to his own seat as though nothing had happened.

Months later, the Clowns bus pulled over for repairs in the blackness of an Everglades night on Florida's Tamiami Trail. Goose hit Lugo on the back with a bat then, and had it raised a second time, but dropped it and jumped on the bus when someone hollered, "Gator!" Lugo returned to Cuba, and never played in this country again.

Buster Haywood relates how Goose jeopardized two lives—Buster's, then Goose's. "Goose said he had a strained muscle in his leg, but could play because it was Chicago and Chicago was a big game, so I played him. Afterwards, on the sidewalk in front of the hotel, Goose pulled a bat on me for making him play, and Sam Hairston saved me with a razor on Goose's throat. I never heard of Goose trying to put wood to anything but a baseball after that. And I never brought it up to Goose. My place was to solve problems, not add to them."

Ego never affected Richard King. Everyone loved Tut and people clamored to be near him. A team leader, during his time he taught every Clowns player something new about baseball, laughter and life. He taught everyone something about the road. All Clowns players felt Tut inspired and night after night laughed harder at him than they had the night before.

Tut sometimes picked up an opponent's thrown bat after a foul ball, handing it toward the batter, dropping it as the batter reached for it. Other times when an opposing hitter swung and missed, Tut dragged a young child, boy or girl, from the stands to the plate, trying to insert the youngster as pinch hitter. He often mimicked exasperated opponents, umpires and sometimes fans. Tut's spontaneity was best in the stands. Clowns crowds contained pockets of laughter with Tut in the middle lying on a fat woman's lap or sipping a fan's pint whiskey bottle or running from an exploding firecracker. Once, in Indianapolis, a shot, louder than Tut's firecrackers, blasted out of a pocket of laughter. A fan had shot his girlfriend. Clowns players thought Tut was victim. "The Clowns would have folded on the spot," Sherwood Brewer said. "Tut was our most valuable person."

Juggling Joe Taylor, a nonplaying performer with the Clowns during the 1948 and 1949 seasons, juggled six balls at once. The P.A. announcer informed fans Tut would equal the feat, and Tut juggled two batches of three balls each glued together. The gag could only be funny performed by Tut. His face froze with concentration, sagged with a missed batch falling to the grass, erupted in smiling pride when, at last, he had both batches airborne. It was fun to watch every time.

Two of Tut's funniest routines drew complaints and did not survive the '40s.

Some complained of the dice routine as unfit for children. Tut shot craps against an invisible opponent. The game started with Tut hot. Kneeling on the diamond, he blew on the dice, rubbed them against his thigh and made pass after pass with happy results, scraping in his winnings with sweeps of his arm along the grass. Then he lost the roll. In craps, one suspecting loaded or tampered dice grabs the toss in midair, and that's what Tut did, scowling at his invisible foe as he suspended non-existent dice above the ground and examined them. Unable to prove foul play though, Tut proceeded and lost his winnings plus item by item of clothing, sometimes including spats or a girdle, ending with Tut in huge, flowered boxer shorts.

Some, including Mom, complained of what Clowns players called "The Saturday Night Whore Act" as unfit for women. Tut in drag, wearing lipstick, tight dress, wig and heels, sashayed and tripped through foul territory toward home plate. As he moved, he adjusted straps holding up his low-cut neckline, checked that his pocketbook was safely closed, checked that the seams in his stockings were straight and powdered his nose with a puff three times normal size, replenishing it in a small bucket. Great clouds of white rose as Tut patted his face. Then, delicately lifting each arm, he slapped gobs of powder onto each armpit. The grass beneath him whitened like hard ground under a January blizzard. He opened his purse, took out a mirror, and checked face then armpits in the mirror, satisfied. Finally, he lifted the hem of his dress high, revealing lace panties, and daintily applied the powder into each shoe. One of the Clowns players approached Tut from the dugout, and offered his arm, which Tut graciously accepted, and the player escorted Tut, still sashaying and tripping, off the field. Most times the routine left male fans and Clowns players laughing with tears rolling down their faces.

As a fringe benefit, Dad gave Tut postcards with Tut's photo on front to sell for a dime each as he passed through the crowd. Tut used his money well. He was one of the few who had Dad put part of his salary into a special bank account for off-season use. Players referred to Tut as "our bank" because he so frequently gave them interest-free loans.

Tut and the sport had a way sometimes of making the past become the future. During a 1947 Minneapolis appearance, Tut tripped as part of a routine. "Do that again, nigger, and I'll give you ten dollars!" a white fan shouted. Immediately, nearby patrons booed the fan. Word spread, and thousands, white joining black, booed him. The booing grew louder and louder until the fan got up and left, to cheering.

"Funniest thing I ever did see," Dirk Gibbons said, "was Tut grabbing a white boy out the stands and dancing with him in Greensboro, Mississippi. I couldn't understand it—the death risk. But the crowd howled with laughter, black and white together. I figure Tut was the only man in the world could do that there and then. King Tut seemed cut out to lower barriers with fun."

Because of illness, Tut missed the Clowns ten-inning win in Flint, Michigan, in 1944. Other than that, no one recalls him missing a game.

He came close once. He came onto the Polo Grounds field ready made in striped suit, ball and chain.

Jim Colzie recalls that the Clowns bus broke down the day before in Harrisburg, Pennsylvania, en route to the Polo Grounds game against the New York Cubans. Thinking Tut might want to see his wife, Bea, in nearby Philadelphia, Bunny said, "Tut, go on home and meet us tomorrow in New York. No sense you sitting around here with us."

Tut declined. It was a tall tales trip. Clowns players enjoyed Goose-Tut-tall-tale trips. Every few weeks on a long jump Goose and Tut became temporary seatmates, and exchanged lies, one more exaggerated and funnier than the next, loud enough so all players could enjoy. The Harrisburg breakdown came during a tall-tale jump, and most figured Tut didn't go home so tales could continue. Bea would be at tomorrow's game anyway.

Next day at the Polo Grounds, as the Clowns batted in the top of the first, two men in suits flanked Tut on the bench. "What's goin'?" asked Goose.

"They got me," Tut said. "They got me." The pain in his face read like Bebop just drowned in the fishing sketch. Police in Philadelphia had issued a warrant months earlier when Tut failed to appear for court in connection with an off-season numbers charge. He had gone to spring training. Waiting for the Clowns' New York appearance, police arrested Tut on the bench at the Polo Grounds. He had been right; police had staked out 2227 Catherine Street, Philadelphia, the day before, figuring Tut would stop to see Bea on the way to New York. Refusal to go home from Harrisburg delayed the arrest one day.

No one cleaned off the dust of the road well as Tut. The arresting officers stayed for the game and Tut's show before hauling him off. Bunny went bail and paid applicable fines from his bank. Dad reimbursed Bunny and wrote it off as an ordinary and necessary business expense. Tut didn't miss a game. And that's how Uncle Sam helped fans see Tut.

14

Life on the Road

Life on the road was difficult and had its own vagaries, its own set of rules, and its own math. Bunny Downs spoke of the road. "Shuckin' corn, hoein' taters, pickin' cotton ain't no tougher than this business. No, sir. For a real hardworking business day in and day out, you gotta take this here whatchacallit, tourist baseball."

So did Sam Hairston. "In the bus league, you played the game looking forward to a rough ride." And the road was not paved with gold.

In the flatland cornfields from western New York to Nebraska and in the low elevations of Florida and the seaboard South, boredom was the greatest danger. Driving with the mesmerizing rhythms of flat fields day after day, hazy skylines of destination cities sometimes on the horizon seemingly forever, was like tightrope walking half awake. Curves and mountain cliffs along the narrow roads of the '40s terrified Clowns players. Before each season started, some players from the Northeast gathered at our home to board the bus for spring training. I remember them saying, year after year, "Syd, don't book us through the Smokies this year. Don't want to ride those cliffs."

During the early '40s, the Clowns played south at the end of each season closing the year with a postseason tour against Monk Silva's Miami Giants. Monk then stored the bus for the winter. After the war, though, the bus was housed in a barn in rural Westchester County, about 15 miles from Tarrytown. Buster Haywood came to town each spring and drove the bus from the barn to our house, to be thoroughly cleaned and re-outfitted by Dad's hired crew: my friends Jimmy Richardson, Ed Pollak and Jay Cohen, and me. Annually, we spent about eight hours each doing whatever Dad had on his checklist.

Next day, Buster drove players from our house to Bunny's Harlem apartment. "Most of Harlem knew Bunny," Jim Cohen relates, "and seemed like half Harlem turned out for the gathering of the Clowns in front of

Bunny's." The bus picked up others en route south from New York to spring training. The rest came in by plane or bus or train from all over the country and Latin America.

In 1944, pitcher "Willie Burns drove the bus day in and day out," according to Sam Hairston, "and won a good many games." He had pitched for the early Miami Ethiopian Clowns. Primary drivers during the mid and late '40s were Charlie Rudd, formerly with the Memphis Red Sox, and M. H. Winston, a Memphis resident. All called Rudd, then Winston, "Chauff." Both were nonplayers, and Winston a first-rate mechanic.

Tut most often rode milkcan, a crucial safety valve. Every player took his turn there, but Tut always rode milkcan tough jumps. The can was a large, metal, milk keg, placed at the top of the stairwell, across the bus from the driver's seat. Whoever road milkcan was like a co-pilot, responsible for reporting all road conditions in detail aloud to whoever was driving the bus. Every road sign was read to the driver. An arrow bent right was read "Curve to the right." Parallel vertical lines were reported "Divided highway ahead." Signs with words were literally read. Converging lines were read "Merge ahead." A stop light was verbalized as "Red light ahead." Shifts on the milkcan were generally more frequent than changes of drivers. Tut had the added virtue of knowing every stretch of every highway everywhere. By 1945, he'd been all over twice, most places more.

During the decade, Buster Haywood, Jim Colzie, Big John Williams, Jim Cohen and catcher Leonard Pigg, all licensed chauffeurs and all players, took their turns as primary or backup drivers.

Sometimes the backup was insufficient. Jim Colzie recalls a Clowns rarity—three straight nights in the same hotel.

We played a four-team doubleheader in Yankee Stadium, involving the New York Black Yankees and Kansas City Monarchs. Next day we played the Monarchs in Cedarhurst, New Jersey, the next the New York Cubans at the Polo Grounds. Now Buster and Winston never drank, and I seldom did. Night before the Cedarhurst game, Buster, Big John, Chauff and I went out on the town together. Next day, dawned on us one of us had to drive to the Cedarhurst ball park. I was in best shape, but I was still heavyheaded. No one riding milk can, 'cause it wasn't a jump. Came to a traffic light. Syd on the bus too. I tapped the car in front of me. Caused a five or six car collision. You know, Satchel traveled in his own car, always a brand new Cadillac. Police got us all pulled to the side sorting out the havoc I caused, when Satchel comes flying by at 55 to meet the rest of the Monarchs at the ball park. We were downtown in a 30 MPH zone. Sees it's the Clowns bus and pulls his hog on over and backs up. Police come up to Satchel. Write him a $50 ticket for speeding. Satchel gave the officer a $100 bill. Said, "Keep the change. I'm comin' in same way I'm goin' out."

When Dad bought the new Flxible bus in 1948 for $12,000, he flew into the Flxible plant in Loudonville, Ohio, from New York, and Buster flew in from a game in Birmingham, Alabama, to share driving duties to join the team in Indianapolis. "We split the driving all right," Buster said, "but Syd got a bit enthusiastic at the start. Had a wreck before we got off Flxible property. Just leaving their lot, Syd cut too hard coming out of the gate, sheared off the rear view mirror. Had to back up for repairs."

Dad reserved hotel rooms when possible and mailed complete information to Bunny in advance. But Dad couldn't always get rooms, because of either lack of time or room availability. Bunny kept a black book on the bus, listing black hotels and white hotels accommodating blacks, and, for cities where there was no such hotel, private homes willing to house black players. Sometimes players rode the bus nights for long jumps or want of housing—rarely, but occasionally, weeks at a time. Bus riding pay was two dollars a player a night. Players picked up extra spending money other ways, too. Some ate sardines or peanut butter sandwiches or otherwise dined cheaply in transit, avoiding restaurants most meals, saving cash from daily meal money, which was raised from two dollars daily to three dollars daily during the '40s. Sam Hairston was paid $25 per month extra to bat pepperball. Dad gave players besides Tut postcards to autograph and sell. Speed Merchant got extra pay for comedy. Bunny got off-season bonuses based on prior season's gates. The more bus nights the greater the number of games played, the more games played the larger the gates, and the larger the gates the bigger Bunny's bonus.

Usually the black book was just part of daily life, accepted as a thread in the fabric of Clowns' existence, but Bunny misplaced the black book once, and phoned Dad for hotel listings in the next town. When he hung up, Dad told me, "Disgrace we have to have a black book. Such things should have died with the Underground Railroad. Sometimes the Emancipation Proclamation, Constitution, all the freedom documents—are still just words, white words on white paper, ought to be bound with a cover says 'white only,' like a God-damned Mississippi bathroom."

Major leaguers complained of grueling doubleheaders, played occasionally during a three- or four-game stand in one city with next day train or plane travel to another city for another three- or four-game stand again spread over two to four days. Buster Haywood recalls a day Satchel Paige pitched for the Clowns. "I caught both games of a doubleheader in Cincinnati. Satchel pitched the first three innings of the first game. Whole team was still in uniform, and I drove the bus to Dayton, Ohio, for the game that night and caught Satchel the first three innings there." Once, the Clowns beat the Monarchs on a Sunday afternoon in Kansas City, leaving town at 11:00 that night. Buster drove halfway, then managed and caught the Clowns 2-1, 14-inning loss to Satchel and the Monarchs the next night in Denver. Jim Colzie recalls a July 4 three-game set, one midday in Niles, Michigan, the next twilight in Benton Harbor, Michigan, the last a night game in Michigan City, Indiana. Black teams were mudders. Rainouts, virtually non-existent, resulted only from true storms, the kind that get named in the tropics, and, absent booking error, something Dad didn't make, Clowns players were only off rainouts. "Travel date" was a white phrase.

With few exceptions, though, as Buster Haywood said, "We had too much fun to be homesick." If Negro leaguers didn't love the game, the only highway was the road home.

And the summer road could sizzle and burn you home too. Fitzgerald, Georgia, Jim Colzie's hometown, had a three dollar street tax assessed each resident for road improvements. Jim went to spring training before the year's notices were distributed. When the Clowns came to town, Jim, the number one local celebrity, was arrested, and held until Bunny paid ten dollars total tax plus fine for late payment. Augustus Felton, one of seven Felton brothers of Fitzgerald, all lawyers, had the town refund all but the three dollars. But over the years the story changed, and Clowns rookies didn't want any part of Fitzgerald, Georgia, "where you got to pay a tax to walk the streets, or you get arrested."

Space limitations restricted clothing and other comfort items carried traveling. But adjustments were made. "Finest suits in the United States," Jim Colzie recalled, "were made by a black tailor owned a dry goods store next to the hotel in Birmingham. Man had a working relationship with Syd.

We'd watch for Birmingham on the schedule, save up, get to town early or leave late, and go in and pick out our suits and get fitted. Couldn't wait for the suits. No room on the bus anyway. Man would send them along to Syd in Tarrytown, and Syd held them for us till the season was over."

Spec Bebop, Tut's dwarf companion, had his own problem on the road. "His little legs didn't reach the floor," Sam Hairston remembers. "Had to stand more than his share to keep the circulation running."

Once in the '60s, Dad booked a jump too long through the mountains, and the team rode all night and next day, and arrived at the park just after the last ticket refund was made. But for that, none of Dad's teams ever missed a game. The Clowns were in two memorable bus wrecks, both in the Flxible. Mom and Dad and I were at the Charleston, West Virginia, park, but word came that Tut was seriously hurt in a bus wreck, and that the team would not make the game. It turned out to be a rainout anyway. If it hadn't been stormy, the Clowns might have had a new slogan, "We're idle hurricanes and bus wrecks."

Nearing West Virginia, the bus was coming off a one-way bridge in the mountains. A speeding truck rounded a corner and pinned the bus to the bridge. While a half dozen Clowns were injured, including Tut, none was seriously hurt; however, damage to the bus was extensive. For weeks during repairs, the Clowns made dates by chartered bus and train. Dad borrowed to make paydays, but never missed one.

An earlier accident was more serious, especially for Jim Colzie. Sunday games in the Negro leagues were the most important and most festive and were almost always played to big crowds in league stadiums in large cities. Top pitchers pitched Sundays, and players called the best of each staff Sunday pitchers. Three in the morning on July 20, 1947, the Clowns bus pulled off the road on a rural stretch of highway near Elwood, Indiana, en route to Indianapolis from a night game in Ft. Wayne. Jim Colzie was scheduled to pitch the first game of a doubleheader that day in Naptown. As next starting pitcher, he was lying down next to Bunny on the allotted place: the bus-wide back seat.

The main tank had run out of fuel. John Brown, chauffeur then, wasn't sure where to locate the outside switch to the auxiliary tank. He wanted the oil checked too. Bus lights remained on as players awakened sleepy-eyed or nodded back to sleep. One player began placing flares. Another moved forward to check the oil, when Gail Harris, with a carload of partying friends, roared down the highway toward the bus. Hearing the sound, Bunny poked his head out a side window. "Man's gonna hit us!" he shouted. Harris swerved out to pass a car, but another vehicle came at him head on. Overadjusting back, Harris crashed into the rear side of the Clowns bus before any could react to Bunny's warning. Colzie was thrown to the floor, and his knee slapped into the post supporting a side seat. Harris' car spun three or four times before he corrected its path and fled down the highway, following the car that nearly hit him head-on, which had made a quick U-turn and happened to be filled with party friends of Harris. He was apprehended down the road.

On the bus, the crank case or motor block was cracked, and the storage compartment door fell off. Body repairs of metal damage, folded like accordion bellows along the storage compartment, were left for postseason. The bus was sidelined for motor block repairs and door replacement. Dad paid for transportation into Indianapolis and round-trip train fares between Indianapolis and Toronto for a Clowns Canadian appearance. Years of investment of Dad's time and money followed the wreck. So did more loans to make payroll. Colzie's career as a Sunday pitcher was over. The lawsuits lasted for years.

Colzie recalls that he beat the Monarchs the day after the wreck, but his knee swelled. Dad had him examined, treated and fitted in Indianapolis with a temporary brace. A permanent brace was ordered out of Akron, Ohio. Colzie missed an 11-day tour, including Cleveland and Chicago, after which Dad reappeared on a Sunday to see how Jim's knee reacted in his next start, and personally had Jim removed late in a 16-2 win over the Chicago American Giants. The knee had worsened. In Nashville, Jim bunted and twisted the weakened joint. A subsequent start in Kokomo, Indiana, resulted in emergency room and follow-up treatment, fittingly enough, by Kokomo's first black doctor.

Colzie's season was done, and he returned home to Georgia, though Dad paid his regular salary through September 15, season's end. There was surgery.

Again Dad borrowed to make paydays. He retained an Indianapolis law firm to file suit for himself and Jim in Anderson, Madison County, Indiana.

Then desk calendar page days began a slow roll, as if a forgetful old man turned a sheet along the rounded posts of the holder every week or two.

Suit was filed July 12, 1949. Jim's case was set for trial May 31, 1950, Dad's for June 6, 1950. Then a systematic series of delays and postponements kept pushing the trial date progressively farther into the future. It would be almost five years after the accident before the case finally came to trial, and another year before the $4,000 awarded by the jury was actually paid.

At one point, Dad wrote to counsel, "As for Mr. Colzie, don't think it practical to have him examined in Georgia due to color discrimination in that part of the South."

There was never a settlement offer in the Colzie case. Jury voir dire may have revealed why. Jim recalls:

Syd sat there with me day after day until six jurors were picked. Until they were picked, one after the other said, "Shoot, I wouldn't be from Madison County if I wasn't prejudiced." Syd and I were as out of place there as could be. But he sat right with me. Syd was the best person in the world, and those people either didn't like blacks or didn't want to sit there. It's an easy thing to say you're prejudiced, gets you out of a lot of thinking, eliminates responsibility you turn your head and say, "Hell, don't give me problems. I'm prejudiced." Works for any race.

Dad testified early after jury selection, then returned to Tarrytown. The team was on the road. On May 24, 1952, the jury returned its verdict in favor of Colzie, the amount $4,000.

On May 4, 1953, nearly a year later, the judgment was paid, attorney's fees were deducted, Dad was reimbursed for most expenses, and James Colzie received his net recovery. In April, 1956, Dad accepted $300 to settle his own case, $68 less than he spent to repair the engine block and baggage compartment door nearly nine years earlier. It made more sense than traveling from Hollywood, Florida, to Muncie, Indiana, for a trial with a chance of recovering perhaps $600 more.

"Clowns played North and South Dakota where I first met whites never saw a black," Buster Haywood said. "Kids stared. I told 'em they could touch, it don't rub off, the color. You know, sometimes they touched and rubbed and looked at their fingers."

Chin Evans described his pitching style as a mixture of cunning and confidence. He lived like he pitched.

Chin was alone the summer of '40 when he bought the hammer in Richmond, and no one saw it in his belt next day in Washington when the Clowns left the bus for lunch.

Evans approached the restaurant. "Not that one, Chin. That's the one we told you the maitre d' ordered the dishes smashed after we ate last year."

"I know," Evans said. "Been there before myself and had it happen."

He entered alone. A few teammates watched long enough to see the scowling maitre d' grab the menu from a waiter and toss it down in front of Evans, then they silently walked away.

"You from the nigger ball club, bus out front?" the maitre d' asked.

"The Clowns."

"Right. Nigger clowns. Name says it. Painted on there big as life, too. Ethiopian."

Chin ordered and as he finished each course, set the dishes aside. "Now don't you remove nuttin', Boss," said Evans, a graduate of Atlanta's Morehouse College, who would later teach and coach both high school and college. "Doesn't want you lookin' like a servant haulin' off a colored man's trash."

And at the end of the meal, when the check came for under a dollar, he gave the maitre d' a twenty dollar bill. Not wanting to give change, the maitre d' said, "Pretty big tip for a nigger clown."

"Not a tip. A waste riddance fee," Chin said, and he wrapped the tablecloth around the dishes, took the hammer from his belt and smashed the lot. "Just throw the nigger dishes out in the nigger tablecloth and keep the change," he said.

❖

Though teammates were not allowed, Armando Vasquez was served in some restaurants in the Deep South so long as he spoke Spanish.

Sometimes doors were opened, sometimes locked, and occasionally, they swung back and forth.

George Ferguson's Ferguson Hotel at Capitol Avenue and 11th, Indianapolis, was a black establishment in a mixed neighborhood, and the closest thing the Clowns had to home. Across the street was a white-owned and -operated delicatessen players loved. The owner kept the deli open late game nights for postgame Clowns' meals. One off-season the deli changed hands, and when the Clowns came into town for their home opener against the Cleveland Buckeyes, Preacher Henry and Jim Colzie led the club across the street to "eradicate some giant sandwiches and dills."

As the door opened, the new owner shouted, "You niggers ain't supposed to use the front door! Use the side!" Stunned, the religious seatmates led the team's temporary retreat.

Minutes later, part of the team returned through the front door, the first two with weapons drawn like Old West gunslingers. "We in our own home, and I think we got the right door, don't you?" Goose Tatum asked the gelatinous owner.

"Sure do. Take what you want on me," the owner responded, sliding the cash register open.

"We just want to come through the proper door and eat," Henry Merchant assured him, "same as we do whenever we're here."

The old owner was back before the next homestand.

During a mid-'40s tour against the Monarchs, Buster Haywood and Jackie Robinson were ordered around back for service in a Mexican restaurant in a black neighborhood in a small South Texas city. Jackie refused, and the manager was called. Jackie smiled, nodding toward the streets, and said, "Man, surely you don't intend to send us back out hungry in our own neighborhood, do you?"

The manager seated them and made sure they were served.

Most times were less dramatic. Like other Negro leaguers, the Clowns generally knew where they were accepted and where they weren't, and road life was tough enough without testing hostile tables.

Dad's philosophy was that the joy the Clowns gave superseded discrimination and racial tension. In 1931, Colonel Charles B. Franklin broke the color line in Louisville, Kentucky, by booking a black game there and integrating the crowd. Before that, blacks sat in the right-field stands, and whites everywhere else. He first booked the Clowns in 1936 and returned them to Louisville two to four games annually until Dad retired. Late in the depression, officials considered banning black teams in Louisville or returning to segregated seating. "Then the Clowns came in. Drew a huge integrated crowd, peaceful and joyful, blacks and whites slapping each other on their backs, laughing and cheering one big roar," Franklin said. "That ended forever meaningful talk of segregated crowds here or no more black baseball."

But life on the road differed from life elsewhere only by being less predictable. During the early '40s, Royal Oak, Michigan, ballpark officials ordered the Clowns, playing there free for a charity appearance, to use the men's room, not the ballpark dressing room. Bunny objected. When the officials suggested if the Clowns didn't like the bathroom, they could change in the jail. Bunny was frantic and wondered if the intent was to provide the players an alternative place to dress or imprisonment. He called Dad.

Cancelling the game, Dad had Bunny and the players at the gate to tell fans the reason. There was no arrest. Dad mailed a check to the charity.

The same summer, the Clowns played a local team in Gary, Indiana. One of the locals loudly used a racial slur. The Gary manager immediately benched him.

"Clowns saw more love than hate on the road," said Jim Colzie. "But things came up when and where you least expect. Like I was a Yankees fan, 'til once on the bus. Figure on the bus with just teammates, racial thing won't come up. They're interviewing the Yankees' Jake Powell on the radio. He's a policeman off-season. Ask him about his job, he says how he beats niggers over the head."

Recalling a Len Pigg home run, Colzie said, "And sometimes there was God-given justice." From the roller coaster atop an embankment outside the ballpark in Dayton, Ohio, teenagers hollered pregame racial insults at ballplayers. Police arrested the youngsters at the end of the ride. During the game, Clowns catcher Len Pigg lofted the longest home run in the history of the park. The ball first hit ground beneath the roller coaster.

Sometimes silence was the racial comment. In 1947, the Boston Red Sox arranged tryouts for Clowns players Ray Neil, Jim Colzie, Sam Hairston and

Goose Tatum. When the foursome arrived at Fenway Park, the gates were locked. There was never a tryout.

And sometimes there was white-made justice. In 1947 the Clowns completed a night game against the Chicago American Giants, and Dad gave Abe Saperstein money for tickets next day at Wrigley Field so the Clowns could watch Jackie Robinson play against the Cubs. "Cubs were calling Jackie terrible things," Colzie recalls. "Their shortstop Roy Smalley was trying to shut them up, but no use. Then Eddie Stanky and Pee Wee Reese came out of the Dodger dugout angry and told the Cubs to say whatever they had to say to them because they were Jackie's teammates. Cubs stopped that talk."

The 1943 Clowns toured New England, parts unfamiliar with blacks. "Some places we could stay at white hotels, some not," Pitcher Jim Everett recalls. "Some places, black churchgoers put us up; some places, were no blacks." The Clowns bus broke down in Skowhegan, Maine. "Players climbed up top of the bus to sleep. Pulled a tarp over themselves," Everett recalled. "Middle of the night there's a thump and loud metallic rumbling. Skunk fell on them, and they cleared the roof like birds out of the roost."

Whites traveled time-free in Birmingham, Alabama, in the 1940s, but blacks had a midnight curfew. "In Birmingham wasn't no Midnight Hour, the good-time kind you sing about," Tut once said.

The Clowns stayed at Mrs. Perkins' Hotel, and those spilling over stayed in her house. Jim Cohen pulled up at Mrs. Perkins before dawn of a game date following a long nighttime jump. Dropping the team off at the front door, he parked the bus and was walking to the hotel, about a block away, when a police car, siren screaming, red light flashing, bounded along the sidewalk at him and screeched to a stop, leaving rubber feet from Jim, who froze still. Two officers leaped out, guns drawn.

"Goddamned nigger, what you doin' out?" one shouted.

Jim explained.

"We're gonna park. You got half a minute to get your brown ass in the hotel, and you best be in pajamas in bed that thirty seconds is up." Jim recalls it was the only time he felt he moved fast as Henry Merchant.

From the hotel window, he watched more squad cars speed in, and at least a half dozen patrolmen, weapons drawn, searched thoroughly for him, including alleys, trash bins and parked cars.

"Man outside wanted me to argue so he could shoot me," Cohen concluded. "I guess punctuality was a black man's virtue in Birmingham back then. Best thing after that was silence. Next best thing was natural quickness."

And sometimes there was black-made justice. Hypocrisy was often more frustrating than outright bigotry. Jim Colzie explained:

In the South, you plain didn't go in restaurants. In the North or along the border, most all restaurants let you in, but some just part-way. For part-way places, we had a policy—three strikes you're out. Waiters and waitresses had a way of ignoring you once you were seated. We call out once, say in a minute. We wait, they ignore us. Twice, say be right there. We wait. They ignore us. Third time, say coming, coming. We wait. They ignore us. We pocket the silverware and leave. Save it up till we could give it to George Ferguson when we hit Naptown. The Ferguson Hotel had some of the finest silverware in the United States. And some of the seventh finest. And some of the thirty-first finest. And some of the fiftieth finest. Most, of course, was just durable.

15

At the Helm

Player managers were favored in the Negro leagues. Having a player manager was like having two men in one bus seat.

During 1947 and 1948 the Clowns had a farm team, the Havana La Palomas. Patterned after the parent club, the team featured the between-innings comedy of Ed Hamman, who also served as road business manager. The field manager was Ramiro Ramirez, who had been a player manager for Dad's Cuban teams in the '30s. Dad owned both teams, so players could be moved between teams as circumstances dictated.

Livingston "Winkie" James was shortstop for the early Miami Ethiopian Clowns. Dad felt about as comfortable with Winkie as the British felt with Rudolph Hess. But Winkie was a better shortstop than Hess, and played the position from time to time with the Clowns for nearly a decade, and, the whole time, Dad heard rumors about a knife, ready, handkerchief between blade and handle. Then one game Dad attended at Comiskey Park, the Chicago American Giants were rattling the fences off Roosevelt Davis. "Cut ball ain't hopping," Dad said to Bunny.

"Maybe the ring's not cutting deep enough, Skip. Maybe Winkie ought to let him use his blade," Bunny said, laughing. And that's how Dad confirmed Winkie carried the blade at all times, in his side pocket on the street, in his back pocket during games, under his pillow nights.

Dad farmed him out to the La Palomas, and Winkie quit.

Winkie James was a piker compared to a player that Dad once hired as a player manager. Fred Wilson was born more than two centuries too late to lead a pirate ship on a Caribbean tour, but he drank, fought, intimidated and thought like a privateer captain. One of baseball's best hitters for average with power, he was as feared on deck as William Kidd, the pirate captain. He handled a razor or knife as well as he handled a bat. Evil was his disposition. Evil was his nickname. Evil was how others perceived him, even teammates. "Fred Wilson played best half drunk," Clowns pitcher Jim Everett said, "and he was a dangerous man to be around." Everett should know. He pitched for the 1943 Clowns, and Fred Wilson was right fielder–manager of the Clowns that year, and sometimes took his turn on the mound.

He was the first Clowns player to be named an all-star for the East-West Game, which highlighted the Negro leagues' season and annually drew crowds of 20,000–50,000 paid to Chicago's Comiskey Park, including thousands arriving from other Negro leagues cities by chartered trains.

Wilson, who played several years for the Miami Giants and was the original Miami Ethiopian Clowns right fielder, also managed the Clowns during the late 1930s, but his horrendous disposition, frequent flashing of switchblade knives (as often at friends as at others), and vampirish hours, combined with nightly gin-mill fever, dictated short-lived leadership stints.

He was replaced as Clowns' manager before the 1944 season by his opposite, Jesse "Hoss" Walker, a feisty infielder, clean-cut and intellectual. A teacher and coach during the off-season, a team man who sometimes cried when the Clowns lost close, Hoss was loved and completely respected by his players. Clowns catcher Len Pigg rated Hoss Walker baseball's all-time best manager. He led the Clowns during the 1944, 1945 and 1946 seasons.

By 1947, Jim Oliver was no longer Clowns shortstop, and Coco Ferrer had been sent to play short for the La Palomas. Before the season started, Dad hired two of baseball's all-time great infielders, shortstop Willie Wells and second baseman Newt Allen, both in the twilight of their careers. It was the latest example of Dad's combination of altruism and name recognition. Wells, who had been a star for several teams for decades, and Allen, who had been the Kansas City Monarchs second baseman for more than two decades, needed jobs, and both had well-known names. Wells was hired as shortstop-manager.

Wells' glove was nothing more than a second skin. Jim Colzie described it. "Tiny glove, hardly bigger than a winter dress glove," Colzie said. "More than 30 years old. No padding. And the man used it like no one else. He could cover the earth!"

Allen played second behind Ray Neil and short behind Wells that year. "Either way," Colzie said, "we had the best double-play combination in baseball. One of the best plays I ever saw, Wells made a stop in the hole. Momentum would have tied most anyone else up without a throw. Willie tossed it behind his back to Newt, who pivoted perfectly and got the double play."

But playing skill didn't always translate into managerial ability. Forgetting how many years Wells had played in Latin American winter leagues and not realizing he was therefore fluent in Spanish, Clowns lefthanded speedballer Angel Garcia sat next to Wells on the bench in Baltimore explaining to Leo Lugo, Coco Ferrer, Juan Guilbe and Tomas Quinones how poorly Wells was running the game against the Elite Giants, concluding that it was too bad the Clowns had no Class D team for Willie to manage. Wells sent Garcia back to Cuba.

Within weeks of that, Jim Colzie was driving the grueling jump from Nashville to Kansas City, and Big John Williams was riding the milkcan, when Wells casually asked how far they were from Kansas City.

"Dunno, Skip," said Colzie.

"Well, hell. Is it 2,000 miles or more like two miles?" Wells asked.

"Dunno, maybe 250," Colzie said.

An hour later, Colzie saw a sign. "Skip," he said, "Sign says Kansas City 225 miles."

"Lyin' son bitch!" Wells shouted. "We made more than 25 miles in an hour!"

"Shit, Skip. You pressed him for an answer. The man was only estimating," said Big John Williams.

"Gonna be some changes we hit Kansas City, Williams," Wells said. "Get off the goddamn milkcan. Tut, replace him on that goddamn milkcan."

Willie Wells was going to fire James Colzie and Johnny Williams. From Kansas City, Bunny broke the news to Dad long distance.

"He cost me Garcia from the left side. Now he wants to lose me two Sunday pitchers from the right," Dad said. "Can't you reason with him, Bunny?"

"No, Syd. He's firm."

"Then relieve him," Dad ordered.

It was one of the worst days of Dad's career, and he often told me over the years, "I'm so proud that Willie Wells was with the Clowns, if just for a few months. He was the best there ever was at short. He was a good and decent man."

Ramiro Ramirez was interim manager until Dad named Buster Haywood manager during the 1948 season when Ramirez requested to be relieved due to bad legs.

Buster grew up in Portsmouth, Virginia. His father worked at the train station until he was laid off when Buster was 16. Buster then worked odd part-time jobs to help his mother, a hospital dietician, support the family, but he didn't stop playing baseball. In 1935, at age 25, he was released by the Newark Eagles after a brief stay. Someone less determined might have quit baseball then, but Buster stayed with the game on the semi-pro level. He declined an offer from the Mohawk Giants because he suspected financial problems. He was right. The team, once a powerhouse, soon folded. In 1939, the Birmingham Black Barons appreciated Buster's talents during their visit to Virginia and signed him.

A fair, gentle, religious man, Buster managed the Clowns from 1948 through 1953. A proponent of one-on-one management and self-motivation, he never had a team meeting. His six seasons as manager were marked by an intensifying rivalry with the Kansas City Monarchs, led by his counterpart, John "Buck" O'Neil. Both were about the same age. Both were great players as regulars. Both were religious and considerate. Both still filled in, particularly effective as pinch hitters. Both were honest and loyal. Buck would become Ernie Banks' first professional manager, Buster Hank Aaron's. Buster would manage Toni Stone as the first female player on a male major league team. Buck would manage her the next year.

Buster managed the Clowns to three Negro American League championships, and played and managed as an all-star in East-West games. He is the manager most often associated with the Clowns. Only Tut and Verdes Drake were with the team longer. Just like Dad and Bunny, Dad and Buster were like brothers. But if Buster and Bunny were like brothers to each other, the sibling rivalry was Freudian in scope and grandeur. Clowns people cared about the Clowns, and that, coupled with the comedy element and the road, compounded and magnified the difficulties that would have been involved managing some other, ordinary team. Buster explained:

Syd put baseball ahead of show. No conflict there. But the comedians had to be handled special. Wouldn't have no paydays without Tut, Bebop, Goose and Peanuts. Whole league depended on our comedy. We were their payday and their lunch money. I couldn't make a move would lose a comedian. We had young kids, never been away from home, and we had the road. Had Bunny and Tut. I loved 'em both, especially Tut. We couldn't exist without Tut. Bunny's Syd's right hand. I'm his left. But damn, Bunny and Tut thought they was managers. Sometimes I'm sitting on the bench, Bunny one side saying do this, Tut on the other saying naw, naw, do that. I do what I want, and they don't let up. It don't work out.

The Clowns finished next to last in the Negro American League in 1943, second in 1944, fifth and fourth the two halves of 1945, third in 1946, about the same in 1947 though no standings were published, fourth in 1948 and 1949 and first in 1950.

It seems like daily Mom said, "Sydney, you're too good-hearted."

Players couldn't have agreed more. At one time or another, they all were recipients of Dad's generosity.

Jim Colzie said, "Win or lose, Syd would shake your hand, and when you took back your hand, you had a twenty or fifty or hundred."

Chivo Smith said, "Anytime Syd's at a game, you got a handshake with a five ever you score a run."

"Players always asking, 'When's Syd coming out?'" said Sam Hairston. "We loved to see Syd coming with his briefcase. It was bonus time. Always asked me, 'How much you need for your family?' I'd tell him the number. He never turned me down."

After games we waited and waited in the stadium for Dad. Night games we waited until warned the lights were being turned off. Then we waited outside the clubhouse in the car, as Dad roamed the locker room discussing salaries and disbursing bonuses. It seemed like early morning, and probably was, when Dad finally appeared at the clubhouse door and started toward the car. Then Tut intercepted. "Skip, I need a raise." Both men laughed, then entered the shadows for serious talk.

I always told Mom the same thing, "When I get big, I'm never going to wait for anyone or anything."

Tut emerged from the shadows.

"Mom," said Valaria. "King Tut's leaving, call Dad."

"Too late, Val," Jerry said. "Here's Bunny. Mom, wake me in New Jersey when we get to White Castle."

"Hamburgers sound good," Valaria said. "Wake me too unless it's breakfast, then I may as well starve."

"There goes Bunny," Jerry said. "Call Dad."

"Not now," Mom answered, "There's Speed Merchant."

"Are we gonna be here forever?" I asked.

"Just have patience. Daddy will be here before you know it," Mom said. And he was. Until we hit a certain age, none of us can remember staying awake until Dad got to the car.

Once we were old enough to stay awake until he reached the car, we were rewarded with Mom's greeting line, "Syd, did you keep enough for gas to get home?"

On the way home from games to the south, like Philadelphia, Wilmington, Baltimore, Washington, he woke us all when we got to the White Castle just before the Holland Tunnel. As baby of the family, I carried on the tradition of the youngest—waking every five minutes and asking if we were at White Castle yet, complaining when we weren't, then being too tired to leave the car when we got there.

Simultaneously, Dad had the large, interest-free loan outstanding to Abe Saperstein for the Globetrotters; court costs and fees advanced interest-free in Jim Colzie's personal injury suit; attorney's fees paid to defend against the Minot, South Dakota, injunctions against the continued career of shortstop Len "Preacher" Williams, this without expectation of repayment; and a $1,000 interest-free loan to George Ferguson to keep the Hotel Ferguson going in Indianapolis.

The loan was made on July 23, 1948. There were probably interim payments negated by future advances, and the loan was finally repaid in full on July 7, 1952, by an offset against room rents.

During the same period, Dad constantly had numerous $10 to $50 loans to players outstanding at any given time, always without interest, often without request for repayment, and he loaned one pitcher $700 to buy a $6,500 house, all without a note, interest or security. The return payments were spread over four years. That's how Dad and Clowns players did business.

Dad sat next to Buster on the bench one night in Cincinnati in 1949. "Syd, my Daddy needs a car, and I don't have the money," Buster said.

"Don't worry, Buster. Your Daddy's got a car and you can pay me back, no interest. How much you need?"

"Priced a Chevy today, $900," Buster said.

Next morning, Buster bought the car, and Dad gave him a week off to drive it home to Portsmouth as the team played toward Richmond. Buster left Cincinnati with $300 in his pocket and drove straight through to Portsmouth without stopping for sleep. Buster's father drove that '49 Chevy until he died in 1972, at age 90.

"The Clowns were like the Yankees. Drew big crowds," Buster said. "Clowns played more charity games than anybody. Syd booked us many times each season free at prisons, mental institutions. Syd always wanted to replace misery with fun, do something good for somebody else."

Following the 1943 season, Dad laid groundwork to switch the club's base, for the limited number of home games Negro leaguers played, from Cincinnati to Indianapolis. Abe Saperstein's brother, Morrie, wanted to acquire the Chicago American Giants and move them to Cincinnati, and Abe asked Dad to make room. Abe had exclusive booking rights in Indianapolis too, where the Clowns had always drawn well. When Dad verified player complaints that, because they were black, they were not permitted to use the dressing rooms at Cincinnati's Crosley Field, Dad's decision became irrevocable.

Indianapolis Indians general manager, Owen L. (Ownie) Bush, was inclined to permit the Clowns to use Victory Field in Indianapolis as home, but he met traditional racial resistance, and for two seasons, the Clowns played as the Cincinnati-Indianapolis Clowns. Because of denial of Clowns' use of Crosley Field dressing rooms, Bush, ignoring all local opposition, insisted that the Clowns use Victory Field as home whenever Dad wanted to schedule it and the Indians were on the road. Bush had been courageous enough to hold firm and racial opposition diminished. In 1946, the Clowns became the Indianapolis Clowns.

Cliff Robinson of Indianapolis, Clowns 1948 batboy at age 13, was first a fan. "Blacks sat quietly way in back at Indians games then," Robinson said, "but when the Clowns came to town, Victory Field was ours for one day, and the place rocked with joy without restraint. Before the game, there were placards everywhere. Sound trucks rode the streets for days announcing the game. It was special—an event. Kids flocked to the Hotel Ferguson for a chance to see the Clowns."

Most games it seemed like 90 percent of the crowd was Clowns fans, except in Indianapolis, where the percentage was higher. Sometimes performers in Clowns crowds outnumbered those on the field. Jesse Owens and entertainers such as the tap dancing Step Brothers, Mantan Moreland (Charlie Chan's movie chauffeur), Judge Pigmeat Markham, Eddie "Rochester" Anderson and Stepin Fetchit were Clowns fans. Band leader Lionel Hampton was the Clowns number one show business fan. Whenever his band appeared near a Clowns game, he attended the game, and, when he did, he wore a Clowns uniform and coached third base an inning. According to Dad, Hampton planned to bring his band on tour with the team one summer until his wife and agent intervened. He earned more elsewhere. Buster Haywood remembers Hampton got so caught up in one Clowns game, members of his orchestra came to the ballpark to get him so he didn't miss his show.

Fame is relative. Dad related that, introduced to the Mills Brothers at a Clowns game, he was about to say he couldn't believe he was actually meeting them, when one of them said, "Can't believe we're actually meeting Syd Pollock."

Kansas City Monarchs shortstop Othello "Chico" Renfroe often spoke of the money Clowns crowds put into league coffers, and he called the Clowns "the league's bankroll."

Clowns crowds were never consistently larger than during the '40s. The Clowns and Monarchs drew a standing-room-only crowd of 31,323 to

St. Louis' Sportsman's Park, home of the Cardinals. Satchel Paige beat the Clowns there the second game of a another doubleheader 6-1 after an opening game Clowns win before more than 16,500 paid. There were more than 12,000 paid at several Clowns games in Washington, more than 15,000 at the Polo Grounds, more than 14,500 in Philadelphia's Shibe Park, more than 31,000 in Cincinnati, and consistently more than 12,000 in Chicago. It was like that in every major city.

According to Buster Haywood, Branch Rickey's decision to integrate the Dodgers followed years of the Clowns outdrawing the Dodgers in Brooklyn. "Once the Dodgers-Giants had 5,000 paid at the same time we had over 15,000 across Brooklyn against the Bushwicks. The man didn't want to integrate to make history. He was a smart businessman. The first game Jackie played for the Dodgers, the crowd was half black."

Someone once said a batting slump for Sam Hairston was a hitless hour. Sam was a hitting machine. His wife was pregnant as the Clowns played south during 1944. Mired in a prolonged slump, he asked Bunny about returning to Birmingham for the birth.

"You stayin' put," Bunny said. "Got no call to be there. You ain't no doctor." Sam stayed put, and the slump continued.

On August 29, 1944, in Nashville, Nathaniel Pollard, pitching brilliantly for the Birmingham Black Barons, was victim of the birth. As Hairston came to the plate to face Pollard, the announcer said, "Let's have a hand for Clowns third baseman, Sam Hairston, now batting. He just became father of an eight-pound boy, and mother and son are just fine." And that's how Sam learned of the birth of John Hairston. Sam blasted the first pitch over a light tower for a titanic home run.

Clyde Nelson died playing first for the Clowns in 1949. He was 32 years old.

Annually, the Clowns played the tough Studebaker team in South Bend, Indiana. An excellent hitter, Nelson, a Chicagoan transplanted to Miami, was acquired from the Studebaker team to back up Goose at first and to play third base for games Sam Hairston caught.

Among Clowns players, the all-star night-lifers were, in order, Fred Wilson, Peanuts Davis, Goose Tatum and Clyde Nelson. Bunny once said, "Sunlight made Fred Wilson's soul squint." Goose, Peanuts and Clyde Nelson loved the dark almost as well.

"Night before he died," Buster Haywood said, "I caught Clyde Nelson and Peanuts in a room with a couple women. Wasn't something I would have done, but I can't make my morals theirs. Thing is, all this party noise woke everybody. We got a doubleheader next day."

Next day 7,248 paid attended the Clowns–Philadelphia Stars doubleheader at Shibe Park. The Clowns won the first game 6-4. Len Pigg, who captured the Negro American League batting crown that year, caught both games for the Funmakers, and Hairston played third. Goose played first in the opener, but became moody between games, said his stomach ached and refused to play the second game. We were there, and Dad fined Goose. Buster penciled Nelson in at first for the nightcap. Nelson had pinch-hit in the first game.

The Clowns had a 2-1 lead in the bottom of the ninth of the second game. No one was on. Nelson had a hit, ten putouts and no errors. Stars second baseman Milt Smith popped a foul right, toward the Clowns dugout.

"Nelson and Pigg both ran for the pop-up," Sam Hairston said. "Pigg was overweight, and fell apart as he ran. Flipped his mask off. Cap flew off. Chest protector rose up over his belly and started flapping. Shin guards came loose, flailing out and banging on and off his legs as he ran. But he made the catch, and when he did, Clyde Nelson collapsed beside him."

In the stands, we cheered, but Mom said, "Somebody's down."

By the time I noticed something was wrong, Clowns players were crowded around, and we couldn't see who was on the ground. A doctor came from the crowd to help. Within minutes a fire rescue squad arrived. Nelson was hidden by players as the rescue squad carried him from the field, Dad at his side.

In part of his column subtitled "Laugh Clown, Laugh," *Philadelphia Inquirer* reporter W. Rollo Wilson described the locker room:

Shocked players of both teams stood in the crowded quarters while efforts were made to revive him. (I say "crowded" because, for some KNOWN reason, all Negro teams, whether there be two or four, must use the accommodations arranged for the average twenty-five player major league unit.)

Most visibly shocked of the Indianapolis group were owner Syd Pollock, business manager Bunny Downs, King Tut, Goose Tatum. . . .

Mom sent Jerry to the locker room, and he ran back and forth with reports on his own. Each time he told us, "Dad says he hopes not but he knows Nelson's dead, but the doctor won't say so." Mother asked us to pray for Clyde Nelson, and we did. On his last trip, Jerry gave us the certain news; it was a fatal heart attack.

Dad had the body returned to Miami by train, and Goose went from irritation to burden.

"Next night," Buster recalls, "we went through the motions and lost 19-4 in New Castle. Liquor and loose women killed Clyde Nelson same as they killed Peanuts."

We rode back to Tarrytown numb inside as if we'd been drinking Novocain.

When the Miami Ethiopian Clowns started the 1936 season, Miamian Buster Scott was mascot, batboy and equipment manager. Dad liked him and worried about what Buster would do without the Clowns. The players liked him and felt he brought good luck. Despite the chronic need for bus seats for players, Dad kept Buster Scott with the Clowns until 1950.

Short, Buster Scott was powerfully built, more like a football player than a baseball player. Called Keg by some, he told players his sport was boxing. Year after year, he claimed to be waiving his chance at being a top pro boxer by taking the road with the Clowns. "This team's everything to me, but, damn, costs me a title, great a fighter as I am."

According to Sam Hairston, Monk Silva arranged a Buster Scott fight in Miami's Dorsey Park with a pro the night the Clowns gathered for one spring training. Fred Wilson bet a hundred dollars on Buster and felt safe for two reasons. One, for years he had heard Buster talk championship and figured the mascot could take any stiff Monk Silva might have booked. Two, Fred Wilson signed to referee.

Thirty seconds into the first round, Buster Scott hit the canvas, victim of a snapping right cross. Fred Wilson began the slow count. "One. Two. . . . Get up, Keg. Damn! . . . Three. . . . You got him, Buster. He was reelin'. . . . Four. . . . Up, Keg. I got a hundred on you!"

Buster Scott arose. Wilson shook him lightly, making sure there was at least minimal awareness and that nothing rattled. He jiggled Buster's arms, then pinched his cheeks like a mother tweaking her baby. "Finesse him, my brother," Fred said, "like you was before you was hit."

Buster nodded knowingly, listening to this referee like he was a corner-man. The other fighter looked quizzically at Wilson and danced gracefully and impatiently from one foot to the other.

Wilson stepped back from Buster, and Buster danced heavily, like a man about to lose waltzing at a marathon ball. Then, he lumbered forward, landed a soft jab, and took a vicious left hook that sounded like the crack of a bat. He went down for the second time. Wilson leaned over him. "One. . . . Two. . . . Get up, Keg. A hundred dollars. . . . Three. . . . You got him. . . . Four. . . . Get up. Think championship! . . . Five. . . . "

"You can count to a thousand, I ain't gettin' up," said Buster Scott, and he didn't, until he was counted out.

16

Remembrance of Players Past

As part of growing up, children should view parents as strong and sacred, powerful and everlasting, perpetually vibrant and joyful. At least, that's how my brothers and sisters and I saw ours. And it was good. Besides our parents, we had others we perceived as larger than life: King Tut, Buster Haywood, Bunny Downs, Verdes Drake, Speed Merchant, Ray Neil—men the heart of the Clowns, a "great group of men," remembered forever strong and young, sacred and, above all, joyful, always deflecting the worst the road had to offer, taking the extra base, slashing one more line drive, earning one more massive ovation. And with them—cigarette between teeth, record ash curled—charting it all in his scorebook on the bench in the dugout, Dad.

Second baseman Ray Neil and shortstop Jim Oliver, friends from Florida, joined the Cincinnati Ethiopian Clowns to start the 1942 season. They grew up together a double-play combination in St. Petersburg, Florida.

Oliver played short until he went into the service. When he came out, he signed a contract with the Cleveland Buckeyes but wanted to play for the Clowns. Dad found an inequity in the standard Buckeye contract, and C. Richard Fulmer, the Clowns' Indianapolis lawyer, persuaded Cleveland to transfer Oliver's contract to the Clowns. Oliver covered plenty of ground, and his powerful arm beat runners from deep in any hole. Homesick daily throughout his career, Oliver constantly missed his wife, who never wanted him to travel, and he left the Clowns for home, having played a total of less than three full seasons.

But while Oliver was with the Clowns, according to John "Buck" O'Neil of the Monarchs, "Neil and Oliver were as good a double-play combination as ever played baseball."

Most often, Ray Neil is the first player mentioned by those recalling the Clowns. He was a quiet, determined leader, who played the game smoothly and hard. He was as great with the glove as with the bat and as great on the basepaths. One winter in Venezuela, Neil set a record that might never be broken. He had 19 putouts and assists in a single game without an error. He was as fine a second baseman as ever played the sport.

Tut was loved as the joy of black baseball. Henry "Speed" Merchant too was loved, not just because he was a great player, but because he was happy. To Merchant, life was a rally about to start, soon as the next Clowns hitter entered the batter's box. Fans loved him because if black baseball was played on the run, Merchant galloped. If the Clowns played with fire, Merchant was an explosion, a conflagration.

Recalling Merchant's chronic "soft cough" and occasional shortness of breath, Jim Colzie said, "Some thought Merchant had TB. Way I see it, fast as he was, he sometimes outran his own breath is all."

John "Buck" O'Neil said, "Merchant ran like poetry; Merchant running was a thing of beauty. Only Jesse Owens was as beautiful to watch. Merchant was every bit as fast as Cool Papa Bell or Tetelo Vargas."

Clowns 1945 infielder Leroy Cromartie called Speed Merchant one of the greatest players he ever saw. "He could field, hit and throw with the best," Cromartie said. "And he ran like no one else. Long, long strides. He skimmed the ground like a piston-driven machine."

My brother Don could not pick an all-time major league–Negro league team without including Merchant.

Buster Haywood said, "Merchant made great catches coming in and going out. He was a great ballplayer with quick moves. He was always on his own to run. Often scored from second on an infield groundout."

Sam Hairston was surprised no major league team signed Merchant after integration. "Sure, he was older, but he had the perfect baseball body, the perfect baseball hands, and Good Lord, could that man run." Hall of Famer Monte Irvin, who played for years with the Newark Eagles of the Negro National League, considered Merchant the best of all Clowns players.

During the war, when Goose and Peanuts were in the service, Merchant performed the fishing and dentist sketches with Tut, and Buster Haywood recalls a serious moment the irreverent mind-set paid off:

> Don't recall who we played, but it was fog thick as day-old grits. Out-fielders about hitting each other tossing flies between innings. Merchant decides not to throw again. Might hurt someone. He puts the practice ball in his pocket. Blast hit over Merchant's head in straight-away center during the inning. Rolled under the fence. Nobody saw it roll under but Merchant. He pulled the practice ball from his pants, threw a liner out of the fog and got the runner at third.

Usually, when my brothers and I sat in the dugout, Speed Merchant was the first player next to us, treating us like fellow travelers, not owner's sons, pointing out nuances of the game, asking how school was, asking what we thought Clowns strategy ought to be, asking how Mom and our sisters were and whether they were in the stands, telling us game highlights since the last game we'd seen and asking us our batting averages. Everyone was Speed Merchant's friend.

Whatever Maximo Sanchez told Dad in 1944 after Sanchez first saw Reinaldo Verdes Drake play center field, no matter how many minutes of superlatives he used, he understated. There could have been no way to describe what he saw. Drake's ability could be conveyed only by eyesight, and often, after one of his catches, witnesses doubted their eyesight. I've seen two athletes do the impossible, defy vision and suspend disbelief: Michael Jordan in basketball and Verdes Drake in baseball. Drake was small and thin and quick as a hummingbird's wings. I didn't see every center fielder who ever played baseball. I did see DiMaggio, Mantle, Mays, Piersall, Ashburn. To me, it is impossible to imagine another outfielder as good as Drake. He remains a classification of one. He caught flies the next best couldn't reach in day-dreams. For example, in 1949, he led the Negro American League in put-outs with 211. Willie Mays was second with 200. After that, the numbers dwindled to 180 and below.

Clowns players always cite a Drake catch as the greatest play they've ever seen. But each one describes a different catch. Jim Cohen recalls an impossible running catch Drake made against the Homestead Grays in Pittsburgh as the greatest play he ever saw. Ray Neil flatly calls Drake the greatest outfielder ever, and said, "He played shallow 'cause he went back like nobody else. You hit to deep center on Drake, you're out if it don't clear the wall, and maybe you're out if it does clear the wall."

Dad described the greatest play he ever saw:

We had an SRO crowd in Sportsman's Park, 31,323 paid. Monarchs pounded us the first game. Second game we lead 2-1. Late inning, seventh or eighth, they load the bases, two out. Hank Thompson comes up. Drake sometimes broke before the crack of the bat. Knew his batter, saw how he's stepping into the pitch and where the pitch is headed. Thompson strides into the pitch, and I catch movement in center. I watch Drake take off top speed to straightaway center field. I hear the shot off Thompson's bat. Drake hits the warning track in full stride, turns and looks back for the first and only time until he climbs the fence on the run, five, six feet off the ground. Caught the ball over his shoulder up there, back to home plate. The crowd gave him a 15-minute standing ovation. Gave me goose bumps inside my chest. We won 2-1. I'd been worried we'd be forgotten in St. Louis if we dropped two. We only had one chance every couple years in there. Watching Drake do that, you knew there was no limit to what a man can do.

Batboy Cliff Robinson described a 1948 catch Drake made in Cleveland's Municipal Stadium as an "over the shoulder breadbasket catch . . . the same catch that later made Willie Mays famous."

I recall watching Mays' famous World Series catch off Vic Wertz and replays for years with Dad, and Dad always said the same thing as he did watching other great catches or long chases ending in near catches, "Drakey woulda caught it in his back pocket."

Sam Hairston said no one had an arm like Drake's. He laughed loudly as he recalled the first game Reuben Jones managed the Memphis Red Sox against the Clowns with Drake in center: "Reuben Jones was coaching third. Man on second. Flyout to Drake in deepest center. Jones gave the tag sign, and the runner tagged. Time he's to short, the ball passed him on by. Jones is waving him back and shouting, 'Go back! Go back!' Jones never seen an arm like that and never sent a runner on Drake again."

Drake hit line drives as naturally as a duck floats on water. A spray hitter, he batted from as low as just above .200 to well above .300, but was probably a lifetime .275–.280 hitter. He was never without his golden crucifix on a golden chain around his neck. It was not for show. John "Buck" O'Neil of the Monarchs said, "Drake could hit to all fields. He was a smart hitter and a good man."

As Bunny was a buffer between Leroy Cromartie and potential evil forces, Verdes Drake was that and more for Clowns Latin rookies. He was surrogate father, tour guide, interpreter, intermediary, social mores analyst, and whatever else he needed to be to ease the pain of international adjustment.

Jim Colzie told me his special memory of Drake:

Let me tell you about how Drake got me a $200 bonus from your daddy.

In St. Louis, Satchel Paige beat me 2-1, and Satchel hit in the winning run. As we're leaving the field, I said, "Satchel, next time we meet I'll beat you."

Now, he was scheduled to pitch freelance that Sunday for the New York Black Yankees in Yankee Stadium. Asks Hoss Walker "When Colzie pitching against us again?"

Hoss says, "Sunday, in Kansas City."

Satchel tells Frank Duncan, the Monarchs manager, "Well, cancel my plans to go to New York. I'll whup Colzie Sunday in Kansas City."

Sunday in Kansas City, we had a 3-2 lead late against Satchel. Bases loaded. No outs. Bonnie Serrell comes up, best spray hitter in the league. Buster comes to the mound. Asks, "What you gonna throw him?"

"Changeup outside," I said.

"Good idea," Buster said.

Drake's shallow—50 to 75 feet behind second. I threw my pitch as perfect as I saw it in my head. Thing is though, Serrell lines a clean single up the middle. All three runners running. Problem for them was, Drake makes an impossible catch off his foot, throws to Ray Neil for two, over to Goose doin' a split at first for the triple play.

We won 3-2, and it turned out I hit in the winning run on a single I sliced had two sets of eyes, one lookin' at Gene Baker at second, one peekin' at Buck O'Neil at first, and it just avoided them both.

And that's how Drake got me a $200 bonus from your Daddy.

After the game, we're all strolling out to the buses together, both teams, Satchel and everybody. A beautiful woman comes melting along the sidewalk, man walking behind her. Satchel looks her up and down. Says, "Hey, lady, want to get married?"

She says, "You best ask my husband. That's him behind me."

Satchel ducked into a building, but the man smiled and said, "Hey, get him back. We came for Satchel's autograph."

During the '40s, many Clowns players played winter ball, most at jobs Dad found.

Monk Silva recalls that, during the early '40s, the Clowns sometimes played the Deep South out of Miami until as late as November.

During the mid-'40s, Buster Haywood helped Monarchs pitcher Chet Brewer gather players for the Negro league Kansas City Royals All-Stars' postseason tours of California, the Southwest and Mexico against Major League All-Stars. Satchel Paige's catcher on such tours, Buster was selected most valuable player for the Negro league stars on the 1946 tour against Bob Feller's Major League All-Stars. In 1947, Buster and Tut joined other Clowns players on a Jackie Robinson all-star team touring the same area against Major League All-Stars. Clyde Nelson, Ray Neil, Big John Williams, Sam Hairston, Goose Tatum and others joined Buster and Tut representing the Clowns on the Negro league teams. According to Jim Colzie, players, more ecumenical than organized baseball, sometimes integrated their own all-star games by switching teams.

In addition to postseason barnstorming tours, Dad helped place players in winter leagues in Puerto Rico, Venezuela, Mexico and Panama. Dad didn't let go once he placed a player for the winter. He kept in contact through letters and newspaper clippings that players sent him, and offered advice and encouragement in return.

Chivo is Spanish for male goat. Part of constant immigration from the Bahamas, Lauretta and John N. Smith, seeking economic advantage, sailed to
Key West, where their son, Eugene, was born November 28, 1911. Before his
voice changed, his shout sounded goat-like, and the nickname Chivo stayed
as his baseball skills sharpened. But for road baseball, he lived his whole
life, parts of nine decades, in Key West, less than a half mile from "the
southernmost point of the United States." Chivo and his brother, Allen
Smith, were the last surviving members of the original Miami Ethiopian
Clowns. Then Chivo died in 1996.

In 1935, Chivo and Allen joined the Miami Giants and were charter
members when the Giants became the Miami Ethiopian Clowns the following season. Allen pitched; Chivo played third. Allen retired after the '38 season, but Chivo played on at third, short and wherever needed. During the
war he caught in the service, and afterwards signed with the Cleveland
Buckeyes. But he played all nine positions for the 1946 Clowns, the last year
any of the original Clowns players appeared with the team on the field.
Then, there was only Tut.

During the 1946 and 1950 seasons, Jesse Owens toured with the Clowns,
racing Speed Merchant in pregame exhibitions. On August 14, 1946, the
Clowns won 7-2 over the New York Cubans before more than 9,000 paid in
the Polo Grounds. Owens and tap dancer Bojangles Robinson, who had an
unusual natural talent for running backwards, appeared at this game. The
Amsterdam News reported activities:

Pregame ceremonies brought out two popular heroes, Jesse Owens,
American star of the 1936 Olympics in Berlin, and Bill (Bojangles)
Robinson.

Owens, running 100 yards over hurdles, finished second to Henry
(Speed) Merchant of the Clowns who ran the century on the flat. Jesse
was beaten by a scant foot. Robinson sprinted backwards and with the
aid of a 30-yard handicap he beat Orestes Minoso, Cuban third baseman, by a good 15 yards. Owens then ran around the bases against

four runners and finished five feet in front of the anchor man even though Jesse must have covered an additional ten yards by circling the bases very wide.

Owens was generally clocked running the bases, then Tut would clip several seconds off Jesse's time, by concentrating, motioning for quiet and waiting till he had it, scratching the ground with each leg like a horse, digging in, leaping two feet in the air with fright as the starting gun sounded, and using an unannounced shortcut—home to first to third to home.

Sometimes Merchant and Owens raced a straight 100-yard dash. They were virtually even. Of course Jesse was older and generally won, but he ran in a track suit, while Merchant wore his full flannel baseball uniform.

On June 15, 1949, in New Castle, Pennsylvania, the Clowns beat the City League's All-Stars 15-0 before a paid attendance of 3,402. Jim Cohen and Peanuts Davis combined for a one-hitter, and Verdes Drake's two triples and Sherwood Brewer's two doubles led a 19-hit Clowns onslaught.

Next day the local paper carried the story plus a news photo of Goose Tatum sitting on an apparent pillow on the ground, a U of boys gathered around him for autographs. Goose's head is back in laughter, pen in mouth. He has a paper to sign in his hand. The picture is unremarkable but for two things: Goose's infectious grin and the cutline, "GOOSE TATUM—First sacker for the Clowns plays a unique game of ball as the Clowns defeated the All-Stars last night. Goose thoroughly 'covered' first base as he played ball and signed autographs for his avid fans as the game was in progress." Sitting on first base, Goose simultaneously played his position and signed autographs for the laughing fans.

Following the 1949 season, Goose played basketball with the Harlem Globetrotters full time. In late September, Dad wrote to George Ferguson at the Hotel Ferguson in Indianapolis, "We've been catching poor weather on after season games but otherwise things are going OK and team is going better since we got rid of our chief worry, Goose, as he had the team upset too much."

Age and illness so decimated Peanuts Davis that he retired after the 1950 season. The complexion of the Clowns had changed. Comedy was on the sidelines until Natureboy Williams joined the Funmakers in 1955.

In the spring of 1950, Dad phoned Alejandro Pompez, owner of the New York Cubans, and Dad and Jerry picked him up in Spanish Harlem to ride together to a game in Philadelphia.

"Syd, 1949 was a bad year for me," Alex Pompez said during the ride. "The numbers 949 came up and about broke me."

Pompez' lament could have been considered a prophetic representation of black baseball's future. The elimination of baseball's color line had "about broke" the Negro leagues. The Negro National League had already folded following the 1948 season and the final year of the decade proved to be the beginning of the end for the Negro American League as a viable major league.

PART FIVE

THE FIFTIES

The Jody Transition

In 1954 Oscar Charleston guided the Clowns to the Negro American League championship, their fourth in the last five years.

By the end of the decade, the Clowns were the only touring team capable of performing on an organized baseball level.

—Alan Pollock

17

First Pennant

As an attraction, the Clowns swelled Negro leagues attendances to unprecedented numbers during the 1940s. At 11:59 P.M., December 31, 1949, I called my friend Jay Cohen for our phone conversation planned to last from the 1940s into the 1950s. Our discussion ended at 12:01 A.M., January 1, 1950. During the two minutes, we had spoken from the Golden Gate era of the Negro leagues into their dying decade.

Organized baseball slipped through the back door as Jackie Robinson went out the front, and before black baseball knew, it was no longer master of its own home.

As stingy as organized baseball was in accepting the trickle of blacks, the Negro leagues were terminally damaged, like an electric fan with a slightly unbalanced blade whirling imperceptibly, then visibly, further and further out of control, eventually busting the fan. Followers of black baseball now wanted to watch blacks in the major leagues. Like a constrictor swallowing a piglet whole, by 1950, the Negro American League had expanded to ten teams, adding the clubs that had survived the death of the Negro National League.

More and more, black teams became financially dependent on funds from sales of player contracts into major league systems. Rents charged black teams for major league parks escalated rapidly. Clowns' gates provided the last hope for Negro American League fiscal freedom and added years to the existence of black baseball.

Major league rosters were built for major league conditions, and Negro league rosters fit Negro league circumstances. Either set of leagues likely would have been superior in its element. Both were big league caliber before integration, and most of the best black athletes in the United States were still playing Negro American League baseball in the early '50s.

Beginning in 1955, the ability of Clowns teams, pounded by economic forces, diminished rapidly into upper, then middle, then lower minor league levels. The Kansas City Monarchs ceased playing top-notch baseball once Tom Baird sold the club to Ted Rasberry after the 1955 season, and the roster scattered.

By the end of the decade, the Clowns were the only touring team capable of performing on an organized baseball level. There was still something called a Negro American League, but teams were ragtag collections of washouts and young sandlotters, changing players at times daily, and missing most paydays and numerous playing dates. Drawing only a few thousand people, the annual East-West game was moved during the late '50s from Chicago, where it was born and raised and had once thrived, to New York, where it drew no better. Dad told Ed Hamman, "It's sad. It damages the Clowns. The Monarchs and Black Barons miss dates because they can't afford bus repairs or don't have enough players after a no-pay payday. Used to be called a bus league. Now it's a broken-down-on-the-side-of-the-road bus league. It's better they don't show than they do. They show, they're so weak, they hurt the Clowns worse than if they hadn't gotten their bus started."

Television didn't help the Negro leagues; it competed. The major leagues fed on television revenue and the additional interest generated by wide exposure.

Black baseball had no TV revenue. The growth of television in the late '40s and early '50s kept fans home. Why go see the Bushwicks and Clowns? Black fans in Brooklyn could watch Jackie and Campy and Newk compete against whites on TV. Theaters at the tail end of vaudeville closed. People were living-room-bound for entertainment. There was no immunity in our house. I camped in front of the television and ate supper on the living room floor while watching the Yankees, my favorite major league team.

The Clowns won their first Negro American League championship in 1950. Negro league statistics were never complete and lacked the significance of statistics in organized baseball. Negro league standings did not necessarily reflect the quality order of the teams. Manager Buster Haywood and Clowns players confidently believe they had the best team in black baseball during 1948 and 1949. Negro league statistics often provided insufficient numbers for meaningful analysis. Most games for Negro league teams, even among each other, were not league games, and league games were not equal in number against each league team. Problems meeting and exchanging opponents on the road, breaking jumps and playing more than 100 cities a year in far-flung states precluded uniform scheduling.

Unlike major leaguers, bus league teams could not play three games in one city, take off a travel date and go to the next three-game stand. They were like nomads eating up oasis after oasis, traveling with the same opponents to towns and cities everywhere with one opponent, until scheduling niceties, devised by owners at numerous league meetings in Chicago each season, allowed them to exchange opposition where they intersected another tour. Weekday games in small towns between league teams were not league games and did not count in league statistics. The Clowns most often played the better teams. Partly because of the friendship between Dad and Tom Baird, the Clowns' most frequent opponent was the Monarchs.

Clowns catcher–third baseman Sam Hairston, in 1950, had a statistical year almost unparalleled. At the end of each season, the Howe News Bureau issued final league statistics out of Chicago, and, at the end of the lists, gave season highlights. After the 1950 season, the bureau summary read, "There is no need to write about anyone else but Sam Hairston of Indianapolis. Sam was top man in five departments of specialized play among them being the most important of all, that of leading hitter with a mark of .424 in 70 games. In the others he excelled in hits with an even 100, total bases with 176, home runs, 17 and runs batted in with 71."

For the batting crown, Hairston beat out future major leaguers Bob Boyd (.356), Willie Mays (.330), Elston Howard (.319), Jim Gilliam (.265) and Ernie Banks (.255).

The bureau statistical narrative cited other Clowns: "Granville Gladstone of Indianapolis bashed out the most triples, 13. Henry Merchant of Indianapolis, [won] just what his name implies in the way of speed, by top-ping them all with a total of 45 thefts. Raul Galata struck out the most bats-men, 120."

Nat Peeples of the Clowns and Clyde McNeal of the Chicago American Giants were second behind Merchant's 45 stolen bases; each had 20.

"Before the 1950 season started," Sam Hairston recalled, "Syd told me he'd sell my contract to the majors if I had a good season. I did, and he did."

That winter, Sam hit .380 in Venezuela, and in 1951, he was called up with Minnie Minoso as the first blacks with the Chicago White Sox. He batted five times, and had two hits for a .400 batting average. Dad and I watched game after game on television, waiting for Paul Richards to play Hairston again. He never did. Sometimes, we saw Sam warming up pitchers in the bullpen. It was sad; he couldn't hit from the bullpen, and Sam Hairston was a hitting machine.

He was farmed out to the White Sox Colorado Springs Western League team, where he batted over .300 four times, leading the league with a .350 average in 1955. That season, he struck out but 30 times in 546 at bats, typical of his contact-hitting style. His last year in the minors was 1959, when he hit .330 for Charleston in the Sally League.

Sam's son Jerry played years for the White Sox and his son John for the Chicago Cubs. Sam and his sons constituted the first black father-son combination ever to play major league baseball. While his sons spent more time in the major leagues than he did, Sam coached the White Sox in spring training and in their minor league system for more than 45 years. There is no question that only in the Negro leagues and the minor leagues was Sam Hairston given the respect due him.

Dad's efforts to improve the Clowns going into the 1950 season included acquiring some new players, including three Latin American players. Cubans Pablo Sama, rookie shortstop, and Pedro Naranjo, southpaw hurler, were joined by Granville Gladstone, an outfielder from the Panama Winter League.

Nat Peeples, acquired from the Monarchs during the season, joined veteran holdovers Verdes Drake and Speed Merchant in the outfield. Charlie Peet, a promising youngster also saw spot duty in the outfield, but hit only .214 , and Dad sent him to the Canadian Mandak League in 1951 for seasoning. Never returning to the Negro leagues, Peet caught on in the minors, and improved his hitting yearly, until, in 1956, he moved up to the St. Louis Cardinals, where he batted only .190 in limited action, but was considered as fine a prospect as Dad once thought. Flying to Venezuela for winter league play following the '56 season, Peet was killed in a plane crash.

There were also changes in the infield. Goose Tatum was replaced by all-star first baseman Archie Ware, for years a Cleveland Buckeyes mainstay, and Johnny Britton, a fine infielder, returned to the Clowns. Britton had a clean-shaven head that figured in his own routine for guaranteed tear-provoking laughter. Once a game, he batted with a wig softly stuck on his head under his cap. Taking a call strike, he'd confront the umpire face-to-face, hollering loudly and angrily, kicking dirt. Then he pulled his hat off and threw it to the ground and kicked it, growing more and more vocal and animated. Finally, face contorted with anger, bobbing and puffing kiss-close to the umpire, Britton tore off his wig and threw it hard into the dirt, kicking it high into the air in a cloud of dust.

When Britton jumped the club in mid-season, Dad purchased the contract of Benjamin "Honey" Lott from the New York Black Yankees to play third base when Sam Hairston was forced behind the plate due to injuries to catchers Piggy Sands and Buster Haywood.

Sam "Piggy" Sands became starting catcher as a rookie in 1950, and, except for injury late his rookie season, was the Clowns regular backstop for four seasons. Monk Silva remembers a phone call from Dad during the winter of 1949.

"Let me ask this," Dad said. "You ever hear of a catcher name of Sam or Piggy Sands?"

"Nope, Syd."

"Supposed to be related to you. Home run king of Sing Sing Prison. Sands is not a family name?"

"Nope, Syd. Never heard that name. Sing Sing, you say?"

"Home run king there. Played against us twice last year, we played Sing Sing. If he's a good man, I'll do my best to get him out and with the Clowns."

"Can't say one way or the other, Syd. Don't know the man."

Monk hung up, and, when his wife came into the room, said, "Syd Pollock just called me as a reference for some convict in Sing Sing. Thinking of signing him. Syd thought he was a relative."

"Piggy Sands! He's my cousin."

"What is he, bad or good?"

"Good man. Good family anyway." Monk called Dad back with a favorable report. Dad helped Sands get early parole.

I asked Dad once about Piggy and Sing Sing. "Professor," he said, using a nickname he had given me as a child, "Piggy says he was driving a car and two buddies asked him to stop at a gas station so they could get cokes from the coke machine. The first Piggy knew they knocked off the station was when he thought he heard a blowout behind him and then a ping on the side of his car and looked in his rear view mirror and saw the station owner, gun raised, shooting at the car. At Sing Sing, they tell me every getaway driver tells the same story, but I believe Piggy."

"So you don't think he knew?" I asked.

"Good man with us. That's what counts," he concluded.

The catcher played four Clowns seasons with honor, and when his baseball career was done, Monk got him a job with the Miami Recreation Department. Dad vouched for his character. He worked there in exemplary fashion until he retired, returned to New York and died.

Clowns pitching was strong in transition in 1950. Raul Galata, with an 11-6 record and a 2.82 ERA was steadiest. Harry Butts and left-hander Raydell "Ray" "Black Beau" Maddix joined veterans Preacher Henry, Henry McHenry, Peanuts Davis, Jim Cohen and Andy Porter. Cohen was in his prime, but Porter had lost something on his fastball and Peanuts was a shadow of the pitcher he had been. Another pitcher that year was Tom Johnson, who later coached baseball, swimming and and football at Howard University.

The Clowns opened their 1950 league season May 7 with a doubleheader against the New York Cubans at the Polo Grounds attended by all-time great pitcher Smokey Joe Williams, then 64 years old. The games were played in his honor. Pregame coverage referred to Williams as "rated in many circles as the greatest pitcher of all times. In his day he tangled with the likes of Walter Johnson, Grover Cleveland Alexander and Satchel Paige in scintillating hurling duels, and more often than not emerging as the winner."

Williams' career, from 1905 to 1932, was primarily with the Lincoln Giants of the Bronx and the Homestead Grays. His masterpieces against National League champions are legendary, one a no-hitter against the New York Giants. Against black teams, he won as many as 41 games in one season, and once struck out 27 Kansas City Monarchs in a 12-inning game. His fastball and control at least matched Satchel Paige's, and many consider him baseball's all-time best pitcher.

Smokey Joe spent a good part of May 7, 1950, in the Clowns dugout, and Dad introduced us, but then, as close to him as I wanted to get, I could get no nearer than the far side of five or six players continuously lined up on either side of him soaking up his thoughts and black baseball lore.

Two days later, our family went to a doubleheader in Philadelphia that typified the Clowns season.

By 1950, Goose was gone from the Clowns, and Peanuts no longer had the raw athletic skills that earlier enabled him to play with uninhibited comedic flare. Comedy was mostly on the sidelines in the capable hands of King Tut and Spec Bebop.

Partway through the 1950 season, Dad's efforts resulted in potential Pathé News coverage of the Clowns. Before homes had televisions, and even after most homes had television, any visual news, usually Pathé Newsreels, was seen at movie theaters. Pathé coverage had popularized the Globetrotters, and in 1950 Pathé and a lesser known newsreel outfit came to the Polo Grounds to cover a Clowns-Cubans doubleheader. Dad's mistake was thinking the public wanted a copy of the Globetrotters, and the 1950 Clowns were not that. They were the best team in the Negro American League. But they were no longer suited for comedic baseball. They were structured for baseball and comedy. Even in 1936, when Tut was in his prime as a player, he was acknowledged as a great fielder, but a sub-par hitter. Bebop was never a baseball player. Peanuts was nearly a decade past his finest pitching.

Pathé News should have been presented with top-notch baseball, Tut's comedy sketches and shadowball, and it would have shown well and represented reality. Instead, with full knowledge of the newsreel people, Dad met with Cubans owner, Alejandro Pompez, before the game, and contrived an inning in which Peanuts, Tut and Bebop would compete, with the acquiescence of the New York Cubans. After each out, Tut and Peanuts would perform pepperball on the diamond. Pompez concurred with the idea but never really intended for the Cubans to allow the comedy.

Cubans crowds were late crowds. The opener started with only a few thousand in the stands as backdrop for a film. Instead of providing a great start with great entertainment, even the off-field comedy turned sour. Maybe Tut and Bebop were nervous, pressured to perform as players in a major league setting. Warming up before each game, Bebop always threw to Tut as Tut lay on his back resting with his glove on his foot. Tut caught nine of ten of such throws by foot. For Pathé News, Bebop threw wide the first time. Tut dropped the second throw, and caught the third hesitantly. Fans who'd seen them time and time again scratched their heads. Mother stated aloud, "This is going very poorly."

Once the game began, Tut struck out on blooped pitches. Bebop singled a lobbed pitch to right, but looked clumsy doing it, barely beat it out and was picked off. A single, a walk from Peanuts and a bunt toward Tut loaded the bases, which were then cleared by Minnie Minoso's triple to the center field wall. And when Dad complained, he was told it all counted. The result was that (a) the Clowns spotted the Cubans a three-run lead, (b) Ralph "Spec Bebop" Bell amassed a lifetime Negro American League batting average of 1.000 and (c) Pathé News left immediately after the triple, expressing no interest whatsoever in waiting until shadowball after the seventh inning.

The irony is that the win was one of the most exciting I ever recall seeing. The team wanted to beat Pompez for his treachery. Pablo Sama's homer into the right-field seats in the top of the ninth, capped the comeback and proved the game-winner. Tut's double-peaked cap spun through the air like a maple seed pod in spring, and players jumped for joy in front of the Funmakers' dugout. Every Clowns player joined Tut kissing the top of Sama's head as he crossed home plate. Great defense in the bottom of the ninth preserved the victory. Everyone who saw that game saw baseball at its best.

KING TUT

With his charisma, creativity, and acting ability, King Tut was the essence of the Clowns and the heart and soul of black baseball. He wasn't just watched and enjoyed, he was flat out loved by everybody.

GOOSE TATUM

Goose Tatum earned his greatest fame with basketball's Harlem Globetrotters, but he began his career as an athlete-entertainer with the Clowns. This picture was reproduced on postcards and as 8×10 glossy photos which Syd Pollock sold by mail for 25 cents.

CLOWNS PEPPERBALL

The pepperball staged by the Clowns prior to the game was a treat to watch. King Tut (*left*) was a master and originated almost all the comedy in the routine, including the ball that rolled down the back and was flipped off the rear end to the waiting teammate. The other players are Thaddist Christopher, Sylvester Snead and Goose Tatum.

KING TUT, SPEC BEBOP AND ED HAMMAN

King Tut sometimes worked solo and other times in tandem with another entertainer. His most memorable companion for rehearsed two-person sketches was
Spec Bebop, a dwarf standing just over three feet tall. The duo is pictured with
Ed Hamman, a comic and part owner of the Clowns, who conceived the idea for
the oversized mitt and bat shown.

JUGGLING JOE TAYLOR
Juggling Joe was an exceptionally good juggler, but his talent didn't relate to baseball.

PRINCE JO HENRY

Prince Jo Henry said his ideas came from God. He began his Clowns career as a third baseman before turning to comedy to seek a raise and assure his presence in the starting lineup.

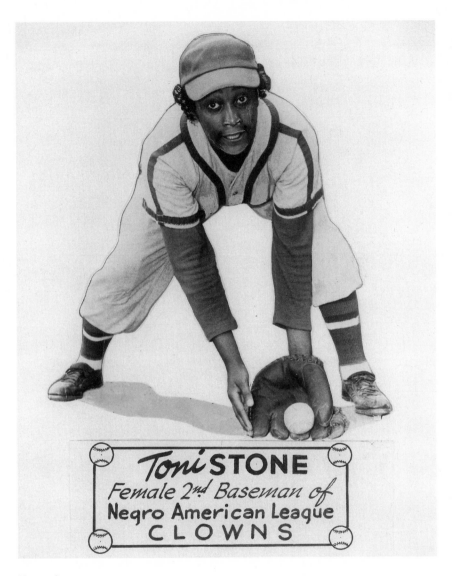

TONI STONE

Toni Stone, signed by Syd Pollock in 1953 as a gate attraction, was the first female in any sport to compete on a male major league team. She played the first three innings at second base each game, and fans flocked to see her.

TONI STONE (ACTION POSE)

Toni Stone sought no favoritism and received none. On the field all treated
her like a ballplayer. Men came at her hard to break up double plays. They slid
spikes up when she made the tag. She wanted action and she got it.

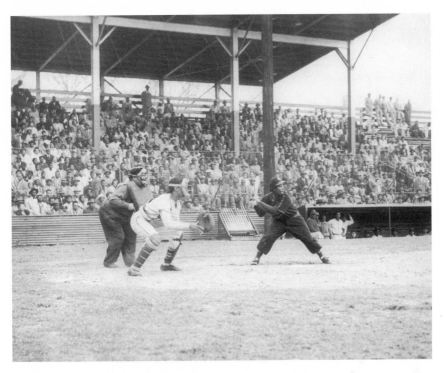

Toni Stone (at bat in game)
Toni Stone was to male baseballers what Jackie Robinson was to white baseballers. Most men resented her success but loved to watch her play. She was first
a ballplayer, then a lady. (Courtesy of Virginia Union University)

RAY NEIL, TONI STONE AND SPEED MERCHANT
Toni Stone (*middle*) is flanked by Clowns stars Ray Neil and Henry "Speed"
Merchant.

CONNIE MORGAN
Connie Morgan played second base for the Clowns in 1954, after Toni Stone was traded to the Kansas City Monarchs. Later in the season, she was joined by a second female, Mamie "Peanut" Johnson, but the novelty of a female on a male team had worn off.

JACKIE ROBINSON AND CONNIE MORGAN
Syd Pollock arranged for Connie to try out during the Clowns postseason 1953
tour against Jackie Robinson's Major League All-Stars, where she was photographed with Jackie.

KING TUT, OSCAR CHARLESTON AND CONNIE MORGAN
Clowns' manager Oscar Charleston (*middle*) is flanked by the inimitable King
Tut and female second baseman Connie Morgan. As a player Charleston was a
fierce competitor, but at the Clowns' helm he was a father figure.

CONNIE MORGAN (BATTING WITH KING TUT CATCHING)
Connie Morgan demonstrates her batting style, with King Tut serving as her catcher with his trademark oversized mitt. Press releases stated her salary as $10,000, but Syd Pollock sometimes exaggerated her salary for publicity purposes, as he had done with Toni Stone. (Courtesy of Malcolm Poindexter Jr.)

SIX ETHIOPIAN CLOWNS
Standing second from the left wearing his trademark sideways hat is Eddie "Peanuts" Davis, who joined the Ethiopian Clowns in 1938 and was given the Clowns name "Nyassas." The knuckleball artist was an ace pitcher, as well as a superb comic second only to King Tut. He often outdueled Satchel Paige in head-to-head matchups and remained with the Clowns, except for military service during World War II, through the 1950 season.

Three Clowns All-Stars

Photographed on the field at Chicago's Comiskey Park at the 1948 East-West game are the Indianapolis Clowns three all-stars, second baseman Ray Neil, catcher Sam Hairston and pitcher Jim Cohen. Five years later Neil won the Negro American League's batting title. Hairston learned that he had become a father when it was announced over the PA system while he was at bat. He then blasted the first pitch for a home run. Cohen earned the nickname "Fireball" because of his blazing fastball.

Leonard PIGG
of Indianapolis CLOWNS

Ray NEIL
of Negro American League
CLOWNS

LEONARD PIGG

Leonard "Fatty" Pigg (*left*) was a hard-hitting catcher who joined the Clowns after being discharged from the army following World War II. He batted well over .300 in his two full seasons with the Clowns in 1948–1949.

RAY NEIL

Ray Neil (*right*) was a good hitter and smooth fielder who enjoyed a long career with the Clowns. In 1953–1954 he surrendered his second base position to female players for the first three innings of each game because they were a gate attraction.

TED RICHARDSON

Ted Richardson was a small left-handed fastball pitcher from Orlando, Florida, who signed with the Clowns in 1952.

JIM TUGERSON
Jim Tugerson and his brother Leander were both signed by Syd Pollock and pitched for the Clowns in 1951.

DAVE AMARO
Dionisio "Dave" Amaro pitched for the Clowns in 1954.

H ANK A ARON
Hank Aaron, who became the major league career home run king,
joined the Clowns in 1952 as a 17-year-old shortstop. Prior to joining the Clowns, he had batted cross-handed.

SYD POLLOCK AND HANK AARON
Syd Pollock and Hank Aaron shaking hands after Hank had joined the Milwaukee Braves.

ED HAMMAN AND SYD POLLOCK
Clowns' co-owners Ed Hamman and Syd Pollock are pictured at a baseball meeting in St. Petersburg, Florida, in 1959.

ACTION SHOT TAKEN AT THE 1941 *DENVER POST* TOURNAMENT
In a game against the Kansas City Life of Denver team, the Clowns scored
13 runs in the first three innings and cruised to a 16-1 victory in route to
winning the 1941 *Denver Post* Tournament championship. The photo shows
Clowns left fielder "Tanna" being thrown out at first base, with Al Kavanagh
taking the throw. (The photo appeared in the *Denver Post* and was furnished
courtesy of Jay Sanford.)

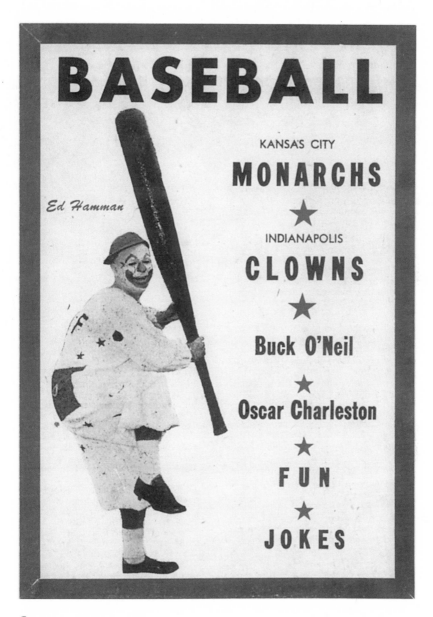

GAME PROGRAM
This program was sold at a 1954 game between the Indianapolis Clowns
and Kansas City Monarchs. The Monarchs were the defending champions
of the Negro American League, but the Clowns, who had won the previous
three pennants, reclaimed the title in 1954. Ed Hamman was co-owner,
business manager and entertainer for the Clowns.

STADIUM SCENE

This crowd shot was taken at a game at Chicago's Comiskey Park between the Clowns and their 1964 touring partners, the Brooklyn Stars. A crowd of 15,779 enthusiastic fans enjoyed an evening of fine entertainment and saw the Clowns take a 6-2 victory.

THE ETHIOPIAN CLOWNS' TEAM PICTURE, 1934.
The early Ethiopian Clowns grew out of the Miami Giants. This photo shows the Clowns suits, fright wigs and war paint that the team wore to enhance the entertainment element of their games. Two of their star attractions were Dave "Skinny" Barnhill and King Tut (*fifth and sixth from left*).

THE 1940 ETHIOPIAN CLOWNS' TEAM PICTURE
The Ethiopian Clowns have their eyes on batboy Buster Scott (*left*). In the front row are Dave "Impo" Barnhill (*second from left*) and Buster "Khora" Haywood (*fourth from left*). The first two players standing (*from left*) are Fred "Sardo" Wilson and Felix "Kalihari" Evans.

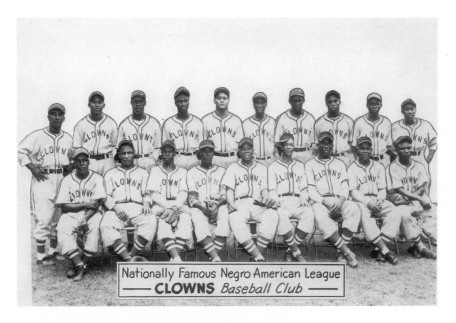

THE INDIANAPOLIS CLOWNS' TEAM PICTURE
This Clowns' team picture includes ace pitcher and star comic Peanuts Davis (*seated fourth from right*) and future manager Buster Haywood (*standing second from right*).

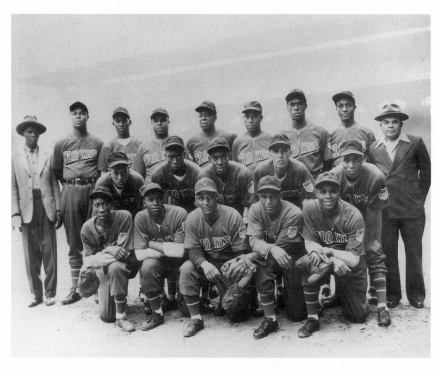

THE 1943 INDIANAPOLIS CLOWNS' TEAM PICTURE
This Clowns' team picture includes Buster Haywood (*standing far left in civilian clothes*) and business manager Bunny Downs (*standing far right in civilian clothes*). Also pictured are King Tut (*kneeling far left*) and Roosevelt Davis (*kneeling far right*).

THE INDIANAPOLIS CLOWNS' TEAM PICTURE
This Clowns' team picture in front of the team bus includes King Tut (*standing far left*), "Pullman" Porter (*standing second from left*), Jim Cohen (*standing sixth from left*), business manager Bunny Downs (*standing far right in civilian clothes*), Ray Neil (*front row far left*), and Buster Haywood (*front row fourth from left*).

THE INDIANAPOLIS CLOWNS' TEAM PICTURE
This Clowns' team picture includes entertainers Juggling Joe Taylor (*kneeling far left*), Spec Bebop (*front row fifth from left*) and King Tut (*kneeling second from right*), along with business manager Bunny Downs (*kneeling on far right in civilian clothes*).

Indianapolis CLOWNS *Negro American League Champions*

THE 1952 INDIANAPOLIS CLOWNS' TEAM PICTURE (POSTCARD)
This Clowns' team picture was taken at Memorial Stadium in Baltimore.
Standing (*left to right*): unknown, Jim Tugerson, Frank Ensley, Woody Small-
wood, Ray Neil, Bill Cathey, Leander Tugerson, Jim Cohen, "Speed" Merchant,
Preacher Jenkins, "Piggy" Sands, Frank Carswell. Kneeling (*left to right*):
Elzie Todd, Jimmy Wilkes, Ted Richardson, Reuben Williams, unknown, King
Tut (with his trademark oversized mitt), manager Buster Haywood, Curtis
Hardaway. Sitting (*front*) with bats: Spec Bebop.

THE 1953 INDIANAPOLIS CLOWNS' TEAM PICTURE
Clowns' owner Syd Pollock broke the gender line when he signed female second baseman Toni Stone (*kneeling fourth from left*) in 1953. Also pictured are entertainers Spec Bebop (*front row far right*) and King Tut (*standing far right*). Players include Verdes Drake, Frank Ensley, Ray Neil and Buster Haywood (*standing eighth through eleventh from left*) and Henry "Speed" Merchant (*kneeling sixth from left*). This was the only season from 1950 to 1954 that the Clowns failed to win the Negro American League pennant.

18

Repeat Champions

American life in the '50s was not all drive-in restaurants, rock and roll and idyllic family life. National psychology in the '50s was framed early by the Korean War and throughout by the Cold War. The inconclusive police action against North Korea and Communist China, which lasted from June 1950 through July 1953, took lives and hinted to us that our nation might well be as mortal as its men in service. Fear of the Soviet Union and of the bomb dominated American life. The resulting need to escape may have helped provide the social setting for the growth of rock and roll and the carryover of the romantic movies and novels of the 1940s. Certainly, the Clowns were still useful.

During the '50s, the draft was a focal point of young male adulthood. Most draft-age men either volunteered for the service of their choice or were drafted. Others had wives and children or educational deferments, and did not serve. Some baseball players played baseball in the service. Others didn't. Between baseball years lost to World War II and Korea, Boston Red Sox great Ted Williams missed his chance at baseball's career home run record.

During the summer of 1951, I made a fool of myself over Ted Williams. It began over card flipping during 1950. One-on-one, my friends and I flipped bubble gum baseball cards spinning from hand to ground, heads up or heads down, and if the second boy matched the first, he won all cards. If not, he lost all cards.

If nothing else, memories of aching jaws and wrists told me I had the entire Bowman Gum Company 1950 baseball card collection. I slept easy nights. Almost. Teddy Wilcher and Leon Evans both told me they had the 1950 Joe DiMaggio, that their fathers had put their cards in safes, that they weren't allowed to show Joltin' Joe. Somewhere in my mind I doubted the completeness of my collection. I awoke sweating from dreams of flipping The Yankee Clipper away. Not every night, but some. The Bowman Gum Company was in Philadelphia.

In 1951, Mom and Dad and I went to Philadelphia for a Clowns–Philadelphia Stars game. Next night the two teams were part of a four-team doubleheader in Griffith Stadium in Washington. I didn't notice when we checked into the Broadwood Hotel in Philadelphia that Dad reserved not just one, but two nights. I was too excited with the prospect of two straight Clowns games in different settings and my plans to somehow edge Mom and Dad toward the Bowman Gum Company to verify the non-existence of a Joe DiMaggio card.

After we arrived back at the hotel following the Clowns Shibe Park game, Dad informed me I wasn't going to Washington, a matter he thought Mom had told me and she thought he had previously mentioned.

"Wait a minute," I said. "Yes I am."

"No. I'm going with the team on the bus, and you and Mother will stay here."

"Why?"

"We expect more than 15,000. Some will be drunk. I have three other owners and all my players to talk to. I want to talk to Buster and Bunny and Tut on the bus, and I don't want you and Mother alone in the crowd remnants after the games."

"Then we'll have to leave Mom here, but you and I can go down to Washington in the bus."

"You need to stay here to protect Mom."

"If I can't protect her in Washington, what makes you think I can protect her here?"

"There won't be 15,000 people milling around the hotel."

"Besides," I persisted, "you're going to the drugstore where they have my favorite malteds."

"They're my favorite malteds, not yours. You always say the malteds in Tarrytown are better."

"Until last year. The last one in Washington last year was pretty good."

"You stay here. I'll have Mother get you a malted, Professor, but it's going to be a Philadelphia malted."

It was hard to believe this guy was not only my father, but my best friend!

Before bed, I negotiated one of the worst days of Mom's life. I would stay to guard her in exchange for her taking me to the following places: (a) a drugstore for a malted; (b) the Bowman Gum Company; (c) the Boston Red Sox–Philadelphia Athletics doubleheader next day at Shibe Park. It was still a bad deal to me compared with Washington and the Clowns. Dad was reluctant, but Mom agreed. The price of my protection ran high.

As much as Mom loathed baseball, the Red Sox–A's doubleheader had to be a new low point in her life, especially after the diminishing excitement of our visit to the Bowman Gum Company plant following the malted. She couldn't root for the Clowns. Bea King, Tut's wife, had wisely declined Mom's invitation to join us. I was Mom's company, and I sat beside her in my Clowns cap, glove ready for a foul, totally concentrating on baseball. Each game was rain-delayed numerous times. Mom probably later had weeks of nightmares involving suffocation under tarpaulins or murders by groundskeepers or being hit by wild pitches or maybe of being married to Noah and helping to ready the animals for the ark. As the evening-like afternoon darkened into night-like evening and intermittent showers beat down with metronomic regularity, Mom begged more frequently to leave. The Red Sox had won the first game and led the nightcap by four or five runs. "We can leave when they take Ted Williams out, Mom. Ought to be after his next at bat, this size lead." Ted batted and left the game, and we caught a cab back to the hotel. Mom smiled the whole ride like she was being honored in a convertible in a Manhattan ticker-tape parade.

We went out to eat and returned to the lobby to wait. At least we weren't waiting outside Griffith Stadium. That was the one good thing about not going to Washington. Here, we talked to an old Civil War veteran who was staying at the hotel. I kept running out front to check if the Clowns bus was coming, and there was plenty of action in the lobby and out front. I still wore my Clowns cap and glove, and I waited patiently for someone to see me and assume I was a major leaguer and ask for my autograph.

One time I went out front and stood at the curb next to a tall man in slacks and an open dress shirt. I looked south toward City Hall. No sign of the Clowns bus. "Baseball fan?" the tall stranger asked.

"Yes."

"At the Red Sox game today?" That should have been the first clue. Philadelphians would have called it the "A's game".

"Yes. With Mom. We left when they took Ted Williams out."

"Me too," he said. Clue two overlooked. "Nice glove you have there. Can I see it?"

I'd gotten into a fight with a classmate, David Robinson, over trying on that glove. Dad had told me not to let anyone else use it, but when he learned David and I had fought he said, "I meant no one should catch with it. You needed to break it in for the way you catch. You can let someone try it on."

I'd already broken Mom's rule about not talking with strangers, so I handed my glove to the tall man. Besides, he was skinny well-built, like Goose Tatum, and powerful enough to rip me in half and make off with my glove if he wanted.

"This is a professional glove," he said.

"Right. Would cost you $36 you walk in off the street to buy it. Cost my father half that 'cause he owns a baseball team."

"What's his name?"

"Syd Pollock."

"The Clowns," he said.

I was amazed. "You know Dad?"

"No. I've heard of him is all. I'm in baseball too."

He handed me back my glove. And I looked close. Closer. Closer still. I stared into his face. And I knew. Then I said it. I pointed up at his face, and said, "Hey. Wait a minute. You know who you are? You—you're Ted Williams!"

"Yes, I know."

Further fulfilling my role as jester, without another word, I ran into the lobby for Mom. "Hurry, Mom, hurry! Ted Williams!" I shouted, pulling her up from the couch and across the lobby by her hand to the sidewalk. But, of course, he was gone.

If the Clowns were to repeat as Negro American League champions in 1951, Dad had to solve preseason and in-season problems. Sam Hairston was in the White Sox organization. Peanuts was suspended for not reporting to camp and never played again. One of the top pitchers, Raul Galata, jumped the team in mid-season, signing with the outlaw Canadian Manitoba-Dakota circuit, which honored no contracts but their own. Other players from last year's lineup who went to Canada were Charlie Peet and aging Archie Ware.

Benjamin "Honey" Lott was back at third at the start of the season, but Curtis Hardaway replaced him late in the season when Dad sold Lott's contract to the White Sox organization. Because Dad felt he would sell Sherwood Brewer's contract to a major league club early in the season, the Clowns had three solid shortstops: Brewer, Len "Preacher" Williams and Willie Brown.

The Clowns ace pitcher was Jim "Fireball" Cohen but more help was needed on the mound. Dad purchased veteran pitcher Frank Carswell's contract from the Chicago American Giants for $7,500, and the young Tugerson brothers, Jim and Leander, had matured on the mound.

To plug some the other holes on the roster, Leonard Pigg returned after a year in Canada to back up Sam "Piggy" Sands at catcher; Buster moved Speed Merchant to first base, settling the issue there; and Dad signed Erwin Ford and Lincoln Boyd to battle for the third outfield spot vacated by Merchant. Returning starters Nat Peeples and Verdes Drake completed baseball's fastest outfield.

The Clowns had a sharp competitive edge that season, and it flashed like a razor one Sunday at a mid-season loss in Forbes Field, Pittsburgh.

The Funmakers were home team, had beaten the Monarchs in the first game of a doubleheader and went into the bottom of the ninth of the nightcap behind by one. They tied the score with runners at first and third, no outs. Buster selected his bat to pinch-hit, when the game was suddenly called, the score at the end of eight declared official.

An equipment manager's nightmare resulted—flying through the air like swarming insects, thrown bats, caps and gloves immediately littered the dirt in front of the Clowns dugout.

Tut stormed the plate umpire through the litter, followed closely by Bunny, Dad, Buster and the rest. I stood amid the thrown bats, caps and gloves partway between the dugout and the plate. At first, the stadium was eerily quiet in shock (Mom later described hotdogs suspended halfway to mouths), except that Pauline Downs, Bea King, Aunt Winnie and Mom shouted arias at the umpires from the box seats behind the Clowns dugout, and their protest rippled out like water from a stone thrown into a smooth pond and eventually riled the crowd up into frenzied decibel levels.

"Blue law!" the plate umpire shouted. "Ain't my fault."

"What you mean, blue law?" Tut hollered, face inches from the umpire's. "Can't play past five P.M."

"Shit you can't," said Tut. "I played here more years than your mama's had hair on her chest, you son of a bitch. Rule is no inning can start after five. It's just now God-damned five. Ninth started ten, twelve minutes ago. This whole inning's legal even if we rally till damn midnight."

"You don't know shit, Tut," the umpire said. "This is my town."

"I got to know everybody's town. Know your town better than you do. That's obvious. I know every rule from Key West to Vancouver. I got to know the rule," Tut said. "My damn act delays the game, so I'm well aware of the rule. It's the inning can't begin. Call the damn Mayor."

The third base ump said thoughtfully, "Mayor's not available Sunday."

"Pittsburgh don't close Sunday," Tut said. "I hear damn horns honking in the streets right now. Get the damn Mayor on the phone. I always wanted to give him shit about the smoke here anyway. Get the son of a bitch on the phone! We got a damn municipal emergency!"

"Got to quit at five," said the first base ump. "Blue law." It was unanimous among the three officials.

"You ain't gonna have a blue law, you gonna have black and blue balls, Ump," said Lincoln Boyd, and Buster, Bunny and Len Pigg combined to hold Lincoln back.

Dad said, "Look it up, ump. Look it up. It's in the book one way or the other, right?"

"It's in the City Code," the plate ump said. "Don't carry that around with us."

"Well," said Buster. "You can't effect the outcome of a game on something ain't here. You got it, let's read it. You don't, let's play ball."

"My job's to know it, not read it," said the plate umpire.

"You probably can't read anyway, you illiterate son of a bitch," said Lincoln Boyd.

He was ejected from the now non-existent game. It was as superfluous as tossing a belly-full man from a pie-eating contest.

"You're job's to run a ball game, not run a damn religion," said Tut. "Let the game go on. God wants to see how it ends. You already ruined this Sunday. Listen to the language you causing."

"You don't tell me my job, Tut. I'm throwing you out. You're out!" If the blue law didn't end the game, the plate ump would end it by attrition.

Another 15 minutes of arguing and four or five more ejections made no difference. The game was over; the loss in the books.

The Clowns protest was denied later that summer by J. B. Martin, president of the Negro American League. The game was officially a win for the Monarchs.

John Marvray was a Clowns right-hander during the 1951 and 1952 seasons. Early in the '51 season, he had a 3-2 count on the Monarchs' player-manager John "Buck" O'Neil in New York's Yankee Stadium. Marvray described what happened:

I was a fastballer. Came with the Clowns 'cause they had a big league reputation, a big league pitching rotation. I had a 90 mph-plus fastball, so when I had 3-2 on Buck O'Neil and got a curve signal, naturally I shook it off. I wanted fastball. I got fastball. I threw smoke. Buck O'Neil hit it right back at me too hard for me to react. Hit me square in the mouth.

They hauled me off to the hospital and admitted me. I lost three teeth and a month of pitching.

That night, Buck come to see me at the hospital, said, "Didn't mean to hurt you. I was trying to hit it out of the ballpark. It's just you're so fast, I topped it."

"Topped it?" I asked.

"Topped it," he repeated.

"Well damn!" I said. "You hit it solid instead of topped it, you'd have killed me!"

The whole 1951 season was like a 3-2 count and a shot back at the mound between the Monarchs and Clowns, but in the end, the Clowns repeated as champion, Merchant as leading base stealer. Ray Neil led the league in batting at .346. But Clowns legs were aging. Their quick bats were slowing as the season wound down. The nucleus—Ray Neil, Speed Merchant, Verdes Drake—needed more and more horse liniment. During the season, in which they won both halves, they unraveled and diminished in quality, and were resewn several times by Dad, who became a master stitcher just keeping a coat together. Dad was like Tut near home plate putting on his tattered tux coat, feeling his way with a flashlight and a road map.

During the season, Nat Peeples' contract was sold to the Dodgers. Lefthanders Harry Butts and Pedro Naranjo jumped to the Manitoba-Dakota League. Promising righthander Whit Graves jumped to South America and was suspended. The *Chicago Defender* reported that "raids on the Clowns were made by representatives of Canadian and South American clubs, with the latter making such tempting offers that General Manager Syd Pollock nearly lost his entire team when each individual player was offered a large bribe to finish the summer in San Domingo. Only Graves took the bait, the remainder feeling that they had too many opportunities to break into organized baseball to breach their contracts."

Dad felt that jumping players inflicted irrevocable self-damage. According to the *Defender,* Dad said jumpers could feel secure only until they had off-days, "which every player is bound to have . . . They then find themselves without a job and slapped with a ban when they try to return to the United States. We're paying good salaries . . . based on our drawing capacity and a number of our players stand an excellent chance of making the grade in Organized Baseball before another season rolls around. Those who miss this opportunity will find that they have cut off their nose to spite their faces."

Dad received offers for Harry Butts' contract from both the Dodgers and White Sox the day after Butts jumped to Canada.

Pablo Sama had jumped to his native Venezuela.

Honey Lott's contract was sold to the White Sox. At the time, he was leading the Negro American League in runs scored, total bases, doubles, home runs and runs batted in.

Even with their ever-evolving roster, the Clowns ended their 1951 pennant-winning drive with six consecutive wins over the Birmingham Black Barons.

Each year into the '50s, the difficulties of maintaining a quality roster compounded. While players became available as other Negro American League teams folded, loss of players and prospects to organized baseball and to Canada and South America seemed to increase faster than they could be replaced. Dad had three advantages though. Players loved him because he was color-blind, fair and honest, and he never missed a payday, so when teams disbanded, unemployed players sought Dad out. Players too knew the advantages of Dad's connections in organized baseball. And the Clowns were still the best draw and could afford the best players.

Buster Haywood managed the east in the 1951 East-West All-Star game in Comiskey Park, Chicago. After the game, Dad, W. S. Martin of the Memphis Red Sox, Ed Gottlieb and Tom Baird left Comiskey Park together. Dad's money belt, tied beneath his pants, held the Clowns' cut of the gate. His briefcase contained business papers. Dad had plans if robbed. Plan A was to give robbers the briefcase and walk off into the sunset with the money belt full. Plan B was to give up the money belt and, if necessary, walk into the sunset pantless, but alive.

That was on paper. As the four owners walked down the block toward the parking lot, a man coming from the opposite direction pulled a gun and ordered them to give him their briefcases. Terribly frightened, and not knowing what the other three had in their grips, Dad laughed as if part of a joke between him and the gunman. "Right. You're IRS?" Dad asked. "Confiscating our records? Checking hotel receipts? J. Edgar Hoover, Jr., street auditor, right?" He laughed again, never breaking stride, and the others followed his lead, laughing and walking past the gunman. As the gunman turned toward them in disbelief, a police car rounded the corner in front of them, and the gunman ran off. "Dumbest thing I ever did," Dad told me years later. "I could have gotten us killed. Of course Tom, W. S. and Ed thought I was a courageous genius, and they didn't believe me when I told them how scared I was, said courage was acting to confront your fears anyway. I just didn't think to stop was all I did."

Dad confronted the coming 1952 season the same way. He walked right on toward it. He just didn't think to stop.

19

A Shortstop Named Henry

The approaching 1952 season presented more roster problems. The quality of the league and of the Clowns was diminishing rapidly.

The major off-season problem occurred in September 1951, when Dad sold the contracts of Sherwood Brewer and Len "Preacher" Williams to the Braves, leaving the Clowns without a shortstop. Dad thought first of Carl Dent, but, back from Canada, Dent had signed with Ed Gottlieb to play second for the Philadelphia Stars.

Reuben Williams was part of the solution. Growing up in Florida, Williams, who could play second and third as well as short, was a long-time teammate of Jim "Schoolboy" Tugerson. Tugerson recommended the young infielder, who was playing army ball at Fort Totten on Long Island, and Dad signed him.

The other part of the shortstop solution was a quiet, serious teenager playing for a men's semi-pro team in Mobile, Alabama. He had learned hitting by swinging a broomstick at flung bottle caps. Sam Hairston once said, good hitting depends on seeing the ball. A pitched ball is a whole lot easier to see than the sides of a speeding bottle cap.

Ed Scott had played a brief barnstorming tour in center field for Dad's 1939 Miami Ethiopian Clowns shortly after Dad bought out Hunter Campbell's interest and purchased the new school bus refitted with reclining seats. Then, Scott played for the Norfolk Stars, managed by Bunny Downs, until the Stars disbanded late during the 1940 season. After the demise of the Stars, Scott returned home to Mobile, Alabama, where he got a job, but continued to play baseball locally with the Mobile Black Cubans and the Mobile Black Bears.

By 1951, Scott managed the Mobile Black Bears. For years, Dad had booked the local Mobile teams for owner Willie Davis, who in turn, with Ed Scott, promoted the Clowns in Mobile each season. Before the 1951 season, Dad and Ed Scott reached an oral agreement for Scott to act as a bird-dog scout for the Clowns, to be paid a fixed commission whenever Dad sold a Scott-recommended player's contract to a team in organized baseball.

Over the years, Scott sent Dad some fine players, such as pitchers Percy Smith and Phil Laduna. But his first find was his best and earned him $250, his finest commission ever from Dad. Scott broke into scouting like no one else in baseball history.

During the summer of 1951, Scott phoned Dad and said, "I got a 16-year-old shortstop on the Bears can rip the hide off a baseball. He's not a great shortstop yet and he might be playing out of position, but he hits the ball like few I've ever seen."

When the Clowns played Mobile late in 1951, Bunny gave the high school youngster a pregame tryout and an employment application, then watched him play for the Black Bears against the Clowns and gave Dad a glowing report. Dad filed the report in his "players" folder in his file cabinet along with the completed employment application received from the youngster.

On the application, Henry Aaron reported his height at 5′6″ and his weight as 150. He claimed a .365 batting average for 1951, 20 stolen bases and "good" fielding ability. For "position or positions I play" he listed "Short Stop," then added, as an afterthought, in lighter-colored ink, "or Second Base." In response to inquiry as to off-season occupation, he crossed out his first response, "basketball," and answered "grocery store."

In September, when the contracts of both Clowns shortstops were sold, Dad reviewed the "shortstops" section of the "players" folder, noted that Aaron would turn 18 on February 13, 1952, and that Bunny's report was unusually favorable. Dad decided that Hank Aaron was going to have a chance to be the Clowns 1952 shortstop. On November 28, 1951, Dad wrote Aaron:

Yours received and herein enclosing contract for 1952 season with Clowns. Please sign same (in ink) under my name, and below your address have one or both of your parents sign their approval, and have two parties witness your signatures . . . returning said contract so same may be filed with our League office.

You will receive complete instructions for reporting to Spring Training camp along about the latter part of March or before, followed by transportation to reach camp when the time comes to report.

With kindest regards and best wishes, as well as assuring you of the complete support of our organization in helping you make good in your baseball career.

The contract called for a salary of $200 per month. Henry had written Dad on November 12 that his parents already approved of the Clowns. Now, he discussed the terms with his parents and Ed Scott. "Treat the Clowns like a minor league club," Scott told Henry, "a stop on your way to the big money—$5,000 a year in the majors!" On December 14, Dad wrote to Aaron acknowledging receipt of the signed contract.

On March 18, 1952, Dad, as he had done with so many players so many times over the years, sent the youngster the first of the rules of the road:

Will have ticket delivered to you, or message where to pick same up, with connection via rail arranged to get you into WINSTON-SALEM, N.C. either late Wednesday nite, Apr. 9 or before 9 a.m. Thursday morning, Apr. 10 . . . on which morning we commence training.

You will report to:
HOTEL STEVENS
526 East 4th Street
WINSTON-SALEM, N.C. (Phone 3-9545)

And look up Bus. Mgr. Bunny Downs and Mgr. Buster Haywood on arrival.

Rooms are reserved for your arrival in name of Clowns BBC. . . . your $2 meal expense money per day will commence on the morning after you report to "Bunny" Downs. We do not take care of taxis or meals enroute.

Limit yourself to one handbag . . . do not carry too much clothing . . . only essential items . . . and be sure to bring your own glove, shoes, sweatshirt and sweat sox. Complete uniform will be furnished you.

Ticket should be in your hands on or before April 7th.

Have your mail addressed to you, c/o Clowns, Box 64, Tarrytown, N.Y. Have persons writing you use airmail postage and letters will be forwarded promptly as they arrive here.

If there is any other information I may have overlooked please advise? Appreciate letter immediately acknowledging receipt of this notice, that all is okay, and that we can expect you to reach camp by the morning of April 10.

Aaron mailed back his acknowledgment and assurance dated March 24, 1952.

"I carried Henry down to the train station with his little old grip," Ed Scott recalled. "Took his picture outside the train station. Still have it in my scrapbook. He had his grip with his clothes, whatever Syd said to have and two sandwiches. I waved at him from the platform as the train pulled out for Winston-Salem. He waved back from the window with that shy smile of his."

"The Hotel Stevens in Winston-Salem, Professor, was not affiliated with the Hotel Stevens where we stayed in Chicago," Dad later told me. "It was up over a bar, a pool room, they say, and sure didn't have an elevator or sterling silver, but it was the best accommodation provided Negro League teams in that part of North Carolina. We trained four days there that year. I didn't know it then, but that was the longest spring training the Clowns would have the rest of the way. Played the Winston-Salem Pond Giants a couple exhibition games, then started our tour."

During his first spring training call to Dad, Bunny pointed out in passing that Henry Aaron did not own a dress suit, so Dad had Buster bring Henry to a men's store and buy him a suit from Buster's bank, which Dad had Bunny replenish from the first Pond Giants gate.

In 1963, Dad and I were at lunch with John Mullen of the Braves, and after Dad jokingly made an offer John turned down, Dad laughed and said, "Can you imagine, I signed Henry Aaron for $200 a month and a suit of clothes? And here you are turning down a million."

More than 30 years later, Buster Haywood said of Aaron's arrival, "God done sent me a miracle." Buster described Aaron as a quiet, humble man who just did his job.

> But his job included hitting, and that made Henry something special just doing his job. I didn't change a thing. You don't do nuttin', you don't even look close, you don't breath loud when a man's splattering hits against ball park walls and out into the streets. Bunny called Syd, said, "You got to come out to see Henry Aaron." First time Syd saw Henry, Henry doubled off the wall, and Syd had me tell him, "Henry, you're looking good, but when you're right-handed, you grip the bat with your left hand on bottom." He was leading the Clowns in hitting batting cross-handed, and I hadn't even noticed till Syd saw it.

After watching Aaron hit, Dad raised his salary from $200 to $250 per month without request.

Long after Aaron's playing career ended, Philadelphia journalist/video anchorman Malcolm Poindexter, who was a reporter for the *Philadelphia Inquirer* in 1952 and was the Clowns' public relations director from 1959 until Dad's retirement, wrote to me concerning a 1952 Clowns game he covered: "I remember the day your Dad pointed to one of the Clowns players and asked me what I thought of him. 'Pretty good,' I said. 'Pretty good,' he replied, 'he's Hank Aaron. Remember the name.'"

Ray Neil said, "Already in 1952, Hank Aaron was the best hitter I'd ever seen. He had more wrist strength and a quicker bat at age 18 than most great hitters in their primes."

Clowns outfielder Frank Ensley said, "Henry was so relaxed, he seemed to play without fire. You could fool him once, and next time he saw the pitch, he'd homer."

When the Clowns came to Tarrytown early in Aaron's Braves career, my friend Jay Cohen asked Clowns pitcher Frank Carswell what Aaron was like with the Clowns. "The man ate pork chops three meals a day, two for breakfast, two for lunch, three for dinner, and a spare time to time for a snack. We all called him Pork Chop. Had players thinking about strict pork chop diets so's they could hit like he could."

Fellow shortstop Reuben Williams recalls that in the field Aaron had problems in the hole.

Ray Neil was top-notch major league. He taught me more about base-ball than anyone in the game. Just watching him play was a lesson you couldn't get anywhere else if you paid tuition. Ray and I both worked every day showing Henry how to handle the hole. He had a way of go-ing down and doing a split and tossing weakly to first in between side-arm and underhand. The problem nagged him even with Eau Claire in the Braves organization. Neil and I finally corrected it when Henry came back to us at the end of '52 for our fall barnstorming tour.

But there was good news too about Aaron in the field. The May 17, 1952, *Chicago Defender* reported that

The Indianapolis Clowns turned in seven double plays against the Kansas City Monarchs at Nevada, Mo., last week. The Clowns won the exhibition game, 7-5.

The combination of Henry Aaron at shortstop, second baseman Ray Neil and first baseman Henry Merchant contributed five, while Merchant to Aaron to Merchant accounted for the other two.

The relaxation mistaken for lack of fire noted by Frank Ensley was an everlasting Aaron grace. When Dewey Griggs scouted Aaron for the Braves, he thought Aaron was lazy and couldn't throw, a thought he vocalized to Aaron between games of the doubleheader. "I been throwing just hard enough to get them out," Aaron told him, "I'll show you." He showed Griggs his true arm in the second game, rifling overhand bullets across the infield.

Sportswriter Jim Murray, noting Aaron's easy grace, later compared Aaron to Willie Mays by citing Aaron as a symphony to Mays' rock and roll tune.

Dad said retrospectively that the Clowns wondered how Aaron com-piled the stolen bases he did. "He ran so gracefully, with such long, loping strides—and we didn't time our runners, so I was amazed when Dewey Griggs clocked him and said he had one of the fastest times home to first he'd ever clocked. We knew Henry could hit and throw and field. We didn't know till then he could run."

Before Dad saw Aaron play for the first time, he wrote John Mullen a letter concerning other matters, then added, "P.S. We've got an 18-year-old shortstop batting cleanup for us." Intrigued, Mullen had Aaron scouted, but the initial report was unfavorable. Once Dad saw Aaron, Dad was insistent—the Braves had to re-scout Aaron. Dad granted Mullen's request for a 30-day re-scouting period, and assured Mullen he would not deal with another team during the 30 days.

The Cincinnati Reds sent a scout out to cover Aaron. The same man scouted Ernie Banks with the Monarchs the following year. His reports concluded that neither man would ever hit major league pitching. Dad sent letters touting Aaron to every major league team. Racial barriers in organized baseball, while weakened somewhat, still stood strong. They just weren't talked about so much. As a retired Henry Aaron later noted, more than half the Clowns players were far better than their major league counterparts making the big money. At the time, only six of the sixteen major league teams had ever had black players on their rosters. Former New York Cubans owner Alex Pompez, who had become a scout for the Giants, sent another scout to see Aaron. Aaron played with a cold following a long jump and a sleepless night on the bus, and went one for four. The Giants scout was unimpressed and reported that Aaron would never hit major league pitching.

Undaunted, Pompez had Aaron re-scouted.

Meantime, the Braves sent Dewey Griggs into Buffalo for a May 25 Clowns–Memphis Red Sox doubleheader. Mom and I sat with Griggs part of the time as he scouted, and Dad spent the twin-bill between the Clowns dugout and our seats. Aaron went seven for nine over the two games.

On May 28, 1952, Dad and Monarchs owner Tom Baird were rooming together in Chicago's Sherman Hotel, there for a Negro American League meeting, which is what Mom told John Schwartz, secretary of the New York Giants' farm clubs, when he phoned Dad in Tarrytown.

Schwartz called Dad in Chicago and offered $15,000 for Aaron's contract, $2,500 on league approval of the new contract, $2,500 if the player remained 60 days in the organization or with another organization to whom the Giants might transfer his contract, $2,500 if he went as high as AAA and remained for 30 days and $7,500 if he was retained in the major leagues for 30 days. They offered a salary of $250 per month for Aaron. Dad told Schwartz that Aaron was already making $250 per month with the Clowns, but Schwartz refused to offer more. Dad asked him to wire the offer.

As Dad and Tom were about to leave the room to pick up the Giants' telegram in the lobby, the phone rang. It was John Mullen of the Boston Braves.

"Syd. John Mullen. Sorry to bother you, but Villa gave me your number there. We had Aaron re-scouted. We want him."

"I think I just sold his contract to the Giants. Tom Baird and I were going to the lobby to get the telegram when you called."

"Doesn't your word mean anything, Syd? You gave us 30 days."

"Time ran out yesterday," Dad answered.

"Not the way I figure it. Besides, we need a shortstop. The Giants don't."

"How much?" Dad asked.

"Ten thousand, $2,500 now, $7,500 if he sticks with our organization 30 days."

"Giants offered $15,000."

"Ten," Mullen said.

"How much for Henry?" Dad asked.

"Two fifty a month."

"He gets that from me now. That's all the Giants will pay. Give Aaron $350 a month, you got him."

"Done," said Mullen.

"Done," said Dad. "Send me a telegram confirming." Mullen did.

Aaron stayed with the Clowns until June 15. When his contract was sold, he was leading the Negro American League in batting, runs, hits, doubles, home runs, runs batted in and total bases. He was third in stolen bases. His statistics dropped between the sale and the time he signed the Braves' contract.

Before he left the Clowns, Aaron refused for a time to sign the Braves' contract.

On May 29, 1952, Dad received a second telegram from John Schwartz of the Giants. It responded to Dad's wire the prior day about the Braves' offer: "Your wire received. Will make same deal as outlined in previous wire substituting . . . salary to Aaron to be three hundred fifty dollars per month. . . . Please confirm."

Dad informed Schwartz that he had already accepted the Braves' offer. Angry, Schwartz wrote Dad that he had his scout, Gene Thompson, speak with Aaron about why he refused their offer, only to find out Dad had never told Henry about the $250 per month. The scout told both Aaron and Buster Haywood that Dad had swollen the Giants' offer by stating that part of the payment would go to Aaron, a charge Schwartz later leveled at Dad. That Dad would not have used that as a negotiating tactic is obvious from the precedent such a technique would have set. Amounts paid for Negro league contracts were generally in the $1,000–$5,000 range. The Golden Age of the Negro leagues had ended years earlier. Of the six remaining Negro American League teams, four were losing money, and needed sales of player contracts to break even or better. The Clowns and Monarchs in 1952 made marginal profits, and relied on sales into organized baseball to make reasonable returns on investments. None could afford to give players part of the amounts paid for player contracts. The advantage to the players was moving into organized baseball, where real money could be made. Aside from Dad's inherent honesty, he would have been foolish to use such a promise even falsely to raise the offer. Losing his credibility with those in organized baseball would not be worth the few thousand dollars extra such a trick might have generated.

But Gene Thompson's conversation with Henry and Buster had done the damage. Henry was convinced that Dad sold him out, and he was determined not to sign with the Braves.

On June 3, 1952, Dad wrote a two-page letter to Mr. and Mrs. Herbert Aaron, Henry's parents. Referring to the deal with the Braves as one done quickly, he said that there was a ten-day report date, during which period Henry would be salaried by both the Clowns and the Braves. He then outlined his reasons for the sale to the Braves, not the Giants: (a) the Braves needed a shortstop; the Giants didn't; (b) the $100 per month salary differential; (c) Dad's closer affiliation with the Braves, which would permit more potent intervention in Aaron's behalf.

Dad did not point out that the Giants had offered Dad more than the Braves. He went on to state his opinion that Gene Thompson's discussion with Henry and Buster had their son confused. After citing the low figures organized baseball offered for Negro league contracts, Dad pointed out his investment and the costs and uncertainties of replacing Aaron, stating that "sometimes 4 or 5 [players] must be brought in and placed on salary before we find a capable replacement."

Quoting Bunny as saying that Mrs. Aaron advised Henry by phone not to sign with the Braves based on Henry's belief he should get a bonus for signing, Dad said that the Braves had been specific about disinterest in players seeking bonuses and that "bonuses are not paid Negro players. . . . Jackie Robinson, Sam Jethroe, Campanella, etc., got nothing for signing."

Reciting the vagaries of major league scouting reports and the slump Henry had gone into after the sale, Dad recommended that Aaron sign, indicating a reputation problem in organized baseball if he did not.

His parents and Ed Scott recommended that he sign, and he did.

Henry Aaron's first professional paycheck was for $22.75. It covered four days with the Clowns, with a gross pay of $33.25 and a half dollar deducted for Social Security, nothing deducted for withholding. There was an additional ten dollars deducted for five two-dollar daily advances, probably producing the miraculous change of daily peanut butter sandwiches into a few pork chops. During Aaron's stay with the Funmakers, Dad advanced an additional unallocated $35—$19 for a glove, $22 for shoes, $2 for sliding pads, $2 for a "jock-cup," and an additional $18.95 for shoes.

The payroll record is dramatic in its simplicity. It reads: "MAY 15 . . . $33.25; JUNE 1 . . . 80.00; JUNE 15 . . . 91.94;

SOLD TO BOSTON."

The Braves asked for Dad's patience in allowing time for them to meet some financial needs of their own, and, as he had done all his life whenever faced with similar requests, Dad agreed to wait for his money. On January 12, 1953, John Mullen wrote to Dad:

Enclosed is Boston Braves check #14715 in the amount of twenty-five hundred dollars payable to the Indianapolis Clowns which represents the final payment to you for the contract of player Henry Aaron.

May I thank you again for allowing us to spread the payments on this deal. By all accounts it appears that we have a fine prospect in

Aaron, and your cooperation throughout this transaction had been excellent.

Privately, Dad told all who would listen that Aaron would not only prove to be one of baseball's all-time greats, but would rank second only to Oscar Charleston among the greatest baseball players who ever lived.

During the summer of 1953, Dad and Jerry flew into Chicago for two days, then took the train to Cleveland for Clowns games against the Monarchs. Before the night game in Municipal Stadium in Cleveland, Jerry entered the Monarchs dugout for the starting lineup for Dad's scorebook. Jerry recalls:

Dad had me keep score so he had chance to talk to Buster, Bunny, King Tut and the players. He could look over my shoulder and check my scorekeeping whenever he wanted to keep track of the game.

Twelve of sixteen Major League teams scouted the Monarchs' shortstop, Ernie Banks, that night. Tom Baird wanted $20,000, but expected a top offer of $15,000. His plan, he said was "When I get a $15,000 offer, I'll counteroffer $25,000 and throw in our pitcher, Bill Dickey."

I felt funny taking Buck O'Neil's time just before a big game, and I felt skittish in the opposition dugout. So when Buck gave me the lineup slip, I was copying fast as I could.

Off to my right, I heard a voice, and the speaker was a white man, unusual in the Monarchs dugout, a New York Giants scout, tall and big, and he was talking to another scout. Looking toward the Clowns dugout, he said jokingly, "Oh, there's Syd Pollock. I don't like that guy. I scouted Henry Aaron, and we wanted him, but he let the Braves have him."

Aaron was Northern League 1952 rookie of the year, with a .336 average with Eau Claire in the Braves organization. In the spring of 1953, he was brought into Toledo, a Braves AAA American Association team under Paul Richards. In an intrasquad game, Aaron homered and doubled in two at bats and played flawlessly in the field. During the days that followed, he was benched, then told to sit in the stands and learn by observing. He phoned Dad and said he'd rather play in the Northern League than sit watching others in AAA, and Dad told John Mullen. Responding, Mullen sent Aaron down to Jacksonville, where Henry hit .362 and led the Sally League in batting average, doubles, runs, total bases and runs batted in. He was selected the league's Most Valuable Player. Still nursing inadequacies as an infielder, Aaron was sent to the Puerto Rican winter league, where, at Braves request, his manager, Mickey Owen, converted the mediocre shortstop into a very good outfielder, clearly capable of the excellence he later attained in right field. During the spring of 1954, outfielder Bobby Thomson broke his ankle, and Aaron was brought up as a starter with the Braves.

The rest of the story, of course, is history.

In addition to signing Aaron, other roster changes were necessary for the 1952 season if the Clowns were to defend their NAL title successfully. Late in 1951, Dad signed Ted Richardson, a small left-handed fastballer from Orlando, Florida. He led Clowns hurlers from the left side as Fireball Cohen led them from the right through the 1952 season.

During the off-season, Dad signed fleet-footed outfielders Jimmy Wilkes, released from the Dodgers organization, and pitcher Jimmy Jenkins. Wilkes, a talented veteran, had been leadoff man for the 1946 Negro National League champion Newark Eagles, and his speed and bat control fit Clowns philosophy gracefully. Julio Toledo, a lanky Cuban from Havana, basically held the first base job for the 1952 and 1953 seasons, allowing Speed Merchant to return to the outfield.

Other players appearing with the Clowns at various times during the 1952 season included infielders Armando Vasquez and Andy Watts, outfielder Dewitt Smallwood, and pitchers Willie Collins, Clarence Turner, Percy Smith and Elzie Todd.

Ben Kerner, owner of the NBA's St. Louis Hawks, promoted Clowns games at Offerman Stadium in Buffalo in those days, and crowd sizes there were impressive. For awhile, in 1951, Dad thought of shifting the name of the team to Buffalo, and the team was briefly publicized as the Buffalo-Indianapolis Clowns. During the 1952 season, the Clowns played six dates in Buffalo and only four in Indianapolis, and Buffalo was a pivotal city for the Funmakers that season. Not only was Aaron scouted there, but the Clowns won a round-robin trophy in Offerman Stadium, and in a late season game there, Curtis Hardaway hit a colossal home run that left the deepest part of the park above a light tower. Later Ed Hamman joked that when the ball came down, it had snow on it. Dad and Bunny agreed that it was the kind of home runs that Josh Gibson hit "when he really hit 'em." It remains the longest ball I ever saw hit.

During an interview in Omaha, Nebraska, that August, Tom Baird, always an owner of the Kansas City Monarchs and sole owner after J. L. Wilkinson retired following the 1947 season, provided context for the status of black baseball with comments on the current Negro American League, the Dodgers' signing of Jackie Robinson and the greatness of Monarchs' pitcher Bullet Rogan. The *World Herald* reported the interview:

"We have had many changes in the almost 33 years of Negro ball," Mr. Baird said here Saturday. "Our league has been cut to six teams through the raids of major and minor league ball, and we have been forced to hit the road for more one-night stands. Our salary scale now is slightly above that of Class A.

"However, I can see definite financial hope for Negro American League teams through the dropping of racial barriers. More Negro youngsters than ever before are taking up the game and trying out for our teams. We can make money by selling these players to the majors."

Kansas City, Indianapolis, Memphis, Birmingham, Chicago and Philadelphia are the only teams remaining in the Negro American League. The Baltimore Elite Giants were forced to combine with Birmingham after last year.

Long regarded as a friend of the Negro, Mr. Baird said the Jackie Robinson incident brought him into temporary disfavor with patrons in Kansas City.

Robinson, fans will recall, was signed by Branch Rickey of the

Brooklyn Dodgers for delivery to Montreal in 1946. Jackie went on to Brooklyn in 1947 and has been a star there ever since. "Many Negroes thought I was trying to keep Jackie from getting his chance in organized ball," Tom recalled. "That is untrue, because I got him a trial with the Boston Red Sox before Brooklyn ever entered the picture.

"Rickey never even gave me the courtesy of a call concerning Robinson. When told by the Associated Press that Jackie had been taken by Brooklyn, I made some strong statements. I was not misquoted, but the facts were distorted in some stories. I said then and I repeat now that we should have been paid for Jackie and that I should have been consulted by Rickey before he was signed. Other major league teams paid for Negro players."

The Monarchs, founded in 1920, and the Clowns, tracing their origins to 1929, fought again in 1952 for the Negro American League Championship, and Dad and Tom Baird, the closest of friends, were once again rivals, their rivalry reflected by managers Buck O'Neil of the Monarchs and Buster Haywood of the Clowns: ethical, clean-cut leaders, respecting each other, but both with the fire and will to win.

In July, Buffalo hosted a Negro American League Round Robin tournament, a single elimination affair, held only that year. The Clowns won the tournament, behind Frank Carswell's 1-0 shutout over the Philadelphia Stars and Jim Cohen's 5-2 win in the title game over the Chicago American Giants, who had eliminated the Kansas City Monarchs. The Clowns received a trophy for winning the tournament.

The season ended with the Clowns third straight Negro American League championship. While individual statistics have not been found for that year, Speed Merchant again led the league in stolen bases, and Julio Toledo reportedly led the league in batting.

After the season ended, but before their traditional fall barnstorming tour, the Clowns won seven of twelve games from the Birmingham Black Barons in a tour called the Negro World Series, wrapping up for the Clowns every 1952 Negro American League championship available: the first half, the second half, the Round Robin and the World Series.

20

Toni Stone

During the off-season Andy Watts, both Tugerson brothers, Jimmy Wilkes and Jimmy Jenkins either entered organized baseball or contracted to play in Canada or Latin America.

For 1953, Dad signed shortstop Willie Brown, outfielder Richard Hairston and pitcher–utility man Rufus McNeal. Dad bought outfielder Frank Ensley's contract from the Monarchs, and he joined Drake and Merchant to form another sterling outfield.

That year, the Clowns carried their largest roster ever. But their chance for a fourth straight Negro American League title in 1953 might have retired with Jim "Fireball" Cohen. The loss of Cohen and the Tugersons crippled the pitching staff. To help shore it up, Dad signed Cuban rookie Dionisio Amaro and brought back former Clowns Ray Maddix and Angel Garcia. A fastballing left-hander in his prime, Garcia returned in 1953 as a junkballer whose arm was shot. First time through the league, he had everyone off-stride, swinging early. Second time through they timed him so well, Dad reacquainted Angel with Havana mid-season; his career was over.

Dad secured tough right-hander Willie Gaines from the Philadelphia Stars when the Stars went out of existence after the 1952 season. Ed Gottlieb had realized he didn't particularly need the club's negative cash flow to offset gains his Warriors were netting in the NBA.

The Chicago American Giants permanently adjourned too after the 1952 season, and, in 1953, the league went forward with the force of a tightly spinning hurricane with only four teams—the Clowns, the Monarchs, the Memphis Red Sox and the Birmingham Black Barons. Propelling the force from its eye were Dad and Toni Stone.

Toni Stone was the first woman in any sport to compete on a men's major league team. She played the first three innings at second each game for the 1953 Indianapolis Clowns.

She could run the hundred yard dash in 11 seconds flat, and look as soft and feminine as any woman alive doing it. She traveled with 21–25 lonely men from March through October and was faithful to her husband.

Black bus leaguers had special problems, especially in the South or in rural northern areas. There was no bathroom on the bus. Long jumps were a way of life and were hard enough on kidneys, but when colored-only bathrooms were few and far between, the degree of difficulty became painful. A woodsy bend in the road generally provided cover for team relief. Players lined up facing the side of the bus, dreading sudden headlights in peripheral vision.

Mother once told me that her loneliest moments were after we were grown and she was alone at Mass, and I've often wondered about the loneliness of Toni Stone in the woods in the night by herself while her teammates lined up at the bus during a Clowns rest stop.

She was to male baseballers what Jackie Robinson was to white baseballers. Most men resented her success, but loved to watch her play. She dressed in hotels or umpire's dressing rooms. She sought no favoritism, and received none. Men came at her hard to break up double plays. They slid spikes up when she made the tag. She wanted action and she got it. But as Joyce Hamman said, "Toni Stone was a very brave soul. She was always a lady, playing or not, and off the field all treated her like a lady. On the field, she was first a ballplayer, then a lady, and all treated her like a ballplayer."

She heard the worst language, and, if it was directed at her, hurled it back. She played the game with every bit of love she felt for it, and played it with an intensity that presaged the hustle of Pete Rose. She launched her body at men to break up double plays. She slid spikes up. After her errors, she returned to the dugout and threw her glove off the wall onto the bench. A Toni Stone strikeout on a called third strike was as exciting as a Ted Williams homer. Amazingly, the phrase "in your face" was not invented in 1953 to describe Toni after a called third strike. Immediately after the call, her visitation with the plate umpire was like no one else's. Her bat already thrown to the ground like a Johnnie Britton wig, her face inches from the umpire's or pressed against his mask, her head bobbing with anger and agony, she screamed her thoughts on his call, his ancestry, his body parts and the amazing things she strongly suggested he do with his body parts. Crowds roared.

Toni Stone and Dad were destined for each other. Both did what they loved, and nothing and nobody interfered. Dad worked 18-hour days, immersed in the game. Toni Stone traveled and practiced and played 18-hour days, immersed in the game. They were two lifetime lines heading to intersect.

Every man who played baseball stayed in shape to play baseball. Often even today, after a car ride of 150–550 miles, I think of how it would feel to get out of the car and play professional baseball against top competition. Negro leaguers did it out of a bus, and it took a special kind of conditioning to do that day after day after day, sometimes more than once in a day, without off days, in different settings each time. Toni Stone did it too, and she didn't have menstrual time-outs and she had no supportive female camaraderie. Fans were there to see her, and she played no matter how she felt. I suppose the number of women who could travel and play like that, discriminated against on the basis of race and sex the whole time, would be few. And to do it with the energy and intensity of Toni Stone evidenced the power and beauty of the human spirit and made me proud to know her.

Born Marcenia L. Stone in West Virginia on July 17, 1931, Toni moved with her parents to Minneapolis toward the start of World War II. Boykin Stone, her father, had a job there giving checks to military veterans. Her parents often took her to Midway Field, then St. Paul Stadium, to see black baseball, and Toni fell in love with Showboat Thomas, King Tut and the Clowns. She thrilled to more than one Satchel Paige–Peanuts Davis pitching duel, and, after one game in 1943 or 1944, approached Bunny Downs near the Clowns dugout.

"Mr. Downs, I'm a ballplayer."

"Good for a girl, are you?" Bunny asked.

"Good for anybody. Want to try me out and sign me? The Clowns come first with me, so you have first chance."

Tilting his fedora back on his head, Bunny said, "Tell you what. You're mighty young just yet. You got to finish school. You finish school, and you feel ready, you come back. Ask for Bunny Downs, and we'll sign you."

"See you," Toni said.

Her father early noticed her fine coordination and encouraged her to participate in sports. Toni starred in girls' track, swimming and baseball, but baseball was her love and focus. At 15, she left a girls' softball team and joined a boys' baseball team. Then Gabby Street, manager of the Saints in the American Association and former St. Louis Cardinals player and manager, held a baseball clinic in St. Paul Stadium. Toni showed up, and Street told her it was a boys-only clinic, but she refused to leave. She warmed up after he chased her and tried to bat after he chased her again. Street must have thought she was identical quintuplets. She was everywhere he looked. Partway through the clinic, after he had ejected Toni from the stadium, he heard a solid crack of the bat, followed the path of the ball and watched as Toni leaped high behind second to spear a hot liner backhanded. He invited her to participate in the rest of the clinic, after which he encouraged her to pursue a baseball career.

She played for the Wall Post #435 American Legion boys' team from 1943 to 1945.

Her family moved to Oakland, California, and she played there in 1947 with the San Francisco Sea Lions, a strong semi-pro men's club, famous for producing Bill Bruton, who went on to play center field for the Boston Braves.

From 1948 to 1950, she played for the New Orleans Creoles, a men's team considered a Negro leagues minor league club without affiliation. The Clowns visited New Orleans most seasons to face the Creoles. They did so in 1950, and Bunny Downs was impressed with Toni. After the game, she approached Bunny for the second time in her life.

"Well, I graduated high school," she said, "and you had to be pleased with what you saw of me out there, weren't you?"

"Sure was," said Bunny, his toothpick bobbing as he spoke.

"Then, you gonna sign me like you promised?"

"Damn!" said Bunny, "You're the little girl from Minneapolis, ain't you?"

"Sure am. Now you gonna sign me or not?"

"Got to speak to Syd Pollock. It's his club. His decision."

Bunny mentioned Toni to Dad. Bunny also helped Toni draft a letter to the All-American Girls' Professional Baseball League, but she never got chance to play there. Ironically, the "League of Their Own" was just that— racially segregated. Toni's whole life was something like waiting for American society to call a third strike. She was already black. She was already a woman.

After the 1952 season, Dad felt Clowns crowds would get the team through more years of good baseball, but the league was down to four teams, and attendances were diminishing rapidly for the rest of the league, even the Monarchs. He could not envision the league surviving the season, absent a boost in attendances. He thought of the early 1920s when he booked Maggie Riley and her male Devil Dogs. He remembered the female player Bunny had mentioned.

Toni had married Aurelious Alberga, born in 1885, and a pioneer himself. He was reportedly one of the first black officers in the post-Reconstruction U.S. Army.

Dad's analysis was that no one, man or woman, was good enough to re-place Ray Neil at second for the Clowns. Toni Stone was a good female player though, worthy of a chance to play top-level baseball with men, and certainly flashy and fiery enough to draw fans and hold their interest. It would do black baseball no good to draw fans, then disappoint them. Bunny assured Dad that Toni played the game intensely. Dad decided to have Buster put Ray Neil in left for three innings each game to keep his bat in the lineup while Toni played second.

"We can't sign a player named Marcenia Lyle Alberga or Mrs. Aurelious Al-berga. Her name needs to be short and easy for fans to say and remember," Dad said.

It was our biggest name search since the dubbing of Ralph Bell as Spec Bebop. Dad finally settled on Toni, from the then-current popularity of Toni Home Permanents for the hair, and combined it with Marcenia's maiden name, and she became Toni Stone. She approved. Her husband consented to both her new career and her on-field name.

Advertising her salary at $12,000 a season, which would place her ahead of most major leaguers on the pay scale, Dad signed her for $300 a month, then raised her to $350, then $400, which made her one of the highest paid Clowns players.

Buster Haywood well remembers 1953 spring training for the Clowns: "We stayed at Bishop Plummer's about ten miles outside Portsmouth. He was minister at my church. There was an old diamond near his place. I played there against Buck Leonard and Skinny Barnhill as a semi-pro back before I joined the Birmingham Black Barons. We trained two days. We opened against the Norfolk Palms in Norfolk. Day after that we faced the Portsmouth Merrimacs in Portsmouth. Wish we'd have had more time before Portsmouth. Wish I hadn't had a woman on second for a game like that. Right in my home town too."

TWA flew Toni into Washington, D.C., where the Clowns' bus picked her up and took her to Bishop Plummer's.

Three days later, she walked her first plate appearance in Norfolk, and singled home two runs her second.

The day after that, on April 18, 1953, the Indianapolis Clowns and Portsmouth Merrimacs met at Portsmouth Stadium, marking the first time in history that a black professional team ever played a white professional team in the State of Virginia, although the Merrimacs had recently integrated. Toni Stone played the late innings at second for the Clowns. Following their own spring training, the Merrimacs had fashioned an excellent record, winning a number of games against other minor league clubs and regional teams, scoring 17 runs against the Little Creek Amphibs in their immediately preceding game. The Clowns were 1-0 following their two-day spring training.

The game would typify the 1953 Clowns season. Leading 5-3, they gave up eight runs in the bottom of the fifth, and lost 11-8 before a paid attendance of 5,486. Toni Stone was 0 for 1 at bat. While her fielding for the game was not reported beyond the fact that she participated in a double play, the Clowns made six errors.

The following week in Elizabeth City, North Carolina, against locals,

Toni walked, singled, batted in two runs and scored two. Against the Norfolk Royals in Windsor, North Carolina, she drove in two runs with a first-inning single, scored three runs, and handled five chances in the field without an error. Later the same week, Dionisio Amaro, Willie Gaines and Angel Garcia combined for a one-hitter in a 2-1 win over the Newport News Royals, and Toni slipped behind a runner for a pickoff, tagging him out herself during the rundown.

In July, Bert Nunez of the Monarchs tossed a one-hitter at the Clowns in a 4-0 Monarchs' win, a rain-shortened five-inning affair in Muskegon, Michigan. Toni Stone's single was the Clowns' lone hit.

Teammates gave Toni mixed reviews.

Frank Ensley said, "Toni was great for a female. She had lots of desire. Gave 100 percent. She was flashy, and that was her strength for the Clowns."

Rufus McNeal felt that "Toni hurt us and helped us. She took up a roster spot. She put fans in the stands."

According to Gordon Hopkins, "Willie Brown I think it was on third, took his time getting a routine grounder over to Toni at second. Or let's say the ball was slow coming out of his glove and made it real close at second for the double play. After the game, Bunny told Chauf, 'Don't start this bus.' Bunny stood in the front of the bus facing us in our seats, all of us showered, clean and quiet. Bunny said, 'Ain't no need to naming names. We all know what happened. This lady's putting money in our pockets. We don't want her hurt turning double plays. You men all expendable. She ain't. 'Nuff said?' We took his meaning, and took great care, then on, to protect her."

Toni's presence widened the Buster Haywood–Bunny Downs rift to an impassable chasm, one that finished Buster's Clowns career at season's end. More than 40 years later, Buster recalled:

> I disliked Toni Stone as a player. She couldn't play. She couldn't catch a damn pop-up, and that's why Syd got rid of her. It upset me no end to play her. She drew well for us one year, and that was it. Tut too. He told Toni, "Shit, woman. You can't play no ball. You ought to be home washing dishes." Tut wanted to win more than any man I ever knew.

She'd swear right back at Tut, but he'd walk off and do his act. She couldn't field grounders to her right. She'd make an error, come in and slam her glove down in the dugout. It gave me headaches. I about had a heart attack.

Worse, according to Ray Neil, Tut ribbed Buster about how Buster felt: "We'd have bases loaded during Toni's mandatory innings. Toni coming to the plate. Tut would holler over to Buster, 'Shit, Skip. What you batting her for? We got bases loaded. Pinch hit for her, Skip. Pinch hit.' Tut flashing that gold tooth laughing, and Buster seething at Tut and Bunny, knowing he got to keep her in there for business reasons."

The three Martin brothers were born and raised in Memphis early in the twentieth century. They were black. Dr. W. S. Martin was a world-renowned surgeon, often visiting Europe to consult or to lecture. He built his own hospital in Memphis. Dr. B. B. Martin was a dentist, with a dental clinic in Memphis. Dr. J. B. Martin went north to Chicago where he enjoyed a successful, lifelong political career. Dr. W. S. Martin owned the Memphis Red Sox and built Martin Stadium in Memphis, by 1953 the only home stadium owned by a Negro American League team. Dr. J. B. was president of the Negro American League. Dr. B. B. was a Memphis Red Sox officer and league vice president.

When I attended the 1953 Negro American League mid-season meeting with Dad at Chicago's Stevens Hotel, all three Martins were there, along with William "Soo" Bridgeforth, then owner of the Birmingham Black Barons, and Tom Baird, representing the Monarchs.

The subject of Toni Stone arose, and the exchange was heated. Dad complained that pitchers were throwing her curves, sliders, knucklers, spitters, screwballs, drops and change-ups.

"She's a woman," Dad said, "but she's capable. Just have your pitchers throw her fastballs only. And the other thing is, they shouldn't brush her back."

"Just fastballs?" Bridgeforth asked. "You try telling a man to throw just fastballs so fans can watch a woman hit him."

"Syd, you're messing with the integrity of the game," Tom said.

"She can't hit everything, she shouldn't play," said W. S.

"Look," said Dad, "so your ace throws his arsenal at Toni. What's it prove? He can make a woman look bad at the plate? So what? He makes her look bad, the fans won't come back. Then you can't afford your teams. The league dies, and all these great pitchers got no place to pitch."

"Syd," J. B. said. "You can't ask players to give less than their best. Tom's right. There's integrity. We can't have a league rule says a man can't throw nothing but fast balls to one person singled out."

"Especially when pitchers have major league scouts watching them," B. B. pointed out.

"The Clowns have an advantage with a player getting nothing but straight pitches," Bridgeforth said.

Dad replied, "Would you rather your pitchers face Frank Ensley and Ray Neil back to back or Toni and Neil? Would you rather have Toni at second three innings or Ray Neil all game? I'm benching one of the league's best outfielders and putting the best second baseman in baseball in left three innings so we can all make some money. Tell the scouts your man's throwing just fast balls to give the lady a break." The league voted unofficially to throw hard but straight to Toni Stone.

"Now we have the matter of brushing her back," Dad said. "There's no Smokey Joe or Satchel or Bullet Rogan in this league today. These guys now throw at her head, they may not have the control to miss. They hit her in the head, we lose our meal ticket." And the league voted unofficially not to brush Toni back.

The degree of adherence to unofficial league policy remains uncertain. We attended subsequent games and saw Toni get the same rotation of pitches as anyone else, and, while she was never injured by a pitch, we saw her hit the dirt more than once later that season, and the glare she gave pitchers after near-beanings was worth the price of admission.

That summer, on the day Angel Garcia showed me how to throw a curveball, I nearly died for Toni Stone. The night before, the Clowns played Toledo, where Dad and I had lemonade and stayed with the Powells. We rode the Clowns bus into Michigan for games in Monroe, Detroit, then Saginaw.

At 12, I had a mighty crush on Toni Stone, and I wanted to show her that we had baseball in common and that I was Tarrytown's finest center fielder. After clearing it with Buster, Dad said I could take fielding practice with the Clowns during batting practice. He was unaware of the sexual nuances involved in my request to take the field and that it was my chance to show off for Toni as well as to catch a few next to my idol, Verdes Drake.

The Monroe groundskeeper had lined the field and watered it down prior to our arrival two hours before game time so that when the Clowns checked in, the field was essentially ready. Only the batter's box and infield needed to be smoothed before the game. At that park, the water sprinklers had to be manually removed following use, and the groundskeeper overlooked one in shallow center field. None of us saw it either.

Like Don and Jerry before me, I'd warmed up with Clowns players, even fielded in non-comedy pregame pepperball, but I had no idea about the velocity of a ball headed at me off a pro's bat. The first hit my way was a solid liner up the middle. Drake let me call him off, and as I came in on it, the ball slapped off the sprinkler head and knocked off my cap and grazed my hair as I ducked and it passed me like a Ted Richardson fastball. Later, as Angel Garcia taught me the curve in front of the Clowns' dugout, Toni, walking past, told me, "Little Syd, sometimes it's safer on the mound than out in center," and I knew that while the sprinkler had spared my life, it had killed any chance Toni Stone would squeeze me to her bosom for courage under fire in the outfield.

Toni's 1953 overall batting average, counting games against locals, exceeded her official Negro American League average, which was .243. Officially, according to league statistics, she had 18 singles and a double in 74 at bats, with four runs scored, two walks, a stolen base and three RBIs. She struck out seven times. She was last in the league in fielding percentage at second base with an .852 mark on 29 assists, 23 putouts and nine errors.

Those were the numbers, but the numbers don't convey her zest for the game; the clouds of dust enfolding her slides; her grunts, audible to the stands, as base runners slammed her out of double plays or she did the same to others when she was on base; the sweat on her face as she took her lead dancing back and forth to aggravate the pitcher; her dives sliding along the ground after grounders up the middle; her smile and the wave of her cap from first to ovations after her singles; her rhubarbs with umpires; her leaps in the air for liners; and crowd excitement. It was electric every time she hit the ball or handled it in the field, whether she struck out swinging or look-ing, and even when she missed making a spectacular catch or a stop in her own reckless style. Crowds roared when she knocked the clay from her spikes with her bat at the plate, when she hollered defiance at opposing pitchers. Statistics don't describe the joyous laughter or tears of pride of the women in Clowns crowds that year, screaming with arms extended over their heads in adoration. The numbers don't tell how Toni Stone rode America sitting with her teammates, another of the early '50s Indianapolis Clowns, but built differently—a lady respected as a baseball player by her fellow travelers.

The Clowns drew more fans in 1953 than any black team, including the Clowns, ever drew in any other single season. Toni Stone had probably de-layed the death of the Negro American League by a season and a half.

Those last days of black baseball encased Negro leaguers in a diamond-shaped limbo. The Negro leaguers of the early '50s are not honored as their predecessors because many historians do not consider the Negro American League a major league after 1950, and because ongoing discrimination and quotas within organized baseball and continuing social pressures and ha-treds kept the early '50s Negro leaguers from entering organized baseball or from advancing once they got there. The early '50s Negro leaguers were overshadowed too by blacks in the majors. Often when I think of 1953, I think of the Monarchs' infield of Hank Bayliss on third, Sherwood Brewer on second, Francisco Herrera at first and Ernie Banks at short. Herrera be-came first baseman for the Phillies, and in mid-season 1953, Ernie Banks went directly from the Monarchs to the Cubs, and sometimes when I think of 1953, I wonder where Francisco Herrera and Ernie Banks would have ended up had the Negro American League folded in May for want of Toni Stone.

On May 24, 1953, the Clowns and Monarchs played their league opener at Blues Stadium, Kansas City, Kansas, before a paid attendance of 18,205. More than 300 people participated in 45 minutes of pregame festivities sponsored by the Monarchs Booster Club. There were bands, majorettes and other marching units. There were floats and bathing beauties. Guest dignitary James Cowan of Wichita tossed the first ball, as principal R. T. Coles of Kansas City Vocational High School batted, and Dad caught, a moment certainly cherished for its comedy by Buster Haywood and Tut. In the remaining photo of Toni Stone batting in that game, Tom Baird appears in the background on the steps of the Monarchs dugout. It was the first he'd seen her hit. In another hint of things to come, the Monarchs won 8-5. The Clowns left the bases loaded in the top of the ninth.

The crowds appeared all season long. There were more than 12,000 paid in Philadelphia. The Clowns and Monarchs split four games in back-to-back doubleheaders at Comiskey Park, Chicago, before 14,208 the first day and 6,236 the second. More than 11,000 paid watched the Clowns beat the Birmingham Black Barons 4-3 in Griffith Stadium, Washington. In Baltimore, Negro leaguers played in Westport Stadium, a race-car track converted for baseball use on an ad hoc basis. My recollection is that the stands sat about 4,500 people for baseball. On July 17, 1953, a crowd of 7,345 packed the stands there and spilled over between stands and foul lines and even into the outfield for a 4-3 Clowns loss to the Birmingham Black Barons, and it reminded Dad of the overflow crowds the Miami Ethiopian Clowns drew years before to Dorsey Park, Miami. The paid attendance for the Clowns-Monarchs doubleheader in Detroit that summer was 21,303.

Going into the Detroit games, the Monarchs had pounded Clowns pitching all season in rally after rally. The Clowns had pounded Monarchs pitching too, but Clowns hits were spread out, and almost every series strongly favored the Monarchs. The teams toured together weeks at a time.

Before the Detroit doubleheader that summer, Dad, Tom Baird and I ate in our favorite Chinese restaurant in downtown Detroit, and Dad told Tom, "I hope we take you at least one today. We get these big crowds here and lost last year in that four-team doubleheader. We lose two today, we likely lose fans."

The Clowns dropped the opener, but had a two-run lead going into the bottom of the ninth of the nightcap, when the Monarchs loaded the bases with two outs. Ernie Banks came to the plate.

Dad dumped his curving ash and lit a new cigarette from the old. He doodled nervously at the top of the page in the scorebook in his lap. He slid his black fedora back on his head and squinted toward the plate. Banks stepped into the batter's box and took the first pitch—ball one. As he stepped into the second pitch, I noticed movement in center field, and saw Verdes Drake turn and run top speed toward the left-center-field wall. The wall became screen a few feet off the ground. The sharp crack of the bat followed instantaneously, and still Drake ran, not looking back until he was perhaps ten feet from the wall, and when he looked, he did not break stride. He ran up the wall and the screen fluidly to a height that made return to earth risky as a spaceflight splashdown, and he stretched as he did, and, at the height of his climbing leap, the ball bounded off the screen less than two inches above his glove. The Clowns lost by a run.

To Tut it was an inverse "Casey at the Bat." Detroit became joyless.

"Almost like the one Drakey caught off Hank Thompson in St. Louis years ago," Dad said to Tut, but Tut was silent, barely nodding, and I remember him staring blankly out the bus window next day, speaking only when spoken to all the way into Saginaw, or mumbling, "Sorriest damn bunch I ever rode with."

In early June 1953, black weeklies reported that

> Manager Buster Haywood was a bit worried about the club's batting slump in early stages of the campaign this year. At the start of the NAL pennant chase the Funmakers dropped five consecutive close games to the Monarchs, but recently have snapped out of it as witnessed by their 8-6 win over Kansas City at the Monarchs' home field, and a 9-4 triumph over the same club that night.
>
> Haywood said, "I know I had the hitters, but felt a bit worried when they were leaving as many runners stranded on base when a hit would have meant a victory."

The Monarchs won the first half of the split season. For a while, the Clowns and Black Barons were tied or switching second-half leadership. But pitching and timely hitting faltered and injuries struck.

During 1953, the Clowns consistently carried an eight-man pitching staff, unusually large for a traveling team. Percy Smith, Clarence Turner, Frank Carswell, Willie Gaines, Ray Maddix, Dionisio Amaro, Angel Garcia and Ted Richardson were all starting pitchers. Other players too filled in on the mound, such as Speed Merchant. Rufus McNeal, more a pitcher than a utility man, replaced Angel Garcia in the starting rotation when Dad released Garcia near mid-season.

The Clowns' mound problems were typified by the year of the Clowns ace lefthander, Ted Richardson. An all-star the previous three seasons, he dropped to 6-8 but still led the Clowns pitching staff with a 4.05 ERA.

Speed Merchant personified other Clowns' problems that season. Hitting .348 in 1951, he dropped to .287 in 1952 and slumped to .258 in 1953. His 1953 league play shortened by injury, he stole only five bases, not only failing to challenge for the league lead, but finishing fourth among Clowns base runners.

Bad luck also plagued the Clowns. During their late-July– early-August challenge for the second-half lead, the Clowns took five of eight from the Black Barons, but then Verdes Drake broke his arm in Washington and Percy Smith injured his knee sliding into second base on a double off the right-field wall in Philadelphia. Within a week of those injuries, Merchant was sidelined with a wrenched knee, and Ted Richardson fractured an ankle.

Ray Neil led the league in batting for the season with a .397 average, 50 points higher than Ernie Banks, who finished second at .347. Neil also led the NAL in hits and doubles and was second in total bases and stolen bases. Verdes Drake, as usual, led league outfielders in putouts with 151. Next closest was Duke Henderson of the Monarchs with 124, then Frank Ensley with 114. Drake also led the league in RBIs that season and was second to Frank Ensley in outfielder assists.

But the Monarchs won both halves of the season, and the Clowns finished third.

21

Charlie, Connie and Peanut

The upcoming 1954 season presented a new assortment of problems. Buster Haywood had signed to manage the Memphis Red Sox, where men were men and women were spectators. To replace him, Dad hired the man he considered the greatest baseball player who ever lived, Oscar Charleston. He had last managed the 1952 Philadelphia Stars during their farewell season, spending an interim year retired in Philadelphia, living not far from 1954 Clowns second basewoman Connie Morgan.

"Oscar Charleston was my mentor," Connie said. "Once the Clowns hired me and hired him, he took me off-season and taught me all he could about sliding and running the bases and, when it warmed a touch, hitting and fielding. He was a strict manager, not so you couldn't have fun, but stern enough so you knew to get down to business. He had us self-disciplined. Didn't talk much about the old days. He was interested in winning here and now."

Pitcher Mamie Johnson, the Clowns other female player, recalled that "with Oscar Charleston, you either played ball or you went home."

Charleston's career was summarized in the Clowns' 1954 program:

Oscar Charleston, manager of the nationally famous Indianapolis Clowns . . . has compiled one of the greatest records in baseball, and is well known to old timers as one of the game's greatest natural athletes.

Oscar first broke into baseball while with the 24th Infantry in 1912. Then for a short period in a Manila league, he longed for his home at Indianapolis and hastened there to join the noted ABC's. Still in the rookie stage, Charleston was paid only $50 per month. To show how rapidly he became established as a future star, his salary was upped to $350 the following year.

Charleston switched to the great Lincoln Giants of New York City that same season, and in following years played with such teams as the Pittsburgh Crawfords, St. Louis Stars, Hilldale and Homestead Grays.

A demon on the base paths, he was equally renowned for his tremendous hitting and fielding. As a rookie fielder, he set a Cuban Winter League record, winding up the 1921–22 season with a .960 percentage, and a batting mark of .405 that same year proved tops in the loop.

Of Charleston's speed afoot, one observer exclaimed, "He's so fast, he makes Ty Cobb look like Ham Hyatt." The latter had firmly established himself as one of the slowest runners of the day in the majors.

At bat, Oscar kept opposing pitchers on edge. He possessed an uncanny way of anticipating pitches and meeting them squarely. At bunts, especially the swinging sacrifice, he was a master. On occasion, he would tip off the opposition and smilingly outleg them to first. For those who howled for the long ball, Charleston had that too.

Once in Holland, Pa., a fan approached him before game time and predicted that he'd blast no less than four homers that day. Two promptly landed in the left center field bleachers and two others followed but were foul by inches. However, the fan was satisfied, settling for the pair. This was in 1924 and Charleston, then at the peak of his career, was thinking seriously of accepting a manager's job. His accomplishments became a matter of record and he'd gone as far as he could as a Negro. The majors wouldn't accept him, even though John McGraw watched Charleston play many games and expressed the wish and desire that he would live to see the day when such a player would be given the chance to play in any league.

Probably the closest he got to a major league team was as a member of the St. Louis Stars, who scheduled a five-game series with the Cardinals in 1921. The Cards won three out of the five, but Charleston received a great degree of satisfaction by belting five homers and putting up a tremendous show on defense against the major leaguers.

Remembered by most as a brilliant center fielder, there is no position on the diamond that Oscar didn't play at one time or another. While with the Toledo Crawfords of the Negro American League of 1939, he was billed as the "62-year-old player who knew all nine positions." And so he did. Fans packed the ball park to watch him start the game on the mound, move behind the plate and then make a complete tour of the infield and outfield positions.

These were but a few of the feats which made Charleston the talk of Eastern Negro League as well as Havana Cuban circuits. Greatly in demand because of his scientific knowledge of the game . . . Oscar was later summoned to Hilldale, the Homestead Grays, Pittsburgh Crawfords and most recently, the Philadelphia Stars, as pilot, and now takes over the reins of the Indianapolis Clowns. . . .

Summarizing a brilliant career, Charleston has spent a total of 40 years in baseball to date. . . . When editorials expounding the merits of one Oscar Charleston are read from years gone by, it is easily understandable why they were written.

In the record books, Charleston's versatility, personified by speed and sensational play, will always bear witness to this—one of the most renowned natural athletes in all baseball history, rating with the greatest sluggers the game has ever known.

On January 29, 1954, Dad wrote to player prospect Johnnie Evans, "under our new manager, Oscar Charleston, you will be playing for one of the greatest baseball players the sport has ever known."

I remember that summer well when we went to see the Clowns play in Kingston, New York. Dad introduced me to Oscar Charleston, and Charleston's face matched his reputation. His eyes, clear and intense, below bushy, defined eyebrows, radiated strength, confidence, knowledge. His smile was contagious. He was tall and stately. He had the character and grace inherent to so many who spent their lives on the road in black baseball. He was distinguished and charming. He was competent and businesslike.

"This is my youngest son, Alan."

"I remember Alan, Syd. He's your shadow. He's the one always over on the Philly Stars bench talking basketball with Eddie Gottlieb."

"Right," Dad said, "but what a hitter Alan is. Everything he hits is a line drive." Typical of Dad—he was telling baseball's greatest player that I was about to become his peer.

Oscar Charleston nodded, smiling.

"He's a center fielder too, Oscar, just like you."

"No," I said, "Not quite like him."

Oscar Charleston patted me on the back. "Well you keep up the good work. You want to learn some more about center field, you sit next to me tonight and watch Drake."

"I always watch Drake," I said. "He's the best. He's my idol."

I spent the night watching Drake and listening to tips from Oscar Charleston. I was learning center field in CD stereo from the two masters. I did the same every Clowns game we attended that season. But, of course, I had long since known nobody could do the things Drake did. Some things you could learn; some, you couldn't.

The 1954 Negro American League championship race, with two new teams, Goose Curry's Louisville Clippers and Ted Rasberry's Detroit Stars, ironically came down to a one-two finish by Oscar Charleston's Indianapolis Clowns and Buster Haywood's Memphis Red Sox.

As joyful as Dad was about having Oscar Charleston as manager, he was sad about Buster being in the opposition camp.

Late during the 1953 season, Dad had publicity photos taken of Toni Stone in Philadelphia. For the session, she wore a dress, and leaned against a Cadillac; stood beside it, keys in the door lock; sat on the fender, legs gracefully draped over the side. She told Dad that the car reminded her she needed a raise. He had given her three raises during the season, all unrequested. When the Clowns repeated at cities that season, crowds were smaller. The novelty of a female player, even one as colorful as Toni Stone, was wearing thin. Another raise would make her as highly paid as any roster member, save Tut, and either the team's whole salary structure or its morale would be adversely affected.

Dad reviewed his "Girl Players" folder, thick with applications, and singled out Connie Morgan's. Her photo helped. Her face was sweet and beautiful. During a five-year period, she had accumulated a lifetime .368 batting average with the Philadelphia Honeydrippers, a female fast pitch softball team. A natural athlete, she also starred for the Philadelphia Rock-

ettes, a female basketball team. When not playing baseball, she was a secretary and clerk. She had attended William Penn business school for two
and a half years following high school, so she was intelligent and articulate.

Toni Stone had actually recommended Connie Morgan to Dad initially.
Dad arranged for Buster and Bunny to give Connie a tryout during the
Clowns postseason 1953 tour against Jackie Robinson's Major League All-
Stars. She drove to Baltimore, tried out in Clowns uniform and was photo-
graphed with Jackie Robinson and other major leaguers.

"She's a nice little second base woman," Bunny reported to Dad. "Course
Buster don't want her. Buster wouldn't want Lena Horne if Lena Horne
could play second like Neil, hit like Josh, run like Merchant, talk like J. B.
Martin and dance like Bojangles."

Dad signed Connie Morgan and sold Toni Stone's contract to Tom Baird
for the Monarchs, a move that also spread around the drawing power and
added a new, soft touch to the Clowns-Monarchs rivalry.

Mamie "Peanut" Johnson had pitched some for the 1953 Clowns and joined
them for the postseason Jackie Robinson tour. Born in Ridgeway, South
Carolina, she approached Satchel Paige there at a game when she was nine
or ten years old, and whenever Satchel appeared nearby, she went to see him
and he showed her more and more how to pitch. "Satchel Paige taught me
how to pitch," Mamie reported. "My best pitch was my curve. My control
was patterned after Satchel's. No one had his control. But mine was pretty
good."

Before joining the Clowns, Mamie pitched boys' baseball and girls' hard-
ball and played girls' basketball in Long Branch, New Jersey. She also excelled in countless sandlot tackle football games with boys. An NYU graduate, she was a nurse off-season.

Dad signed her to play for 1954, and pro baseball had its first two-women
roster.

The breadth of Dad's new problems was revealed in his April 1, 1954, letter
to Toni Stone:

First opportunity I've had to write, altho have been in contact with Mr. Baird and know everything has been worked out satisfactorily between you and him.

I'm having difficulty locating a place to make me up some sort of protective bra for Connie and Mamie, who will be with us this season.

Am sure you use one, and maybe you can give me some information as to where same can be obtained and how to go about ordering same and idea of price?

Any information you can give me by return airmail will be appreciated.

Will be seeing you along the way this season as we have many games with Monarchs this season.

Kindest regards to you and your hubby. . . .

"Toni never wore one, and Syd never found one for us either," Connie Morgan told me more than 40 years later.

After the usual perfunctory spring training, neither woman was a positive factor until the Clowns defeated the Greensboro Red Birds 6-3 in Greensboro, North Carolina, on April 19, the fifth game of the season. Connie Morgan singled. Six days later, in a one-inning appearance, Mamie Johnson retired the Winston-Salem Pond Giants in order, striking out the first man to face her in a 10-2 Clowns loss.

Early in the season, the Clowns beat the Kannapolis, North Carolina, Giants 9-4. Connie Morgan walked and scored on Erwin Ford's homer. Next night she drove in a run during the Funmakers' 10-3 win over the Rockingham Giants.

Two nights later the Monarchs ended a three-game Clowns winning streak with a 7-6 win in Wilmington, North Carolina. During the loss, in her initial pitching effort against an NAL team, Mamie Johnson pitched one inning, retired the side without a run, and left the game with a one-run lead. According to the *Baltimore Afro-American*, a mid-July Clowns winning streak featured improved hitting by Connie Morgan, and "her excellent fielding figured in two important lightning-fast double plays to break up rallies."

By mid-May, Mamie Johnson had pitched four innings, three of them against local competition and had not been scored upon. On Mother's Day, she pitched another scoreless inning, this against the Monarchs, and, in what must have been a great crowd-pleaser, gave up only one hit—a single to Toni Stone, whom she promptly picked off with a quick move and crisp toss to Speed Merchant.

By mid-June, Mamie was released, and Connie was mired in a batting slump. "I had a baby to take care of at home, and just couldn't stay on the road," Mamie recalled.

Connie highlighted her career citing two particular memories. In Laurel, Kansas, during the beginnings of a dust storm, the wind swirled dust across the field as she came to the plate. She connected on a fast ball, sending a long drive to left, and it would have been a home run had the wind not blown it foul just before it left the ballpark. "Another thrill," Connie remembered, "was once I tagged Toni Stone out sliding in. Whew, was that woman upset! Hollering at the umpire. Hollering at me. Hollering at the world. That was Toni's style, all right—excitement and aggressiveness."

Connie Morgan was generally considered the best of the women who played in the Negro American League. The clear consensus is that none would have played based on merit, absent gate value. All three competed with total effort. All three were accepted by the Clowns as teammates. Toni never felt fully accepted by the Monarchs.

Officially, Mamie had no NAL decision; therefore, she was not included among the official league statistics. Toni Stone batted .197 for the Monarchs in 1954 with 13 singles and a double in 71 at bats. She had three RBIs, walked seven times and struck out eight times. Connie Morgan batted .178, with seven singles and a double in 45 at bats. She stole a base, had an RBI, walked six times and struck out six. Connie fielded .885 with six errors. Toni fielded .778 with ten errors. They had the two lowest fielding percentages at second in the league.

It was the last season for any woman on a black major league team.

During the early 1950s, when he was in his early teens, Arthur L. "Junior" Hamilton was catching semi-pro men's baseball in Jacksonville, Florida. Preacher Henry and Peanuts Davis, both retired, pitched semi-pro in Jacksonville. Hamilton recalled:

I caught 'em both. Peanuts had the finest knuckle ball I ever did see. Not a blooper. Came in moderately fast. Jumped and hopped and swung in and out all the way into the glove, and I never had to move the target. Peanuts had absolute control over the knuckler. Even in the wind. Wind never affected the action on his knuckler either. You know, it's windy, most knuckleballers may as well stay in the dugout, but not Peanuts.

Now Preacher Henry had the drop. Not what you call just the drop. What you call the six-foot drop. Thing would come up to the plate sinking slightly like any other pitch, then suddenly the bottom fell out, and it was like the ball dropped right out of the sky.

Sometime in the early '50s an old man came into town with an old bus. Man's name was Charlie Henry. Used to run the Zulus back in the '30s, a team Tut told us about. Charlie Henry took a bunch of us in that bus down to St. Pete. Hired us for the day. We played down there. Went to the gas station after. Charlie Henry filled the bus. Got in. The thing wouldn't even turn over. Had it fixed. Said, "Men, there went the last of my money." That's the last we saw of Charlie Henry too. Had to hitchhike back to Jacksonville.

So after the 1952 season, Preacher Henry told Syd Pollock about me, that I was just 16, but I was ready. Syd had me come out to the ballpark when the Clowns played Jacksonville that spring. Buster had me work infield practice. Loved the way I threw. Said I reminded him of him as a young man. Had me warm up a tiny lefthander name of Ted Richardson. I never knew a man could throw that hard or do that stuff with the ball. Best screwball I ever saw. And his curve was just as good. Threw so hard, he had me stabbing at the pitches. And he's just warming up. Later on with the Clowns, Dionisio Amaro, Percy Smith and Ray "Black Beau" Maddix threw maybe as hard, but not with that curve and screwball. Amaro was hardest to catch though. His fastball moved and dropped. He threw what you call a heavy ball.

Bunny asked if my mama would let me sign. I said yes, and so did she. So Bunny signed me from the tryout. Bunny was some business-man on the road, a fine secretary. Handled the money for Syd. Paid us. Gave us the meal money. Settled up with the promoter and the ball park. Made sure everything ran smooth. Picked up the mail Syd for-warded and handled each mail call. Left management on the field up to Buster, then Charleston.

My first game was in Miami. Tut told me about the early Clowns, about how Skinny Barnhill had the same velocity as Satchel Paige. We didn't play in Dorsey Park, though, where the Clowns started. Miami had the AAA Marlins in the International League. We played in their Miami Stadium. Drake climbed the right-center-field wall and turned an Ernie Banks home run into a long putout. I was young and small. They played me shallow. Richard "Flip" Phillips was on the mound for the Monarchs. I tripled off the center-field wall first time up and singled the second.

Piggy Sands retired following the 1953 season; his batting average had dipped to .217, and Arthur Hamilton became the Clowns starting backstop. Hamilton recalls:

I was learning in 1953, scarcely played, and still learning in 1954. But in 1954, it was what we now call hands-on learning. I was the starter.

How good were the 1954 Clowns? Best in black baseball. Charleston didn't add much. He was old and had old ideas. Wasn't up to date like Buster. But we had George Wanamaker, Erwin Ford, Frank Ensley, Ray Neil, Verdes Drake, Speed Merchant—all those guys could start on any major league team. We had the fastest outfield in baseball, and speed throughout the lineup. Outfield was Ensley, Drake, Ford. We're not even talking about Merchant, Neil, Willie Brown. We had some speed. Neil was the best I ever saw on second, terrific hitter. Drake was the best outfielder I ever saw. Could stroke the ball too. From the heart of the Clowns, only Buster was gone. King Tut, Buster, Merchant, Neil, Drake, Bunny—those guys were the Clowns. They were the Clowns. The '54 Clowns had maybe AA pitching on a scale of D on up to major league. Only thing about the Clowns that year wasn't major league was the pitching.

When you evaluate black teams you got to consider conditions. We traveled sometimes 400 miles between games. We played several games a day sometimes in different towns. We'd do without showers. Sometimes, we'd go two, three days without a bed—nights on the bus. Some places, the only black hotels were in big cities, so we'd book the big city hotel for a night game we had in a small spot 50–60 miles away. So maybe 11, 12 at night we'd come out the locker room, and have an hour, two-hour ride ahead before we slept. Highways then were two lanes, you know. No expressways like you got now. We never had home field advantage, except everybody everywhere loved the Clowns. We got two dollars a day meal money. Ate three meals a day and saved some off that. Hard to believe now. No fancy restaurants like the white clubs.

The Clowns could draw crowds. We had more than 18,000 to the 1953 league opener in Kansas City. Everybody wanted to play the Clowns every chance they got because we were the biggest draw in black baseball.

Seven players were gone from the 1953 team: Richard Hairston, Julio Toledo, Piggy Sands, Frank Carswell, Raydell Maddix, Reuben Williams and Curtis Hardaway. George Wanamaker replaced Curtis Hardaway at third. Other new players included Erwin Ford, who returned to right field for the Clowns after spending two years in the Braves' organization, utility infielder Bill Holder, 16-year old backup catcher James Portier, and pitchers Pedro Quintana, Phil Laduna, John Wright, Vince Husband and Howard Coffey. Coffey and Husband were both released before the end of the year. Dad also brought back Big John Williams, with spitter and cut ball, from the '40s Clowns. Williams also backed up M. H. Winston driving the bus.

Even with the flux of roster changes, Oscar Charleston guided the Clowns to the Negro American League championship, their fourth in the last five years.

That winter, Oscar Charleston died.

A few days after the death of Oscar Charleston, Dad told me, "Professor, last season may have been my last. I think I'm going to retire, maybe sell the Clowns to Ed Hamman."

"Why?" I asked. He didn't know it yet, but a few months earlier, I had decided to make the Clowns my life's work, to take over when Dad was done.

"It's not certain. Maybe it's just with Buster gone. Now Charleston. But you know, every year there's fewer minor leagues, more ballparks are parking lots. Crowds are down. Negro leagues never got space in the white press. Can't now. Look at the Jimmy Powers thing. Hometown owner. Hometown promoter. Guy like Hank Rigney. We should fill Yankee Stadium. Every New Yorker ought to have chance to see Verdes Drake, Ray Neil, Speed Merchant, King Tut. Who knew they were in town? What'd we have five, six thousand? It's a shame, people always throwing up a corner others got to go around to get to the fun. Cost of staying on the road keeps going up. Profits are small for the risk. We never had a major bus wreck. What if we did? League quality's down. The Louisville Clippers had trouble fielding a set of uniforms that matched. That reflects on us."

Mom wanted Dad to retire. I didn't. Dad seriously discussed the Clowns' future with Ed Hamman. Ed wanted the team eventually, but realized he wasn't ready without Dad. Ed had run road clubs on and off since 1933, but always as road business manager.

Even though W. S. Martin wanted Buster Haywood back to manage the 1955 Memphis Red Sox, Buster retired, but Dad and Buster corresponded, and on December 22, Dad wrote Buster:

> As a necessary conservative move plan on naming Bunny manager next season. . . .
>
> Don't know at this time whether I'll stay in league or not, as it's a costly operation, jumps are too long if an even schedule is to be maintained, and may decide to operate independently, permitting carrying fewer men and keeping salaries in line with actual receipts. . . . to cover overhead one must keep on the move and eliminate long jumps as much as possible.

Ongoing operation required on-field comedy and reduced expenses. There were no more women players after 1954; the novelty had worn off. Black fans were major league fans now. Black baseball had to entertain fans or die, and Negro American League competition was no longer enough. The level of NAL competition, while diminishing rapidly, precluded hiring of comedic players. Release of aging players, who had become like family, reduced payroll, as did hiring younger players at lower salaries, a move which also allowed for profit potential from player contract sales as skills developed. If the Clowns left the league, scheduling would be easier and more profitable. The Clowns could play where Dad wanted, not where other owners wanted. Opposition would be assured if the Clowns carried their own opponents, as the Globetrotters did.

The hard decisions were made. The Clowns would leave the league. Ed would establish his own club, the New York Black Yankees, as touring partner for the Clowns. Player comedians would be hired. Bunny would be Clowns' field manager, Ed the road business manager. Dick Lundy was hired to manage the Black Yankees.

As a result, 1955 became a year of abrupt transition, and on-field quality suffered. If the Clowns had major league ability in 1955, it was marginal. Dad released Ray Neil and Speed Merchant following the 1954 season. He got both jobs as welders and ballplayers with the St. Joe Caterpillar Tractor Company in St. Joe, Michigan. Merchant married and rejected the job. At first Neil was resentful, but then thanked Dad, realizing he now had a trade for when his playing days were done—he had known nothing but professional baseball, and bad knees limited his play. He stayed with the company the remainder of his working career. More than 40 years later, Neil recalled the last time he saw Dad:

I came with the Clowns in 1942. Last time Syd saw me play was 1954, Philadelphia. We were one behind, one on. Manager marched out to the mound, Tut hollered, "Conference!" and popped out of the dugout and ran to the mound. He always did that for a conference. Never told us a blessed thing was said. Cupped his ear, leaning in like he's listening. Ran to me at the plate like he always did, pretending he's whispering. Pointing out at the mound, all exaggerated. Then he walks into the dugout, never looking at the pitcher, but pointing at him every two, three steps.

Next pitch I homered. Crowd went crazy. As I crossed home plate, Tut pulled off my hat and kissed my head. Syd was still laughing when I come in the dugout.

We kept the lead and won by one.

In his wisdom, J. B. Martin, when he learned Dad's intentions, invited the New York Black Yankees into the league. But the decision was final. In 1955, the Negro American League proceeded without the Clowns. The Clowns played independently, touring with the New York Black Yankees. Often, the teams split up to play local semi-pro or minor league opponents. Sometimes, they played three-team doubleheaders involving locals. The Black Yankees didn't draw many without the Clowns, nor did the Negro American League teams. The Clowns still drew the crowds. And some of the Clowns' greatest honors and most interesting days lay ahead.

I clearly recall Dad of the '50s on a couch near the window in a train men's room, talking baseball and smoking, long curved cigarette ash bobbing rhythmically and gracefully, miraculously intact, on the cigarette dangling from the corner of his mouth. He is wrapped in summer sun and lacy wisps of white cigarette smoke.

Unless the early '50s games were near home or in certain cities, we went by rail. Like a kid, Dad loved trains. Every trip, Dad brought mail and special orders to players—always a bat, always equipment, sometimes a gift wanted for someone along the road, sometimes suits ordered from the tailor in Birmingham. Whenever just Dad and I traveled by train, I wore my Clowns warmup jacket and Clowns baseball cap and voluntarily carried the bat, hoping girls my age would mistake me for a major league child prodigy.

On train trips, whenever Dad visited the men's room, Mom said, "Alan, go make sure your father doesn't sit on that couch and start talking baseball or I won't see him again till Denver." I always wondered why Denver. We never traveled west of Chicago by train. She said, "And he was so shy when we married. Almost scared to talk to your Aunt Sadie." Trying to keep Dad from talking baseball on the train was like trying to stop the ocean from making waves. I happily walked the aisle because my presence was always futile, and I heard great baseball stories.

But that summer, on the way to Detroit, Dad was as close to judgmental as I ever heard. His men's room companion was a white man, previously ignorant of black baseball, apparently ideal for Dad's monologue. "Well, then," said the man, "owning a colored team, you must have heard the one about the bunch of niggers at the back of the bus."

"Certainly," Dad answered. "Punch line's 'the last shall be chosen first.' Let's go back to Mother now, Alan. She doesn't like me talking baseball."

When I told Mom, she said, "God bless us and save us—a Catholic comeback, from Sydney no less. God bless your father. All your life you'll hear about dirty words. There are two: 'hate' and 'nigger,' and both stand for the worst in the people who use them."

And those were the two words absolutely forbidden in our family.

22

Jackie Robinson's All-Stars

During the four years 1950–1953, the Clowns toured postseason against Jackie Robinson's Major League All-Stars. Legendary New York public relations man Ted Worner ran the tours.

Worner knew Dad from the mid-1930s, when Ted was sports editor of his hometown *Yonkers Statesman*. He explained:

> It was the middle of the depression . . . and I got to know Syd. I was the sports editor up until the outbreak of World War II . . . and I went into the P.R. business after the war. . . .
>
> WMCA said to me, "You seem to know sports . . . did you ever produce a radio show?" I said "No" and they said, "Well, you're going to now 'cause we just signed Jackie Robinson up to do a six-nights-a-week baseball show." . . . Our first guest was Campanella. The guests we had were unbelievable . . . Durocher, Branch Rickey, Sugar Ray Robinson. Nobody could turn us down.
>
> Jackie was awful, absolutely awful. First of all, he hadn't been up in the big time long enough to have the sharpness he had later. He had a high-pitched voice. It wasn't working out. Show didn't get any ratings. I finally came up with an idea [for a system that worked] . . . and he got to be pretty good. . . . Jackie said to me, "How would you like to promote my barnstorming tour? . . . We went last year . . . and it was completely disorganized. . . . I'd like you to take it over."
>
> Alex Pompez, who owned the New York Cubans, ran the first barnstorming tour . . . and it was a fiasco. . . . So I contacted [Syd], and I made a deal. . . . We were allowed by Ford Frick, the commissioner, to start the day after the World Series and were allowed 30 days [to tour]. No more. Those were the baseball rules.

Major leaguers who didn't know, the touring All-Stars were about to learn the math of the road.

Traditionally in the South in those days, crowds sat separately, whites filling prime box and grandstand seats behind the plate, behind the dugouts and along the near baselines, and blacks relegated to distant sections in the outfield or along the far baselines. Ted Worner reversed that. For the Deep South Jackie Robinson All-Stars games against the Clowns, a section was reserved for whites in the deepest outfield, or, if there was no seating there, along the third-base line from third to the fence. The most seats and the best seats went to the blacks.

> All I had to do was put up the posters, and they'd bring down the gates. . . . Campy [Roy Campanella] could walk into a field and take one look and tell you within 50 how many people were there. They played what they used to call p.c., percentage. . . . the Clowns were getting a little unhappy because they were playing for maybe $400 a month . . . a lot of money in those days. . . . I paid their salaries, I paid their hotel rooms, I paid their food, pretty much what [Syd] did.

The promoters got 40 percent of the net gate. Ted paid the Clowns and his expenses from the 60 percent teams' share, then divided the balance with Dad and the major leaguers on agreed terms, with some major leaguers receiving sizeable flat guarantees against a percentage of net.

I remember in Baltimore when the Clowns threatened to strike. They wanted to go on p.c. the same as the major leaguers. Dad eventually convinced them that, while fans came for Tut and the Clowns and for the Negro leaguers–major leaguers clash, Jackie Robinson was the big draw in the fall, and without the major leaguers the tour would fail.

According to Ted Worner, at least six Jackie Robinson All-Stars now grace the Hall of Fame. The major leaguers' roster during the four years included Jackie Robinson, Roy Campanella, Don Newcombe, Larry Doby, Willie Mays, Luke Easter, Ray Dandridge, Monte Irvin, Henry Thompson, Charlie Neal, Sam Jethroe, Maury Wills, Mickey Vernon, Gil Hodges, Ralph Branca and Bobby Young.

The white players—Young, Vernon, Hodges and Branca—played only in 1953.

Some Clowns players avoided postseason tours because of interference with off-season jobs. Because of winter league play in Latin America, Verdes Drake and Ray Neil missed most, if not all, the Jackie Robinson tours. Dad supplemented the Clowns postseason lineup with other Negro leaguers. Ernie Banks of the Monarchs made the 1950 tour with the Clowns. After Hank Aaron finished the 1952 season in Eau Claire for the Braves, he returned to the Clowns for the postseason tour.

Competition on the tours was friendly, but tough. Ted Worner recalled an incident with Peanuts Davis in 1950:

> The games were close. We had 18,000 in New Orleans and I wanted the fans to get a little thrill, so I said to Peanuts in the dugout, "Peanuts, groove one and let Larry Doby or Jackie hit one out of the park."
>
> He drew himself up his full length, and said, "Mister Ted, I play to win."

Jackie Robinson was the force behind the enterprise. He handpicked his teammates among the major leaguers and gave complete energy and commitment to the tours. Leaving the 1950 tour three days early, he returned to New York 20 pounds lighter, suffering stomach problems that would plague him the rest of his life. Ted Worner gave reasons for the love and respect given Jackie Robinson over the years:

> To show you what kind of a man Jackie Robinson was, you can take all the players, bar none, and not one of them could carry this man's glove. . . . He made himself outstanding. He didn't even like baseball. . . . His love was football. He was an All-American mention at U.C.L.A. . . . He never graduated. . . . He had to go to work to support Rachel and his son, Jackie, Jr. He took a job playing with the Kansas City Monarchs. . . . He made himself a great baseball player, an exciting baseball player, but he was a man besides that. And it was unbelievable the things he would do and the way his mind worked. For example, he'd never quit before the full nine innings. . . . Doby would take a rest, the others would take a rest, but not Jackie. . . . we used to get people to spend money from the mattress, old crumpled-up dollar bills. . . . some cities we had to sit them in the outfield behind second

base. . . . They weren't really there to see a baseball game. They were there to see a legend. And when Jackie had to go to Puerto Rico for some award . . . he insisted I make five announcements telling the people he wouldn't be back for the return game on Monday. He just wanted everything above board. Tremendous man.

A great Matisse is beautiful colors wonderfully arranged and blended with masterful strokes and points. Jackie Robinson's greatness as a person surpassed race, but race was a color in the painting. The setting of the time shaped Jackie Robinson's strokes and points. Ted Worner discussed events in Birmingham involving a local ordinance prohibiting whites and blacks from appearing on the same team:

> [Having] the white guys on the team was a big, big draw. The black audiences just loved seeing the white guys playing with the black team . . . five cops at a game they usually had one, that was at Birmingham. . . . [The white players from] my team didn't even come to Birmingham. They stayed in Nashville or Chattanooga or something like that and they skipped Birmingham altogether.
> . . . Hodges called me and he said, "Ted, we're for you. . . . you're sticking your neck out, and we'd like to help you, but we have families, and we can't take a chance that they'd be a riot, we'd get hurt."
> I went to see a lawyer there, and he said, "Ted, you've got every constitutional right to play . . . but I wouldn't test it if I were you."
> We knew there was going to be trouble, and I stayed at the Tutweiler Hotel . . . knock on the door. I'm on the phone calling all my promoters and answering all those who wanted games and so forth, and two guys walked in, announced they were from Sheriff Bull Connor's office. Said, "We understand you got some Negras . . . playing on your team."
> I said, "Yes, we've played all over the South with no incident whatsoever."
> "Well, you can't play white and black on the same team in Birmingham."
> I said, "They're my team."
> He said, "You better not show up with those players. If you do, you're in big trouble. . . . Look, mister," and he called me an epi-

thet, "We're not afraid of you 'cause you're nothing, you're just a big man from New York, you think. We shoved a . . . cigar," I was a cigar smoker then, "down the mouth of a United States Senator . . . Glen Taylor of Idaho." Because he wanted to go in the front door of an auditorium, they wanted him to go around the back, and they arrested him. "So you know we're not afraid to do it to you."

. . . so now we come out to the game. There was about five or six cops there. One cop came over to Maury Wills, and looked at him, he says, Maury Wills is quite light, he says, "Are you a black man?"

And Wills started laughing, he said, "If I'm not black," he said, "I've been laboring under a misapprehension all my life."

Now I didn't have my stars—Branca, Hodges . . . Bobby Young . . . and my missing man was Al Rosen. . . . Rosen I signed to a contract to come, put him on all my posters and everything, and the day before the tour was to open up in Baltimore, I get a wire from him saying the doctor says his back was bad, he couldn't go barnstorming. What had happened was that Hank Greenberg gave him five thousand not to go barnstorming. He thought he might get hurt. Rosen had come off a good year. He led the league in slugging, he led the league in home runs, and never had another year like it. In the end it turned out he saved me $10,000 because nobody missed him. Not one person said to me you advertised Al Rosen and we didn't get him.

I had to do something, and what I did was I got hold of Willie Mays' father. Willie was at Ft. Eustis in Virginia, and I got Willie . . . to play. I said, "Willie, I'll give you $5,000 . . . and I'll give you an extra $500 if we draw more than X number of people . . . I ended up paying Willie Mays at that time more than any man had ever paid him, something like $7,000 to play one game.

. . . The Negro fans around the country felt that Jackie should have refused to play. . . . Jackie felt the people bought their tickets to see a game, to see him, and that it would cause less things if he showed up and didn't fight with the cops or defy them.

23

On the Road Again

On April 10, 1955, the Indianapolis Clowns, billing themselves Negro World Champions, opened the season against their touring partners, the New York Black Yankees, in Greensboro, North Carolina. The fastest outfield in baseball remained intact—Frank Ensley in left, Verdes Drake in center and Irwin Ford in right, but Ensley often played second, leaving left to DeWitt Smallwood, Shad Green or Rufus McNeal. Orlando Lugo was back at short. Jim Portier caught, backed up by former minor leaguer Ike Quarterman, Jr. Junior Hamilton was in the Army. George Wanamaker returned at third. Pitching was a strength. Phil Laduna was in the Air Force, but Rufus McNeal, Dave Amaro and Willie Gaines were back on the mound. The notable 1955 signings included two pitchers, two comedians and a catcher–first baseman.

Jim Proctor was a rookie right-hander, who would spend several seasons with the Detroit Tigers. John Wyatt, who had run a 100-yard dash in 9.5 seconds and a 220 in 21.1 seconds as an undergraduate at North Carolina A&T College before joining the Funmakers, would become American League Fireman of the Year as top reliever with the Kansas City Athletics and Boston Red Sox.

Clowns and Black Yankees players were interchangeable, with the accent on Yankees pitchers moving to the Clowns for games against locals.

One reason the Clowns left the league was to reunite baseball and comedy as part of the game. Dad first signed James "Natureboy" Williams, a 20-year-old, and Prince Jo Henry, formerly with the Philadelphia Stars, for the 1955 season.

Dad and Ed Hamman perceived the financial strength of the Globetrotters as dependent in part on remaining undefeated season after season against stooge traveling companions. Dad reasoned that fans came to see the Clowns, not their opponents, and that if they saw the Clowns only once or twice a year or once every few years, they might not return if the team clowned but lost.

So the team's first year outside the league, the Funmakers roster was substantially stronger than the Black Yankees, and Clowns victories resulted from Darwinian survival.

The Clowns policy of borrowing the best Black Yankees to play locals was impractical when each club played locals the same night in different cities, rare occasions generated by special request of favored promoters. Dad preferred playing the Black Yankees because they were familiar with Clowns comedy, which made the game more entertaining. For example, the Black Yankees catcher always threw to third when he saw the signal for the Clowns switch steal, first to second and second to first. Besides, the Black Yankees were no drawing card on their own.

James "Natureboy" Williams eventually played like a partially squashed Goose Tatum. Goose was tall, lean and graceful; Natche was 5'8", 220 pounds and graceful. Natureboy ran faster, and eventually hit better. Goose was a better fielder. Both received throws while performing splits. Both taunted runners with the last-split-second toe tap of first, but sometimes Natureboy did it while sitting on a chair. Natureboy developed the ability to hit with his back to home plate, leaping around to face the mound as the pitch was being delivered. Once he developed that talent he hit that way one at bat a game, and several times hit category-five home runs that way. He generally played in a dress, switching to baggy pants with suspenders for the bats-in-the-pants routine, his once Prince Jo Henry was gone. In the dress, his legs looked fat, but they were all muscle, and, as Dad once wrote in a Clowns release, he could "run like a scared gazelle." Natureboy Williams had center fielder speed.

Having the Black Yankees as traveling opponents allowed Natche and Prince Jo full comedic reign, and with Ed Hamman, Tut and Bebop working the sidelines between innings, the Clowns funshow was never better than 1955, 1956 and 1957.

During 1955, the Clowns consistently beat minor league and local semipro teams, and such teams must have felt intimidated coming to the plate and seeing Prince Jo playing third, dressed in top hat, tux coat and giant circus clown shoes, sitting on a chair with his legs crossed, and Natche on his chair at first. The batter was something like a burglar being given keys to a house along with assurances he'd screw up the job anyway.

In fact, Prince Jo was a better than average fielder, but not so strong at the plate, and Natche was a great athlete with comedic flair, but not yet a pro caliber player. Natche developed quickly. By 1960, baseball treated him as a comic mainstay, not as a serious baseball player, but in my opinion, from 1960 until he lost his eye after the 1963 season, Natureboy Williams was one of the best first basemen in baseball. He was one black player born too late for the glory years of the Negro leagues and too soon for full acceptance in organized baseball, but, as Dad said, more than a million fans were entertained because Natureboy Williams was born precisely on his birthday.

On June 30, 1955, the Clowns played in Independence, Kansas, and the *Independence Reporter* provided coverage:

> Whether you like horseplay or baseball, there was plenty of both at Riverside Stadium last night as the Indianapolis Clowns and N.Y. Black Yankees tangled in an exhibition tagged as one of the best ever to be played at the local ball park. The Clowns won, 8-6.
>
> Few in the stands cared who won or lost. All they wanted to see was some slam-bang baseball and that's exactly what they saw.
>
> . . . [F]or combining clowning and baseball, Prince Jo Henry, the Indianapolis third baseman, and "Natureboy" Williams on first gave the local diamond fans an exhibition of comic diamond artistry the likes of which they've never seen.
>
> Prince Jo appeared at the hot corner in a number of different uniforms and rapped the ball to the tune of three for five. Sometimes he took a nap while the batter was in the box and once he took a hot grounder, ran most of the way to first base before he threw just in the nick of time to catch the runner.
>
> Natureboy was a master around first and offensively he, too, could

hit the ball. Each time he got up to the plate, he took off his shoes, dug his toes in the dirt and swung from the heels. He played the entire game in a grass skirt.

Briggs Stadium, Detroit, was scheduled for July 31, 1955, a date pivotal in the lives of our family and the Clowns. The Clowns won a doubleheader, but sadly it was the last time the Funmakers would play in Detroit.

Four hours before game time, Dad and I left our hotel to walk the half mile or so to the Clowns hotel for the bus ride to Briggs Stadium. The weather was sunny, hot and still. As usual, Dad walked fast. A block from the team's hotel, he said we'd have 20,000 to 30,000 paid weather considered, then suddenly, he stopped walking, grabbed his chest with his right hand, holding his briefcase out to me with his left, and, as I took the briefcase, staggered against a chain link fence in front of a lot-wide parking area between two buildings.

"You OK, Dad?"

"They must have served me your old pancakes at the hotel, Professor," he answered, leaning against the fence. "Terrible pain in the chest. Must be indigestion. I'm out of breath—the food, the heat and walking fast, I guess. Feels like I might have torn something in my left shoulder too, catching the fence or holding my briefcase out."

"What should I do?"

"Just hold my grip, we'll rest a minute. I'll be okay. Watch down the street. You see the bus filling up, you let me know, don't want Chauff leaving without us."

We stayed there for more than a minute, less than two, before Dad announced ready. He took his briefcase back, but we walked slowly toward the hotel. I had never seen Dad walk slowly before.

I was there that year in Montreal when Dewitt Smallwood first died.

Thanks to Smallwood, brisk advance sales indicated a crowd exceeding 2,000 for St. Jean. A fill-in outfielder on and off for the Clowns, Smallwood was released in the early '50s. Then one season, he won the triple crown as an outfielder for the minor league club in St. Jean, after which he advanced to the Texas League.

In the high altitudes of the Texas League parks, Smallwood apparently hammered out 27 home runs one season. "Hell, air was so thin there," Smallwood said, "once I homered trying to drag bunt my way on with a fungo." In 1954, he batted .300 with the Philadelphia Stars before adding some comedy to his game and returning to the Clowns for the 1955 season.

Dad's St. Jean releases featured Smallwood's Texas feats and reminded fans of his Canadian triple crown. A fine man, Smallwood was loved in St. Jean.

Chauff was the law of the bus. If he said the bus left at 4 P.M., it did, whether the manager, the starting pitcher or Syd Pollock was late. Stories were told in which the door closed and Chauff drove off leaving players halfway across the sidewalk. "I told him he can marry couples on that bus," Dad once said.

M. H. Winston had a way of giving signals like a third base coach. He'd tap the steering wheel, shift his black, horn-rimmed glasses, adjust the pencil wedged behind his ear, and scowl out the open door at players scurrying busward.

That Monday in Montreal, Chauff's glare stopped Smallwood cold in his tracks halfway across the walk, in the leave-'em zone. Smallwood followed, his gym bag falling to the concrete, clearly dead or dying.

Dad and some players carried him into the hotel and placed him on a couch. The bus horn sounded. Chauff's hands glided quickly as a magician's— steering wheel to glasses to pencil to forearm to wheel. Without quick action, the Clowns would not field a quorum that night in St. Jean. Dad had the desk call an ambulance.

As Winston glowered and tapped like an impatient hangman, we re-entered the bus and left.

Less than an hour later, Dad negotiated with Chauff to buy five dollars worth of gas. Dad went to the pay phone.

Back on the bus, Dad announced, "I called the hotel. Smallwood revived before the ambulance got there. He's okay. Went to a movie." The team cheered like pennant winners. Dad muttered, "Miraculous resurrection."

Of approximately 1,800 adults in the St. Jean ballpark that night, hundreds brought notes to the dugout, only the amount on each note varied. "I owe you $1—Dewitt Smallwood." "I owe you $5—Dewitt Smallwood."

"I would have died too," Dad said.

The Clowns ended the 1955 season with their last series against a club in organized baseball, though there were some individual games in later years. In September, the Funmakers played the AA Nashville Vols a three-game series in Sulphur Dell, the classic ballpark with the hill running up to the left field wall. The Clowns swept the series with Johnny Wyatt winning the clincher and aiding his own cause with a home run.

On September 23, 1955, Dad wrote to Johnny Wyatt:

> I had Detroit scout our team when we played the Nashville Vols. . . . Their scout thought we looked very good against them and was surprised we could beat a double AA club. I told him with right kind of pitching and with Drake covering center field for us, we could beat many of the major league clubs if given the opportunity to play them, especially in the bigger parks like Yankee Stadium, Polo Grounds, etc., where our outfielders had plenty of room to roam around and pull down those long fly balls, that in many parks go for home runs.

The Clowns had played Yankee Stadium July 12, 1955, and the fixed expenses, game or rainout, were $912.41, the sort of gamble making major league parks less and less desirable to play. Crowds had shrunk, expenses were up, and payroll had to be reduced. The Clowns were unraveling as a baseball power.

Bunny Downs' diabetes worsened as he aged, and he decided to retire. "Syd, you need to tighten payroll, and bus baseball ain't right for anybody, but old as I am, it's downright intolerable." Clowns '40s pitcher Big John Williams was hired to replace Bunny for the following season. As Dad pointed out to Ed Hamman, Big John could also relieve Chauff driving the bus and could still "cut the ball and throw enough junk to stop most white locals."

Dad tried to secure less demanding work for Bunny. He contacted every major league organization, but baseball had no room for him, so Bunny Downs simply retired.

Tarrytown taxes, reported to be the highest in the nation, led to Dad's position that once annual real estate taxes on our house exceeded $1,000, we would move to Florida. It happened during the winter of 1955–1956.

If the Clowns would go down with Dad at the helm, the first real chance was during the first quarter of 1956. We arrived at Hollywood February 1, 1956. Our movers arrived nearly a month later, and the Clowns home office, crated somewhere in transit, was unavailable to Dad. He had no files, no books and records, no phone numbers or addresses, no mimeograph machine, no publicity or photos. The Clowns were a rudderless ship during a time crucial to early season bookings. Dad used a portable typewriter on plain typing paper and answered incoming correspondence as it arrived, and he took phone calls, and a schedule began to form on the back of a poster Ed Hamman sent over from St. Petersburg. The 1956 season was safe and in the offing.

Our first month in Florida, I threw a tantrum one day when Dad went deep-sea fishing while I was in school. "Damn it, Mom, he could have waited till Saturday when I could go! I won't even talk to him when he comes home!"

"Yes you will, Alan," Mom said. "That time in Detroit, when you carried his briefcase, was a heart attack. It wasn't just cost of living made us move. It was health too."

I talked to Dad when he came home.

The 1956 Clowns were the same old character with new faces. Dad was still there. Tut was still there. The bus was still there. M. H. Winston still drove it. The blend of good baseball and comedy remained. But the Clowns had never changed so much.

In 1956, Dad was 60 percent owner and Ed was 40 percent owner of the Clowns and Black Yankees, a combined operation, one presented to new players as a traveling baseball school. The concept was to sign the best available young, black talent for the fastest possible development into major league quality, and to do it on a budget set by dwindling attendances and increased road costs. The two teams traveled in two buses, but players were almost totally interchangeable. Except for comedians and one veteran, players knew that they were hired for no more than a season or two, to be released if their contracts were not sold into organized baseball, that scouts from every major league team would see them, that they would see high-level competition daily all season long in a baseball world still constricted by racial quotas.

Rookie salaries were reduced to $200 per month. Veterans either signed contracts in organized ball or were given releases. Gone from the outfield were Frank Ensley, Irwin Ford and DeWitt Smallwood. Gone from the mound were Ted Richardson, John Wyatt, Jim Proctor, Dave Amaro, Willie Gaines and Charlie Mapp. Orlando Lugo and George Wanamaker were gone from the infield. And Rufus McNeal, an infielder-outfielder-pitcher, was gone from every position.

New players were on tour. Of real veterans, only Verdes Drake remained. "I once let Willie Wells go, the best shortstop ever," Dad said. "Now I have the best outfielder ever. And nobody in organized baseball wants him. I just can't let Drakey go." The only other players on either team with Negro league experience were Big John Williams, Jim Portier and Prince Jo Henry. Big John barely played now, managed the team and drove the bus as needed. Jim Portier was still young enough to keep for organized ball.

The quality of the Clowns as a baseball power had dropped far below that of any prior Clowns team, but they still played at mid-minor-league level and were the best in black baseball, and they still beat almost every team they faced.

Roberto Herrera played on the 1956 team, so the Clowns tradition of strength and depth behind the plate remained. Al Fletcher and Chester Moody caught for the Black Yankees, though Herrera and Portier took turns there as well. The fifth catcher in the organization was rookie Clarence "Choo Choo" Coleman, who would become the charter catcher for the original New York Mets.

Choo Choo studied baseball like an absent-minded professor works out theoretical physics.

Dad and Ed considered Choo Choo smart, but dizzy. "He focused on things others might not," Dad once told me, "and when he did, he'd overlook something simple. Like once he was running a mental film of the Black Yankees, figuring pitches for each batter that night. Well, that was fine, except he was alone on the way to a movie matinee with this imaginary game running through his head. So after the movies, he couldn't figure the route back to the hotel, and when he asked a police officer for help, Choo Choo didn't know the name of the hotel and said to "call around to colored hotels asking for the Clowns."

The spring training before the Mets first National League season, Dad and I had a game on the radio. Choo Choo was catching, bottom of the ninth, one out, men on first and third, game tied. Someone topped one straight up in front of home. Choo Choo picked it out of the air, touched home and threw to first, and the winning run scored. Apparently he forgot that there was no force play at home. Dad figured Choo Choo was running the next day's game through his head.

According to Joyce Hamman, Choo Choo Coleman was the only Clowns player fluent in Stengelese. She described the journalistic counterpart to a game between the Miami Ethiopian Clowns and the Zulu Cannibal Giants:

> It was Casey Stengel interviewing Choo Choo Coleman in St. Petersburg during the Mets spring training. It was the only interview I ever heard probably only two people understood—Casey Stengel and Choo Choo Coleman. The thing I remember is that Casey asked Choo Choo who his roommate was with the Clowns.
>
> "Number 16," Choo Choo answered.
>
> "Nice guy, was he?" Casey asked.
>
> "Sure was," said Choo Choo.

The Clowns made one of their few talent errors with Choo Choo Coleman. On February 22, 1958, Dad and Ed released him for lack of speed and hitting ability.

Carl Forney was born and raised in Gastonia, North Carolina, and played semi-pro ball a few miles away with the Belmont Blues. Like Hank Aaron, Forney grew up hitting bottle caps with broomsticks. In 1955, ex–Negro league catcher Quincy Trouppe loved Forney as a pitcher and signed him to a contract in the Cardinals organization. He pitched a year for the Decatur, Illinois, Commodores in the Cardinals system, but was released with bursitis in his arm in the spring of 1957.

Later that spring he was an outfield mercenary for the Pepsi Cola Giants of Charlotte, the best black team in that part of North Carolina, when they played against the Clowns. Sylvester Snead, who was the original second baseman of the Miami Ethiopian Clowns, had returned to the Clowns as manager for 1957 and 1958. Friends of Snead advised him of Forney's talent, and two nights later, Forney pitched for the Clowns in Rockingham, North Carolina.

From the time the Clowns left the league in 1955 until Dad's retirement after the 1964 season, only one player besides Natureboy Williams played for the Clowns more than four years—Carl Forney. He pitched and played outfield for the Funmakers from 1957 to 1962 inclusive and also managed the team the last three seasons. For the Clowns, he once hit eight home runs in seven days. Once, in Poughkeepsie, New York, he blasted a record home run off former Philadelphia Phillies relief star Jim Konstanty, over the left-center-field fence and over a tennis court behind that. His last year with the Clowns he hit 26 home runs.

Not all thought Forney a great hitter. As Forney told it: "We played a game here in Gastonia. My boy, Aaron—I guess he was about two years old—was there, and I struck out three times that day. They said my son shook his head, 'My dad can't hit.'"

"If you could go back in the towns where we played ball," Forney said nearly 40 years later, "and ask them which was the best team ever to come through for the Clowns, what year, I believe some people could tell you that team in '57. That's the year I think we won almost all the games . . . almost everybody hit over .300."

The 1957 Funmakers were certainly not the quality of Clowns teams 1955 or earlier, but they were a very good team, a definite improvement on the 1956 group. Tut inspired, counseled and entertained. Drake played center field. Natureboy improved daily. Choo Choo Coleman and Jim Portier were back, and Art Hamilton returned from the service to play the season before entering organized baseball with Elmira. Other players from that season included Mike Franks, Clarence Turner, Walter Landy, Mitchell Bell, and George Smith. Carl Forney said, "The best ballplayer we had out there during my time was George Smith. That man could play some second base."

Dad offered Smith to the Braves, but their scouting reports were not favorable and they declined the opportunity to sign him. But Dad was persistent in bringing him to the attention of the major league franchises, and in July 1958, the Detroit Tigers purchased his contract. Starting in 1963 he played several years for the Detroit Tigers, then the Boston Red Sox.

Verdes Drake was featured in the 1957 Clowns program, which reported that "he is probably one of the greatest ball hawks in the history of Negro baseball but his small size (5'6", 140 pounds) kept him from ever becoming a star in the big leagues." Dad wanted the Braves to give Drake a chance in 1957, though with age, his speed and quickness had diminished to high-normal levels.

Of all baseball people, only Dad would have written the letter he wrote to John Mullen of the Braves on July 21, 1957. The Braves were in the thick of the National League pennant chase when Braves center fielder Bill Bruton was injured. Dad wrote:

This may sound "crazy," but noting Bruton will be out of the lineup for 30 days, if there is anyway you can bring in Clowns' centerfielder, VERDES DRAKE, and play him immediately, believe this player could help your club in pennant drive.

Drake has the experience, has a good arm, can field among the best in the business, and do believe he can outhit Bruton.

Everyone seems to pass Drake up because of his small size, but in my book this player is big league in every respect and do believe he could help you.

He's yours gratis, if you actually can use him as a regular in your outfield.

Am positive he can hit major league pitching, and can save many a ball game with his outfielding.

John Mullen did not accept the offer, and Verdes Drake finished 1957 as the only true veteran with the Indianapolis Clowns.

When the Clowns left the league, motivation took on a different spin. There was no league championship. There was no league batting crown or RBI leader or ERA king. There was no slot open in an East-West game. There was no substantial roster continuity. Players had roommates for months, not years. Double-play combinations rotated without the smoothness of familiarity. Salaries shriveled. In-game comedy increased. Most conditions of the late '50s inhibited enthusiasm.

Lower salaries actually benefitted morale. Players willing to accept such pay toured for the love of the game and belief in themselves. The Clowns, no longer a final stop, had become a means to an end for some, a brief love affair for others.

As Carl Forney said, "You'd be surprised the kids came out there to play ball when they put one of them Clowns suits on. Then again they'd say this is where Hank Aaron started. You got it in your mind that you know you gonna be like Hank, which ain't but one Hank, but every day, you enjoy yourself when you put one of them Clowns suits on."

Players played efficiently too to keep their jobs and to see the country.

There was a player pool into which each player put a dollar or two a payday, with monthly statistical leaders taking percentages of the pot.

Against locals, there was Clowns pride, and M. H. Winston, Tut, Drake, Dad and Ed provided links to the past. Those threatened by common foes bond. The Indianapolis Clowns still faced old adversaries: game opponents, the road, ignorance, racism and something other baseball teams didn't face—to borrow a phrase from Dad's 1933 integration letter to Bill Veeck, Sr.—"social pride." Social pride included not just white racism, but elements in the black community, heirs to the anti-minstrel show philosophy espoused by Wendell Smith and Cum Posey against the Miami Ethiopian Clowns during the late 1930s and early 1940s—social pride that found fault with the Funmakers' entertainment. Although in the entire 35-year history of Dad's black comedy teams, there was never a moment of fan protest over entertainment at a Clowns game, Clowns players were aware of the greater tolerance given white comedians than black. They knew no white columnist had ever demeaned white baseball comics like Al Schacht, Nick Altrock, Bobo Nickerson, Ed Hamman or Jackie Price for being white baseball comics. They knew no white sportswriter had ever called the House of David a parody of the white race or the European heritage.

But controversy or not, road burns or none, wins or losses, segregated or integrated hotels, eating whatever they could wherever allowed, the Indianapolis Clowns rode united in their love of the game and their blessed ability to play it.

During the late '50s, more than ever, Dad dealt with change, and, almost impossibly, his workday lengthened.

Determination, hard work and flexibility allowed Dad and Ed Hamman to carry the Clowns successfully through the late '50s and into the '60s.

Inflation, union costs and organized baseball's myopia made costs of operation almost fatal. Decreasing news space hurt attendances.

To play in major league stadiums, the Clowns had to pay escalating rentals plus unionized grounds crews and stadium staffs, who received the same wages whether the game was played or whether there was a rainout before the park even opened.

While aging gracefully, Big Red, as Clowns players called the bus, purchased in 1948, was becoming more expensive to operate, almost by the mile. Only the fact that M. H. Winston was an expert mechanic, capable of overhauling the engine without help, prohibited net losses several years.

Mat Pascale had promoted baseball in Omaha, Nebraska, from the days Dad started in Tarrytown, and Mat promoted the Clowns and their predecessor teams from the start. The two men were lifelong friends. Just before the 1960 season, Dad wrote Mat that he had given nationally syndicated columnist Red Smith "my personal opinion why in the last ten years the minors dwindled from 59 leagues to 21, and number of clubs skidded from 446 to 150, only 139 operating in U.S.A."

As non-major league baseball withered, ballparks were fewer and farther apart. Ghost parks, where minor leaguers once played, now abandoned and idle, had weeds in outfields and cobwebs in grandstands, and unused fields left gaps in local baseball interest. Conversely, many existing teams in organized baseball considered the Clowns a rival for the entertainment dollar and kept the Clowns out through high rentals or lack of cooperation. As Dad said, "When we come in and outdraw the locals by five times, three things happen: one, they rent an otherwise idle park; two, they make concessions money; and, three, we generate baseball interest and the habit of fan attendance. Every club in organized baseball should be fighting to save itself and the sport, and part of the fight should be bringing in the Clowns. But no, organized baseball always seems intent on cleaning a loaded gun pointed at its own foot."

Clowns costs were cut in salaries, and, by having Ed as partner, Dad eliminated the expense of a salaried business manager. With the traveling opponent also owned by Dad and Ed, the teams' net gate was not divided, and the Clowns and their touring companions typically received 65–70 percent of net gate proceeds.

Purchasing cheaper uniforms and setting up traveling companion losses to the Clowns were two mistakes Dad and Ed made. The cheaper uniforms, which showed the soot and missed cleanings always a part of bus life, detracted from the team's professional appearance as much as the reckless base running of the Clowns' opponents, which not only reflected on the apparent ability of the opposition, but sometimes caused Clowns fielding errors.

One important change of the late '50s was the use of an advance man. For decades, circuses had used advance men, salesmen who drove the United States lining up local sites for future appearances, particularly in small cities or towns not usually visited. The advance man's job was to locate money-making areas to break jumps between big dates and to locate sponsors and local promoters. Part of the job with the Clowns was to find playable ballparks with securable gates.

In 1958, Dad hired retired Ringling Brothers advance man Bobby Burns and his wife, Jeanette, who, for four seasons for the Clowns, together revisited every place the sun shined in the mainland United States and southern

Canada. The advance man received traveling expenses, a small salary and a share of each game he booked, and, as years accrued, shares of return games.

As part of the '50s adjustment, the search for entertainers was easier than at any time since Dad had an interest in the team, because now, while in-game entertainers still needed professional baseball ability, major league quality was no longer required. Circumstances made acquisition of entertainers imperative facing the 1958 season.

By 1958, Goose Tatum was finished as a star basketball comedian. Ted Rasberry, owner of two of the four teams remaining in the Negro American League, signed Goose as first baseman for the 1958 Detroit Stars, and changed their name to the Detroit Clowns. Lured by promises of big money, Prince Jo Henry also signed with Rasberry.

On February 1, 1958, Ed Hamman suffered a major heart attack. While Ed recovered sufficiently to function as road business manager for the '58 season, a Clowns player was paid extra to chauffeur Ed's car for the rest of Ed's career. Ed was finished as an entertainer.

For 1958, the Clowns hired white juggler/baseball comic Frank "Bobo" Nickerson to replace Ed, and signed Ulysses Grant Greene of Tobaccoville, North Carolina, as a player entertainer.

A gifted dancer, Greene joined Natureboy as understudies to Tut and Bebop for the post-shadowball dance. Sometimes, when crowds became particularly involved with Tut and Bebop, Natche and Greene joined them near the plate in an impromptu two-couple spike hop that made everyone who saw it cry laughing. No one stole the spotlight from Tut, but the biggest laugh came from Natche's shocked and angry expression when he caught Greene dancing lower and lower, eventually low enough to daintily pull the hem of Natureboy's dress out just high enough for a peek.

But the 6'1", 195-pound Greene had other talents. He was a reasonably good hitter who could play anywhere but behind the plate. More important, he was an ambidextrous pitcher, who threw right-handed to right-handed batters and left-handed to left-handed batters.

For 1958, the name of the Clowns traveling opponent was changed to the Los Angeles Hawks. The Hawks made a name for themselves early in the season in Memphis before more than 4,500 paid. While trying to lose, the Hawks beat the Clowns 6-4.

Time and return to independent play had not been kind to the Clowns.

24

Farewell to the King

The Clowns were an anachronism. Black baseball was essentially dead. The Clowns had a pulse because Dad willed it so, and because he could adapt to almost anything. The Clowns still served at least three functions: entertaining people; bringing baseball everywhere; and creating baseball interest and providing a proving ground for young black baseball players.

The problems of the late '50s were major, and many converged in the social-pride press coverage of a catcher named John Gray during the Clowns' June 22, 1958, Yankee Stadium appearance.

On June 23, 1958, the *New York Mirror* published Ben Epstein's account of the game:

Baseball spiked with burlesque was on exhibition in the Stadium yesterday. And at the comedy's end, the score had the Indianapolis Clowns beating the Los Angeles Hawks 7-5, a score that didn't bother either of the Negro clubs which tour the country like rasslers on a picnic.

Yes, the farce featured such diamond items as hitting homers and a catch or two but a crowd estimated at 5,000 derived most of its fun from the following acts:

The Clowns boasted a first baseman, "Nature Boy" Williams by name, who played in two different "uniforms." The first outfit was an "Aunt Jemima" attire and the second like a hill-billy Al Schacht. One thing for "Nature Boy": He really could glove that ball.

INDIANAPOLIS, which at one time had Hank Aaron in its act, came up with a switch pitcher, Ulysses Greene, as a reliever in the sixth. Uly threw righthanded to righthanded batters and lefthanded to lefthand batters. All one can report is that Greene needs a little more experience from both sides. . . .

One King Tut and one Bebop, a 38-year-old midget, who stands 38 inches, regaled the crowd with a hippy dance to the tune of rock and roll. . . .

Clowns Johnny Gray and Byron Purnell each hit two-run homers. . . . Gray, a promising young catcher and watched by White Sox scout Dave Holly, smacked an inside-the-parker in the fifth.

GRAY, ONCE the property of Cleveland, was released after a 60-day trial with the Indian's Daytona Beach farm in 1956. Purnell banged his into the left field stands in the sixth. . . .

In the *New York Post*, Milton Gross used his full-page column as follows:

This is the story of a 19-year old named John Gray. It's the story of empty ball parks, ancient and disheveled uniforms, short rations, bus trips and the sad state of Negro baseball. It's also the story of ambition which continues to burn with the pure white flame against the background of disappointment.

Johnny Gray is a kid with fuzz on his chin and two kids of his own. He's a catcher for the Indianapolis Clowns, a sort of baseball counterpart of the Harlem Globetrotters, who appeared at the Yankee Stadium yesterday against a team of traveling companions called the Los Angeles Hawks. For this Gray is paid $200 a month.

"We got to buy our own food out of that, too," he said. It seemed such a meager return in the vastness of the Yankee Stadium, where 5,000 watched the so-called game. But Gray said, "They picked Hank Aaron up from the Clowns and you keep hoping somebody'll come and see you and pick you, too. This is the only way I know how to make the big leagues."

"You can make more working at a job," it was suggested.

"I know I can," Gray said, "but I can make the big leagues if somebody picks me up again. Right now I'm good enough to catch triple A or maybe double A, but this is the way I got to do it now."

Gray had played class D ball back in 1956. He had a year at Wilberforce College, where the Dodgers had first seen John Roseboro, and when a Cleveland Indians scout made a pitch to sign him, Gray leaped at the chance. He was offered a $2,500 bonus, $500 down, $2,000 after 90 days, but after 60 days with Daytona Beach in the Florida State

League, Gray was told by Manager Hank Majeski that he was going to be released.

"The only thing," said Gray, "was they were going to release me to a team in the rookie Nebraska State League, LaPlatte, but I still would be tied to the Indians. I asked about the $2,000 and they said I wouldn't get it, so I demanded my release and I got it. I wasn't going to play without the rest of the bonus."

That was two years ago. In the time between, Gray played semi-pro ball around his home in Ft. Lauderdale.

"There was no chance to go anywhere that way, so I decided to sign on with the Clowns about two months ago," he said. "Aaron only played six weeks with the Clowns before the Braves saw him and bought him."

We stood there near the Yankee dugout, where Mickey Mantle, Joe DiMaggio and Babe Ruth had walked, and Gray's hope was almost something physical to behold. It was in every syllable he uttered. It was the dream that youth won't relinquish, ambition that shouts you're another Campanella, maybe tomorrow, maybe next week they'll see you and grab you and say sign the checks, the steaks are on the house.

His uniform was Navy blue, with red stripes and red letters. The blouse and the trousers were wrinkled and faded and the salt of the sweat never will be washed completely from it. But neither will the desire that the road to riches and fame lies in this game he plays for a team that is called the Clowns.

"Suppose," I said, "some scout saw you and signed you. What sort of contract do you have with this team? Would you get a part of the purchase price?"

"No," he said, "the club would get it all. That's the contract I got with this team."

"That would satisfy you?"

"It's the best I can do, but I know I'm going to do it," Gray said. "I played a lot against Willie Mays' barnstormers. I played with Jim Grant, who's with the Indians. I know I can make it if I get the chance."

A few innings later you had to wonder how all this ambition will be spent. You watched the tomfoolery on the field, where a dwarf named Bebop, a clown named King Tut and a first baseman named Nature-Boy Williams tried to amuse the few fans with comedy antics. Williams played first base in a ladies' gingham dress, a red bandanna wrapped around his head and red and white spiked shoes. Later he came out with another outlandish costume and it was all right because ever since they left the Negro American League four years ago the Clowns do not profess to play straight baseball. Unlike the Kansas City Monarchs and Memphis Red Sox, who play next Sunday at the Stadium, the Clowns are strictly exhibitionists.

Thus what is it like for Johnny Gray, with the fire still burning in him, when he must become part of the act? There was a point, for instance, when Bebop came to the plate with a bat three times his length, hit a rubber ball back to the pitcher and then proceeded to run the bases until he came to the plate where Gray had to make the play. Bebop pointed to the stands. Gray turned away and then Bebop slid under him.

It is a job, like all other jobs and if this is the way Gray must do it then it is right for him. But you think of Jackie Robinson, who opened the door to organized baseball for Negroes, and you recall all those great Negro ballplayers who never had the chance before Branch Rickey undertook his adventure in human relations, Mule Suttles, Josh Gibson, Ray Dandridge—they spent their lives in this sort of thing with all their talent, but never had the chance to use it. Now here is a boy who believes he has talent and believes he knows how to use it, but the chance seems so slim, even though the barriers are irrevocably down.

Dad was angry when he read the story, and he asked John Gray how the youngster could betray the Clowns. Gray insisted that things he said were twisted, that Gross went beyond what he said, did his own research, drew his own conclusions and published half truths. By day's end, Dad realized that he had been angry at Gray for doing what Ed Hamman had asked him to do—to answer whatever he was asked. Dad knew that Gray was not a P.R. man in a catcher's mask, and that all he had done was to tell the truth. Dad was no longer angry.

A few days after the article appeared, Malcolm Poindexter, a leading black journalist, penned a response to what he perceived as a "direct attempt to discredit what I know to be one of the finest teams in the Negro American League in years past."

Black baseball was in a sorry state. On August 7, 1958, the Clowns drew more than 11,400 paid to Forbes Field in Pittsburgh, the largest crowd in baseball that season outside the major leagues. If not for that gate, Dad and Ed would have lost significant amounts of money for the year.

Verdes Drake was the only Latin American player on the team in 1958. He finished the season with the Clowns, but after that year did not play again in the United States. Drakey accepted his life as it was, without complaint. He was also the most memorable athlete and the greatest baseball player I ever saw.

Mom was major league pregnant with Jerry during late summer, 1933, when Dad had a flat tire heading to Troy along the Taconic Parkway. As Dad jacked up the car, Franklin Delano Roosevelt halted the presidential motorcade taking him home to Hyde Park to rest. Luckily for the family, I was unborn because I'd have run up to his limo and begged him to veto Dad's reservation at the Hotel Troy.

"Good morning, young lady," the President said. "My chauffeur will change your tire." Introductions were made and Mom assured the president of two future votes. In the talk that followed, as was customary then, Mom's pregnancy was not mentioned.

After the tire was changed, Mom said, "Mr. President, I don't know how to thank you."

"If it's a boy," said FDR, "name him after me."

Jerry's middle name is Franklin.

During 1936, a campaigning Franklin Delano Roosevelt, riding in an open convertible, cruised Bedford Avenue, Beekman Avenue and Cortlandt Street from the main gate of the estate of the Republican Rockefellers down the hills of the Tarrytowns to the train station on the Hudson, a clever campaign use of the opposition party. As Mom told it: "The sidewalks were full, both sides of the Avenue. I was with Marguerite in front of the Strand packed in the crowd. As the president rode by waving his fedora, he saw me. 'Hello, Villa!' he shouted through the din. He not only managed a visit to the best-known Republicans during a presidential campaign, he never forgot a name or a face."

Tut had the same gift. As early '50s Clowns outfielder Frank Ensley said:

> Tut met everyone and he met only friends. And he never forgot names or faces. Tut would say how he got to send an autographed postcard of himself to Joe Johnson. When you ask who Joe Johnson is, Tut says, "Now you know him, don't you? Remember the five Monarchs fans we met at 12th and Vine last year in Kansas City? He was the quiet one stood by hisself at the back. Tall, bald man. Got a coconut head." We'd be amazed till next time he'd talk the same way about someone he met once at a Miami Ethiopian Clowns game in 1938 or in Cincinnati in 1942.

Tut was in full stride with life. I remember sitting transfixed in the dugout watching Tut, legs crossed, long fingers wrapped around a big fat cigar, shouting out profanities or one-liners at the ump or the other team or, during bad games, at the Clowns. He was like God directing the world. Sometimes Dad smoked cigars, and when he did in the dugout, he lit up off Tut's. Every cigar I've smelled since brought Dad and Tut back. Some can't stand the smell of cigars. I say there's nothing better.

Clowns catcher Art Hamilton recalled:

> Bus pulled up outside the hotel was the best publicity there was. Crowds gathered all around us, before we even lit on the sidewalk. First one off was always Tut. People hollered, "There's King Tut! There's King Tut!" Tut puffing on that big old cigar he always had. You know everybody loved Tut. Love was something you could almost see around Tut alongside the cigar smoke.

Bunny checked us in, and he'd be signing the register, and the desk clerk look up, and Bunny tell him the same thing he told everybody. He'd look him up and down real serious, shake his head sadly and say, "I want you to meet me in Milwaukee, Wisconsin, to join me on the All-Ugly Team."

Of course, Tut set the pace for all Clowns humor, on field and off.

According to Clowns infielder Gordon Hopkins, Tut was always first in a restaurant, and he said the same thing every time he entered, "I want a neck bone sandwich and a pint of wine."

Tut created laughter everywhere about everything. As Frank Ensley said, "Tut carried laughter on the bus, to the hotel, in the stands, on the field. The world today needs Tut and Syd, needs to see 'em again side by side."

Reuben Williams, who played in 1952 and 1953, still tells friends about Tut:

My favorite is, once a man in a box seat sees Tut strolling toward the Clowns dugout, and he cries out, "King Tut you know you ugly! Look like you been whooped with a ugly-stick!"

Tut said, "That's okay. I get paid to be ugly. You don't get a damn thing for being ugly."

Even the man laughed, harder than anybody.

Gordon Hopkins said, "Tut was a joy. Like Bob Hope comes on the stage and people laugh, Tut comes on the field, the crowd laughs. The players laugh. Tut was like magic."

Perhaps Carl Forney of the later Clowns described Tut best:

You could go to a ball park in a bed, a sickbed. Before you leave, you'd get out of the bed walking with Tut doing stuff in the stands 'cause Tut gonna get you up and make you laugh. . . .

Tut would go through the stands during the whole ball game, and pick out kids, pick out the old women and have everybody up there laughing. Sometime, you be out there playin' ball, you be lookin' up at Tut, 'cause Tut's up in the stands got everybody laughin', 'cause you want to know what Tut doin'. . . . When Tut go up in them stands, you come to the plate to hit the ball, Tut had you laughin'. You're supposed to be playing ball, you be laughin' at Tut. . . .

He'd ask people if they have money or something, he was gonna do a trick and make it disappear, and then he'd walk off with their money. . . .

One night we were playing, and I was coming up to bat, and Tut was up there in the stands, and all at once he had everybody quiet. I looked over there, and he said, "Hey! Hey! Look at that woman with them two left shoes on." And she looked down, say, "I ain't got no two left shoes." Tut just start laughin'. . . .

Then he's set there and a man and his wife would be huggin'. Wife be settin' there tryin' to enjoy the ball game. Tut say, "Well, I'm gonna go tell your husband you settin' up here with another man."

Tut was more than funny, more than joyous. The Clowns 1958 program pointed out that the man who traveled more than a million miles with the Clowns had helped hundreds of young baseball players with his baseball knowledge. As Frank Ensley said, "Tut was a great motivator. He treated everyone with humor and understanding. Even though he could get down on us, he taught us never to get down on ourselves." Rufus McNeal said, "Tut inspired everybody. He was the Clowns." Carl Forney said, "Out there playing ball . . . you can't see your mistakes. Tut could always tell you what you were doing wrong. Correct that, it made a better hitter out of you." Forney also described the 1958 King Tut:

But you know, after I got out there, I guess over the years, he had wore himself down because he couldn't do what he used to do. A lot of times Tut would get kind of tired. I think he was forcing himself. I believe Tut was sick a long time before he took sick. A lot of times we'd get on the bus, he wouldn't hardly say much. When I first went out there, he kept you laughin', talkin' all the time. But he got to where he didn't say much on the bus. I figure then that Tut might have been sick then.

June 15, 1958, was King Tut Day at Connie Mack Stadium in Philadel-phia. Tut was honored at home plate by the Clowns and given gifts before a modest hometown crowd on a warm Sunday afternoon, a true baseball day. Bea stood in the sun by his side, and, with a field mike, Dad, Bunny and others briefly expressed their love and appreciation. As he had been for years, King Tut was the most beloved figure in black baseball.

"I'm so glad we had Tut Day when we did," Dad said the next April.

If the Clowns would go down with Dad at the helm, the spring of 1959 was the second chance, and, sadly, this time, Tut could not spit out a mouthful of water and swim away across the infield.

When he arrived at the airport in St. Petersburg, Florida, for spring training for the 1959 Clowns, Tut uttered one of his favorite tag lines: "Where's my Cadillac?" But this time, he meant it. Totally disoriented, he was suffering a serious chemical imbalance. Ed had Tut treated locally, and Dad had him flown back to Philadelphia under supervision. He was taken to the State Hospital at Byberry.

And it was there Tut passed.

Outfielder Irwin Ford, who roomed with Tut part of 1954, said: "He was a teacher. He talked with you like a daddy if you's down. Wasn't a thing wrong you couldn't take to Tut. Told us what the Clowns meant to him and what the Clowns could mean to a young player if the young player kept himself under control. I loved Tut. There was a greatness about him as a person you can't explain to somebody unless they been around him."

Nobody has to explain that greatness to me.

It's hard to say whether the Clowns would have gone on had Tut died in December 1958, before the 1959 season took shape. But as usual, the Clowns' training was done almost as soon as it began, and, ready or not, the team was on the road. It was like Tut had come to St. Pete to see them off. For months, Dad believed Tut would get well and return. His influence never left the Clowns.

25

Bobo, Yogi and Chauff

No longer able to afford a nonplaying manager, Dad hired former Clowns Negro leaguer Lincoln Boyd as player manager. Carl Forney remembered Lincoln Boyd: "During the day, we hit a town, tell you if you're gonna pitch that night, he'd say, 'Brother, I'm going downtown on you.' And he would hit you downtown. He could hit. He could hit. Lincoln was a good manager too."

In addition to Boyd and Forney, the Clowns 1959 roster included Alex Harriday, Byron Purnell, Joe Cherry, Earl Palmore, Ross Linthicum, Al Hooker, Jose Sambrana and Vanity Rushing.

The 1959 outfit was one of the better minor-league-quality teams the Clowns would have. As Forney said, "We had some major leaguers out there then, just in the right place at the wrong time."

Contortionist Yogi Cortez, who performed such feats as hand balancing on a chair while scratching his ears with his feet, was signed early in the season for additional sideline entertainment.

The 1959 opponents were called the Georgia Flyers.

In a four-page pictorial spread on the Clowns, the September 1959 issue of *Ebony* magazine reported that when Dad became involved with the Clowns,

> . . . he noticed that most of the Negro teams . . . were shabbily dressed, scantily equipped, poorly managed and had haphazard business arrangements. But he also noted that Hunter Campbell managed an unusually talented troupe called the Miami Clowns. Pollock further felt that with his baseball contacts and background in vaudeville-type showmanship, he could turn Miami's baseball clowns into a fabulous show and money maker. He did. It was some time before they were

classy enough to play in the Negro American League, but during the last decade, the NAL has been hampered by low attendance, and it was the showmanship of the Clowns that offset the low gate odds for some time.

. . . The Clowns have since withdrawn from the league and remain a major "proving ground" for Negro talent.

. . . Pollock contends that baseball alone is not enough to bring the fans out to the park. . . . The people just want to be entertained, he insists.

. . . Pollock answers the critics of his "undignified" baseball with insistence that "this is good business and baseball is a business." And with Clowns-type baseball, there surely is no business like show business.

Ever presenting fresh ideas, Dad wrote to Bill Veeck, then with the Chicago Cubs, on May 19, 1959:

Would you be interested in a 30-minute Pre-Game Funshow Presentation featuring our nationally famous INDIANAPOLIS CLOWNS-versus-the GEORGIA FLYERS in an inning or two of baseball and comedy, as a preliminary attraction to your game on Thurs. July 2 or Tues. July 14?

We can condense our entertainment into a fast, entertaining 30 minutes of action and laughs, exhibiting the Clowns' newest "Shadowball Infield Workout" in slow motion; the popular routines of Bobo Nickerson, the "screwball of baseball"; the ambidextrous pitching of "Two-Way" Ulysses Greene; and the sensational "Rock n Roll" jitterbug dancing of Natureboy Williams and Greene, etc.

The Clowns, always a big drawing card in Chicago, who haven't appeared in your city during the past four years, this year have the greatest and funniest baseball Funshow ever presented on any diamond.

. . . If interested, we would consider a flat guarantee, or a straight percentage proposition based only on the increase in attendance over your average week-day crowds. . . .

In the spring, the Clowns toured north through Georgia and were booked into Forbes Field, Pittsburgh, June 26. It became the night that conflict between Ed Hamman and Bobo Nickerson erupted like a furniture-spewing volcano.

If earlier conflicts between Bunny Downs and Buster Haywood drew sparks, feelings between Bobo Nickerson and Ed Hamman torched a conflagration. Bobo hated bus travel. Ed suggested Bobo ride in Ed's Cadillac, and Bobo accepted the kindness. From then on, they were daily as close to disaster as Mrs. O'Leary's cow was to the lantern. They were magma seeking a fault through which to boil up and out.

Ed was short and puffy, Bobo tall and muscular, with minimal body fat. Both had played for the House of David. Ed was an ex-performer, disabled by his heart attack. Bobo was an active entertainer. Ed had worked the World Series. Bobo had not. Ed was boss and had responsibilities and didn't drink; he wasn't paid for rainouts or small crowds. Bobo was paid daily with no responsibility other than to perform. Bobo was bitter; other entertainers, not as talented, regularly worked organized baseball, but Bobo was stuck with those he called "a bunch of friggin' colored semi-pros." But worse, Bobo was a wounded war hero, an Army Ranger, who took part in the landing at Leyte Gulf and saw most of his best friends blown to bits. He told me that on one island, when the Rangers were overrun by the Japanese, he was wounded, conscious, but playing dead as American forces counterattacked to save the Rangers. One of the few survivors told Bobo that a Japanese soldier bayoneting bodies to certify death had his bayonet raised above Bobo when he was leveled by a bullet fired by an advancing American soldier. Bobo worried about all that and tried to drink away his worries. Nightly, he spent the remainder of his daily pay on beer. Bobo was a child at heart, and Ed wanted no part of child psychology.

It rained all day in Pittsburgh. By mid-afternoon, the game was called. Dad and I had a room adjoining Ed's on the twelfth floor of the Pittsburgher. Bobo's room was immediately above ours on the next floor up, numbered fourteen to avoid bad luck. After supper, Dad and Ed met in Ed's room to discuss teams problems and needs. Bobo entered, wanting to discuss Bobo, and instantly Ed and Bobo argued.

Dad said, "Look, Bobo. We can talk with you later. Right now Ed and I have dozens of other things need our attention." Dad pulled a twenty from his wallet. Handing the money to Bobo, he said, "Here. Go out and see live acts at a nightclub. I saw two or three ads in the paper. Quality entertainers. Look at stage presence. A good entertainer can have a headache. He can have a wife fooling around. He can be stuck on the Borscht Circuit while someone with half his talent's working Ed Sullivan. But Bobo, the good ones look happy when they work."

Bobo snatched the bill and left, slamming the door. He didn't look happy.

I awoke at 3:30 A.M. to Bobo's voice thundering from above, like the squawking of some dyspeptic, malcontent, slightly obscene angel heralding the apocalypse. "Up your gigee, Pittsburgh, you son of a buck! Max Patkin and Al Schacht ain't worth a pimple on my ass!"

"He's right, you know," Dad said, "far as talent. It's attitude holds Bobo down. It's anger in his stage presence."

Though to hear Dad critique Bobo's act under pressure somehow calmed me slightly, I was terrified. There was anger in Bobo's stage presence, and, at the moment, the world was his stage. There had been a loud crash in the alley below, and Dad reported, "I saw a chair go down past the window. Bobo's throwing his furniture out." I was afraid Bobo might come to our room angry and throw more things out, starting with Dad and me.

I needed assurances and it turned out Dad too was afraid, but his fear was different.

"Friggin' colored bunch a damned semi-pros! Nick Altrock ain't fit to clean my toilet! Up your friggin' gigee, Pittsburgh, and have a lick on my wing-ding nuts!" Bobo yelled. A TV flew by the window, followed by a popping explosion on the alley below.

"Are you scared, Dad?" I asked.

"Yes."

"Of what?"

"I think the couch may be next, then Bobo, poor guy."

Through the floor, we heard Bobo arrested. Dad wanted to bail him out. Ed didn't. "Syd, he'll never learn, he don't learn now." Ed prevailed.

Later Bobo claimed he wasn't drunk, but just "blew my top." Later too we learned that, before he came to Ed's room in the hotel that night, he had read a news item about an appearance Al Schacht had just made or was going to make with the Pirates. That had set him off.

Bobo's wife, Marilyn, bailed him out. It was a season-ender. Dad and Ed didn't want him back, and Bobo felt they had betrayed him by abandoning him and were not his friends. It looked like Bobo was already part of Clowns history.

From Pittsburgh, the Clowns rolled on to Columbus, Ohio. I drove Dad and Ed in Ed's car. We arrived at Jet Stadium, Columbus, ten minutes late, and, as we pulled up to the locker room gate, so did the Clowns bus.

"What happened, Chauff. Why you late?" Ed asked.

"Yogi ain't with us," Chauff said.

Purportedly an eastern mystic, Prensuanta "Yogi" Cortez claimed mind-over-matter ability. "Some mystic," Carl Forney said 37 years later in describing how Yogi, drinking like Babe Ruth and dressed like Superman, had once hollered the mystical word "Shazaam" and leaped from a second-floor banister, cape flying in the wind, onto the floor of a Connecticut hotel lobby. "If he was diving, he'd have gotten awful marks on his entry," Forney said. "We thought he'd killed himself. He was treated at the emergency room and released."

Forney continued on the subject of Yogi: "The best job he had was at night when he'd go to the clubs. You'd go to the clubs, you'd see Yogi. He's up on the stage. That's Yogi up there! He's got himself all up in knots there. He made more money with the clubs than he made with the Clowns."

Ed asked Chauff the significance of Yogi's absence, and Lincoln Boyd answered, "Russell Patterson's riding with the warmup jacket draped on his arm 'cause he's pitching tonight. Yogi's his seatmate. Wants the window open. It's an eastern mystic's way he said, fresh air and all. Patterson said the damn window stays down, he don't want no draft on his arm. Yogi takes umbrage. Says we don't care about him, stop the bus, he wants off. So we stopped, and he got off. We tried fifteen minutes to get him back aboard, offered a seat behind Patterson, but didn't do no good. Then we came straight here, top speed so's not to be late."

"Where did you leave Yogi?" Dad asked.

"About fifty miles out. Farm country," Chauff said.

"Damn!" Ed said. "You mean you left Yogi all alone in the middle of nowhere? He's advertised tonight! Bobo's gone, now no Yogi!" Ed held his chest, "Syd, get me to the locker room. It's my heart."

One arm around Dad's shoulder and one around mine, Ed hobbled into the locker room assigned to the Clowns. "Thought you'd never get here. My uniform's on the bus," said the Great Yogi from a bench in front of the lockers. "You look pale, Ed. Terrible in fact."

Later, when Ed was refreshed, we asked the groundskeeper how long Yogi had been at Jet Stadium before us. "About ten minutes," he said.

"How'd he get here?" Dad asked.

"Walked," said the groundskeeper.

"But walked from what?" I asked. "A cab, a tractor, what?"

"Didn't see anything," the groundskeeper said. "The man just walked."

That, more than anything else Yogi ever did, advanced the cause of mysticism in my mind.

By 1959, the Clowns were the only traveling team still listed in the "Baseball Blue Book" and recommended by both the National Association of Professional Baseball Leagues and the National Baseball Congress.

The diminishing quality of the remnants of the Negro American League had become more than a mere annoyance to Dad and the Clowns. NAL teams were hurting Clowns' bookings and gate receipts.

In his May 10, 1958, "sport-I-view" column in the *Philadelphia Inquirer,* following an inaccurate announcement that Goose Tatum had purchased the Detroit Clowns from Ted Rasberry, Malcolm Poindexter wrote: "Promoters here and in other sections have put the 'thumbs down' sign on Goose Tatum and his newly purchased Detroit Clowns baseball team. First, they resent Tatum's using a name that has meant top-notch baseball and showmanship to the game via Syd Pollock's Indianapolis Clowns. Secondly, they refer to Tatum's past history in business in a most uncomplimentary way."

Poindexter then listed examples of Goose's disreputable business dealings (false adverstising, failure to make scheduled appearances, refusal to pay debts), difficulties with the IRS, and marital problems before concluding, "In brief, Tatum left a bad taste in the mouths of promoters throughout the country. It only takes one or two fiascos to sour them on a guy permanently. Perhaps that is why no one in Philadelphia has made a bid to play the former Detroit Stars here."

A year later, the April 18, 1959, the *Chicago Defender* reported:

> The Indianapolis Clowns . . . leading Negro independent club, will this season take legal steps to protect their 30-year-old name if any club, league or non-league, uses the name Clowns in advertising an attraction.
>
> Syd Pollock, president and general manager of the original Clowns, said that steps will be taken in Federal Court to seek an injunction against any club which does this. Pollock was specifically referring to the Detroit Stars of the NAL who last year played under the name "Detroit Clowns."
>
> Fans were confused as a result, and when Detroit missed an engagement Pollock's team was blamed. The Detroit club is owned and operated by Ted Rasberry, a businessman. The club features Reece (Goose) Tatum as the star comedian; however, his performance was limited during the 1958 campaign and again Pollock's club was accused of misrepresentation.
>
> Pollock stated, "The Clowns, in the thirty years we've been in business, have always given the fans what was advertised. We never missed a booking, and there's no city we can't play."

Dad had built a reputation that was well known throughout black baseball. His own players knew it better than anyone. Dad was a constant source for a "helping hand," even in later years when times were hard.

Dad agreed that Ed Hamman became a partner too late. "The big money days of the Clowns became history with Toni Stone," Dad said. There was seldom Clowns money to loan after 1953. Ed didn't give personal loans and seldom gave favors. Dad made personal loans and gave money and favors to players, usually to an extent irritating Ed. The gifts took two forms— forgiveness of debt or cash on the road, designed not to look like a gift. For instance, alone with a player, Dad would hand him a ten or twenty and say, "That's for the catch you made in Kokomo, one of the best I ever saw." The road gifts got to Ed the worst.

"Syd, you spoil these players," Ed would say. "You come out giving them extra money and it's weeks again to get them back in line. You can't give 'em sardines and peanut butter three weeks, then take 'em for steak and lobster and expect them to eat like they did before they surfed and turfed."

Dad would say, "We don't give 'em real salaries any more, not most of 'em. All they get's enough to stay on the road alive. What I give 'em when I see 'em comes out of my pocket, not yours."

"Yeah, but then you go home and I'm out here with a bus fulla prima donnas and weeks of headaches. Ain't right, Syd. Two and two don't make four on the road. Ain't right."

Smaller than earlier loans, though still significant in a pre-inflation economy, advances in the '50s were fewer too than in the past. Clowns life was shorter for all but comedians. Players moved into organized baseball in mid-season, and sometimes even when they made major league rosters, they didn't take care of past debts. Dad became increasingly reticent about parting with money.

When Dad and Ed argued over loans, and the organization didn't advance funds as Dad wanted, which generally happened since Dad wouldn't advance funds without Ed's agreement, Dad did so personally. Dad's motives were always what they should have been and decisions were even-handed.

Dad also gave advice. Being consistent, he gave players the same kind of advice he gave family—how to be positive, how to better themselves, how to get along. More than 40 years after he played, Frank Ensley recalled: "Syd was always positive. A confidence builder. Said, 'You owe doing well to yourself and your family.'"

Of player thank-you notes over the years, Dad's favorite was the one Mike Franks sent him in 1959, which ended: "Thank you for your kind consideration and understanding heart. I just hope someday I'll be able to repay you for all you have done for me and my family."

Economic realities in the '50s put extra bumps in the road. As Tom Baird wrote Dad in 1955, "if it wasn't for sale of players, we could fold any time." Daily meal money was reduced from three dollars to two dollars and, before the end of the decade, was deducted from salary. Ballparks disappeared as minor leagues died, and jumps increased in length.

And the features on the map were occasionally formidable. During their 35-year history, Dad's team never failed to appear for a game, although they missed one in Hagerstown, Maryland, in 1958.

John Gray recalled it nearly 40 years later:

> We jumped from Lexington [Kentucky] to Hagerstown over the Appalachians—you know, the Smokies and the Blue Ridge. Big Red huffin' and puffin' and going up slow, whirlin' and twirlin' and whippin' on down. You look out the window going down, you see drive-off ramps for runaway trucks. Chauff thinkin' same thing we are—don't want Big Red a runaway bus on a drive-off ramp tryin' to slow down before we fly off the side of the mountain. So he came down slow as he could.
>
> Got dressed on the bus on the way into Hagerstown, but got there late. The lights were still on, but the last of the fans were leaving. We played Griffith Stadium in Washington next day.

In 1959, when a promoter questioned Clowns integrity, Dad told me, "It beats all, doesn't it? For decades road teams blow dates, show up late or not at all, or advertise Satchel and Satchel's off fishing, and they muddy things up for the Clowns. Finally, we're late one game, and we're lumped right in with the rest. Like Ed says, 'Two and two don't make four in road baseball.'"

Yet, as Clowns catcher John Gray said, "The road was an experience and education you couldn't buy, to see the way people everywhere lived, to see the way we lived on the bus."

Clowns player-manager Carl Forney summarized:

> I enjoyed it because you had time to ride and see things. You get to stop and enjoy people. . . . like Chauff. Only problem Chauff had, when you leave a place, you had to go to the bathroom before you leave, 'cause Chauff gonna take you four hundred miles before you stop at another bathroom. Natureboy would stop, but Chauff slept all during the ball game, so he could probably drive . . . till six o'clock that next morning.
>
> Chauff—good man, good bus driver and dependable. I'll tell you, Chauff pushed a lot of miles before he would turn loose. He'd get about half sleeping, and I'd tell Chauff, 'cause he was my roommate,

I'd say, "Chauff, anything you do, try to drive long as you can 'cause I'm afraid of Natureboy driving." Natureboy thinks he's driving a car instead of a bus.

A lot of times, Natureboy, he'd say, "Alright, Chauff, you're getting sleepy, let me take the hack now."

And I'd say, "Well, since you're going to do that, I'll get up there on the can. I'm gonna be the lookout man 'cause I ain't going to sleep with you driving, Natureboy."

Chauff . . . he'd tell you if you ain't there at six o'clock, if somebody was sick, what time the bus gonna leave. But the funny thing though, I messed around and went crosstown, and I didn't get back till around seven o'clock, and they say Chauff worked on the wheel, he worked everywhere to keep from leaving. I came back . . . I said, "Chauff, I really appreciate that."

He said, "Man, you really had me over a barrel. You got everybody mad at me."

I said, "Well . . . I just couldn't get back."

Liquor and women were easy ways to deal with the road and within walking distance of rooms. There were other ways. One involved Chauff, the man who, next to Tut, best knew the road. Carl Forney explained:

We'd get to the ball park. Instead of Chauff just going back there and lay down and get some rest 'cause we're leaving, got another 300 miles to go that night, Chauff rolled out the dominoes. He cared more about them dominoes than he cared about sleep. 'Cause we could play dominoes sometimes two, three hours a day. Then when we get to the hotel or motel, we'd play dominoes. Chauff get up next morning early, he'd go eat his breakfast. He'd look for Natureboy or (Leo) Gray or Carl Forney to play dominoes. I told Natureboy, "I'm getting tired, dominoes in the morning, dominoes in the evening, dominoes at night. Chauff love them dominoes."

And Natureboy said, "He can't play."

He wasn't any good either. Sure he swore he could, but Chauff couldn't play no dominoes. Hey, I was a beginner and whupped him.

. . . That was an everyday job for us, just like we got to play ball, we got to play dominoes. Soon as we checked in (we rode all day and night), played ball, get to the motel, Chauff say, "You want to play some dominoes?" We'd play dominoes until curfew time. A lot of times we'd go through curfew time. 'Cause we were kinda strict on that curfew. We didn't have too many guys break it neither, 'cause they knew what they had to do.

Chauff talked about baseball. A lot of times Chauff sat up in the stands. You never knew Chauff sat up in the stands? Chauff be sittin' up in the stands, he'd tell you, and the first thing he'd always say, "Natureboy can't hit." Old Chauff would sit up there with that toothpick in his mouth, driving down the road say, "Natureboy, you can't hit."

During the 1950s, segregation was still entrenched in America. In the South, it was de jure, while in the North, it was de facto. But the seams of segregation were unraveling.

Baseball had been on the cutting edge of this change, when Branch Rickey signed Jackie Robinson to a Dodger contract in the winter following World War II, but residual racism still persisted in our national pastime. The Clowns had preceded organized baseball in helping break down these barriers by spreading fun, laughter and good will everywhere they appeared. We dealt with the racial aspects of life on the road however and whenever it was necessary.

As a white, Ed Hamman's wife, Joyce, had her own recollections:

We had the black book for no-hotel towns, had names and addresses of private homes where the Clowns could stay. Don't know whether we called it the black book because of its color or its purpose.

One time, I was outside the Clowns hotel in Birmingham waiting for Ed, who was inside talking with ballplayers. A white man told me to move, said a white woman had no right standing outside that hotel.

... Sometimes, when restaurants wouldn't serve the players and I was around, I'd buy food and bring it to them in the dressing room at the ball park. ...

On the road, we generally ignored prejudice as a fact of life. The men were out there to play baseball, and people came to see them play.

At home was sometimes different. Twice we had bomb threats on our home in St. Petersburg because Ed was involved with a black team, and once Chauff spent some time with us, and police trailed Chauff and me to the grocery store. Can you imagine? Who in this world would be the last one to hurt anybody? Maybe Syd Pollock, but after him, Chauff.

PART SIX

THE SIXTIES

A Section Reserved for Whites

Almost every problem ever plaguing black baseball intensified during the '60s. There was still a section reserved for whites in every Deep South ball park, but the Clowns bus continued carrying joy and love of the game down the road.

—Alan Pollock

26

No Camelot for the Clowns

In 1960, the nation elected John Fitzgerald Kennedy president despite his Catholicism. Dad had followed John F. Kennedy's career for years and was convinced that the young politician, committed to civil rights, would become president and make the sixties special.

If Dad expected a promptly integrated Camelot, he knew differently before the 1960 season opened. Thirteen years after Jackie Robinson integrated major league baseball, former Clowns pitcher Jim Proctor began his rookie season for the Detroit Tigers, and, in response to Dad's recommendation that the Tigers look at Clowns pitchers Jerry Singleton and Ross Linthicum during the upcoming season, Ed Katalinas, chief scout for the Tigers, responded by letter dated March 12, 1960: "At the present time, we are having a large number of Cubans report to spring training who have been thoroughly scouted during the winter leagues and as a result, will have more colored players than our system can handle. If, at any time, you have an outstanding colored player who is a prospect, I will scout him personally and we will try to make a deal for him on the spot."

Almost every problem ever plaguing black baseball intensified during the '60s. There was still a section reserved for whites in every Deep South ballpark, but the Clowns bus continued carrying joy and love of the game down the road.

Dealing with morning mail, Dad put the Katalinas letter under his heavy, domed paperweight with other letters. The sun sparkled through the glass-blown white and blue flowers inside the dome. It seemed business as usual.

But it really wasn't. Business was more difficult daily. New changes had begun beside old changes accelerating. The Clowns had problems, and so did baseball. Clowns problems were terminal, not preventable. In at least one way, the Clowns' death knell was worthy of celebration, because the end of the Clowns was so firmly based on integration.

Baseball's problems though were curable, if baseball would cure them, but refusal to learn and to adjust to change would eventually hurt the game. Refusal of professional baseball to address its needs was a catalyst to the death of the Clowns.

Dad saw it all coming. He saw it in press coverage of major league baseball, in lack of press coverage of other baseball. He read the truth between the lines beneath major league letterheads. And he heard promoters, made skittish by the irresponsibility of other road clubs. The Clowns were earning new fans for baseball, but baseball was hurting the Clowns. The Clowns were plagued by the trifecta of high park rentals, shoddy performances or no-shows by patchwork outfits calling themselves Negro leaguers and poor press coverage. Dad fought it all like an Olympic swimmer, caught in churning rapids, seeking smooth water, but pushed backwards.

Goose Tatum had few peers as a sports comedian, Satchel Paige few as a pitcher, but neither Goose nor Satchel rivaled the Rothschilds or Moynihan for business methods or economics expertise. But then, the Rothschilds couldn't pitch and Moynihan couldn't play first. And they had sense enough not to try. But Goose and Satchel had no pensions, so they considered the world of business and figured a bit of dirt economics.

By the '60s Goose was well beyond his athletic prime and had ruined his reputation by nonappearances with Ted Rasberry's Detroit Stars (Detroit Clowns), and Satchel, in 1961, was 54 years old and still loved fishing or women in lieu of pitching or being at a ballpark on a given game day. Yet Goose and Satchel were readying the world for operation of their own road club. On February 25, 1961, Dad wrote Tom Baird: "fact Satchel & Goose as per clippings you sent me . . . intend running their own club. . . . already heard from Toad Franklin [Colonel Charles B. Franklin] . . . saying Satch and Goose would both like to play with N.Y. Royals on tour with the Clowns. . . . life is too precious to fool around with either of these guys . . . plus Clowns still have too good a reputation."

The August 13, 1962, *St. Petersburg Times* reported:

Old Satchel Paige allowed six hits over two innings and Goose Tatum made one brief appearance as the Kansas City Monarchs defeated the Harlem Stars 12-9 in a Negro American League baseball game at Campbell Park yesterday afternoon.

By the time the Stars and Monarchs had finished their three-hour-plus marathon, the crowd estimated at 300 was glad to see their own St. Petersburg Braves take the field. . . .

It was a tough day for the promoters and the fans expressed their disapproval of the Stars-Monarchs game throughout.

Tatum, a basketball clown trying baseball, came out of the dugout only once—to place a firecracker behind the plate umpire.

Paige, onetime famous pitcher for the St. Louis Browns and Cleveland Indians, who admits to being 47 years old but is more like 67, showed that old familiar shuffle when he took the mound.

But in his prime it was a cocky shuffle. Yesterday it was because of old age.

The line score showed seven errors made by the two traveling teams. Acknowledging the article to Ed Hamman, Dad noted, "These publicized appearances, where Clowns have to follow 'em in same parks, have 'killed' baseball for us and everyone else . . . and hurt attendances tremendously."

The problem spread nationwide, and Dad stayed up later nights writing extra paragraphs to promoters to distinguish the Clowns from other touring teams. Clowns success in the '60s relied to a large extent on new promoters in new cities or in cities not played for years. Minor leagues and playable ballparks continued to diminish. The road between games lengthened. And if Goose and Satchel got to fresh promoters first, Dad or the Clowns' advance man faced prejudice against all road clubs.

In 1960, Satchel Paige pitched in Philadelphia's Connie Mack Stadium before a paid attendance of 349.

Problems predated the straw aggregation Goose and Satchel built in 1960. In 1959, Dad wrote promoter Andy Cohen:

[Clowns advance man] Burns tells me they swore off colored teams at Paris as Ted Rasberry and Goose Tatum failed to show up for a game there. . . .

You'll recall how I advised you last season about the unreliability of these teams. . . . you've been lucky they've shown up for your engagements . . . but we run across cities where they've failed to show. We ran across Rasberry's team at Washington, where they watched us play to 6,000, and players said they weren't being paid off and the league was folding after the East-West game in Chicago on August 9th. . . .

. . . These other teams are making it tough in spots we have to follow them in, because of their unreliability or showings when they do appear.

Dad also wrote former Monarchs owner Tom Baird about complaints from one of Ed Gottleib's associates about the current Monarchs' failure to show for bookings and poor performances when they did appear: "This fellow Ted Rasberry of Kansas City Monarchs ruined things. Had terrible team, bunch of kids, no opposition to home clubs." Dad also mentioned the decline of the Birmingham Black Barons: " . . . [promoter] doesn't seem to realize this isn't the Black Barons of old with Willie Mays, Piper Davis, etc., no names that anyone can recall or mean anything . . . new fly-by-night management."

Lining up the Clowns' 1964 tour of western Canada, Dad wrote Vancouver promoter Nat Bailey:

. . . The Clowns remain today the only salaried professional road baseball attraction out of over 100 that once traveled the highways of Canada and the U.S. While there are some pickup teams knocking around under the names of some of the old teams of the long since defunct Negro American Professional Baseball League, these teams are totally unreliable and have nothing to do with the teams that originally played under their banners.

. . . The Clowns are just the opposite of these fly-by-night clubs. We have a proven reputation for reliability, drawing ability and topnotch entertainment. Last season our bus had three major breakdowns immediately before and during our tour of Western Canada. By chartering Greyhounds and encountering extra travel and repair expenses over $5,000, we were able to make each of our eleven Canadian bookings without missing a single date. This season we have another bus, and have installed a new diesel engine, more suitable for traveling the terrain encountered in the West last season.

By taking such measures to protect our reputation and to insure fans, promoters and sponsors the maximum efficiency possible in an operation of our type, the Clowns have always operated successfully.

The Clowns were only minimally salaried during the '60s, but they were always paid. They didn't play the quality baseball once their trademark, but they played at a professional level, and they generally played well. They traveled efficiently. Particularly after Natureboy and Birmingham Sam teamed up, the Funshow was major league. The Clowns were still an attraction to be proud of.

As sports editor Jim Wechsler wrote Dad from White River Junction, Vermont, on July 11, 1960: "Regarding our game with the Clowns July 5th— As always they put on a fine show and were most co-operative and we all enjoyed their stay in town. It's a shame that so many of these other so-called touring star . . . teams aren't the same. Instead, the others seem to carry on something awful, thus giving all the star touring teams a bad name. Once again, thanks. We were all most happy over the performance and conduct of the team as always."

Press coverage became an even greater problem as the Clowns lost familiar terrain and played new places or towns last visited decades earlier. Dad blamed the press in part for the shrinking popularity of baseball.

On April 23, 1960, in language timely today, Dad wrote O. K. Blauvelt, president of the National Association of Fans, Inc., in Ft. Wayne, Indiana, summarizing baseball's problems:

[the] thing, nationally speaking, which has taken the family spirit out of baseball, rather pointedly has been the cause of decline of the Minor Leagues, ruin of semi-pro and college and H.S. baseball, as it was in the old days, is that sports writers of majority of big city papers, including AP & UP, ignore almost entirely, the activities, the achieve-

ments of individual star performers in the latter category, and dwell almost entirely on building up about a dozen Major League 'name players,' day in and day out, which players no longer need such publicity, already have filled their scrap books, and helps only to get such players extra commercial endorsements and pay. Our "national sport" has become too much big business.

27

The Clowns in Cooperstown

For 1960, the Clowns signed two important pitchers, right-hander John Whitehead and left-hander Freddie Battle. A power hitter as well as a power pitcher, Battle also played first and outfield and served as bus barber and as one who made bus society palatable. Any society preserves sanity by relying in part on those laughing at societal problems. Freddie Battle was such a stabilizing force in the early '60s society of the Clowns bus, or Big Red, as the Clowns now called her. He lightened the drag of the road.

Whitehead managed the 1960 and 1961 New York Royals and the 1962 New York Stars, all Clowns touring partners. The Clowns and Royals carried 28 players between them on the Clowns bus in 1960. Throw in The Great Yogi and Chauff plus occasional tryouts, and a sizeable society rumbled down the road inside Big Red. Carl Forney managed the Clowns for the first time that season.

On June 8, the Clowns played in Niles, Michigan. The *Niles Daily Star* reported:

Last night before a large crowd at Thomas Stadium, an independent baseball team known as the Indianapolis Clowns played up to expectation, as it thrilled and amazed those who watched them perform. The Clowns toyed around with and practically made a rout of the game in downing the out-classed South Bend Sherman's Cleaners team by a sound 9 to 4 margin.

Getting right off to a slam-bang start, aided greatly by fabulous "Natureboy" Williams, there was almost never a dull moment in the entire game. . . .

The third inning saw Natureboy pull his famed bat routine, as he pulled all sorts of odd-shaped bats such as a huge coke bottle, a midget bat and even a wooden leg from his pants. . . .

He also taped a "for rent" sign on the ump. . . .

From the fifth inning on, the pranksters from Indianapolis went into their world-famous funshow, with almost everyone getting into the act at one time or another. . . .

June 12, 1960, was a day unique in baseball history. Before more than 2,000 paid in Louisville, Clowns ambidextrous hurler Ulysses Grant Greene pitched a complete doubleheader, the first game a 3-2 win over the New York Royals, left-handed, the second a 5-2 loss to the Royals, right-handed. That was the only loss for the Clowns in 33 straight games.

On August 1, 1960, the Clowns became the only black team ever to play in Cooperstown's Doubleday Field in honor of Baseball's Hall of Fame.

For the record, Grant Greene pitched an ambidextrous two-hit shutout in Doubleday Field and Ed Craig homered as the Clowns beat the Coopers-town Indians 10-0 before about 500 fans. The *Oneonta Star* reported:

The Indianapolis Clowns presented their two-diamond circus Monday to the squealing delight of fans in Cooperstown and Oneonta who for a change didn't seem to mind that their local heroes were getting clobbered.

. . . Holding their attention instead was a weird brand of baseball that featured rock 'n' roll dancing, a shadowball show and a guy named Yogi who could teach his Yankee namesake a thing or two about the art of squatting.

. . . The piece de resistance was the Clowns' famed shadowball show. While a record player blared out dixieland jazz rhythms, the infield went through a perfectly executed practice session—without a ball. Then followed an Elvis Presley number that had Nature Boy and an ambidextrous pitcher named "Doubleduty" Greene swinging like coed cats at a Hartwick Hop.

But the more important story was how the Clowns players felt about it all. In 1996, Carl Forney described that:

> When they found out they was booked in Cooperstown, I ain't never seen nobody in my life so happy as those Clowns ballplayers, 'cause, you know, that's something you can talk about the rest of your life. . . . I tell people now, I've been to Cooperstown you know, they don't believe me. . . . I'll tell you though, that Cooperstown was really something. That made me feel good. . . . the thing special to me was the ball park. . . . When I went to home plate . . . that's the best feeling I ever had in my life 'cause the big boys had been there, Mays and all the Hall of Famers, and, if I had money now, I think I'd go up there to Cooperstown. I'd just want to see it again because it's been years. If I wasn't a Clown, I never would have gotten to Cooperstown.

In 1960, Vanity Rushing was 19 years old, 5'9 1/2", 173 pounds, a catcher from Chicago. He could run like the wind and switch hit for average with power. He thought well behind the plate and stopped ill-thrown pitches like the Berlin Wall kept people in the Soviet Bloc. With an arm slightly less impressive than Buster Haywood's, he ranked with Sam Hairston and Paul Casanova as the Clowns finest backstop since Buster. The Boston Red Sox purchased Rushing's contract from the Clowns in August 1960 for $22,100, the most ever paid to a black baseball team for a contract. By contrast, the Cubs paid the Monarchs $20,000 for Ernie Banks' contract; the Giants paid the Black Barons $10,000 for Willie Mays' contract; and the Braves paid Dad $10,000 for Hank Aaron's contract. At the time of the Rushing sale, Tom Baird told Dad, "Syd, we should have said they didn't have to pay us a dime for Banks and Aaron, just send us $100 for each major league home run. Maybe you can get rich doing that with Rushing."

Sales terms allowed Rushing to finish the '60 season with the Clowns and to report to the Red Sox camp in the spring.

Assigned to the Red Sox farm team in Wellsville, New York, Rushing was second in the league in stolen bases and was batting .296 his second season there, when he suffered a severe knee injury. He never regained the ability he had before the injury, though he stayed in the Red Sox organization until he was released from their Waterloo, Iowa, affiliate in 1965.

The Clowns played the Kansas City Giants in Kansas City, Kansas, on August 17, an appearance promoted by ex-Monarchs' owner Tom Baird, who promised fans, "It will be like old times." And it was. There were bands, drill teams, majorettes and a paid attendance of 9,503, more than 10,000 in the stands. Alex Harriday had a triple, two singles and four RBIs, and Natureboy Williams stole home during the Clowns 8-4 win.

As far as I know, old-time Negro league players were honored by black teams only at Clowns games. The first time was the 1950 Smokey Joe Williams honorarium at the Clowns–New York Cubans game at the Polo Grounds in New York City. The 1960 game in Kansas City was the second. Honored attendees at the Clowns-Giants game included some all-time greats: Bullet Rogan, Frank Duncan, Newt Allen, Buck O'Neil, Hilton Smith, Army Cooper, Jesse Williams, Dink Mothel and Eddie Dwight (father of America's first black astronaut). There were more Clowns games later in Chicago honoring old-time Negro leaguers.

The Clowns closed the season September 12 in Atlanta, Georgia.

The 1961 Clowns had power hitting and power pitching. Natureboy Williams, Carl Forney, Haley Young, Freddie Battle, Joe Cherry, Alex Harriday and Paul Casanova could all give the ball a ride. The hard throwers included Forney, sidearmer Henderson Horton, Earl Palmore, Al Hooker and Joe Cherry from the right side and Battle and Charlie Middlebrooks from the left. Newcomer Billy Parker, who would stay with the Clowns through and including Dad's last year, 1964, was both a hitter and pitcher. A small line-drive spray hitter, Parker played second, and sometimes hit with surprising power. He took a regular spot in the Funmakers' pitching rotation. One of the quietest, warmest, most positive and diligent of all who ever played for the Clowns, Parker pleased everyone ever associated with him in 1971, when he became rookie second baseman for the Los Angeles Angels.

Clowns "midget" shortstop–third baseman Billy Vaughn, talked about that 1961 team 35 years later: "It was the best I saw my years on the road. Few beat us. . . . You know lots of my teammates 1961 and after, with things as wide open as now, would have played in the majors."

The 1961 Clowns opened the season April 9 in Pensacola in the cold and rain, and about six weeks later the weather got hotter but things got jail-house-floor colder.

Late in the preseason, Dad had decided to intersperse the May Texas tour with a dip into Mexico. He booked Juarez for May 23.

The trouble in Juarez, Mexico, was that tequila was more of a rumor in 1961 than the fad it became later when margaritas were fashionable. Three Clowns players—outfielder Louis Ringo, pitcher Al Hooker and pitcher-catcher Joe Cherry—victims of Juarez heat, had heard of tequila, but never tried it. So they went to a Juarez bar to sample the product.

Before they even put salt to their lips, they were arrested for using and dealing drugs, not by police, but by a gang who prepaid local police to use the jail for the scam. It wasn't subtle. The phony officers didn't even bother to plant drugs. They just accused, charged and apprehended the players on the spot; hauled them off to the vacated jail; slammed them into cells; and asked who should be called for release money.

They called Ed Hamman at the team hotel, and Ed brought the $200 fine to the jail; paid the gang; watched as the players were freed; and said farewell as the Mexicans wandered off down streets dimly lit by Juarez city lights.

Dad didn't need a note as to why Juarez would not be booked again. He had the reason memorized.

On June 4, 1961, the Clowns drew more than 7,000 paid to Municipal Stadium, Kansas City, Kansas, for the benefit of the NAACP Freedom Fund. Charlie Middlebrooks tossed a two-hitter (only one hit left the infield); Carl Forney had four hits, including a triple; and Paul Casanova went five for five, including an inside-the-park homer, against former Kansas City Monarchs greats Jim LeMarque and Frank Duncan, as the Clowns pounded the Kansas City Giants 14-0.

That Casanova was even in uniform was a tribute to Dad. It was custom for the old-time Negro leaguers to gather at the main gate at Clowns games in Kansas City, discussing old days and current lives. Dad always joined them. Afterwards, when Dad and I arrived at the Clowns dugout maybe 15 minutes before game time, Paul Casanova was sitting on the bench wearing a T-shirt, blue jeans, sneakers and a frown. I had never seen him before, nor had I ever seen a man more powerfully built. There was no visible body fat. But he was a study in inert energy. He was motionless but for a slight facial quiver, obviously the result of the effort of whatever facial muscles had the awesome responsibility of holding his frown in place.

"Why isn't Casanova dressed?" Dad asked Carl Forney.

"He's Latin is why, temperamental. See the white guy two rows up in the box next to the dugout?"

"Yes," Dad said.

"He's a Cardinals scout. The Cardinals released Casanova. The scout hollered hello to Casanova before batting practice. Casanova went to the clubhouse and got into his clothes and came back out. He's been sitting there catatonic ever since. He says he ain't gonna play with no Cardinals people looking at him. The guy leaves the ballpark or Casanova says he don't play."

"Where's Ed?" Dad asked.

"Probably off buying Casanova's ticket back to Havana. Told him he was finished with us if he didn't get up and go to the clubhouse to dress by the ten-count, which, of course he didn't." In fact, Ed had passed us in the crowd unseen on the way to unhinge Dad from the old-timers we had already left.

Dad sat beside Casanova. I sat next to Dad.

"Look, Paul," Dad said, "the Cardinals make mistakes. They didn't, they'd win the series every year. If we didn't know their mistake on you, you wouldn't be with us. We rarely take a guy's been cut from O.B."

"He leaves," Casanova said, pointing his thumb back at the Cardinals scout like a hitchhiker, "or Ed Hamman can go buy my ticket home."

"You're young, like Alan here. I'm telling you like I would my son. You got nobody here. You're in a foreign country. Got nobody to look after you. Nobody cares you're mad at this guy. If he doesn't like you, worst thing you could do is let him beat you, make you go home. Best thing is to make the big leagues and show him up. Your future's in getting in uniform, coming out here and knocking one out to the cows and throwing a couple runners out stealing. Show the guy how bad his organization screwed up."

Casanova smiled and looked out toward the Municipal Stadium cows grazing on their hilly meadow just outside the right-center-field inner fence.

Dad continued, "I got at least six scouts I know of all from different teams out here to look at you. There's two new teams coming into the National League, the New York Mets, the Houston Sports. Wid Matthews is here for the Mets, just to look at you. He's the best there is. Don't let him miss his chance to see you."

Paul Casanova rose slowly and walked down the steps to the clubhouse tunnel.

"With our luck," Dad whispered to me, "cattle rustlers will make off with the cows and Casanova will lose focus." As it happened, Casanova's inside-the-park homer bounced off the wall in front of the cows.

Billy Vaughn joined the Clowns on July 3, 1961, in Huntsville, Alabama, before a large, joyful crowd. He was billed as the only midget in the world playing professional baseball, but in truth he was not a midget—he was a small man. "When I joined the Clowns," Vaughn said, "I was 17. I was 4'6" and 145 pounds and still growing, and I never did stop growing until I hit 4'11"."

In 1955, Billy saw the Clowns when they played his hometown, Decatur, Alabama: "The Clowns were major league quality then. I was just 11, a small 11, and the guys took a liking to me, and let me sit on the bench, teasing me and Bebop, telling Bebop how I was going to grow up and replace him. . . . From the moment they let me in that dugout, I said I got to play pro baseball, just got to. And all them teasing me about Bebop."

Bebop was a dwarf comic. Billy Vaughn was a small athlete, with great foot speed, a strong arm, decent fielding ability and a nice batting eye. His ability to play baseball was no fluke. He lettered four years of high school football and played two years of semi-pro football, all as a running back. He was a quiet, serious student of both sports. And crowds loved him, amazed that one so small was a player, not a joke.

Billy Vaughn would remain with the Funmakers through the rest of the time Dad had an interest in the team. Rumors spread now and then of Bebop or some other dwarf or midget playing for the Clowns. I've talked to people who swear they saw Bebop make one of the greatest plays they ever saw or Dero Austin double. None of that is true. But Billy Vaughn was a real baseball player. He played well, sometimes made spectacular plays and stroked out a few game-winning hits. And that is true.

On July 18, the Clowns beat their traveling partners, the New York Royals, in Haverhill, Massachusetts, 5-0, before more than 2,000 fans. The Haverhill game was a landmark because it was likely the only time in history a black team was given the press it deserved. Game coverage took up nearly an entire page plus overage on another, including articles of game highlights, attendance, the comedy, local and Clowns' thoughts on the ball yard and concessions sales, photos of the Flying Nesbitts in action, the Clowns in action, Natureboy signing autographs, the seated crowd, the standing-room-only crowd on the field, and cartoon drawings of game and entertainment highlights. The *Haverhill Journal* wrote of Natureboy:

> ... He played first base with a glove the size of a pup tent; he played first base while seated in a chair; he went to bat with a war club ten feet long.
>
> When he walked up to the dish with the big bat Ump Paul Gilbert said, "No dice." So he pulled seven more bats and a plastic woman's leg from his pocket.
>
> He pulled a hat hoister when he threw two balls from home to second from behind his back. You had to see it to believe it.
>
> During the shadow ball drill he had them in the aisles. He jitterbugged, uttered wisecracks and had every kid in the park yelling for him.
>
> And when it was over and he was still perspiring freely he still took the time to sign many autographs for the kids who climbed all over the dugout.

Wid Matthews was in Municipal Stadium that afternoon to scout Paul Casanova once more for the New York Mets. Dad asked me to sit with Wid at the game, a Clowns win over the Royals before about 4,500 fans. During the game, Wid asked me who I thought was the best natural hitter in the major leagues. "Moose Skowron," I said. "No one thinks so but me."

"Why do you think he's best, better than, say, Mantle?"

"The guy's back is so bad, he wears a corset and can't follow through. But he still hits .280 with thirty homers, a hundred-plus RBIs."

"Al," Wid said, "No one in this world thinks Moose Skowron is the best natural hitter but you and me—and Moose's mother. Now let's go over who you think the best Clowns are and why."

Wid rented a car, and drove Dad and me to the Clowns game that night in Lawrence, where Charlie Middlebrooks pitched the win, and Casanova caught one stealing and picked another off, both from a crouch.

"Don't think I've ever seen a better arm," said Wid Matthews candidly.

"You never saw Buster Haywood then," I said, and he admitted he hadn't.

"Casanova's got it all though, doesn't he?" Wid asked rhetorically. "Hits, runs, blocks high and tight and low and outside, throws bullets—could probably pitch, just throwing fastballs."

So after the Clowns had dressed and were on their way to the bus, Wid requested Dad's consent to ask Paul Casanova one question, and Dad called Paul over to Wid's rented car. "You do a nice job behind the plate," Wid said, and Casanova nodded. "What are you going to do once the season's over?"

"Go home."

"To Havana?"

"Yes."

"Family there?"

"Yes."

"Thank you."

As Paul Casanova walked toward the bus, a lone figure in lightbulb night, Wid said to Dad, "We offer $5,000 for Charlie Middlebrooks, usual graduated scale, $1,000 down, something in between you work out with us and the rest when he makes the majors 30 days. We'll submit it in writing."

"Done," Dad said. "But what about Casanova?"

"Don't want him, Syd. Don't get me wrong, I like both Middlebrooks and Casanova, and I'd like to keep them together. But Casanova goes to Cuba, Castro keeps him there, and the Mets have nothing. Things in Cuba are like things in Russia. Nobody gets out anymore. You can't keep the kid from his home and his family."

It was one of the few mistakes Wid Matthews ever made scouting. Casanova emerged from Cuba into Mexico for the 1962 season, and by 1967, he was the starting catcher for the American League All-Stars and finished his career catching for the Braves, a teammate of Hank Aaron.

On August 6 in Wichita, Ray Dumont of the National Baseball Congress awarded Dad (Ed Hamman accepted in Dad's behalf) the National Baseball Congress plaque for outstanding contribution to baseball, the first of two Dad received from the National Baseball Congress. The awards reflected the popularity the Clowns had gained for baseball over the years through their live appearances everywhere.

The Clowns ended the 1961 season on September 4 at Wilmer's Park, Brandywine, Maryland, along with blues singer Little Willie John, part of Arthur Wilmer's Labor Day celebration.

28

Bobo Revisited

In the spring of 1962, Dad and Ed made amends with Frank "Bobo" Nickerson, who had appeared briefly with the Clowns during 1961. Bobo suggested that he was going "to catch a ball from an airplane flying at 1,000 feet this season." Dad questioned the ambiguity of Bobo's language. "Does he mean the ball will be thrown from a plane at 1,000 feet and Bobo will be on the ground to catch it or that he'll be flying in a plane at 1,000 feet when he makes the catch?" Bobo ultimately caught a ball dropped 650 feet from an airplane.

But no matter what Bobo did, Ed Hamman and Bobo Nickerson just could not get along. Whenever they looked at each other, they did it like two gunslingers squaring off on the streets of Tombstone. So when Bobo returned to the Clowns that spring, he did so as an independent contractor at $20 a day, $8 a day accrued and sent directly home twice monthly to his wife, Marilyn, $12 paid in cash daily to Bobo. From his $12, Bobo paid for travel in his own car, food and hotel. (If you wanted to see Bobo cringe, you used Ed Hamman's expression "You pay for travel, eats and sleeps.") Unlike Ed and the players, who ate economically, Bobo dined in nice restaurants, not fine places, but good clean ones serving large portions of pure Americana. As we discovered the days I roomed with him that year, Bobo and I shared pedestrian gastronomical tastes. We preferred peanut butter and jelly on rye to veal cordon bleu. We sought baked chicken and green peas, not beef Wellington and asparagus tips in cheese sauce. We would pass a mile of cherries jubilee or baked Alaska to attack a sliver of chocolate cream pie from the Roubidoux (but that reverence is a story of its own). For the moment, it is enough to say that once Bobo paid for travel, food and room, he spent the daily balance on beer, which, depending on the cost of living where we were, might buy him a single can of the worst or schooners of the finest draft.

He was able to more than double his daily intake the days I traveled with him dividing hotel costs. (If I really wanted to irritate Bobo, I would ask him if we were going to share the bill for sleeps that night, and if that didn't get him, I'd ask, "Well what about eats?")

In June 1961, Ed Hamman wrote Dad candidly of Bobo, after Dad had prevented Ed from firing his nemesis. After pointing out Bobo's attitude deficits, Ed wrote:

> We can't afford incidents like . . . the army camp Fort Hood. Swearing is never funny and if one has to drop to this to get laughs it is bad. With his great talent he doesn't have to. His pepper, ball handling, and bat juggling is the greatest ever done by any human being. His going thru the stands changing hats is one of the warmest personal touch act any one could see. He rarely ever does it. His audience loves it. . . .
>
> The only enemy is Bobo himself. . . .

On May 30, the Clowns played a game in the rain for the troops at Fort Hood, Arkansas, and Ed Hamman was soaked. On June 2, I graduated from Florida State University. I had no job as of June 6, when Joyce Hamman called with the stunning news that illness had chased Ed Hamman down the road from Ft. Hood, and he was hospitalized in critical condition with double pneumonia in Enid, Oklahoma. Freddie Battle was acting road business manager, and Danny White, a utility player and Ed's driver, was working the P.A.

"Alan," Dad said. "You're always saying how you love the Clowns. Now you get to show it. You're taking over for Ed till he gets back, at least two weeks, Joyce says, probably more."

Dad bought two tickets to Kansas City, and on the plane, he simulated setting up the gates pregame and showed me how to do daily reports, replenish banks, do my bookkeeping and handle hypothetical problems he created.

Marti and I were to marry December 1st that year, but in late May when Mother and Dad brought her to Tallahassee for my graduation, marriage was just a thought. Mom wrote Marti a letter, mailed June 14, in which she told her that I was on my way "to run the team for Dad." Then, inviting Marti to our house the following weekend, Mom added, "Dad said, 'I promise I won't tease Marti.' Never the less he will, that I'm sure of."

Bobo was unhappy. A former Army Ranger, he had fought bravely in the Pacific in World War II, and his fiery days on the Pacific islands were the nearest thing to Bobo's mind next to baseball and his wife, Marilyn. There were days Hell was a short jump down a fast highway for Bobo.

As a pitcher with the House of David, Bobo learned juggling and pepperball. He incorporated comedy into his act, but had difficulty making a living on personal appearances. Infinitely more talented than his counterparts Al Schacht and Max Patkin, he received far fewer bookings in organized baseball. As Dad said, Bobo's anger and disappointment showed in his stage presence. When he wasn't touring, he earned money as a pitching instructor at Art Gaines' Baseball School in Hunnewell, Missouri, and those who observed him there said baseball had no finer teacher. During his time with the Clowns, Bobo freely helped Clowns pitchers.

When I traveled with him, Bobo spoke often of the war, and, when he did, he eventually became sullen and quiet, then he would drive hundreds of miles without another word. Joyce Hamman recalls sitting in the press box with Bobo one July 4th Clowns appearance in Chattanooga, and as the fireworks roared, he covered his head with a Clowns jacket deflecting memories.

Dad complained that Bobo too often strolled foul territory without purpose during games, when he should either be entertaining with sideline comedy or out of sight, yet Bobo complained of being made to arrive before games and stay until the end. "Hell, boys," he told Dad and Ed more than once, "Ole Bobo can arrive twenty minutes into the game, do his act after the bottom of the third and have his gigee showered, powdered and on the road to tomorrow by the top of the fifth."

"Shouldn't perform till we have four and a half in," Ed said. "Complete games prevent refunds, unless you'd like us to deduct rain refunds from your pay."

"You mean you don't do that now, $20 a day is my regular pay without rain refunds? Son of a Buck! That's all I get? Well, no wonder—I ought to be playing the major leagues and I'm out here like a wandering gypsy with a bunch a colored semi-pros."

In Kansas City that day, Bobo's act went on and on like he'd been hired just to give Tom Baird ammunition with which to blast Dad during his end of the next Clowns-pervert-the-game dialogue.

By contrast, the Clowns now had Sam Brison, and the Kansas City game was the first Dad and I saw him.

Sam, in his early twenties, had received a playing tryout with the Clowns in Rickwood Field in his hometown, Birmingham, on April 29, and Carl Forney and Ed Hamman were sufficiently impressed with his baseball ability to sign him at the standard Clowns salary that year, $125 per month. A few days later, Sam began his comedy career with an intuitive freestyle swimming slide, and within ten days began receiving $2.50 a day extra for comedy.

Because of Sam's resemblance to Tut, Ed called him King Tut, Jr., and Dad publicized him with that name.

Sam stole the show in Kansas City with impromptu comedy, good baseball and spectacular sliding ability. Dad knew that Sam was the best Clowns comedy find since Natureboy Williams and maybe better than that.

After the game, Dad raised Sam to $250 a month. I asked Sam if he had sliding pads, and he didn't. He had a strawberry down his right hip and thigh like I'd never seen. Dad bought him a couple pair of sliding pads. Then Sam said, "Got one more problem needs resolving, that's my name."

"King Tut, Jr.?" Dad asked.

"Yeah. Problem is, I didn't even know the man. Seen his picture on the bus. He musta been popular as God. Fans keep asking me, 'How your Daddy?' and I got no answer. Ain't gonna lie, ain't gonna say, 'My Daddy fine, I'll tell him you be asking.' These people feel strong about King Tut. Other problem is, I got to have my own identity, establish myself. I ain't no Tut."

"Okay," Dad said, "You just want to be Sam Brison."

"No. I figure Birmingham Sam be good. People ask me about how Birmingham is, I can answer that."

And Dad wrote "Birmingham Sam Brison" on a piece of paper, and told Sam, "Well, that's who you are, Birmingham Sam Brison. I got about two, three weeks of advance publicity out to promoters says you're King Tut, Jr., so play along till it runs out. When I get back to Hollywood, I gotta do one release covering today and another in a week or so, and I'll still call you Tut, Jr., in case Ed reads them, then all that's gonna say, Birmingham Sam. Thing is, this name's a big sticking point with Ed, so wait till he's a bit better before we tell him you're not Tut. Time he gets back out here, I'll tell him."

Dad once said, "Handling baseball comics is about as much fun as bare-handing uranium—the exceptions, King Tut and Birmingham Sam Brison." As unhappy as Bobo was, Sam was happy. Totally devoted to his young wife and new child, Sam rode the bus down a straight, narrow road that didn't include women or drinking or anything that interfered with family, baseball, comedy. He was kind to all, almost always with humor. He was the last player to tour with the Clowns summers and the Harlem Globetrotters winters. He was welcome back anywhere, any season.

Creative, after his playing days, he later starred in the shadowball sequences in the Hollywood movie *Bingo Long and the Traveling All-Stars and Motor Kings,* rated by every black baseball player I've ever spoken to as a disaster film that totally misrepresented black baseball and comedy baseball. But the shadowball sequences were good.

As a technical advisor, Ed Hamman had a heart attack on the set in Georgia, and when Sam, who was quite dark, went to visit Ed at the hospital, he was intercepted and told by a coronary care nurse that only family members were allowed to see Ed. "Shoot," Sam said, "he's my father," and when the nurse did a take, he added, "Course my mother was light."

Sam's comedic mind rivaled Prince Jo Henry's, his timing Goose Tatum's. His comedy was quick, over in an instant like a close-up magician's card tricks, but never forgotten. Dad's last two years with the Clowns, Billy Vaughn sometimes pitched an inning or two, and Sam caught. Sam's between-the-legs throws to nail runners stealing second became legend. One game, Billy kept waving off signals because each signal became increasingly more ludicrous and funnier than its predecessor. As Billy described it: "So then he pulled off his cap, and I shook that off. And he patted his butt, and I shook that off. And he stood up and faced away from me and pulled down his pants, flashing bright red underwear. I nodded yes, and he pulled his pants on, turned and crouched. When I threw a strike, the crowd went crazy. So we did that from then on."

Sometimes, memories define the man. Billy Vaughn said:

Bobo Nickerson. I always picture Bobo finishing his act in Sheboygan, Wisconsin, telling that crowd, "Goodbye, Sheboygan, and if I never see you again, it'll be all right with me." He was anger, disappointment, despair.

Birmingham Sam Brison. I picture Sam, strikes out swinging, looks up in the stands, smiles at the prettiest woman there, says, "Now that's out of the way, I'll be right up, baby." Grace and timing and smiles. That was Sam.

After the Kansas City game, Bobo drove Dad and me to Lawrence for a night game. Dad showed me how to handle the gate and settle up in a small park, and after the game we went back to Kansas City. On June 11, I was on my own. Dad wrote Ed about it June 13th from Hollywood:

. . . put on great show at K.C., but Bobo arrived at park early . . . arranged for field mike . . . made his own announcements . . . did not put on pre-game show (which he should) . . . but did all his stuff in 4th inning (before game was official) . . . did too much talking knocking A's, etc., and drew out his act for 25 min. to half-hour . . . much, much too long . . . then at Lawrence . . . drove Al and me there . . . did a lot of crabbing that he was major league . . . this road traveling biz was no good for him . . . felt like quitting . . . no reason for him, he says, to get to parks early . . . he could report before 5th inning to do his act . . . then leave park . . . why should he put in so many hours . . . he went on in third inning . . . did his juggling act . . . that's all. . . . White announced his next number . . . but he just walked off the field. . . . if he didn't appear at all, probably wouldn't have been missed . . . altho N.B. [Natureboy] got sick or said he had stomach ache around 5 innings . . . plus p.a. system went on the fritz . . . and I was at office with Alan checking when shadowball and dance went on to borrowed record player . . . after eating on way back to K.C., Bobo cooled off a bit . . . was to meet us at Street Hotel at noon to take Alan to Marysville . . . showed up at 12:30 in room where I was going over figures and financial reports with Battle, Alan and Forney . . . told him he was half hour early and we'd be thru by 1 . . . said he'd wait downstairs . . . we came down at 1:30 p.m. and N.B. told me he had left . . . so made room in bus and Alan went with team.

My idea is not to fire Bobo . . . but he should be fined for his action in not doing at least his ball juggling and bat twirling acts at Lawrence . . . and not doing at least one number pre-game. . . . TYB [Tom Baird] is writing you how he ruined things at K.C. . . . it wasn't quite that bad . . . but he didn't help himself or us either. . . .

I fixed Battle [team captain] and Forney up with NEW BANK . . . also Alan has NEW BANK and hope we have sufficient Friday to pay-off. . . . incidentally . . . Bobo . . . handed in one bill for $4.13 for a hotel room just to change uniform in . . . which I didn't like . . . said he's done that several times in past . . . as places where teams dress isn't good enough for him . . . paid same but told him I didn't think it was good policy. . . .

29

My Roomie

Turned out, there was much more to Bobo than the disgruntled juggling Army Ranger he projected. It's just his bad moments were as easy to read as the top three lines of an eye chart magnified. He was joyful to travel with and daily some new positive part of Bobo emerged. It was like watching a rose bloom in time-lapse photography. I understood early why Dad had suggested I split travel between Bobo and the teams. There were things to be learned from both.

All Dad and Bobo had gone through about Bobo arriving before game time was a residual argument between Bobo and Ed. Beginning the next day in Marysville through the time I returned to Hollywood, whenever I traveled with him, Bobo never resented getting me to the park two hours before game time. I would have known if he had a problem with that. Bobo was incapable of deceit, to a fault. He said whatever was on his mind whenever it was there, regardless of his sensibilities or the feelings of those around him.

On June 11, Bobo and I went to eat before we were due at the park in Marysville. It was there I made the culinary faux pas that ranks me all-time Clowns record holder for food blunders. And I did it my first day on the road.

Whenever I went to Morrison's Cafeteria in Tallahassee, I ordered the shrimp salad. Made with fresh Gulf shrimp, Morrison's shrimp salads were among the most beautiful things on earth. So, when I saw shrimp salad on the menu in Marysville, Kansas, I ordered it. Cactus dying of thirst had seen water more recently than the two shrimp resting on my tossed salad, half a continent from the nearest ocean and as at home as penguins in Quito, Ecuador. My two shrimp looked like twin plankton swollen by some horrible nautical plague. But Bobo seemed to relate to me after that night, and, often during our travels, he pointed out to absolute strangers, "This here's my roomie, loves them Kansas shrimp."

At the game in Marysville that night, I wondered about Bobo. Here I was, the boss's son, and a college graduate, granted one who orders shrimp in Kansas. But what would make a well-tempered road warrior like Bobo comfortable around me?

At the end of four and a half in Marysville, the answer came; he was already comfortable. On the bench, Bobo rested a hand on my shoulder. "Okay, Wing Ding Nuts," he said, "time for old Bobo's act. You go settle up—then we take two, hit to right, and go back to the motel. We keep playing these friggin' semi-pro parks without clubhouses, I got to ride sweaty with the boss' son. You tell Syd to think about how that smells next time he books."

On June 13, we drew a decent crowd in Lincoln, Nebraska. We were more than holding our own with two more days to payday. I wore Dad's money belt, with two specific instructions. Once I got a few hundred more than I needed, I was to send a cashier's check home in the amount of the extra money. If I was robbed, I was to lower my pants and give up the money belt at the slightest threat of violence.

On the 14th, we played in Norfolk, Nebraska. Bobo and I checked into the local hotel early. "Marble lobby," Bobo observed. "Perfect. Norfolk's another semi-pro ball park without dressing rooms."

Natche had ripped his tux coat sliding in Lincoln, so I took it and promised I'd have it repaired in Norfolk, and I wanted to send money home. Dad had left me $300 of his own money in case I needed it for payday, and I was nervous carrying the couple hundred extra from Lincoln. While I was waiting for the cashier's check, I asked the teller about a tailor.

"You want the Jew. His place is the next block left, this side the street."

After I left the bank, I walked left to the next block and saw no tailor shop, so I asked a pedestrian. "That'd be the Jew," he told me. "That's the next block."

By this time, I realized I was about to meet probably the only Jew within a hundred miles of this township and range. On the next block, I still didn't see his store, so I asked a shopper, "Where can I find the Jew?"

"Right there," he said, pointing two storefronts away to the tiniest, most unobtrusive shop in town.

Inside was the Jew, looking stereotypical. His gray hair fringed baldness as far back as the yarmulke tilted across the back of his head. He wore rimless half-glasses, and spoke with a Lower East Side New York–Eastern European accent. Sewing the coat while I waited, he commented on the fine quality and the extraordinary wear and tear, and showed little interest when I told him its use.

I didn't want to single him out because he'd obviously been singled out enough, so I never asked him how he got to Norfolk, Nebraska, and I've often wondered since.

When we arrived back at the hotel after the Norfolk game, Bobo was still in full uniform, a gray, flannel baseball suit with red letters "BOBO" in an arc on his chest where team names normally appear. As I approached the door, I noticed he wasn't beside me, then I heard his voice from the middle of the street. "Hold the door open, Roomie."

I did, and Bobo, lit postgame cigar in his mouth, ran across half the street, the sidewalk, and the lobby, then did a perfect hook slide along the last 15 feet of marble, shoe coming to rest against the golden oak of the check-in desk. "Room 408, Chief," he yelled from the floor, holding his left hand aloft to catch the key toss. I eased sideways across the lobby to the elevator like I had no idea who Bobo was. Whenever we stayed in a hotel with a marble lobby and there was either no dressing room at the ballpark or one Bobo felt was meant for rats, I held the hotel door and Bobo slid across the lobby to get the key. I became expert at easing sideways across marble lobbies toward elevators and denying that I knew the man. Once, in Lafayette, Indiana, I was asked if I was with him, and before I admitted I was, I paraphrased St. Peter, "I knoweth him not."

I never had to use the extra money Dad had given me. He couldn't recall whether he gave me $100, $200 or $300, so he was pleasantly surprised when I reimbursed him $300 after returning to Hollywood in July.

But that payday, road baseball economics of the '60s created a problem neither Dad nor I anticipated. Had I known how short player funds were, I would have paid off at the hotel before we got to the ballpark. The players were so short of money, they chipped in and split sardines and crackers for supper in their rooms that evening (something I didn't find out until next night in St. Joseph, Missouri), then arrived at the ball park extra early, exiting the bus on arrival and reentering one by one as we settled up and I distributed the mail I'd picked up at General Delivery. From gross pay, I deducted income tax and Social Security and any advances made since the prior payday, counted out the cash into prepared envelopes and had the players sign the pay slips I'd printed up in duplicate as receipts.

As each player was paid, he took his gear to the clubhouse to change into uniform, but when I was done, Leo Westbrook, a capable left-handed New York Stars pitcher from Chicago, was standing outside the bus with George "Sugar" Brown and John and Hal King from the Clowns. They were dressed in traveling outfits and holding suitcases and gear bags.

"This here's a strike," Leo told me. "You get us more money or we catching a train to Chicago. Gonna hook up with some other team."

"There is no other team. Not any more. Just the Clowns, unless you're in O.B. You doing this because I'm new out here, you figure you'll take advantage?" I asked.

"We're doing this because we need money. We're underpaid," Leo said.

"Everyone knows you're underpaid. I know. Dad knows. Ed knows. You knew when you signed. You think Dad likes that? He deplores it. He wants to keep the team going, he's gotta underpay you. He's underpaid too, more than you. All you really get's a chance. Why didn't you talk to him? He was out here five days ago."

"We're talking to you," said George Brown, a Florida A&M graduate.

"Well, let's go in the ballpark to a phone, and we'll see what Dad says."

After I spoke to Dad, I gave the four my report: "Dad agrees with me. He can't pay more. Says whoever leaves, he understands, but whoever leaves signed a contract for what he's getting, and Dad won't give anyone who leaves a good reference. He thinks you King brothers are both major league prospects and particularly hopes you'll stay. That's it, gentlemen."

Hal King stayed. His brother John left with Leo Westbrook and Sugar Brown. I climbed to the top of the stands and watched the trio walk down the road with their grips until they were lonely silhouettes, then shadows, then gone, and for the first time on the road, I wished I weren't there.

Of the two King brothers, I felt John, a third baseman, was the better player; in fact, I felt he was the best prospect on the 1962 Clowns. But he never made the majors. Hal King, however, went on to a successful career catching for the Houston Astros and Atlanta Braves.

Both teams played just okay in Grand Island, perhaps due to the strike, perhaps due to the powerful winds that eventually blew the lighting system black, delaying the game. But there's knowledge to be gained even on such a night. During infield practice, I heard Natche holler, "Light! Tenth row, 1 P.M. Light! Light! Light!" I asked Freddie Battle to translate, but before he did he walked halfway out to the plate, turned just to the right on a line from home plate to the stands, looked up into the stands and smiled.

Back in the dugout, Freddie said, "Stands here are about a 180 degree arc, so each digit on the clock's 15 degrees. Line from the plate back bisecting the stands is noon, P.M.'s to the right facing the stands, A.M.'s to the left. When Natche says tenth row, 1 P.M., he's saying look ten rows up 15 degrees to the right of noon, and you'll see a beautiful woman with a leg shot."

"How do you know it's a leg shot."

"Light means leg shot. He says leg shot tenth row, and points, she covers up, we don't see anything. He says light tenth row 1 P.M., we know quickly and accurately where to look and what we're gonna see, and the woman has no idea what he said."

Because of the delay for repair of the park lighting system, the Grand Island game dragged deeply into the night. Bobo and I woke extra early and headed for St. Joe. "Bobo, how come you want to leave so early?" I asked.

"Can't wait to get to St. Joe, is why," he said.

"Oh yeah," I said, "I forgot, Marilyn's gonna be there." Bobo's wife was traveling over from Independence to spend the night.

"That too," Bobo said.

"What do you mean, 'That too?' What else is there?"

"The chocolate cream pie at the Roubidoux."

To begin with, I didn't even think of a hotel with a French name in St. Joseph, Missouri, so I thought he had in mind some dive called the Ruby Dew. But I should have known better. Like gold running through a mine, there was a vein of those who loved to eat in the Clowns organization that year, beginning with Dad, widening with Billy Vaughn, Freddie Battle, Natche and me, and wearing off into a small point with Bobo. By that I mean while the rest of us ate like gluttons, Bobo didn't eat huge quantities, but he certainly savored what he ate. So I should have known the Roubidoux chocolate cream pie was special—Bobo spoke of it many times hourly during this particular jump, and thinking back, he had talked about it on and off for days before that. And now I understand. Probably at least once a month since I've been married to Marti, I've told her, "I'd give almost anything for one more slice of chocolate cream pie from the Roubidoux sitting across from Bobo."

We ate at the Roubidoux that night, saving room for the chocolate cream pie, which was to other chocolate cream pies what *Gone with the Wind* was to Civil War movies.

At the ballpark, I spent our two pregame hours trying to get the groundskeeper to water the drought-dusted field and worrying about the whereabouts of the Indianapolis Clowns and New York Stars.

At ten minutes before game time, I phoned Dad in Hollywood. "Dad, I'm sorry, I've been optimistic and trying to delay this, but we got ten minutes to game time, and the teams aren't here. I figure at best, they're all out on strike and commandeered the bus; at worst, there's been a serious accident. I think you ought to call all the highway patrols, troopers and police headquarters between Grand Island and here." About that time, Bobo hollered, "Here comes the bus, Roomie!"

"Dad, the bus is here. I'll call you back."

Carl Forney was the first one off the bus. "Skip, everything all right?"

"Yes," he said, "Tell you 'bout it later. We got to get dressed. Got a ball game." He walked head down toward the clubhouse.

As Clowns players filed into the locker room, they looked drawn and unhappy. Finally Chauff came out of the bus. "Chauff, what happened?" I asked. "How come you're late?"

"Didn't serve us is all. Ain't et since sardines we had before the game in Grand Island."

"What do you mean, didn't serve us?"

"White men. Every restaurant beginning in Grand Island, right here into town, refused to serve us food. We ain't et nuttin' all day. Stopped everyplace. Don't worry, Little Syd, not the first time, won't be the last."

When the Clowns and Stars took the field, fans had no inkling that anything was wrong, and the clubs put on one of their finest games and shows. In fact, it was during that game, Sam Brison pulled off the funniest sight gag I ever saw, the slide into the dust cloud at home on Billy Vaughn's triple.

The teams next ate the following morning on the way to Des Moines, Iowa.

By contrast, Bobo and I had a food problem of our own. We thought about a Roubidoux chocolate cream pie midnight snack, but then decided that Heaven was a whole Roubidoux chocolate cream pie on the way to Des Moines. So we deferred until morning. Next morning, Marilyn and I could hear Bobo singing chocolate cream pie lyrics in the shower, and all breakfast Bobo and I talked about the pie to come. After breakfast, Bobo ordered the biggest chocolate cream pie on inventory to go.

"Sorry," said the waitress. "We only have them evenings."

"You got any from last night?" I asked.

"We never keep them. Gave some away to stragglers at the end of last night."

"Looks like we shoulda straggled, Roomie," Bobo said.

I nearly cried. Bobo's face reddened to the point I feared a stroke. "Only other time I felt this bad," he said, "was first time I read Casey had struck out with Flynn a-huggin' third."

But down the road, Bobo said. "You know, Roomie. We ain't got it so bad. The poor players ain't eaten in a day and a half. I know a place in Des Moines makes one of the best vanilla butter cream layer cakes you ever tasted, vanilla icing, chocolate filled. Son of a buck it's good."

Des Moines proved anything but a butter cream layer cake. At 2 P.M., the Des Moines Merchants began dismantling the New York Stars for the honor of meeting the Clowns at Sec Taylor Stadium at 8 P.M. The Merchants played as well as the Stars did poorly, and, at night, the Clowns fared little better. Around the fifth inning of the evening game, Natche batted with his back to home plate, and the Des Moines pitcher threw at his head (back-of-the-head music). Flopping to the ground as he spun around to hit, Natche saved himself. A lesser athlete might have been hit. Natche wore no batting helmet. As part of his costume of the moment, he had only one of the do rags he often wore around his head on the bus.

The Clowns were upset, made a slight comeback, but were doomed by the momentum of the day and didn't really make it a contest.

While Dad preferred to aid the show by avoiding locals, when I returned to Hollywood, I begged him to book Des Moines and the Merchants again before season's end, and he did.

The Clowns and Stars played an excellent game in Waterloo on June 18 before a crowd of 2,180. We tried to figure on the way in that day whether a giant storm spawning tornados along our route from Des Moines the night before would swell the crowd or keep fans home. One fan told us in a small town on our way into Waterloo, "We had a nothing tornado last night. Won't affect your crowd in Waterloo one way or t'other. Only thing it took here was one good farmhouse and a few old barns. You want to avoid a real tornado." Bobo felt I had a point when I asked if it would have been a real tornado if Dorothy had been in the one good farmhouse. The same storm

injured seventeen in Waterloo; ten of the injured were hospitalized overnight.

We drew well in Cedar Rapids on the 19th and Clinton on the 20th. But on
the 20th we'd either had a mixup with one city following daylight sav-
ings and the other not, or Bobo's watch was mis-set, and we got to the
ball park in Clinton three hours before gametime instead of two. For a
few minutes, the groundskeeper entertained us with a trained deer, then
Bobo said, "I'll tell you, Roomie, old Bobo could use a tall, cool one. Seen a
lounge down the road a mile or so back, downtown. Let's go eat. We got the
time."

But Bobo was more than a year early. Prohibition ended on the federal
level in 1933. In Iowa, legislation terminated Prohibition in 1934, but individual drinks could not be ordered again in Iowa until July 1963. There was
no liquor for Bobo at the lounge. In Black Hawk County, Iowa, in those
days, a lounge signified that the restaurant had a counter as part of the dining room. I sat with a dismal Bobo as the nearly empty restaurant filled
while we ate. Afterwards, we paid at the counter and as we crossed the restaurant toward the front, Bobo cut in front of me and blocked the door, and
I knew there was going to be some horrifying sequel to his slide across the
marble lobby in Norfolk.

Catering primarily to families, the lounge was noisy and filled with at
least 150 diners. At the door, Bobo raised his hands like Moses parting the
Red Sea. "May I have your attention please," he boomed over the din, again
and again, until more and more patrons looked at us. Bobo was parting the
noise, and, when it was silent, he nodded his head toward me and announced, "My partner here and I enjoyed eating with each and every one
of you, and we hope you'll turn out at to see the Indianapolis Clowns
play the New York Stars at Riverview Stadium at 8 P.M. your time, 7 P.M.
ours, but, of course, ours don't matter. Now the Clowns are world colored
champs, but that don't matter as much as you'll thrill to my juggling; the
Clowns' shadowball; shortstop Billy Vaughn, the homeliest midget in the
world playing professional baseball today; Birmingham Sam, who plays
third in a chair; Natureboy Williams, who plays first in a chair; Derek the
trained deer, who sits on a potty seat; and my roomie here, who loves them

Kansas shrimp." Bobo patted my shoulder. "That about cover it, Roomie?"
I nodded. There was no elevator to ease off to sideways this time.

"So that'll do her," Bobo announced. "I repeat. My partner and I enjoyed
eating with each and every one of you, and hope to see you out at tonight's
game, and hope you enjoy the rest of your meal."

As we walked to Bobo's car, he told me, "Pretty effective p.r. Ought to do
this every town."

After Clinton, Iowa, June 20, and Peru, Illinois, June 21, Bobo and I headed
down Route 35 toward Indianapolis, and as we approached Logansport, Indiana, early in the afternoon, I decided I needed a new shirt, and we left the
highway downtown to locate a men's store. After I bought the shirt, we left
on the wrong road, and got six or seven miles out of Logansport, well into
the cornfields, before we realized it. From the map, it was clear that Route
35 headed southeast, but we were going southwest.

"Be 14, 15 miles, if we turn around back to Logansport," Bobo said. "Got
to be a straight line here to 35, shortest distance, you know."

So we stopped alongside an idling tractor and asked a farmer the quick-
est, most direct way over to Route 35.

"Dirt road on the left two cornfields down," the farmer said. "Take you
right on over to 35."

We passed two dirt roads within 200 yards, then another a half mile later.
"Bobo, how big's a cornfield, and how do we know when we've traveled two
of them?" I asked.

"Beats me, Roomie. This whole part a Indiana's one big cornfield. But I
been on the road long enough to have a feel for these things. I'll know our
dirt road when I see it."

This was no Proustian tea party. There was no sign "The Guermantes
Way." It was not me and Swann. It was Bobo and me. And we picked the
next dirt road and entered the rows of corn.

A half hour of decisions-at-forks-of-dirt-roads later, we still faced an
endless world of very tall corn. What had been an amorphous feeling we
might never find our way out began to seem like a certainty.

"Looks like you should have studied agriculture, Old Buddy," Bobo said.
"So what do you think of the road now?"

"I'd just like to find it, is all I think."

And as suddenly as we were lost, we popped out of the corn and bounced onto Route 35, but whenever anything perplexed me the rest of my time on the road, Bobo said, "Guess you're confused as two baseballers in an Indiana cornfield." And only the two of us understood.

Ed Hamman was out of the hospital and rehabilitating, and he was waiting for us when Bobo and I arrived at the hotel in Indianapolis. Bobo exhibited no evidence of joy at Ed's survival, and Ed seemed to pale into relapse when he saw Bobo.

Still too ill to handle the game, Ed stayed at the hotel, and I drove his Cadillac to Victory Field. Delayed by Ed's review of my most recent daily reports, I arrived less than an hour before game time and could park no closer than 50–75 yards from the ballpark.

When I reported to the Indianapolis Indians' offices, there was a party in progress celebrating the upcoming marriage of a club official's daughter, and I was introduced to more than fifty people and offered beer. I declined the offer in the offices at Victory Field on the basis that I wanted to be clear-headed when we settled up after four and a half.

I had called Dad the day before from Peru, Illinois, because we'd drawn a record of more than 1,000 paid there, adding to the list of large crowds in small cities since I'd been on the road, and when I spoke to Mom, she joked that Dad ought to leave me on the bus for good luck even after Ed was back to full strength.

Settling up in Indianapolis that night in the middle of a party was not easy, and someone poured me a beer, then another. After we'd settled up, I had over $5,000 in my money belt, more than enough to send thousands home and still carry the teams through some rainouts. Outside the ballpark, following a well-played 7-6 Clowns win and an excellent funshow, about 2,500 milled around waiting for city buses. Many of the adults had downed much more than I had during the game, and it showed. Things were noisy and animated, but I wasn't worried, because the mood was joyful and the Clowns and Stars were still signing autographs and carrying equipment from the clubhouse to the bus. A few paces from Ed's car, though, I remembered that I had left some baseballs in the office and went back to the ballpark to get them. After I retrieved them and got back outside, the Clowns were gone, and I walked through about 1,000 remaining fans, hands on my belt, ready to drop my pants and give up the money belt at the first hint of trouble. All I received was a few pats on the back from some fans as I passed, "You the man with the Clowns. Seen you in the dugout. Man, they something else. Really enjoyed it."

On June 24th, the Clowns beat Pop Sheridan's Fletcher's Phillies in Niles, Michigan, 8-4, and in the morning, I woke up as a fly on a ceiling. I had roomed that night with Bobo, and before I awoke, he had turned everything in the room upside down, including lamps, all furniture, paintings on the walls, our suitcases. He had planned it in so much detail, he even had an upside-down glass filled with wax beer perched on the window sill.

After the Clowns' 5-4 win over the Lafayette Columbians in Lafayette, Indiana, on the 25th and a hook slide across a marble lobby, Bobo missed several pedestrians with water bags lobbed from our hotel window. "Tell you, Roomie," he said, "either I'm loosing my touch with age, or there's a perspective problem here caused by that overhang we got just below our window, and I ain't that old."

"So put it off till tomorrow in Kokomo. You're just menacing Lafayette's water supply. Could be a drought here, same as St. Joe."

"No. I'm a damn pro, and it's perspective. I'm going down there. Gonna back out from the building across the sidewalk, and you holler out when you see me. That'll tell me the distance from the building I need."

As Bobo went downstairs, I got the next water bag ready, and once he backed into sight—beginner's luck—I soaked him with a perfect toss.

On June 26, I rode with the team to Kokomo, sitting with center fielder Reuben Howard on the left side of the bus as we traveled down the right lane on our side of the median of a four-lane highway. "Light to the left!"

catcher Pete Jones hollered behind us. The bus nearly tipped. Players leaped over each other from right to left to get to our windows as a blond wearing a hiked-up skirt passed to our left driving a convertible.

I stayed that night with Bobo. I had suspected he'd wait out my suspicions before seeking revenge for the Lafayette wetting, but I was almost asleep when he whispered from his bed, "You awake, old buddy?" I quickly converted silence to near-snoring. He arose quietly and went to the hall.

"Hey, bellboy, where's the ice machine?" he loudly whispered.

I draped my sheet down the length of my bed over my pillow and spare pillows from the closet and jumped into Bobo's bed.

His shadow entered the room quietly giggling and hauling a large bag brimming with chipped ice. Like a sneaking cartoon character, he tiptoed quickly across the room to my former bed, pulled my sheet off the pillows and poured the ice.

"Freeze, Wing Ding Nuts!"

"Bobo," I asked from the warmth of his bed, "You gonna sleep in that?"

"Son of a buck! Guess I am."

Word came from Dad that he was near booking a postseason tour of Japan, and I discussed it confidentially with Carl Forney next day en route to Vincennes, Indiana.

"We'll be on old-time pay, Carl. Dad'll pay everyone like when the Clowns were in the league years ago. What do you think?"

"They best have time to build a bridge that long between now and postseason, 'cause I ain't going to Japan unless they do."

"Why not?"

"Let me put it this way. A ship go down, I can maybe swim enough to get to a lifeboat, but I don't much feel like floating the Pacific in no dinghy for no two weeks. But I'd say Syd would fly us there."

"Yes. He said we'd fly."

"See. Chauff drive off the road and I survive, I can walk or crawl away. Plane start going down, I damn sure know I can't fly."

In Vincennes, Bobo was surly. He wouldn't talk to any of us. Vincennes was one of the few small country cities with a portable batting cage, and Bobo spent the Clowns' infield practice in the batting cage with a dozen balls, burning them into the screening from one side of the cage to the other and back.

Ed had skipped the games since Indianapolis and kept Danny White with him to drive him to meet us in Mayfield, Kentucky, on the 28th. Although Bobo helped Clowns players with tips, he was close to few, maybe only to Haley Young.

Early in the Clowns' 13-1 win over the Vincennes All-Stars, Haley sat next to me on the bench. "Your roomie's living in the Pacific today. He's on Hell's front porch. Best you ride with him into Mayfield soon as you settle up. If he won't talk, you talk your head off about joyful things. Tell him about funny stuff happened on the bus or business you saw King Tut do. Something you say's gonna get through, and Bobo will be in shape for Mayfield."

I followed Haley's advice, and by Mayfield, Bobo was okay.

After the game at Mayfield, I chauffeured Ed from Mayfield into Nashville for our June 29 game at the Sulphur Dell.

Working at his pull-down desk in the back seat of his car, Ed said, "I'm feeling better daily, Alan. These reports of yours look fine. You run everything into Columbus, Ohio, July 3, then stay with me until Munhall Independence Day. Those will be two big gates. Then you can fly home. I'm gonna keep Danny White with me to drive, and meander up to meet you and the teams in Columbus. I ought to be fine by then."

We had more than 1,800 paid in Nashville, and next morning, payday, June 30, Bobo and I headed up the highway to Central City, Kentucky, early, so I could pay off the players in the parking lot outside the ballpark.

"Tell you what, Roomie," Bobo said. "You settle up quick in Central City,

I'll work my act the five minutes Syd says I ought to work, we'll have our gigees on the road to Chattanooga quick as Jesse James died when he was shot in Central City. We got a long jump, you know, into Chattanooga, then out to Mason, West Virginia, Sunday night. Mason's over 500 miles from Chattanooga."

"Jesse James died in Central City?"

"Dunno. Either died there or was born and raised there or maybe he just took a leak there. Did something in Central City. It's all the same for a man that bad: living or dying or taking a leak."

"But this seems so far east, I thought Jesse James was way out in Colorado, Arizona, Utah, California."

"In his time, this far east was west."

I was so fixated with Jesse James being so far east, I barely heard Bobo about the Chattanooga-Mason jump. Later, when I thought about my time on the road, I saw everything else as preliminary to the Chattanooga-Mason jump and the game that followed. The whole thing was like a fresco that never made a scene until the last painted tiles of that jump were in place.

As I sat alone in the bus that evening, as isolated and contemplative as a priest in a confessional awaiting penitents, I thought of the players waiting to enter the bus one by one for their pay.

Funny, the teams moved around the map quickly as a gnat on a hot summer night, but waiting dominated road life. Waiting till all showered and dressed. Waiting to settle up with promoters. Waiting across highway heat waves, past miles of plains and lakes and beaches, past phone poles and trees and Burma Shave signs, over rivers and creeks, over deserts, through mountains and hamlets and towns. Waiting with aching bladders, so long that gas stations looked like the good side of the River Styx. Waiting in the fumes of morning traffic jams leaving towns for the privilege of waiting hundreds of miles to wait in other towns in the fumes of evening traffic jams. Waiting for the next room. Waiting for sleep on night jumps. Waiting for the next letter from home and hoping it would tell only good things. Waiting for the stands to fill. Waiting to see family. Waiting for the next laugh. Waiting for a rally. Waiting for the next win. Waiting hungry for next payday, eating light on meal money. Waiting to break a slump. Waiting to be recognized, or at least for someone to say you could eat any place you want.

Sometimes, a man didn't have to take to the road to wait, like the old, black man I was about to meet in Central City.

A lifetime resident of Central City, he was outside the bus when I finished paying the players, and he asked me what was going on tonight, and, when I told him, he said that in all his eighty-plus years, he had never heard of colored baseball. Like Dad on a train, I began a dialogue about the Clowns, which branched out into stories about our families and lives, and ended more than an hour later. As some early fans approached, I realized I was late setting up the gate. As part of excusing myself from my new friend, I shook his hand. And he cried.

"What's wrong?" I asked.

"First time in my whole life a white man done shook my hand," he said. "Your skin don't feel no different than mine, only just younger."

30

On Being Black and on the Road

Even leaving Central City after Bobo's show in the middle of the fifth, Bobo and I didn't get to bed in Chattanooga until early morning hours. The teams, of course, were later.

Freddie Battle pitched a no-hit win over the Stars 2-0 in a 2 P.M. tilt, and after the players showered and changed and loaded the bus, we drove into black Chattanooga to eat before our bus money jump into Mason, West Virginia. As we emptied the bus, Chauff announced a 6 P.M. departure time, giving us an hour to eat and reboard the bus.

The place specialized in pint-sized paper cups of draft beer, and Natche bought me one while I was in the men's room. When Haley Young saw me drink it, he bought me another. Billy Parker bought me a third, half of which I rushed at 5:55 P.M. Haley said, "You best hit the men's room, Al, we got all night before Mason, and Chauff gets vicious if you want to stop, especially he gets tense once we enter the Smokies."

"I know, Haley, but I don't have to go yet."

During the following four minutes, Natche and Billy Parker, Billy Vaughn and Leo Gray, John Whitehead and Charles Stanton, Robert Kelly and Charles White, all warned me to visit the men's room, each in his turn looking at my three empty cups, then fearfully at Chauff. I was a crisis waiting to happen as we entered the bus at six, Chauff drumming his hands on the steering wheel and otherwise giving signals that he already felt tense hours before seeing the first looming mountain of the Great Smokies.

Less than an hour out of Chattanooga, my kidneys began nudging me, then bothering me. "Chauff, how many more miles we got to go?" I asked. The question was to become a refrain.

"About four fifty," he said slowly and objectively. Clearly, there was no intent to stop in the offing.

Before Knoxville, the sun went down. It was like Big Red had entered a tunnel for the night, a bus full of dim light on a lonely highway.

Maybe 10:30 that night, somewhere northwest of Knoxville, my kidneys urged me to tap dance. The legend of Chauff intimidated me. That and my desire not to interfere had kept me from asking to stop. I figured Chauff had an immutable bathroom break scheduled.

Then Freddie Battle said, "Damn, I sure would love a good deli sandwich."

"Easier to find a lion roaming Brooklyn than a good deli sandwich in east Tennessee," said Al "Sokeyok" Carter, a pitcher.

"Didn't say I'd get one, Sokeyok. Said I'd love one."

"Freddie, what's a Sokeyok anyway?" I asked.

"Cambodian for sandlotter," Freddie said.

"They got sandlotters in Cambodia?" I asked before I thought.

"Shit," Freddie said, George Burns to my Gracie Allen, "whole country's sandlotters. Everybody in Cambodia named Al Carter, except some of the women." I joined the bus load laughing.

Then I saw it, about a half mile ahead, a small restaurant, well lit. "Chauff," I said, "You got a cell of hungry ballplayers back here and a temporary road business manager who's got to take a leak. Can we stop at the restaurant coming up?"

Chauff nodded to the hiss of our air brakes.

It was a white restaurant, so I got out alone, went to the walk-up window and began to read the posted menu. "Ain't no use to readin'," I heard. "We see who you're with. Ain't gone be no integration by proxy." Three men looked at me through the window.

"They sittin' at lunch counters and gettin' haircuts today," one said. "Tomorrow, they'll marry your sister."

"Both my sisters are married," I said. "They're not after them." Humor had always softened my hardest situations.

"What the fuck you doin' with them anyhow?" asked one. "You a white nigger or a nigger lover?"

"They're my father's baseball team. I'm temporary road business manager."

"Better get your ass back on the bus," one said.

"No, he shouldn't," said another. "Them boys will slit his throat one night with a razor."

"I go back on that bus without sandwiches," I said, "I'm gonna have to come out at you with my Norelco blazing." My blast of humor was sullenly caught at the warning track.

"Where are the bathrooms?" I asked.

"Ain't no use to telling you. We got one for white, one for colored. Nothin' for you 'tweeners. Both got keys and you damn sure ain't gettin' no key."

Back on the bus, I told those awake, "They saw 'Clowns' printed on the bus and wouldn't serve me. Guess they're New York Stars fans. Maybe we ought to send John Whitehead in."

Chauff shifted the bus in gear. "Happened all along the Grand Island jump to St. Joe. Happened all along the years," he said. "Ain't nuttin' new. Pay it no mind."

The night turned blacker than black, and guessing the number of times I asked Chauff how many more miles we had to go became more difficult than guessing the number of jelly beans in a glass jar. He grew more and more irritated once I began to ask every five minutes, until I asked him one time too many, "Chauff, how many more miles we got to go?"

Looking at me in the rearview mirror, slowly rotating his toothpick angrily with his teeth, he answered: "All of 'em."

That kept me quiet long enough to think. Gas. We'd need gas. Gas stations had men's rooms. We couldn't run all night without gas.

"Chauff, how many miles a gallon the bus get?" I asked.

"Six to eight. Maybe less through the mountains."

I was thrilled until I asked, "How many gallons the tank hold?"

"Dunno. Eighty-five, ninety."

If Chauff wanted to coast a bit, I might not pee until tomorrow in Mason.

Chauff announced he was tiring and wanted Natche to consider driving. Natche traveled on the aisle seat right behind Chauff. Good thing he slept easily, because at least twice nightly, as soon as Natche's head nodded, someone on the other side of the bus would yell, "Light to the right!" And, from a dead sleep, Natche would leap straight across the bus wide awake for the nonexistent leg shot.

I saw my deliverance. When Chauff stopped for Natche to take over, I'd leap off the bus like a train robber in a western, and dash into the woods.

When Chauff finally said he was too drowsy to continue, I braced ready to move, but Natche (a silhouette, head wrapped in a black do rag) and B. D. Bland switched seats, putting Natche near the window, and Natche put his left hand on the steering wheel when Chauff took his off, and one by one Natureboy Williams' body parts replaced M. H. Winston's and we had a new driver without the bus even slowing down.

Finally, in the early morning darkness in northeast Tennessee, Natche pulled over for a break, and we piled out of the bus and lined up facing it. (There were two things that you didn't do with Chauff. One was tell him when and where to stop the bus, and the other was to pee on the tires.) Everyone kept noticeably distant from the tires. It was so dark, no one could see anybody else in any detail, and we were alone in the middle of the mountain forest, but all I could figure was everyone would be listening to hear the sound of three pints of hours-old beer hitting earth. And I couldn't go.

I boarded the bus hunched over like a hundred-year-old man with fresh football injuries, praying no one would say anything funny. I felt like if I laughed, I'd probably jet my way ricocheting backwards around the bus like a balloon spouting air.

Bristol is a city in two states. On its main street, a banner proclaims Virginia on one side and Tennessee on the other. I have fond memories of one state or the other. At roughly 7 A.M., we pulled into a gas station in Bristol. With a sprint rivaling the speed of Cool Papa Bell, Tetelo Vargas and Speed Merchant, I was first to the men's room.

By federal law, they had to serve us on the West Virginia Turnpike, and we ate there.

By late morning, we were at our hotel in Gallopolis, just across the Ohio River from Mason, West Virginia.

Carl Forney formed us in a semicircle around him in the lobby. "Tonight we face Mel Clark's All-Stars over in Mason, and they are good. We got to be our sharpest. So we all get wake-up calls at three, and we gonna meet down here by 3:30 and walk the streets of Gallopolis window shopping until 5:30, and that's when Chauff want us on the bus." We moaned and groaned. "I want you up and about," Forney said, "and I don't want nobody half-awake at 8 P.M. when the game starts up."

Before the midday nap, I considered how different that jump would have been with my family. We could have eaten or slept or peed wherever we wanted along the way—simple and basic. But I had finally seen what it was like to endure a night jump with a black baseball team.

In Mason that night, the Clowns won 1-0 in ten innings when Carl Forney homered well over the left-field fence. From the top of the seventh on, the game was played in a steady rain and probably should have been called, except that not one fan left a seat. Even Bobo stayed on the bench until the end.

I had never been more proud of the Clowns or loved them more.

The deluge started during the night, and rainout was obvious before we reached Columbus July 3. Chauff dropped me off at Ed Hamman's hotel, and I went straight to Ed's room.

"Alan, tonight's game's off. Holland Kelley said Munhall's already flooded, so our game there tomorrow's already cancelled. Syd wants you to fly back home tonight, soon as we review your daily reports. But Syd wants you to call home right now."

When Dad heard my voice he said, "Tom Baird wrote me a June 27 letter.

Told me Ray Dumont's done more for baseball than anyone, then wrote, 'and you come next to Dumont keeping game alive.' "

"That's nice, Dad, for somebody who thinks what Tom thinks about Clowns comedy."

"Alan, you know how you commented once that Tom and I sign all our letters, BCNU, me, things like that?"

They usually used a variety of funny salutations and signatures. "Yes," I said, realizing for the first time Dad didn't sound like Dad, and didn't seem efficiently covering relevant items as usual.

"Tom signed that last letter 'My-o-Me.' Sounds like he was pretty tired, don't it?"

"Yes," I said, now afraid of what I was about to hear.

Dad's voice broke, "Professor, Tom died last night. Had a heart attack and died."

Then there was silence. Ed took the phone from me. "He'll be okay, Syd. I'll make sure he gets out of here tonight, and I'll call you day after tomorrow from Anmore."

Before I left for the airport, Ed shook my hand at the door to his room, and said, "You done okay out here, you know. Syd told me sometime after 1956, said I was the only man in the world left could run the Clowns on the road. I give that a lot of thought, figured, hell, nobody's indispensable. Trained Freddie Battle and Danny White to do my job temporary. Syd trained you. But I learned long ago, when Franklin Roosevelt died, no man's indispensable. Here was a president run the whole world for years, Alan. Here was a man, the whole world said he dies, we stop, we just pack it up. He died, and the world went on. So out there in the hospital in Enid, I rested knowing the Clowns will be here when I get back."

First business Dad conducted when I got home was to review my daily reports with me, beginning with Marysville, Kansas.

"Can you see your mistake on there, Professor?"

"Easy. I made them pay sales tax. We should have. Do I do that again down the line?"

"No. You got it right starting Concordia. So cut a check to the Marysville Jaycees for the sales tax." The amount was somewhere between $30 and $50.

"They wrote you about it?"

"No. But I noticed it preparing to review these with you."

"So they don't know?"

"Not till they get the check, and be sure you do a short transmittal letter apologizing for the oversight."

We were unlikely to play Marysville again, not to draw a couple hundred people. The Jaycees would never realize the error anyway, but Dad sent the money because the Clowns, not the Jaycees, were responsible for sales tax.

For the benefit of the Old Time Negro Leaguers, the Clowns and New York Stars appeared in Chicago's Comiskey Park August 10, 1962. A paid crowd of 6,166 helped honor Negro leagues' old timers presented with plaques. Recipients included Joe Green, Bingo DeMoss, Bobbie Anderson, Sandy Thompson, William Fox Jones, George Bennette, Rube Currie, Thurman Jennings, Alex Radcliffe, Ted "Double Duty" Radcliffe, T. H. Jefferson, Walter Harper, John Donaldson and David Malarcher. Of those honored, Joe Green was oldest, having started his career in 1902 with the Leland Giants of Chicago, the top black team of its day.

The 1962 season ended September 4 in Lake Charles, Louisiana. On August 28, I drove Mother and Dad to Ft. Walton Beach, Florida, and we followed the team to Panama City next day, then to Louisiana for games in New Orleans on the 31st, Pontchatoula the 1st, New Orleans Sunday afternoon the 2nd and Thibidoux that night.

The Louisiana crowds each exceeded 1,500. Thibidoux sheriff Eddie Ste. Marie, the game sponsor there, gave us a police escort into town. But Louisiana was memorable for two other reasons: nickel cokes and the cockroach.

Elsewhere, cokes had gone to a dime or more years earlier, but in New Orleans in 1962, a bottle of coke was still a nickel, and Dad couldn't get over it. We stopped at gas station after gas station and most small groceries in the city that week, sometimes under some other guise, but always to get a nickel coke.

At age 21, I wanted to spare my parents driving, so I took the wheel in Hollywood and never gave it up. The trips to Ponchatoula and Thibidoux and back into New Orleans late each night, followed by walks down Bourbon Street and around the French Quarter, finally caught up with us early Monday morning after Thibidoux and the French Quarter.

When we returned to our room at 509 Royal Street and Dad and Mom were ready for bed, I showered, and, during the shower, spotted the cockroach on the wall tile. Bugs terrify me, and this was no little German cockroach. This escapee from someone's nightmare was what we call a palmetto bug in South Florida. And this particular one seemed nearly big enough to saddle and ride off. If palmetto bugs had their own National Football League, this specimen would have been a dominating all-pro offensive lineman. Sleepily, I reached up and caught him in my hand, squeezed him dead, opened the shower curtain, tossed his hulk into the toilet (it splashed like the distant plop of a deceased gangster in concrete entering the East River). I flushed him.

Next morning was like the day after a Florida State football loss. It's always the same. I wake up happy, ready for the day. Then, suddenly I remember the loss, and it's like someone I knew well died. I suppose psychiatrists call it Gatorphobia or Multiple Cane-o-rhea. But at 509 Royal, the bright light of Monday morning woke me happy, ready for the day. Then, I remembered the roach from the night before with a burst of disgust. "Yuugggghhh!" I hollered, frightening Mom and Dad awake. I shook my hand in a blur, like a hummingbird's wing, as though that could undo the touch remembered during my king of delayed reactions. Washing and re-washing my hands like some insect-murdering Lady MacBeth, I knew I could never rid myself of the wet crunch.

I thought of that roach years later, after Dad retired, when he and I spoke of death and afterlife.

31

Riding into the Sunset

One legacy of the Clowns 1962 season was the flamboyant 1963 home uniforms of Charles O. Finley's Kansas City A's, designed after Finley saw the New York Stars' colorful uniforms during a 1962 Clowns game in Kansas City. The 1962 New York Stars' uniform was cotton, not flannel, was tighter fitting than traditional baseball attire, especially along the upper arms, and was kelly green, orange, royal gold and white. The look forever changed baseball uniforms.

After the 1962 season, Carl Forney retired. He could make more for his family working in Gastonia. Freddie Battle was named manager for 1963.

In his April 12, 1963, letter to Ed Hamman, Dad said to put the best fielders on the Clowns because "Nothing sells better than those Drake catches."

The Clowns added pitcher Ed Kennemore, possessor of one of baseball's fastest (and most erratic) fastballs; second baseman Jim Murrell, considered by Dad and Ed the Clowns best fielder at that spot since Ray Neil; and 6'5", 275-pound catcher Tiny Walke. A professional quality team, still it was probably the weakest team the Clowns had ever fielded.

For the 1963 and 1964 seasons, I worked for Dad in the office for $40 a week. I wanted to take over the Clowns when he retired. He hired me to chart me a different course, to show me that unsubsidized baseball outside the major leagues was dead. It was a fact: the last of the road clubs was getting sucked down in faster, smaller, concentric circles.

I worked 8 A.M. to 5 P.M. and 6 P.M. to 11 P.M. weekdays, and as needed, which was almost as much, weekends. Dad worked his usual hours daily, always at his desk from well before my arrival until well after my departure.

The 1963 and 1964 seasons would present more than the usual array of problems. During 1963, the Clowns played the fewest games of any season in their history under Dad (143) and drew their smallest aggregate paid attendance (103,775) and smallest average paid attendance per game (726).

The math of the road was constant—two plus two still didn't always make four. And a section was still reserved for whites.

The civil rights movement was in full swing, and civil unrest swept the South that spring and summer. In many cases that season, ad hoc taxes and license fees kept black promoters and organizations from renting parks in organized baseball.

The Clowns and their touring partners, the Brooklyn Stars, were scheduled to open the season April 13 in St. Petersburg, Florida, Ed Hamman's hometown. The game was to be played in the black ballpark, owned by the city, which imposed a tax and license fees prerequisite to Clowns' use of Al Lang Field, where the local Class A Florida State League team played, but agreed to abandon taxes and fees for use of "the colored park."

Still, it was not a great opening week. The Clowns lost traditional bookings the first week of the season because black promoters and organizations were unable to secure parks in Miami, Leesburg, Gainesville, Ft. Lauderdale and West Palm Beach. In Palatka, Freddie Battle caught the promoter selling advance tickets (on which the promoter received an extra 25 cents) at the gate.

But the main problems involved segregation. Eddie Pericola, Clowns 1963 advance man from Pensacola, a white man, found organization after organization afraid to book the Clowns in Mississippi or Alabama or unable to obtain the local ballpark. Dad had the same problems by mail.

Bad news mounted. Birmingham, Alabama, where the Clowns were a sure-fire drawing power several times each season, was in jeopardy. In a preseason letter to Ed Hamman, Dad noted nationwide the tension and hurt caused by lack of response to black groups seeking parks. He referred to it in the office as "the agony of no-yes, no-no; the hurt of drifting."

A March 2 *Saturday Evening Post* article titled "Birmingham, Alabama: A City in Fear" cited Birmingham as the largest American city refusing to call its white and black leaders together to work things out.

There was racial repression in the streets of Birmingham in the days before the game: there were demonstrations and arrests, and blacks were beaten and clubbed by police and bitten by police dogs and knocked to the ground with water blasted from fire hoses. Blacks were at least as angry as whites, and they rioted. It continued the day of the game, and it rained as the fans entered Rickwood Field April 28.

Through Ed and black promoter J. Earle Hensley, Dad had expressly requested that the stands be integrated. He wanted nothing aggravating outside forces. He wanted pure comedy baseball, pure entertainment. He wanted, if not a city at rest, at least a ballpark at rest.

Ed Hamman phoned the office during the game, almost in tears of admiration for the players, to tell us that the Clowns and Brooklyn Stars were playing in the rain and in the mud and putting on a great game and show to a wildly cheering crowd. Dad stressed the importance of completing the game with shadowball and the full show, and when we hung up, he said, "Think of this opportunity in Birmingham, Alan. This is what baseball's all about."

Later, Dad wrote the national release in his own words:

As severe racial demonstrations rocked the City of Birmingham, Ala., April 28, the Clowns and Brooklyn Stars took off shoes and sox to complete a regularly scheduled game in a sea of mud during a rainstorm before a peacefully integrated crowd with the idea that baseball's goodwill superseded the risk of playing under such adverse weather conditions.

Following the contest, the Clowns staged their famous shadowball and funshow routines amidst an appreciative standing ovation by the Birmingham fans, who seemed relieved of local racial tensions by the entertaining performance.

On their way to the West Coast, to play their way north into Canada, the Clowns stopped in Bryan, Texas, a town of 20,000, on May 16, and drew a crowd of nearly 3,000 paid to Travis Park for the benefit of the Brazos Valley Youth Association Connie Mack League. It was largest crowd there since 1959, and concessions were sold out by the third inning. The *Bryan Eagle* reported:

> That the Indianapolis Clowns won another baseball game 6-5 . . . was of minor consequence. . . .
>
> Outstanding baseball was spiced by the antics of Natureboy Williams, who stole first from second base and played his first sacker position with a three-foot wide glove while sitting in a chair;
>
> Birmingham Sam, a Clown-prince in baseball disguise who produced a pistol and held it to the plate umpire's temple as a fourth ball was thrown for his walk;
>
> And the celebrated midget, Billy Vaughn—the only one in professional baseball—whose single in the fourth brought a roar of appreciation from the crowd.
>
> SMALL FRY were everywhere, forming a parade behind Pied Piper Natureboy and Birmingham as they strolled through the stands, autographing programs. Two local lads got into the spotlight with the Great Yogi—rubber-jointed contortionist who stood on his hands with his feet behind his head and did the "Twist."
>
> Gales of laughter evoked when Birmingham got caught in a rundown between first and second and dove between Stars second baseman Willie Phillips' legs to reach safety matched applause that welled up from the crowd when Clowns' left fielder Pete Jones twice made hairline throws from deep left to catcher Tiny Walke to protect a Clowns lead.
>
> "I've never seen Travis Park so full," a leading baseball and sports enthusiast, Reuben Bond, said. "If the folks who sat in their cars outside the fence had been inside, there wouldn't have been enough seats for everybody."

The pistol was new for Sam. Sometimes he pointed it at the umpire's head, sometimes he fired a warning shot into the air. When Sam fired his warning shot in parks with upper decks, Ed Hamman tossed a rubber chicken from the upper deck onto the field, and Sam carefully inspected his smoking gun and looked up into the sky, then tenderly picked up the chicken and patted it understandingly and put it into a cooking pot held by the batboy and put the cover on the pot to be carried into the dugout for safekeeping.

As the Clowns approached Canadian customs June 14, the baggage compartment contained players' luggage, baseball equipment, dozens of baseballs and cases of Ed Hamman's programs.

On the customs form, Ed declared 300 of the 3,300 programs carried. The declared programs were in three boxes; 33 more boxes were kept in a locked trunk in the baggage compartment for use in Omaha and Chicago following the Canadian tour, so Ed deemed only the three boxes saleable in Canada.

Officials demanded Ed unlock the trunk, and once they found the 33 boxes of undeclared programs, the Clowns were detained for five hours while every part of the bus and every piece of luggage on it were searched. The team was fined $192.46 and had to pay duty of $19.25, Big Red was confiscated and Ed was charged with smuggling baseballs and programs into Canada and arrested. Hired lawyers freed Ed and the bus, and charges against Ed were dropped, but when the Clowns moved on to Capilano Stadium in Vancouver, they did so without baseballs or programs.

Dad thought the smuggling charges were ridiculous and repeatedly wrote to authorities that the Clowns had made several goodwill tours annually into Canada over the past 33 years, carrying baseballs and programs every time, all without incident.

Dad considered avoiding Canada in the future but noted that the incident resulted from a few officials, either corrupt or mean-spirited, and the Clowns returned to Canada in 1964.

And, naturally, the tail of the same snake that reared its head at Canadian customs to start the Canadian tour appeared at U.S. customs at the finish, and the tour ended nearly as it had begun. At the border, coming out of Canada, U.S. customs had every single item unloaded from the bus, causing a delay of over two and a half hours.

Across the border back home the Clowns beat the Brooklyn Stars before a paid crowd of nearly 8,000 at Chicago's Comiskey Park July 2 in a game for the benefit of the Old Time Ball Players of Chicago and sponsored by the White Sox. White Sox officials rebooked the clubs for August 25.

After Eddie Stumpf raved about Natureboy Williams as a player and an entertainer, Dad revealed to him the unpublicized fact that Natche had lost an eye during the off-season.

Dad decided to join the Clowns for their return engagement at Comiskey Park on August 25th. Had Dad not made the trip, it would have been as unjust as General MacArthur going into a coma and missing World War II, because, in addition to Dad visiting with the former Negro leaguers benefited by the Chicago game, the pregame spectacle at Comiskey Park on the 25th was pure Syd Pollock—more than 3,000 Little Leaguers in uniform, admitted free, gathered on the field and sang the national anthem.

The 1963 season ended in Greenville, South Carolina, September 10 before a paid attendance of 406, and Big Red sputtered from there to her final resting place, St. Petersburg, Florida.

Ed Hamman had Chauff take Big Red across St. Petersburg to a vehicle salvage lot to be mothballed as a backup. Chauff must have felt like he was taking a pet to a vet to be put to sleep. At the lot, Chauff patted the side of the bus a few times and left her for storage. The Clowns would never ride Big Red again. The bus stayed on the lot until moved and sold after the 1964 season. Big Red, which had traveled over half a million miles since 1948 and hauled all the Clowns from Buster Haywood and Peanuts Davis to Billy Vaughn and Birmingham Sam—Big Red, which had done her time in the hands of Canadian authorities—Big Red, which had been given new life time and again by Chauff—Big Red, which had traveled the roads of 48 states, Canada and Mexico and been coated with the salts of the Atlantic and Pacific, the Gulf of Mexico and the sands of the Mojave—Big Red, the way from here to there and back for the Indianapolis Clowns, was at last at rest.

Dad had one more year to go with the Clowns, so he and Ed bought a slightly used school bus, re-outfitted it, had it painted Clowns colors with the name of the team, had a diesel engine installed and had a mechanic certify it fit for the Canadian Rockies. And the two men prepared for the 1964 season.

Dad didn't change. He adjusted.

He and Mom were my best friends, and when I married Marti they became our best friends. We did almost everything together. We ate with them several times weekly, and, during the years I worked with Dad, that helped me keep Dad's working hours my working hours, because I didn't leave their house to eat.

Dad treated others as he treated family, and he remains the only person I've ever met who never thought of himself. Absolutely everything I remember him doing was for someone else. As far as money was concerned, a deal was a deal, and he cared about the money only as a means of being responsible to family and others in need.

While the job of finding available quality Clowns players during the early '60s was not exactly Mrs. Noah searching for a quarter-mile-square litter box for the ark, it was axiomatic that the more black players organized baseball accepted, the tougher it was for the Clowns to recruit. Acceptable Clowns players had to be good baseballers able to travel under tough conditions for little pay in a comedic setting with a strong-willed Ed Hamman setting the rules of the road. With shrinking rosters, the operation could no longer tolerate undependable or temperamental men. While Dad liked second and third chances, Ed did not; Ed dealt with players face-to-face daily, and Dad did not.

In the early '60s, a twist dance contest followed Clowns shadowball, and sometimes hundreds of fans joined Sam and Natureboy (in his dress) following their solo dirty dancing. The two comedians often split from each other and danced the twist with fans. By 1964, the pandemonium of the twist contest was history, but sometimes one or both comedians took a fan from the stands and danced with her. It led to the only tension I recall between Dad and Ed.

Differing on racial issues, both men contributed to black civil rights organizations. Ed wrote and spoke of his belief in the underlying hatred most blacks had for whites, but didn't live as though he thought so. Dad believed people were people, all generally good but flawed, whether white or black. To Dad, all men were at their best in sport, where the flaws and the things that separated people could be forgotten. Dad and Ed never argued race, and neither was ever angry at the other, except that once.

Early in August 1964, Dad and I went to the post office. During the two years I worked with Dad, we went there together probably four times daily. Ed's daily reports were deemed important. Dad read Ed's note. "God damn it, Ed! God damn it!" Dad said. He seldom used such language, and was visibly angry. He slid the note over to me. It said:

Not much to report.
   Had my first trouble with N. Boy in 3 years. Wouldn't let him pull out a white girl by the arm to finish the dance with him. Shut off the music, etc.
   My Dept.

By that night, when he discussed the matter with Ed, Dad had cooled off, and he made his point calmly, but firmly: "If Natureboy can take a black woman from the crowd, he can take a white woman from the crowd. The

Clowns don't measure fan pigmentation. Whether Natureboy can take a woman from the crowd or he can't, that's your department. But if he can, it's no one's department whether she's black or white. And it's the Clowns' department to keep the music playing, not to call attention to racism by stopping the music."

"Syd," Ed said, "Doesn't mean a damn to me Natureboy pulls out a woman black or white, or a little boy, for all I care. Would look funny as hell, a little boy, with Natureboy in his dress and all. Syd, you know I rode hundreds of miles in my car with my daughter Louise sitting on Jesse Owens' lap back when Jesse and me both worked for you in the '40s. What bothered me is, we had a white crowd in New London. Riot's what worried me. Natureboy had that woman by the arm. People look at that peculiar. I'm out here. You're not. And two and two don't make four in road baseball."

"The music's the music, and a crowd's a crowd. You had people out there wanted to forget racial shit, not hear the music stop and see you fuss about Natureboy and some white fan. I bet she was laughing same as anybody. Let me ask this—he didn't kidnap her out there, did he?"

"No, Syd. He didn't kidnap her. Maybe we ought to cut out the dance."

"Your department. I think we ought to keep the dance. If you think it may cause riots, have a policy—no fans allowed. But if you're gonna allow fans, you allow fans. It's like you always say, if only one fan shows up, the show should be the same as for 20,000, because the one paid his money same as each of the 20,000. When we settle up, we don't separate the money a pile paid by white from a pile paid by colored."

"You're right, Syd. We don't."

"So we don't do it with the people who paid the money either."

Passage of the Civil Rights Act of 1964 integrating the road—hotels and restaurants and places of entertainment—would come after that season, Dad's last as a Clowns owner, but the early '60s indicated regression in race relations.

Maybe Dad was right about men at their best in sports. The Clowns regularly toured Mississippi, Alabama and the rest of the Deep South those years, but racial tensions made booking tough. Dad recognized that old ways persisted, even in baseball.

Clowns' attendances had been descending for more than a decade, and salaries were nominal in the early '60s. While the Clowns still packed the stands some places, sparsely attended outings increased at an alarming rate each season.

Perhaps with program revenues and his baseball mail-order business, Ed made a living in those days, but even at prices then, the Clowns had long since ceased to provide Dad a margin worth the risk.

Although they had their bad days, the Clowns teams of the '30s, '40s and early '50s almost always had quality baseball and comedy. During the '60s, it was a struggle for the Clowns to produce both good comedy and good baseball in tandem, but most times, customers got their money's worth.

Some promoters registered varied complaints, many of which dealt with suggestive routines that some felt inappropriate. On the whole, black crowds were more liberal earlier than white about sexual comedy. At times, Natureboy was impishly suggestive pulling bats slowly from his pants during the bats-in-the-pants routine, and, to me, the funniest part of the post-shadowball dance was when Sam, holding Natche close, lowered his hands over Natche's dress to his butt, and a dignified Natureboy, apparently shocked and offended, pushed Sam somersaulting backwards. At times, when they danced several feet apart, especially before primarily black crowds, there was plenty of bumping and grinding, and the laughter increased the wilder things got. Sometimes it irritated Dad (mainly because it offended Mom, who was something of a spectator barometer to Dad), and he complained to Ed, and routines cooled off temporarily.

When I next saw the Clowns, Natureboy's moves were as seductive as ever, and Birmingham Sam was rolled over backwards on the diamond when his hands roamed. As usual, the crowd loved it, and if anyone made a move on a woman as a result, whoever did so probably fantasized about cross-dressed first basemen anyway.

Some people just plain didn't like the Clowns for whatever reason. Maybe they felt the game was a solemn joy, a sacred rite, pure, to be preserved from comedy. Maybe it was racial. Maybe some whites don't like anything blacks do. Maybe some blacks felt Clowns comedy demeaned blacks. Whatever their reasons, their complaints were far outweighed by the fans—black and white—all across America who loved the Clowns.

32

One Last Hurrah

By 1964, Dad was in his 50th year promoting baseball. He felt sure that passage of a Civil Rights Act integrating the road was imminent. James Natureboy Williams was 1964 manager of the Clowns, and the latest find was Dero Austin, a three-foot baseball comedian from Brandfield, Oklahoma, who, like Spec Bebop, did not play the game. With a straight face, Dad typed the following order to J. M. Warlick of Southland Athletic Manufacturing Company, Terrell, Texas:

> Would appreciate you making us one Navy Blue uniform (Clowns) for new MIDGET ball player we have joining us this season. . . . Midget's Waist measurement is 26 inches. . . . Chest is 30 inches. Pants would be made professional style for this smaller youngster, however his legs are VERY SHORT, so length of pants from crotch down, I imagine should not exceed 12 inches. Use own judgment. Numeral on back of shirt . . . 1/4, in same size as used on prior orders, with same lettering on front . . . CLOWNS in script, with tail. . . .

Of the 75 players reporting to the Clowns' usual two-day spring training session in St. Petersburg, 36 warranted at least a further look in the season opener, which, fittingly for Dad's last season as owner, was set for Miami Stadium.

On April 23, Miami Mayor Robert King High threw out the first ball to start the Clowns' 35th season before a paid turnstile count of about 2,100, and Dad's last season began a mile or less from Dorsey Park, where his 1929 Havana Red Sox first played and where the Miami Ethiopian Clowns had originated in 1936. The 1964 Clowns were not the quality of either ancestor, but Dad was pleased with what he saw. Young talent and comedy components appeared ready to jell. Most starters were gone by the 5th inning so that Natche and Ed could judge everyone in action.

Without realizing Clowns history and that this was the team that in 1941 had brought Miami its first national championship, Bill Braucher of the *Miami Herald* was not as pleased as Dad. He wrote:

A new way to make baseball interesting was brought to a ridiculous peak at Miami Stadium Thursday by an organization of buffoons called the Indianapolis Clowns.

The Clowns, perfectly named, played in near privacy. But they fractured their select audience, most of small fry, and nearly fractured themselves while slapsticking through a seven-inning 7-2 fantasy of unearned runs to beat a team of foils called the Brooklyn Stars.

Judging by the reaction of the merry group estimated at 400 scattered about the stands, the Clowns' brand of nonsense is preferred to the three-hour-plus ordeal of the modern game played straight.

. . . Vaughn, the midget, plays it to the hilt. He subtracts from his strike zone, which is approximately the size of The Reader's Digest, by batting from a sitting position. . . .

. . . Birmingham Sam . . . drew his biggest laugh in the fourth inning when a firecracker exploded while Sam was batting. He took off like a dashman down the line and leaped into the arms of the first-base coach.

Natureboy's talents are legion. In the third inning he lugged a bludgeon the size of a mast to the plate. The umpire ruled it out. Natureboy delved into a bulky mass of clothing and produced, one by one, an oar, a golf club, a board, a broom, a model of a shapely leg and, finally, four legitimate bats.

. . . After the game Natureboy and company indulge in shadowball routines, twist dances, female impersonations and similar exercises lampooning baseball.

Those who enjoy this sort of departure would have killed themselves laughing, just as the Clowns killed themselves trying to provide it.

Marti and I and our daughter, Theresa, joined Mom and Dad for the game and enjoyed it. Dad and Bill Braucher were like two blind men describing the same elephant by touch. For the Clowns, and in Braucher's view, it was a pedestrian performance and it is troubling that some judge the Clowns or black baseball by just such an appearance. But, in Dad's view, it was brilliant considering it was a season opener and considering the circumstances leading up to the game. The players were mostly total strangers until three days earlier, and most no more than 20 or 21 years old and away from home for the first time. They also knew they were not training to vie for a championship. Yet nine men at a time tried to mix sport and comedy on a professional level in front of their first crowd.

And the Clowns moved on—and their play and comedy mellowed and settled in—the next night in Tampa, the next in Deland, then Jacksonville. By the next Thursday, they were in Mobile, Alabama, beginning a tour that would take them across the southern tier of states to California, up the West Coast into Canada, through the Canadian Rockies to Chicago and into loops through the Midwest and Deep South. It was the first time Dad could not book a date in the Northeast substantial enough to bring the Clowns into New Jersey, New York or New England.

A fear I had, from the days Dad began talking retirement when the Clowns left the Negro American League, was that Dad wouldn't live much beyond his team. They seemed one, Dad the heart of the Clowns or vice versa. Refusing to acknowledge an end to the Clowns, I thought their salvation lay in rebuilding the team with an upwardly structured payroll and rehiring talented veteran players—bringing back older stars, such as Verdes Drake and Lincoln Boyd—and by accruing the best young players from each season as it elapsed, perhaps with the Clowns as a subsidized affiliate of a major league team, with annual appearances in each major league stadium. I felt that major league interest might be generated by an appearance on ABC's "Wide World of Sports" or CBS's nationally televised "Sports Spectacular" series. While Dad had sent queries to ABC, NBC and CBS Sports during 1962 and 1963, he gave me CBS as a personal project during the 1963–1964 winter, and CBS sports agreed to scout the Clowns in Marietta, Georgia, May 6.

It was a disaster. A representative of CBS flew down to Atlanta from New York for the day for the Clowns game in Marietta that night. Promoter Elmer Knox, Georgia commissioner of the National Baseball Congress, said he paid the recreation director cash for the park rental in March without getting a receipt. Allegedly, the recreation director pocketed the money, and the city then rented the park to the American Legion for a March 6 doubleheader. As Dad wrote to *Ft. Worth Press* sports editor Jim Browder, "They [the City of Marietta] advised Recr. Dir. will be fired, but that didn't do us or promoter any good. [The CBS representative] took next plane to Syracuse, requested we mail his office at CBS our schedule and he'd advise within 2-weeks on next date he could review our performance . . . too late to be televised at Ft. Worth."

If that weren't bad enough, the *Marietta Daily Journal* wrote a story under the headline "INDIANAPOLIS CLOWNS FAILED TO BOOK DATE." Dad had picked up the newspaper article at the post office alone, showing it to me when he returned home to the office. He was calm. I was near tears in anger and frustration.

"Why do they do that? Every day I see more and more what it's like if you're not white. The lead on this story ought to be how they finally write about a colored team because they can say something bad."

"They did us wrong again. That's all," Dad said. "Look, like Ed says, two and two ain't four out there on the road. I told you before, you chip away and smooth things till people learn to get along. You don't join the madness. If you do, you make things worse. Let me say this. It hurts you now because you worked on it. The Clowns and their ancestors have gone against it for generations. Worse than this. You see it now and then. Picture a life of Chattanooga-Mason jumps. You work and work for what you are, but every minute every day somebody's waiting someplace to misjudge you when you did nothing to deserve it. Picture it like that.

"I'm gonna do a letter to the *Marietta Daily Journal*. Maybe it'll go unprinted, but maybe it'll mean something. You got to help people one at a time to see. This whole integration thing's like making a baseball bat from a limb using nothing but sandpaper."

The letter was sent. There was no response.

Dad did not consider a lawsuit.

History blended with the present on June 6, 1964, when former Clowns great Buster Haywood, Clowns ex-hurler Andy Porter and Kansas City Monarchs legend Chet Brewer, all old-time Negro leaguers, attended the Clowns game in Compton, California.

Thirty years later, Buster recalled, "They had some guy trying to be like King Tut. Wasn't but one Tut. They was Clowns, but they wasn't like us.

They had no fire. The fire had done gone out. The years doused it like a damn flood. Didn't play the same quality ball. Didn't have the same comedy. Didn't seem to have the fun we had. They was more like the Globetrotters than the Clowns. They tried hard, sure enough. I talked some to Natureboy Williams and enjoyed that. But things just weren't the same as once."

After touring California, Oregon and Washington, the Clowns headed into Canada for their June 21 Vancouver appearance. A Clowns release tells what happened then:

> The Indianapolis Clowns baseball club lost the first contest of their Western Canada tour. It was a race against death.
>
> The team was coming through customs at Blaine, B.C., en route to the opening of their 35th annual Canadian tour at Vancouver, when a young man rushed into the building shouting for help. The players followed the youth from the building and ran 200 yards down the road to an overturned car, beneath which Sylvia Henry, a 16-year-old Vancouver girl, lay trapped. She had been a passenger in the auto, which had overturned near the Pacific Highway.
>
> They lifted the car from Sylvia, who was rushed to a nearby hospital but was pronounced dead on arrival.
>
> Informed of her death, Clowns playing manager [James] Natureboy Williams, who is known for expressing himself through hilarious diamond antics, summed up the feelings of the traveling baseball troupe. "We are all very sorry she died," he said. "We wish we could have got there sooner and what we did could have been of help to her."
>
> "Humor is said to be sadness turned inside out," the team's comic shortstop Birmingham Sam [Brison] said. "But laughter and tears were never as close together as today.
>
> "It's hard to go out and make fans laugh after something like this, but that's our job," he concluded.

Canadian officials expressed thanks for the effort extended by the Clowns team.

Things seemed perfect July 10, but it was like an answer written across a windy sky in smoke by a skywriter. It was there one moment, gone the next. CBS Sports rescouted the Clowns in Comiskey Park, Chicago, a game played for the benefit of the Old Time Colored Ball Players Association and Fellowship Missionary Baptist Church.

Compared with the Clowns total crowd exceeding 17,000, the Giants-Cubs game across town that day drew a total attendance of 13,556.

Two White Sox observers called it "the best performance ever presented in hilarious and unsurpassed baseball entertainment on any baseball diamond."

"Syd, it couldn't have gone better," Ed said by phone after the game. "We had more than a thousand Little Leaguers in there free plus people on passes, so it was a huge, wild crowd. CBS seen the Clowns in a Big League setting, believe me. Shadowball and the show was perfect; I give Natureboy and Sam and Billy Vaughn some extra cash."

After Dad hung up, I said, "Dad, when CBS tapes this, you gonna sit in the chair for the dentist sketch like with Tut in Brooklyn?"

We laughed. It was euphoric.

There would be no taping. It was difficult for Dad to understand but he wrote "but it's all in the game, like experts who told me Hank Aaron would never hit major league pitching."

While paid attendances for 1964 exceeded 1963, expenses increased, and Dad and Ed netted less than $10,000 to split. On October 17, 1964, Ed wrote Dad that 1963 money from the "[George] Smith sale lucked us through. This year Chicago. Although we did have a record August, without it we would have shown a considerable loss." In the same letter, he pointed out that while $125,000 passed through his hands during the 1964 season, "less than $4,000 has come my way as a profit."

The Clowns returned to Victory Field, Indianapolis, on the night of August 21, 1964, which was declared "Indianapolis Clowns Night" by Indianapolis Mayor John J. Barton by proclamation signed and sealed August 17, 1964. It was the only time in the history of black baseball that a major American city honored a black baseball team.

Funny, I think of sunshine, not rain, when I remember that 1964 season. I think of Dad's second National Baseball Congress award for outstanding contribution to baseball, and "Indianapolis Clowns Night" in Naptown. I picture Dad in our sunlit office, typing with a cigarette dangling from the corner of his mouth, or smiling at me and nodding as we talked baseball, or leaning over to enter the latest booking on a line on the back of a cardboard windowcard, or squinting at distant thoughts during phone conversations or sitting in a dugout with his scorebook open in his lap. I remember him lying asleep on the living room floor after supper, Clowns operations suspended for a half hour as if under a tarpaulin awaiting the sunlight of his awakening. I hear him seeking compromise with his favorite introductory sentence, "Well, let me ask this." I remember the 1964 Clowns only in bright sunlight or colorfully lit night parks. And I remember laughter and applause and the smell of hot dogs and liniment and cigar smoke and the perfume of black women. And I remember the heavy, muscled legs of Natureboy Williams pounding like pistons to the driving rhythms of Clowns dance music and sending clouds of dry clay skyward, and hear the laughter of joyful fans. And I remember Ed Hamman climbing ballpark steps through sparse crowds hawking souvenir programs from a shallow wooden carrier strapped over one shoulder.

The Clowns last game that season was played September 11 in Spartanburg, South Carolina. The next-to-last appearance, scheduled for the afternoon of September 12 in Charlotte, North Carolina, was rained out. Ed wrote Dad from Charlotte, "Sold 9 tickets in advance. Guess the 9 thot it would be hard to get a seat & wanted to make sure." That night, the season officially closed with a rainout in Gastonia, North Carolina.

And soon Dad removed the schedule cards from his desk, as he had done following each season for 35 years. But this time was the last.

PART SEVEN

AS MAILMEN WHISTLE

The day after my father died, I saw the mailman, whistling, coming up our neighbor's walk to deliver letters. Whistling! And I wanted to hit him for being happy. How could he be happy? My father was dead. I don't remember when, but one day again I was glad to see the mailman and to see that the world went on.

—Villa Pollock

33

The Last Whaler

Not long after Dad put the 1964 schedule cards on a storage shelf, Ed and Dad met to settle up and split their minimal 1964 profit, 55 percent to Dad, 45 percent to Ed. The process, in Dad's office, took more than a day, but less than two, and at the end, as Dad waved to Ed, who was headed south toward Tamiami Trail for the day-long ride across the Glades to St. Petersburg, Dad said to me, "Professor, if you're still thinking of running the Clowns for a living, you better consider something with more of a future, like being a Viking or a Pony Express rider or a town crier."

But contrary to Ed, Dad preferred business as usual. While profits were too small for the risk, the Clowns and Dad were part of each other, and Dad still wanted the Clowns to provide black opportunity and to carry black joy across state lines. Elijah "Sonny" Jackson and Dan Berksteiner were two promising Clowns pitchers. Maybe the Clowns could elevate them. Natureboy Williams and Birmingham Sam Brison were two funny men. Maybe Dero Austin would be the next Spec Bebop. Maybe one of the television networks would come through next year.

Dad was convinced that the Clowns needed his talent to survive; conversely, he believed Ed Hamman was the only person who could efficiently handle road operations. Like a dreamer fresh awake and trying to remember a beautiful dream as it dissipated, Dad wanted to go on dreaming, but intellectually he was wide awake.

While I didn't think so then, I now see that Ed Hamman was captain to Dad as owner of the last Nantucket whaler under sail, ready to put to windless seas against steamships and motor vessels.

Dad wrote Ed, "Am proceeding on theory we'll operate on same basis as previously . . . [but] should have your decision on whether we should continue to operate on present basis . . . if you want to take over my share . . . or if we should both call it quits."

Ed wrote Dad, "Regards YOUR DREAM. Sometimes I think it is wonderful to be in business with such an eternal hoper as you are and sometimes I don't. Am thinking me being so practical almost to the point of faultfinding you will get fed up with me."

On November 9, 1964, Ed wrote Dad: "I have gave my future much thot. Quit. That could probably be the wise thing. Especially with my health which is not too good. Buy your share out? Start a white novelty team and play locals? Could hardly do worse than I am doing now."

Then, accurately describing future Clowns road operations, he continued, "Me take my share buy two station wagons and have players drive and save $1,700 a year on a chauffeur enough to pay for the wagons. Lease the Indianapolis Clowns name instead of putting in mothballs and cut down to 13 men and play locals. Yes, I have thot of a million ways."

When it was clear to Dad that Ed considered profit too small to share, Dad sold his 55 percent interest to Ed on January 1, 1965, for $3,885, and Dad followed up with months of letters to Ed and Joyce Hamman and meetings with them live and by phone, providing books and records. He helped them set up and trained them in every phase of the home office, providing lists of promoters and black newspapers and names and addresses of every executive in organized baseball. But Ed knew no one could book and service a date like Dad. Ed was now owner-captain of the last Nantucket whaler, but he was working with incomplete charts, small leaks beneath the waterline, no mate, fewer whales, less use for whale products and little wind.

For a time, Dad considered booking Ice Capades and Dancing Waters. The owners wanted him and he could name his terms. But skating wasn't baseball and while two and two didn't always make four in road baseball, Dad had no interest at all in what two atoms of hydrogen and one of oxygen made on the road, frozen or airborne. It just wasn't the Clowns. So Dad agreed to book the Clowns for some prime 1965 dates for Ed on a commission basis.

And in a December 1964 telegram, Bobo Nickerson, of all people, spoke for many in the sport when he wired, "DEAR SYD SORRY TO HEAR YOU ARE LEAVING BASEBALL THE GAME WILL MISS YOU FOR SURE."

❖

Early in December so Mother and Dad could plan, Jerry gave them their 1964 Christmas gift: a six-day cruise on Cunard's *Carmania* to Nassau and Puerto Rico, and Dad wrote to his friend Joe Progress, sports editor of San Juan's *El Mundo,* so that Progress could meet the ship. According to Mom, on December 29, thousands on the dock cheered for Syd and the Clowns, and a marching band played as the *Carmania* tied up. After nearly 18 years, Dad was back in Puerto Rico, and because his friend Gaspar Bernardini was dead, Joe Progress arranged for the governor of Puerto Rico to deliver Dad's welcome speech.

Home in Florida after the trip, Dad told me, "You're not on top long. Here I'm surrounded by thousands in a place I thought I was forgotten. I was like the hoarded coin in Gresham's law. It was so unexpected, like the time the Mills Brothers said they couldn't believe they were shaking my hand."

Dad fidgeted without competition. During his last years with the Clowns, he encouraged bookings against their touring partners to ensure maximum comedy. But the games he loved were the ones against locals.

So he needed competition, and every Tuesday night now was pinochle, and Dad's road to each annual championship was like a Clowns season because every night we played was pure joy.

Grandpa Pollock had dominated North Tarrytown Firehouse pinochle play. Alive until he was 97, Grandpa was a one-man pinochle dynasty, and he taught the game to Dad early in the century.

So each Tuesday Mother and Dad, Valaria, Marti and I had our pinochle league. While it looked like just any game, it wasn't. Dad's touch made it unique. But pinochle couldn't be promoted and drew no crowds.

In 1965, Ed took the Clowns on the road against the New York Stars. Natureboy Williams, Birmingham Sam Brison, Billy Vaughn and Dero Austin were featured. Dad booked eight games for Ed that year, servicing each with special releases and ideas. That season, Dad earned $1,858.61 in commissions, $1,216.07 on Chicago alone, where the popularity of the

Clowns and the promoting skills of Dad and Eddie Stumpf resulted in a July 2 crowd of 21,194 paid. Adding in press and Chicago White Sox Fun Club members admitted free, the crowd exceeded 22,000. On the same afternoon, the Cubs and Giants drew 5,941 paid to Wrigley Field.

Mom and Dad spent most of their time with family, but hundreds of Tarrytowners moved to the Hollywood area after we did, and Mother and Dad renewed lifelong friendships. A Tarrytowners Club met every month or two in reserved rooms at various restaurants. In addition, Mother and Dad socialized with dozens of other couples.

Mom's childhood friend Sue Monahan married Dad's childhood friend John Kistmas, and, after they moved to Hollywood, Mother and Dad invited them to dinner, along with three other couples. Sue and John arrived at the house with a couple Mom had never seen, and neither Sue nor John introduced them, so Mom was unable to tell Dad who they were. Following a joyful evening, when just Sue and John remained with Mom and Dad, Sue said angrily to Mom, "Villa, it's a shame you never introduced your friends to John and me."

"What friends?"

"The ones got here when we did. Came in with us."

"Our friends?" Mom asked. "I thought you brought them."

It turned out no one knew the couple, and no one ever found out who they were.

"Supposing," Dad asked that night, "they'd come to our door and said they didn't know any of us from Adam, but were hungry or lonely or just wanted to join us—what would you have said, Villa?"

"I'd have invited them in," Mom said. "When did we ever turn anyone away?"

Dad said, "Only thing is, we didn't get their names to invite them back."

Mom and Dad wanted little. Mom wanted three things for as long as I remembered: a station wagon, a trip to San Antonio to see the Alamo and a visit to Ireland. She got the trip to Ireland in 1966, and when they returned, of the two, Dad loved Ireland most. "It's the people," he said, "They're the love-liest, happiest, warmest people I've ever seen. 'God bless us and save us,' they say. No wonder I chose Mother. Ireland's a whole country of Villa Pollocks."

From Dublin, Dad brought me a scapular blessed by a priest and a muz-zuzah for our house.

Twice Dad discussed substantive religion with me, both times answering questions on post office trips.

Surprisingly, in 1959, his answer was that he thought Christ was God. It didn't interfere with his Jewishness. He didn't say what the implications were to him. He simply answered my question with a word.

My other question was whether he believed in an afterlife. "No," he an-swered. "Not when I see a cockroach squashed. When he's dead, he's dead—a splotch is all. Crushed and gone."

Then he smiled. "But you know, Professor," he said, "something in people is never squashed. Something in people just keeps on traveling down the road. There's a joyful something can't be killed."

Dad and Abe Saperstein had been good friends for a long time, dating back to when Abe booked Clowns games in the Midwest. Dad taught Abe plenty about booking and promoting, and Abe elevated what he learned to new heights in international circles with the Globetrotters. The relationship between Dad and Abe extended beyond the Clowns, but unfortunately their friendship became strained when Abe was years repaying more than $10,000 borrowed from Dad during the early 1940s. Correspondence be-tween Dad and Abe from 1947 to 1950 reads like a quick fizzle into the silence of friendship destroyed. Letters exchanged for over two years show a recurring pattern of unkept promises of payment by Abe and entreaties on Dad's part for resolution. These letters remain in Dad's filing cabinets. The final exchange in this series was a letter from Abe, dated April 4, 1950, in which he claimed having made a disputed $500 payment.

There was never again correspondence between the two, either oral or written.

On March 15, 1966, I entered Dad's office and saw him slumped forward, face cradled in his arms resting on his typewriter. He looked up, tears lining his face. "Norma just called," he said. "Abe died."

During early June 1950, Mom told me Grandma Pollock was dying, and asked me to bring my accordion to Grandma's to play for her. Grandma picked out songs of her youth, from the 1890s and early 1900s. She sang as I played, adjusting gracefully to my rhythmic improbabilities. She smiled and bobbed her head happily.

From tricycle age, I often visited Grandma without prompting, alone or with friends. A few days after our homebound duet, it was warm and sunny, and I rode my bike there. For a long time, we talked in the dining room, Grandma, Aunt Sadie, Uncle Gabie and I. When I got up to leave, Grandma called me into her sun parlor, to look down at her garden I thought.

"I'm dying, Alan."

"No, Grandma. I'm saying Our Fathers."

"Nevertheless," she whispered. Then she raised the hem of her dress and showed me pinched black swatches of skin along her legs. "I'm just the second with this disease. A 49er during the gold rush was the other. They study me to help if there's a third person gets it." She released the hem and shoved her sleeves up showing the same sort of patches covering both arms. She was tiny—smaller, more delicate, than ever.

"Does it hurt, Grandma?"

"No more than I can bear. The pain will be not seeing your face. I love you more than my life. Do you know that?"

"I do. I know. I love you too."

She lowered her sleeves and led me to the door. Outside the door in the hall, she kissed me, and I sat on the bannister backward, about to exit at street level after the customary slide originated by Don more than 20 years earlier. "If I never see you again, goodbye, goodbye," Grandma said, and gently closed her door.

Next day, Grandma was admitted to White Plains Hospital, adult visitors only.

Three days after that, it was warm and sunny, and I spent the morning playing baseball. I came home through the back door into the kitchen, and heard Dad laughing or crying in his office. I had never heard him cry. "Is Dad laughing or crying?" I asked Mom. "Grandma died," she answered.

Mom went into Dad's office, and he softly cried to her, "I'll never see my mother's face in this world again." And I understood Grandma's pain.

She was buried before sundown in the orthodox way.

At breakfast next day, Dad spoke of the Clowns game that night. "Who cares?" I asked.

"I do, and before long, you will too, Alan," he answered.

Mom put her hand on my cheek, and said, "The day after my father died, I saw the mailman, whistling, coming up our neighbor's walk to deliver letters. Whistling! And I wanted to hit him for being happy. How could he be happy? My father was dead. I don't remember when, but one day again I was glad to see the mailman and to see that the world went on."

The summer of the Clowns' first Negro American League championship, Dad lost his mother, and I first learned that time was not a healer, but an anesthetic that wears thin from time to time as mailmen whistle. And well before season's end, I cared again about the Clowns.

Dad's last season, he knew there were few more, and he convinced me too that the Clowns were near an end.

"You're right, sir," I said one day, again on the way back from the post office. "The Clowns won't survive long. It kills me, Dad. I love the Clowns. I've wanted to run the Clowns since I was little. I was born too late."

Dad responded, "Does it seem funny to you the world meets our needs? Some play music, some baseball. Some do math. Some make money. Some loan it. Some keep track. Some grow food; some transport it; some review it for the papers. You were born at the right time, Professor, and you'll do what the world needs for you to do.

"Once, we were playing a white team near home, the Port Chester Corpus Christi Club I think it was. You were there, a little boy. We had a nice lead, two outs in the bottom of the ninth. Guy hit a shot up the middle, but Ray Neil hits the hole, makes one of those sweet backhanded stops of his, plants and throws the guy out by a yard. And I think what if baseball was invented, not with a round ball, but a cube. Game would have died right there. Then I figure God made the world round so we wouldn't have corners. The whole thing curves back on itself, kinda like Einstein said about time, and belongs to all of us, and we can go every place. So what do we do? We make corners. Organized Baseball says, like in the Bill Broonzy song, 'You black, git back.' This is our corner. You stay out. So the Negro leagues filled their own little corner.

"I love the Clowns too. Always have. The Clowns brought joy wherever they went, and they went all over. There's joy too in the death of the Clowns, Professor. It's the smoothing of a corner that was created round to begin with. We don't need the Negro leagues corner any more and that's certainly joyful. Everyone, black and white, will know the next Ray Neil, the next Verdes Drake. And that's the way it should be. Round, Professor, like a baseball."

Dad lived with the wonder and laughter of a child, and he loved children. Retired, he spent even more time with us and our children. As Valaria said, "Dad would take all the grandchildren to the post office and for ice cream. We used to say he was like the Pied Piper." Valaria's image of Dad in Florida matches mine, in which he walks briskly down the sidewalk toward the post office with a laughing line of ice-cream-cone-wielding grandchildren.

Mother and Dad seldom did anything alone. In 1965, instead of a vacation alone, they took Marti and me and our daughter Theresa, nearly two, on a cruise to Haiti and Jamaica and, later, took all their five children and all grandchildren above the age of one, on a Bahamas cruise.

Early in March of 1968, I stayed with Mom, while Dad took Marti and our daughters, Theresa and Anna, ages four and two, north by train to visit Estelle and Al in Poughkeepsie and Don and Jane in New Jersey. Marti said Dad refused to use a redcap or let her carry a suitcase. He carried them all.

On the homebound train, shaking his hand in the air, he told Marti that one of his fingers had died. "It's not just numb," he said. "It died."

The following day at home, he had a major stroke, and spent the next eight months relearning to walk and talk, something doctors advised us he would not accomplish.

Valaria wrote of an aspect of the months he spent in the convalescent center: "Dad was so loved by all the children. In his last days in the nursing home, the nurses said every day around three a little boy would come in and go into the elevator. After watching him for days they decided to follow him to see what he was up to. It was our nine-year-old son Dereck who was on his way home from school every day to visit his Pop Pop. They said he must have been a caring man to have this child come by every day by himself to visit."

By football season, Dad walked with a walker, talked more than any doctor thought possible and returned home.

On November 20, 1968, Jerry called us all to Hollywood Memorial Hospital. Dad had suffered a second stroke and a heart attack, and he would not recover this time. Except I knew he would—until I saw his face.

Ten years earlier, for reasons now forgotten, I began to call Dad "Sir Cedric Hardwicke," the name of the British actor. Gradually, I shortened it to "Sir Cedric," then to "Sir."

And after the Monday evening supper in 1962, when Dad sat next to John Jerke in the Kappa Sigma House at FSU, Boyt Elam, a fraternity brother from Greenville, Florida, said, "Al, we were just saying you're the first Yankee we ever heard respect his Daddy like we do in the South."

"How's that?"

"By calling him 'Sir.'"

"It's a different respect than you think. 'Sir's' my nickname for Dad. He's my best friend. It's that kind of respect."

Now, I saw Dad's face and heard his breath rattle and I knew I was losing my best friend.

I looked at his right hand—the one that had touched the hands of King Tut, Lefty Tiant, Josh Gibson, Stringbean Williams, Cool Papa Bell, Bullet Rogan, Spec Bebop, Smokey Joe Williams, Satchel, Thomas Yancy Baird, Skinny Barnhill, Speed Merchant, Ray Neil, Verdes Drake, Roosevelt Davis, Henry Aaron, Chauff, Natche, Sam, Jackie Robinson, Ramiro Ramirez, Hunter Campbell, Bunny Downs, Buster Haywood—the hand that held Mom's, Don's, Estelle's, Valaria's, Jerry's and mine and made the world safe.

Mother had taught us not to say goodbye. "Goodbye is final," she said. "But so long means you'll meet again soon."

I put my right hand on Dad's. "So long, Sir," I whispered.

Then Jerry helped me out of the room, down the back stairs of the hospital and out to my car. He went back to be with the others with Dad until he died.

I could not.

34

Legacy

"Syd ever tell you about Hooks Mitchell?" Ed Hamman asked me outside the funeral home.

"Yes. Pitcher he had in the mid-'30s. Pickoff motion to first so good, he walked men so he could pick 'em off."

"Exactly. Well, Syd Pollock was good enough to walk any ten of the rest of us in baseball and pick us off one by one if he was built that way, which, of course, he wasn't."

"He was the best man I ever knew, anyway," I said.

"You know the Negro leaguers' pension fund ended with Syd."

"I didn't know there was a pension fund."

"You never wondered why Syd had bills in his palm when he shook with the old-timers when they came to the dugout?"

Every Clowns game we attended, retired Negro leaguers came through the stands to the Clowns dugout, and when Dad shook their hands, he passed money.

"Never wondered," I answered. "He did that ever since I remember. It was just part of life."

"Well, Alan, that part of life died the other day. Syd did that since I can remember too. Beginning in the depression, he give cash to Spot Poles or Stringbean Williams or Pop Lloyd, whoever come down to his ball club's dugout, didn't matter they ever played for him or not.

"See, the colored players made no money to save and got no pension. So Syd give them guys money out of his pocket. The worse off he heard they were, the bigger the bill. I seen him give $100 more than sometimes. Nobody else in baseball done it.

"He didn't make it a handout, Alan. He'd give the bill over and say, 'Here's a piece of money for that homer you hit to beat my club in Baltimore in '35 or the time you struck out Josh bases loaded in Philly. Well worth it, for that memory!'"

Twenty-five years later, Othello "Chico" Renfroe, Monarchs infielder during the years of Jackie Robinson, then Ernie Banks, who played for the
Clowns parts of 1949 and 1950, told me:

> Syd came to Atlanta with Mrs. Pollock to see one of those '60s teams
> of his. I didn't need money, but I went down the dugout with some-
> one who did. I'm not gonna mention his name, but this fella was a
> journeyman ballplayer and a bad actor.
>
> Syd slipped the fella a ten, said, "That's for the sacrifice bunt set up
> the winning run that time in New Castle."
>
> Now, I don't even know whether the guy ever bunted in New Castle,
> but afterwards, I took Syd aside and I'm laughing, and I said, "Syd,
> talkin' about some long dead bunt in New Castle. You're the only man
> I know finds something good in everybody."
>
> Syd said, "Chico, you can't find somethin' ain't there from the
> start."

Ninth grade did not presage Dad's success. Before his parents removed
him from school to run the Strand, he was cut from the North Tarrytown
High School baseball team. Arguing with the coach, Dad said he was good
enough to make the team and that baseball meant everything to him.

The coach told him "Sydney, you better get other interests. You'll never
amount to anything in baseball."

Dad accomplished everything he wanted in baseball except ample press
for black teams and earlier integration.

Every player interviewed for this book who played during the brief time
Jim Oliver and Ray Neil worked side-by-side with the Clowns called them
either the greatest double-play combination in baseball history or one of
the greatest. Many felt there was never a better center fielder than Verdes
Drake. Lefty Tiant, Skinny Barnhill and, for a few years, Peanuts Davis,
were among the all-time elite pitchers. Goose Tatum, Lionel Jackson and
Showboat Thomas were certainly three of the classiest first basemen ever

to play. Few were better all around than Tetelo Vargas, and not many could outhit Ray Neil, Alex Radcliffe, Sam Hairston, Hank Aaron and Fred Wilson.

Buster Haywood was a category of one. Not all agree he was baseball's best catcher, but some very knowledgeable baseball men thought so. Buster's aggressive, even abrasive, play and his lack of power at the plate may have stunted his reputation. He was quiet and steady and did not always endear himself to those who played against him.

He is loved by our family, not just because in many ways he's like Dad, but because he's Buster.

At age 84, in 1994, Buster flew to Florida from Los Angeles, and spent five days talking with us about the Clowns. Because of all the children and grandchildren living in my house, most of our time with Buster was in quieter places. But we spent a few hours in my house one Sunday, until it got too noisy.

A few years earlier, Lonnie Wheeler was collaborating with Hank Aaron on Aaron's *I Had a Hammer,* and we communicated by phone and I sent Lonnie Wheeler a copy of the Clowns 1952 schedule and some documentation for the book. Contemporaneously, he was talking by phone with Jim "Fireball" Cohen, whose last year with the Clowns was 1952, Aaron's Clowns season. Buster and Fireball had not spoken since 1952.

At 7:20 P.M. on Sunday, July 31, 1994, Jim Cohen called me while Buster was in our house. I had not spoken to Jim since 1952 either. "Why are you calling me now?" I asked.

"Years ago, when Lonnie Wheeler was working on the Hank Aaron book he called me for background, and said he just talked to Syd Pollock's son. Asked if I wanted your number. I wrote it down in a book I was reading. Couldn't remember where I wrote it when I wanted to call you. I just picked up the same book to read it again, and, wham, there was your number."

"I got someone wants to say hello. Hold on and let me get the extension."

I motioned Buster over, covered the mouthpiece, told him who it was and asked him to wait until I got on the other phone.

"Hello, Fireball. How you doin'?" Buster asked.

"Who is this?"

"Buster Haywood."

"Who is this?"

"Just said. Buster Haywood."

"Who is this really?"

"Buster Haywood."

"Shit, Skip! What you doin' there?"

And for nearly an hour, they resurrected the Negro leagues.

When it was over, Buster said to me, "Now let's go buy a Lotto ticket, because the odds of a win are a whole lot better than Fireball Cohen calling while I'm in your house." We bought our Lotto ticket, and didn't get a single number right.

Before Buster's visit, when I asked him by phone what he thought most belonged in this book, he said, "The thing I'd like most to say in a book is something to bring my race together. We have few blacks at our autograph shows, and they don't know what we were. We ought to put the ways of the past behind us and move on, but to know how to leave them behind, we got to understand what the ways of the past are. You can't shove back something you don't recognize." It was Buster's version of Dad's need to round off another racial corner.

While he was here, Buster told my daughters, Valaria and Karen, "It's absurd how whites and blacks celebrate victory together at the stadium, then leave the ballpark for their own, separate worlds."

Jerry and his wife, Jeanne, and Marti and I drove Buster to Miami International Airport for his flight back to Los Angeles. Two women helped three crying men part.

"This is one of the saddest things I ever done," Buster said. "It's like saying goodbye to teammates season's end, never knowing who's coming back next year and who'll be gone."

On the way back to Hollywood, Jerry said, "It's like you left me or I left you. It's like a brother's gone away."

"Exactly," I said, "and this time the brother took a little bit of Dad with him."

Sometimes, when it's quiet otherwise, and the blues is played galaxies-bright black, I shut my eyes wet and see Dad in a dugout, cigarette ash curved toward the scorebook in his lap, Tut praying aside the third base foul line watching Drakey chase one to the wall, and I hear tens of thousands roar, and above them, Mom and Bea King and Pauline Downs screaming footspeed to Drake, and I smell beer and hot dogs and neat's-foot oil and saddle soap on glove leather and liniment and cigar smoke and the soft, sweet perfume of black women, and I hear Ed Hamman telling a young me in his hotel room in Columbus, "I rested knowing the Clowns will be here when I get back."

Sometime during the mid-'40s, I sat in a Yankee Stadium box with Mom, Pauline Downs and Bea King. The Clowns lost in the ninth, and I cried.

"Close your eyes," Mom said, taking me into her arms. "Sometimes, Alan, you have to close your eyes and wash them to see the truth, and the truth is, the Clowns are meant to make people happy, not sad. Now you shut your eyes and think about King Tut parading around out there, and I bet you'll smile." And I did.

In Hollywood Memorial Gardens Cemetery, Hollywood, Florida, there's a single bronze plate over two graves. Across the plate toward the bottom it says POLLOCK. Above that to the left it reads SYD 1901–1968 and there's a Star of David, and to the right of that, it says VILLA CARROLL 1904–1974 and there's a Roman cross.

Epilogue

During the late 1960s, Ed Hamman invoked his plan of transporting 14 players in two station wagons with a U-Haul to save bus, gas and chauffeur money, and they played local teams only. In 1968, he reverse-integrated the team by signing white players. Roster size was reduced to 10 or 11 during the late '60s, and the team began playing small cities and towns almost exclusively, with a schedule of 65 to 75 games.

After the 1970 season, Ed sold the team to 1960s Clowns Iowa promoter, George Long of Muscatine.

In 1983, Long sold the team to Dave Clark, a Corning, New York, pitcher crippled with polio.

Comedy, crowds and quality baseball had become more and more elusive. The team, eventually all white, survived a while longer.

INDEX

Page numbers in italics indicate photographs.
Teams are listed by nicknames, i.e., Clowns, White Sox, Braves.
The Clowns and Syd and Alan Pollock suffuse this work to the degree that full indexing of
these topics was neither possible nor necessary.

26, 49, 60–61, 74, 81, 84–85, 89, 91, 97–
105, 112, 117–118, 125, 138, 149–150,
159, 161, 167, *195, 207, 208,* 224, 249,
280, 283, 369. *See also* Clowns, Indianapolis
Evans, Felix "Chin," 61, 97, 108, 128, 144, *208*
Evans, Johnnie, 254
Everett, Jim, 147, 149–150

Farrell, Luther, 81
Feller, Bob, 127, 166
Felton, Augustus, 140
Ferguson, George, 144, 148, 154, 168
Ferguson Hotel, Indianapolis, 144–145,
148, 154, 156, 168
Ferrer, Coco, 150, 151
Fetchit, Stepin, 156
Fitzgerald, Ella, 103
Fletcher, Al, 278
Flint (MI) team, 119
Florida State League, 288–289
Flying Nesbitts, 324
Forbes Field, 219, 298
Ford, Erwin, 18, 219, 257, 260–261, 271,
278, 295
Forney, Carl, 61, 66–67, 280–282, 293–294,
296, 300, 304–306, 317, 319–322, 330,
333, 340, 346, 354, 358
Fort Benning team, 82, 111
Fort Knox team, 122
Fort Logan Soldier team, 100
Fort Totten team, 224
Fort Worth Press, 372
Foster, Andrew "Rube," 8, 58
Franklin, Col. Charles B. "Toad," 28–29,
83, 90–91, 127, 132, 145–146, 312
Franks, Mike, 281, 303
Frick, Ford, 266
Fulmer, C. Richard, 161
Funmakers. *See* Clowns, Indianapolis

Gaines, Willie, 238, 244, 251, 271, 278
Gaither, Jake, 115

Galata, Raul, 115, 176, 178, 218
Galves, Cuneo, 77–78
Garcia, Angel, 151, 238, 244, 246–247, 251
Gehrig, Lou, 81
Georgia Flyers, 296–297
Giants, Kannapolis (NC), 257
Giants, Kansas City, 41, 320–321
Giants, Miami, 49, 82, 84, 90, 105, 116,
124, 137, 150, 167, 207
Giants, New York, 157, 179, 230–232,
234, 319
Giants, Rockingham, 257
Gibbons, Walter "Dirk," 106–107, 121
Gibson, Josh, 8, 81, 99, 128, 236, 256, 290,
387, 389
Gilbert, Paul, umpire, 324
Gilliam, Jim, 175
Gladstone, Granville, 175–176
Globetrotters, Harlem, 9, 28, 29–30, 37,
154, 168, 179, 271, 288, 331, 373, 383
Godinez, Manolo, 121
Gordon, Joe, 28
Gottlieb, Ed, 105, 223–224, 238, 254, 314
Grace, Willie, 123
Grant, Jim, 289
Graves, Whit, 222
Graveson, Dick, 75, 77
Gray, Johnny, 287–290, 304
Gray, Leo, 305, 350
Green, Joe, 356
Green, Shad, 271
Greenberg, Hank, 270
Greene, Ulysses Grant, 285, 287, 297, 318
Griffith Stadium, 217, 249, 304
Griggs, Dewey, 229–230
Gross, Milton (newspaperman), 288–290
Grove, Lefty, 46
Guilbe, Juan, 151

Hairston, Jerry, 176
Hairston, John, 157, 176
Hairston, Richard, 238, 261
Hairston, Sam, 111–112, 114–115, 126,

Roque, Jacinto "Battlin' Siki," 76
Roseboro, John, 288
Rosen, Al, 270
Rotary All-Stars, Tarrytown, 75–76, 77
Royals, Newport News, 244
Royals, New York, 312, 317, 324
Royals, Norfolk, 244
Royals All-Stars, Kansas City, 166
Rucker, Joe, 46
Rudd, Charlie, 138
Ruiz, Antonio, 117
Rushing, Vanity, 296, 319–320
Ruth, Babe, 79–80, 81

SABR (Society for American Baseball
    Research), 3
Saints, St. Paul, 241
Salazar, Lazaro, 77
Sally League, 235
Sama, Pablo, 58–59, 176, 180, 222
Sambrana, Jose, 296
Sanchez, Maximo, 115, 133, 163
Sands, Sam "Piggy," 177–178, *213*, 219,
    260–261
Saperstein, Abe, 30, 83, 147, 154–155,
    383–384
Saperstein, Morrie, 155
Saperstein, Norma, 384
Satchel Paige Stars, 98
Sayreton Mines team, 111
Schacht, Al, 283, 287, 299, 329
Schwartz, John, 230–232
Scott, Buster, 159–160, *208*
Scott, Ed, 91, 224–227
Sea Lions, San Francisco, 241
Seay, Dick, 112
Sec Taylor Stadium, Des Moines, 341
segregation. *See* racism and baseball
semi-pro baseball, 48
Serrell, Barney "Bonnie," 165
shadowball, 14–16, 24, 29, 66, 73, 76, 83,
    132, 180, 285, 297, 318, 324, 331, 333,
    342, 360, 365, 370, 374

Shane, Ted, 24–28
Sherman Hotel, 230
Sherman's Cleaners, South Bend, 317
Shibe Park, 157–158, 216–217
Showboat King of Baseball. *See* Davis,
    Edward A.
Silva, Roderick "Monk," 83, 84, 115–116,
    137, 159, 166, 177–178
Singleton, Jerry, 311
Sing Sing Prison, 71, 177–178
Skowron, Moose, 325
Smalley, Roy, 147
Smallwood, DeWitt "Woody," *213*, 235,
    271, 274, 278
Smith, Allen, 167
Smith, Cleo, 76
Smith, Eugene "Chivo," 153, 167
Smith, George, 281, 374
Smith, Hilton, 126–127, 320
Smith, Milt, 158
Smith, Percy, 225, 235, 251, 259
Smith, Red, 283
Smith, Wendell, 95–96, 283
Snead, Sylvester, 84, *183*, 280
Southwestern Iowa Tournament, 98
Spec Bebop, 9–14, 16, 19, 32–33, 34, 38, 90,
    116, 136, 141, 152, 179–180, *184, 212,
    213, 214,* 242, 272, 285, 287, 290, 323–
    324, 369, 379, 387
Speno, Georgie, 72
Sports, Houston, 323
Sportsman's Park, St. Louis, 164
Spurgeon, Fred, 119
St. Joe Caterpillar Tractor Company, 263
St. Paul Pioneer Press, 125
St. Paul Stadium, 240–241
St. Petersburg Times, 312–313
Stanky, Eddie, 147
Stanton, Charles, 350
Stark, Otis "Lefty," 81
Stars, Brooklyn, 206, 359–360, 363, 370
Stars, Detroit, 111, 255, 285, 302, 312
Stars, Harlem, 313